MW00614114

YEARS

SIMON &
SCHUSTER

The

INDISPENSABLE RIGHT

FREE SPEECH IN AN AGE OF RAGE

JONATHAN TURLEY

SIMON & SCHUSTER

New York   Toronto   London   Sydney   New Delhi

1230 Avenue of the Americas
New York, NY 10020

Copyright © 2024 by Jonathan Turley

All rights reserved, including the right to reproduce this book
or portions thereof in any form whatsoever. For information, address
Simon & Schuster Subsidiary Rights Department,
1230 Avenue of the Americas, New York, NY 10020.

First Simon & Schuster hardcover edition June 2024

SIMON & SCHUSTER and colophon are registered trademarks of Simon & Schuster, LLC

Simon & Schuster: Celebrating 100 Years of Publishing in 2024

For information about special discounts for bulk purchases,
please contact Simon & Schuster Special Sales
at 1-866-506-1949 or business@simonandschuster.com.

The Simon & Schuster Speakers Bureau can bring authors to your live event.
For more information or to book an event,
contact the Simon & Schuster Speakers Bureau
at 1-866-248-3049 or visit our website at www.simonspeakers.com.

Interior design by Ruth Lee-Mui

Manufactured in the United States of America

3   5   7   9   10   8   6   4

Library of Congress Cataloging-in-Publication Data

Names: Turley, Jonathan, 1961- author.
Title: The indispensable right : free speech in an age of rage / Jonathan Turley.
Description: First Simon & Schuster hardcover edition. | New York,
NY : Simon and Schuster, 2024. | Includes index.
Identifiers: LCCN 2023052916 (print) | LCCN 2023052917 (ebook) | ISBN 9781668047040
(hardcover) | ISBN 9781668047057 (paperback) | ISBN 9781668047064 (ebook)
Subjects: LCSH: Freedom of speech--United States--History. | United
States. Constitution. 1st Amendment. | BISAC: POLITICAL SCIENCE /
History & Theory | POLITICAL SCIENCE / Censorship
Classification: LCC KF4772 .T85 2024 (print) | LCC KF4772
(ebook) | DDC 342.7308/53--dc23/eng/20240209
LC record available at https://lccn.loc.gov/2023052916
LC ebook record available at https://lccn.loc.gov/2023052917

ISBN 978-1-6680-4704-0
ISBN 978-1-6680-4706-4 (ebook)

Dedicated to my father, John Kenneth Turley, who taught me that life is the unending intellectual pursuit of truth.

And to my mother, Angela Piazza Turley, who taught me that life is an unyielding passionate pursuit of justice.

I like a little rebellion now and then.
It is like a storm in the Atmosphere.
—letter from Thomas Jefferson to
Abigail Adams, February 22, 1787

Contents

Introduction

We are living in an age of rage. It permeates every aspect of our society and politics. Rage is liberating, even addictive. It allows us to say and do things that we would ordinarily avoid, even denounce in others. Rage is often found at the furthest extreme of reason. For those who agree with the underlying message, it is righteous and passionate. For those who disagree, it is dangerous and destabilizing. It is a moment captured in Shakespeare's *The Tempest* when Miranda pleads with her father Prospero to explain a storm that he has literally conjured up at sea to the danger of a floundering ship. She prays for her father to explain his reason "for raising this sea-storm." To her, it is violent and malicious. Yet Prospero insists that his rage had a purpose and "the hour's now come" so that his daughter would open "thine ear. Obey, and be attentive." The inexplicable rage had a design, as it often does, to get others to focus, to listen. Thomas Jefferson made essentially the same point when, after counseling mercy in the wake of the Shays' Rebellion, he explained that such riots, even rebellion, can have a positive, dialogic purpose. He would tell James Madison the same thing, that "a little rebellion now and then is a good thing." Jefferson wanted the "rebels" pardoned not because he agreed with them but because "the spirit of resistance to government is so valuable on certain occasions, that I wish it to be always kept alive. It will often be exercised when wrong, but better so than not to be exercised at all."

In any given age, it is often difficult to see beyond the "sea storm" itself. For many, rage rhetoric is low-value speech with high costs for society. The resulting line drawing has occurred for centuries without rendering a clear distinction of what is rage and what is rebellion. Indeed, this is a question that continues to occupy courts and commentators as political violence increases in the United States. Courts are once again facing claims of sedition by the government and new efforts to criminalize speech. Rage rhetoric is the ultimate stress test for a system premised on free speech. It is a test that we have often failed as the rage of dissidents has produced rageful responses from the government. It is state rage. This history is often dismissed as legal period pieces, unfortunate excesses of the government during times of war or great disorder. Alternatively, the abuses are personified as the acts of evil men. In this way, Jefferson could denounce the administration of John Adams and the Federalists as "the reign of the witches." He would counsel a friend "[a] little patience, and we shall see the reign of witches pass over, their spells dissolve, and the people, recovering their true sight, restore their government to its true principles." Yet it didn't pass. It came back. Over and over again. It came back under Jefferson himself. The problem was never the witches but our own underlying faith—or lack of it.

In looking at our history of speech suppression, prior authors often focus on the historic periods or personalities. This can be a type of rationalization that ignores a common conceptual denominator in how free speech is defined. These periods of crisis are the catalysts but not the cause of that failure. The cause lies more deeply in the foundation for free speech in the United States. All three branches have abandoned protections for minority viewpoints due to a lack of a coherent and consistent theory of free speech. In fact, after rejecting the criminalization of speech in England, the new Republic would quickly reestablish prosecutions for seditious and dissenting speech under the same rationales. More recently, an anti–free speech movement has rejected greater protections as part of regressive "rights talk" or autonomy-based theories. As we witness the revival of American sedition, we need to ask why our body politic continues to be a carrier of this virus, a virus that returns with terrible consequences whenever our political temperature rises. It is a malarial condition that manifests in feverish times and takes hold of all three branches of government, inviting the same rationalizations for censorship and criminalization.

This legal relativism continues to undermine not simply free speech but many of our underlying institutions. While rage and reason may share the same spectrum of thought, rage often leaves only a residue of reason as people strike out at the manifestations of perceived social or political injustice. It is a recurring pattern that stretches back to the colonial times. We are living through another period of such public distemper where our most cherished institutions and rights are being questioned by both the left and the right. The attack on the Capitol on January 6, 2021, was the violent act of people who had lost faith in our institutions and, in its absence, filled that empty space with unrequited rage. Conversely, on the left, even legal academics have joined the call for radical change and portrayed the Constitution as the cause for injustice and inequity. In a 2022 *New York Times* essay, Harvard law professor Ryan D. Doerfler and Yale law professor Samuel Moyn called for the country to "reclaim America from Constitutionalism." The *Nation*'s justice correspondent, Elie Mystal, has called the Constitution "trash" and argued that we should just dump it. They are all voices of doubt in our system and ourselves. The most menacing object of this rage is directed at the one right Justice Louis Brandeis called "indispensable" for the maintenance of all other rights: free speech.

Brandeis was one of the nation's great civil libertarians, one of the "great dissenters" who saw a legal horizon that escaped most of his contemporaries. That horizonal view included core individual rights that define us as a people. The dissents of Brandeis and Oliver Wendell Holmes would become majority views on the Court. Yet even these icons of civil liberties would embrace repressive opinions that denied free speech to political dissidents. The reason for this contradiction brings us back to Brandeis's reference. Most people would agree that free speech is the indispensable right. In 2023, the Supreme Court again emphasized the indispensability of this right to our constitutional system. The question is why it is indispensable. The answer to that question has made a profound difference in the protection or prosecution of speech. One can view water as indispensable for putting out fires, but that is different from viewing water as an essential element for life. Similarly, free speech can be viewed as indispensable to democracy, protected for its ability to foster the forming and advocacy of political positions. Yet that indispensability is cabined as a function of political expression. As such, it can be dispensable in other areas or when the speech is deemed of lesser value. Alternatively, as argued in this book, it can be indispensable because it is an essential part of being human, a natural right. Whether based on a religious view of a divine gift or a secular view of inherent human qualities, this broader view treats speech as indispensable as the manifestation of a creative and expressive impulse regardless of the subject matter. Neither view treats free speech as an absolute. However, the latter view based on individual autonomy allows fewer "trade-offs" through balancing and harm-based tests.

The indispensable reference itself comes from a case that captures the rivaling views of free speech as well as divergent intellectual strains in American society in the early twentieth century. Brandeis's concurring opinion in *Whitney v. California* concerned a suffragist and political activist named Charlotte Anita Whitney. She was a member of a wealthy and distinguished family from San Francisco that included Cyrus W. Field, the magnate who founded the Atlantic Telegraph Company. Her family claimed five ancestors that crossed the Atlantic on the *Mayflower*. One ancestor served as a colonial governor of Massachusetts and others were officers in the Continental Army during the American Revolution. Whitney would often spend summers with her uncle, Justice Stephen Johnson Field, who was put on the Supreme Court by Abraham Lincoln and would prove to be one of the longest-serving justices in history. Notably, he was considered something of a judicial activist who believed in natural rights as a foundation for constitutional law. Whitney would prove an activist of a different kind.

Whitney was exceptionally bright and intellectually curious as a child. Raised in fine private schools, her father, a lawyer, decided that she should go back east for a proper education. In 1885, he sent her to Wellesley College in Massachusetts. When it was founded only fifteen years earlier, Henry Durant had selected the motto "*Incipit vita nova*," or "The new life begins." It was a fitting motto for the young girl from the West who arrived by carriage at the small college. The college would prove transformative for

Whitney, who would be exposed to an array of studies, including political and moral philosophies. She also was taught by a female faculty dominated by social reform advocates. After graduating in 1889, Whitney and other alumna were invited to go for a short visit at the Settlement House at 95 Rivington Street in New York. It was more of a field trip than social work for the affluent young ladies. While scheduled for just a week, Whitney would stay for six months. She wrote how she was shocked as much by the "indifference of the well to do" as she was the crushing poverty that she encountered at the settlement. She later recalled how she saw for the first time "the vicious cycle they were drawn into—the circle made up of poverty, ignorance, sickness, and vice." Upon her graduation, she became part of a new generation of educated women who would matriculate from all-women schools, from Wellesley to Vassar to Bryn Mawr. It was an awakening for Whitney, who returned to California on a mission.

Attractive and reserved, Whitney was expected to get married and start a family. She showed little such interest and wrote, "I made an attempt to have the same pleasures and pastimes as the young people around me, but I was always more or less conscious of a feeling of boredom, coupled with a dread of being thought different." Instead, she began to frequent meetings of socialists seeking radical change in society. She had become disenchanted with settlement work addressing only the surface needs of the poor and oppressed. As historian Lisa Rubens observed, Whitney "became convinced that it was better to prevent rather than ameliorate poverty." She joined the Socialist Party just before World War I and, a few years later, helped found the Communist Labor Party. (She would later run for state treasurer and even the United States Senate as a communist.) Due to her organizational and oratorial skills, she is credited with being a major leader in making California the sixth state to give women the vote in 1911. For many suffragists, the socialist and communist parties represented the most committed organizations to their cause of equality. Likewise, as the late University of Washington communications professor Haig Bosmajian observed, there was no difference in how they were viewed "between suffragists, pro-Germans, and Socialists, between Bolsheviks and anarchists and Wobblies." Whitney was blacklisted by *The Woman Patriot* editor Margaret C. Robinson and, along with figures like Jane Addams, similarly denounced by the Massachusetts Public Interests League as a radical. Also on the blacklist was Susan Brandeis, a recent law graduate of the University of Chicago and daughter of Justice Louis Brandeis.

George Bernard Shaw once said "a reasonable man adjusts himself to the world. An unreasonable man expects the world to adjust itself to him. Therefore, all progress is made by unreasonable people." Like many of the free speech figures discussed in this book, Anita Whitney was that brilliantly unreasonable person. Even when she was a child, a friend (and fellow Communist) said Whitney "was a challenge, a puzzle, even I wonder what made her tick." What made Whitney tick was clearly social justice, but also a deep-seated faith in free speech. Like many radicals in that period, Whitney was wrong for all the right reasons. She saw desperate poverty and wanted to end it. As she explained, her exposure to the settlements gave her a lifelong purpose and "at last . . . something vital [had] to be done and I wanted to have a part in it . . . I wanted to help change it."

Whitney believed that there was an inalienable right to free speech that belonged to all citizens: "A real American cannot be blamed for demanding freedom of opinion and freedom of speech. It's in the blood." On November 29, 1919, Whitney prepared to give a speech at the Oakland Center of the California Civic League. The police originally canceled the speech because she was declared a woman of "known political tendencies." A compromise was reached that would allow her to speak, but only if she consented to having an American flag on the stage—and a police officer. As she walked onstage with the officer looming near her (and other officers in the crowd), Whitney had to know that she was about to give the government what it was waiting for. This woman from a refined and established family from the founding of the country was about to officially become an enemy of the state. She spoke on the "Negro Problem" and denounced the lynching occurring around the country. She declared, "It is not alone for the Negro man and woman." She insisted that "for the fair name of America that this terrible blot on our national escutcheon be wiped away. Not our country right or wrong, but our country, may she be right, because we, her children will it so." She was promptly arrested under the criminal syndicalism law, which made it a crime to support "any doctrine or precept advocating, teaching, or aiding and abetting the commission of crime, sabotage or unlawful acts of force and violence or unlawful methods of terrorism as a means of accomplishing a change or control, or effecting any political change." The Whitney charge was a true Rube Goldberg creation. Whitney was accused of responsibility for violent rhetoric of the Industrial Workers of the World because the Communist Labor Party supported the IWW and Whitney supported the Communist Labor Party.

Authorities used Whitney's work to establish the local Communist Party as the basis for the charge. The media joined in the call for Whitney's conviction. The *Sacramento Bee* declared, "Charlotte Anita Whitney, a woman of education and with all the advantages possessed of wealth and with the opportunity of doing great good to her fellow creatures has prostituted her talents for years to the service of the lawless and disorderly." The attacks were a mix of sexism and sensationalism. The *Bee* insisted that "the urge of these wealthy, well read, but really ill-educated women is the urge of idle restlessness, the crave for adventure, the lust for power—even if it be the leadership of the lawless in the assault upon the citadels of civilization." The trial was a farce. A reporter who served as a witness later admitted that he was ordered by the police to falsely claim that a red flag was draped over the American flag on the stage. The trial occurred in the midst of the raging influenza epidemic. Not only would the epidemic kill one of the jurors (requiring an alternate to be sworn in), but also Whitney's own counsel, Thomas H. O'Connor, fell ill with the flu on the second day of the trial. By the third day, O'Connor could

not function and died a week later. Even with this enormous disruption
to the defense, Judge James G. Quinn refused to allow continuances and
pushed ahead. What remained of the defense team would call only Whitney as a witness. The jury deliberated six hours and found Whitney guilty
on the first count of assembling an organization formed for the purpose
of advocating criminal syndicalism. It deadlocked on the remaining four
counts. Quinn handed down a sentence of one to fourteen years and sent
Whitney to prison. In roughly a dozen years, Whitney had gone from
admission to Wellesley College to a sentence to San Quentin prison. Her
lawyer, John Francis Neylan, said later that, after the decision, was the
only time that Whitney ever broke down, sobbing in his office and saying
"she couldn't take the strain any longer." However, she refused to ask for a
pardon when others were incarcerated. Indeed, she asked, "How can I be
pardoned when I've done nothing wrong?"

Whitney was allowed to remain free during years of appeal. Her case
eventually made it to the Supreme Court but was summarily dismissed
due to a technicality. The appeal was refiled and heard by the Court only
to be unanimously upheld. (Whitney later would be given an uncondi-
tional pardon by California governor C. C. Young and would run for various offices.) The case would become famous for its concurrence by Justice
Brandeis, who articulated the basis for the "clear and present danger"
standard. The decision included a roaring defense of free speech but still
upheld the conviction for a woman who was engaging in pure political
advocacy. This contradiction is often overlooked in recounting the passionate defense of free speech that emerged from the opinion. Brandeis's
supporters have long insisted that the vote to uphold the conviction was
due to the fact that the free speech claim was not properly raised and preserved in the case, a view that others have questioned.

Louis Brandeis had much in common with Whitney. Both saw great
injustice in the world and worked as activists to address it. Brandeis was
born to a Jewish family that lived in Louisville, Kentucky. The Brandeis
family were abolitionists before the Civil War and moved to Indiana.
Brandeis attended Harvard Law School, ultimately graduating as the
school's valedictorian with the highest average in the history of the school.

In 1890, with his partner and former classmate Samuel D. Warren, Brandeis wrote one of the most important law review articles in the history in the *Harvard Law Review*, titled "The Right to Privacy." It single-handedly articulated a new area of constitutional and torts protection.

In 1910, when Whitney was losing faith in social work and becoming a socialist activist, Brandeis was railing against monopolies in Boston, famously declaring that "we must make our choice. We may have democracy, or we may have wealth concentrated in the hands of a few, but we can't have both." Where Whitney became a political activist for equality and justice, Brandeis became known as "the People's lawyer" for his legal crusades. As Whitney was fighting to establish economic and political equality for women, Brandeis was in court fighting for better workplace conditions, including one of the most important Supreme Court victories to improve conditions and working hours for women. When he was later nominated by Woodrow Wilson to the Supreme Court, critics labeled him a radical much like Whitney, and his confirmation was so controversial that it dragged on for four months. It was the first public confirmation hearing held with witnesses. Part of the controversy stemmed from Brandeis's progressive work as a lawyer, but there were also anti-Semitic attacks leveled against the brilliant lawyer. Even on the Court, Brandeis faced virulent prejudice and sought change in society. In fact, Brandeis would go on to serve with one of the most virulent anti-Semites in the history of the Court: Justice James McReynolds. McReynolds was a poisonous, hateful man who even Chief Justice William Taft described as a "continual grouch" and "selfish to the last degree . . . fuller of prejudice than any man I have ever known . . . one who delights in making others uncomfortable." While also appointed by President Wilson, McReynolds refused to go to Brandeis's swearing in and reportedly refused to speak to him directly for years. He would leave the room when Brandeis spoke and later refused to sign the customary retirement letter for Brandeis. When another brilliant Jewish jurist was nominated for the Court, Benjamin Cardozo, McReynolds wrote President Herbert Hoover (with Justices Pierce Butler and Willis Van Devanter) opposing the appointment of Cardozo so not to "afflict the Court with another Jew." It did not work and, when Cardozo was nominated, McReynolds said, "Huh, it seems that the only way you can get on the Supreme Court these days is to be either the son of a criminal or a Jew, or both." Thus, even on the Court, Brandeis defied blind intolerance and prejudice.

There was, however, a difference. Where Whitney became more convinced that the system was fundamentally flawed and incapable of reform without radical political action, Brandeis remained firmly embedded within that system and optimistic that it could achieve social justice. Like Whitney, everything in Brandeis's life seemed to draw him to one particular moment when, on October 6, 1925, Chief Justice Taft called the case of *Whitney v. California* before the Court for oral argument. The radical blacklisted feminist would come before the radical shunned jurist in a battle for the right of free speech in America. The result was historic, as Brandeis saw the opportunity for sharing that horizonal view of what constitutional law should be in a nation committed to individual rights. He wrote:

> Those who won our independence believed that the final end of the state was to make men free to develop their faculties; and that in its government the deliberative forces should prevail over the arbitrary. They valued liberty both as an end and as a means. They believed liberty to be the secret of happiness and courage to be the secret of liberty. They believed that freedom to think as you will and to speak as you think are means indispensable to the discovery and spread of political truth; that without free speech and assembly discussion would be futile; that with them, discussion affords ordinarily adequate protection against the dissemination of noxious doctrine; that the greatest menace to freedom is an inert people; that public discussion is a

political duty; and that this should be a fundamental principle of the American government. . . . They knew that order cannot be secured merely through fear of punishment for its infraction; that it is hazardous to discourage thought, hope and imagination; that fear breeds repression; that repression breeds hate; that hate menaces stable government; that the path of safety lies in the opportunity to discuss freely supposed grievances and proposed remedies; and that the fitting remedy for evil counsels is good ones. Believing in the power of reason as applied through public discussion, they eschewed silence coerced by law—the argument of force in its worst form. Recognizing the occasional tyrannies of governing majorities, they amended the Constitution so that free speech and assembly should be guaranteed.

The statement is as inspiring on the underlying right as it is incongruous with the result in the case in upholding the conviction. It also highlights the subtle tension among those who support the right for free speech but differ on what makes it "indispensable." While Brandeis emphasizes the need to show that speech is likely to cause immediate harm or lawlessness, he still found room to uphold the conviction in this repressive case.

Brandeis states that free speech is both the end and the means, which would seem to affirm that free speech itself is the purpose of the Constitution. However, the rest of the discussion suggests a narrower (and likely more intended) meaning. Brandeis rattles off the classic "functionalist" purpose of free speech to enable citizens to seek change and perfect the democratic system as a whole. Free speech is "indispensable to the discovery and spread of political truth" and "to discuss grievances and proposed remedies." There is no question that he is correct. Free speech does all that and more in protecting other rights and other citizens in our system. However, the focus on that democratic function lends itself to balancing tests based on the value of given speech within that functionalist construct. As discussed below, both Brandeis and Holmes show how even great civil libertarians could accept draconian measures against free speech under this functionalist rationale. If free speech is protected to fulfill the goals of democratic governance, some speech can be barred as inimical to that function. As will be discussed, the British believed that criticizing leaders and judges undermined the system. Thus, in a particularly twisted functionalist rationalization, the British would protect the free speech of members of Parliament while criminalizing criticism of those officials as necessary for good government.

The alternative view is to focus on the indispensability of free speech to individuals as a natural right or a right based on a broader view of individual liberty or autonomy. Often seen as a basis for free speech for centuries, this autonomous view was largely abandoned in the United States in early free speech cases. Yet it offers a clarity that is missing in creating building blocks of past functionalist approaches and also admittedly allows for a broader range of speech that many today find intolerable. Instead, these trade-offs are now used to rationalize censorship and speech codes.

The Court has repeatedly dismissed the notion that "low value" speech is protected in the same degree of political speech or, in some cases, at all. In the case of *Chaplinsky v. New Hampshire* in 1941, the Court upheld conviction of a protester who verbally abused an arresting officer. The Court expanded on the notion of "fighting words" as an unprotected category—a variation on "bad tendency" or rage rhetoric rationales:

> [Exceptions to the protections of the First Amendment] include the lewd and obscene, the profane, the libelous, and the insulting or "fighting" words—those which, by their very utterance, inflict injury or tend to incite an immediate breach of the peace. It has been well observed that such utterances are not an essential part of any exposition of ideas, and are of such slight social value as a step to truth that any benefit that may be derived from them is clearly outweighed by the social interest in order and morality.

Chaplinsky and the fighting words doctrine rested on the same functionalist rationales that some speech is just not valuable in the "exposition of ideas." Any autonomous right to speak was dismissed and the arrest was justified in the trade-off against generalized claims of "order and morality."

Roughly fifty years ago, the Supreme Court in *Brandenburg v. Ohio* sought to limit the criminalization of speech. Yet legislative and litigation efforts continue to push for the criminalization of violent speech. It is a familiar cycling pattern for the free speech community. These fights emerge on the far extremes of our society, where free speech often garners the least popular support. Whether it is Antifa on the left or the Proud Boys on the right, rage rhetoric drives renewed calls for censorship or criminalization. Anti–free speech advocates know hateful or violent speech is hard to defend, but its defense is essential for reasons entirely removed from its content. "Rage rhetoric" is often the manifestation of deep and bitter divisions within our society; social, political, and religious grievances boiling just under the surface of our political discourse. Moving beyond speech used to plan or commit specific crimes, the government has long targeted a wide array of speech as rage rhetoric that can ignite others to actions. It is speech that would be stripped of protections by the Supreme Court as presenting a "bad tendency" for public discord.

As will be shown below, these cases demonstrate how the status of extremist speech has bedeviled leading legal figures for centuries. The temptation to silence rage rhetoric has proven irresistible even for intellectual icons like Justice Oliver Wendell Holmes. The result was transparent rationales for curtailing speech, including the Holmesian mantra of "shouting fire in a crowded theater." With every period of unrest, the same rationales reappear to prevent "bad tendency" speech from inciting others. Yet the choice is not between sedition and stampedes. It is the rationalization found in "bad tendency" cases that has proven the most dangerous tendency in our history. It is the tendency to treat speech as either inherently harmful under sedition laws or inherently worthless under modern doctrines like the "integral speech exception."

In "The Tempest" arising in periods of political discord, rage rhetoric is the very crest of the sea storm; speech that is intended to shock or to motivate others. "Burn, baby, burn!" was used in the sixties as much as an exhortation for radical change as it was for actual arson. It became a common cry for challenging the establishment from politics to the arts. Protesters often demand a reckoning as a prelude to reform. That does not excuse reckless rhetoric that can incite others. However, violent language is often used to capture a sense of urgency or injury. That was evident on January 6, 2021, when former president Donald Trump's counsel Rudy Giuliani warned the crowd that "If we're wrong, we will be made fools of. But if we're right, a lot of them will go to jail. So, let's have trial by combat." Likewise, Democrats have engaged in similarly reckless language in highly volatile situations. In Minneapolis, riots were unfolding when Representative Maxine Waters (D-Calif.) called on supporters to "get confrontational" if a police officer was not convicted. As death threats mounted against justices in 2020, Senate Majority Leader Chuck Schumer (D-N.Y.) went to the steps of the Supreme Court to declare, "I want to tell you, Gorsuch, I want to tell you, Kavanaugh, you have released the whirlwind and you will pay the price! You won't know what hit you if you go forward with these awful decisions." It was all thrilling to supporters who vented what they saw as righteous rage. Some even mimicked violence against those with opposing views. Representative Paul Gosar (R-Ariz.) edited an animated video that portrayed him killing Representative Alexandria Ocasio-Cortez (D-N.Y.), while Trump edited a video showing him assaulting a CNN figure. One cannot discount the impact of these calls or images on those inclined to take violent or criminal actions. Moreover, rage can be addictive. It gives people a license to speak and act with a certain abandon. To protect rage rhetoric is not to condone it. It is to shift the focus on conduct rather than speech.

Rage is a form of speech and, like all expression, it is a matter of both interpretation and perspective. Even the word itself can mean vastly different things from "violent and uncontrollable anger" to mere "intense feelings" or passion. In some circumstances, rage can be considered rational or commendable in the face of extreme conditions or provocation. It can even be celebrated in student protesters at Kent State in 1970 or the gay community at the Stonewall Inn in 1969. The extreme rhetoric used at these moments can reflect a rejection of the status quo or power structures. We "rage against the machine" in music or "rage against racism" in protests. It is the moment captured by the words of Dylan Thomas when he warned us that we must "not go gentle into that good night. . . . Rage, rage against the dying of the light." While Thomas was speaking of the defiance of old age, rage often is the response to what is viewed as inevitable or inequitable in society. The call for extreme change is often matched with extremist speech. That is precisely what rage offers, a license and clarity for many. It is that release that is the reason, to paraphrase Virgil, that "rage supplies [us] with weapons."

Rage captures a crisis of faith within a system. It signals a fundamental break with not only the status quo but also conventional discourse. It can also have a positive element for a society when it remains speech rather than violence. While rage rhetoric is not inherently dialogic, it has a benefit in venting intense and previously unreleased pressures in a society: "people obtain psychological release through the simple process of recounting their grievances. . . . Letting off steam may make it easier to talk rationally later." Sigmund Freud viewed the expression of anger and rage as healthy due to its ability to bring a level of catharsis. Freud believed that repressing such emotions could cause greater and more lasting damage. He viewed rage as residing "on the frontier between the mental and the somatic," or the border between the psychological and the physiological. It has long been a manifestation of political or social pressures that are not being addressed through the political system.

We have a right to rage. It is rageful acts, not speech alone, that the state can punish. Rage rhetoric often captures parts of our society that are isolated or underrepresented in the political system. It is unrestrained and unyielding. While it is often treated as "low value" and inherently threatening to society, it can also be the expression of the most alienated within a society. It is often seditious in the sense of "intending to persuade other people to oppose their government." However, in a democratic society, we have the right to fundamentally change our government and its policies. While most citizens may reject the extreme demands of rage politics, many citizens may view the rage as justified in seeking change. Indeed, yesterday's radicals often find themselves today's establishment figures. Those from Bernie Sanders to Al Sharpton have become mainstream political figures after years of radical political action.

Rage rhetoric has long been the stress test for free speech in society— a test that every nation has failed throughout history. The United States established an unprecedented protection when it barred any abridgment of the freedom of speech. Yet soon after that historic standard was ratified, the courts adopted an abridged interpretation of free speech that allowed seditious libel and the criminalization of bad-tendency speech. This may be due to the same perspective of a beneficent government reflected in English writings, including those of John Stuart Mill. The colonies had been allowed a fair degree of free speech despite the discretionary authority of the Crown. Whatever the intent of the Framers, there is no debate that the criminalization of speech found fertile ground for its application in the new Republic.

Functionalist rationales have long dominated Europe. In countries like Great Britain, there was a highly limited view of free speech and free press at the time of the Revolution. Speech protections were justified narrowly, including the protections of Parliamentarians to be able to speak freely to pursue the public interest. This same rationale would later extend to other citizens who were viewed as using free speech to advance democratic values and participatory government. It resulted in free speech remaining tethered to democratic rationales by a rope that could be longer or shorter in a given country or circumstance. It was a matter of context and conflicting interests. As new avenues for speech developed, from the printing press to the internet, countervailing interests grew for limits due to the enhanced harms from speech, from mass dissent to mass disinformation. In the absence of a deeper foundation for free speech, these trade-offs have worked inexorably against free speech. In the last few decades, this erosion has accelerated as the West has embraced new rationales for limiting the harm of speech to protect against malinformation, misinformation, and disinformation. While the lexicon is new, the purpose remains the same: to control speech in the interests of social order. Whether it is dangerous, destabilizing, or divisive, the benefit of the speech is considered minimal when balanced against the cost.

In any age of rage, free speech is the first victim. What few today want to admit is that they like it. They like the freedom that it affords, the ability to hate and harass without a sense of responsibility. It is evident all around us as people engage in language and conduct that they repudiate in others. We have become a nation of rage addicts; flailing against anyone or anything that stands in opposition to our own truths. Like all addictions, there is not only a dependency on rage but an intolerance for opposing views. The difference between rage and reason is often one's own views. If one agrees with underlying grievance, rage is viewed as passion or justified fury at injustice. If one disagrees with those views, it takes on a more threatening and unhinged quality. We seem to spend much of our time today raging at each other. Despite the amplification of views on both sides, there is also an increasing intolerance for opposing views. Those views are treated as simply harmful and offensive—and, therefore, intolerable. Indeed, to voice free speech principles in a time of rage is to invite the rage of the mob.

As will be shown below, our Constitution was written not only for times like these, but in a time like this. Yet there are few historical periods that match the current level of violent and hateful speech from both the left and the right. With the violent protests in various cities and the January 6th riot in Congress, citizens have turned on each other and increasingly oppose the right of others to be heard. Groups like Antifa were founded as anti–free speech movements and have grown across the country. From college campuses to the pages of the *New York Times*, the voices of intolerance are now amplified against free speech. Writers call for censorship. Academics call for compelled speech. It is a sign of citizens becoming untethered from the values that have defined them and their professions; it is a crisis of faith that reaches every corner of our society. Roughly seventy years ago, Justice William O. Douglas accepted a prestigious award with a speech titled "The One Un-American Act," about the greatest threat to a free nation. He warned that the restriction of free speech "is the most dangerous of all subversions. It is the one un-American act that could most easily defeat us." Many of these officials, journalists, and academics today would be mortified to be associated with "censorship" or an anti–free speech movement. Yet, the use of euphemisms like "disinformation" or "content moderation" does not change the fact that they are part of a comprehensive effort to control and, in some cases, punish the exercise of free expression.

Our history shows that anti–free speech impulses rest in the body

politic like a dormant virus. They spring forward in times of perils or unrest like a fever. This book explores this right and this history in four parts.
First, it explores the basis for free speech and how it has been addressed by
societies ranging from the ancient Greeks to the British Empire to a newly
created American Republic. The United States was premised on a clear
break from its English antecedent. The First Amendment was the single
greatest constitutional commitment to the right of free expression in history. Second, the book looks at how quickly this clarity was lost in the
new Republic. Starting with John Adams, revolutionaries quickly adopted
many of the same abusive measures of the British in crushing dissenting
views as harmful or leading to "bad tendencies." Despite our checkered
history on free speech, this country remains the greatest protector of free
speech in the world. That status is due not to our leaders but to defiant
figures insisting that they had a right to free expression as a right shared
by all human beings. Third, the book looks at the adoption of Blackstonian rationales by the Supreme Court as embodied by the disastrous line
by Oliver Wendell Holmes about shouting fire in a theater. The line is
associated with *Schenck v. United States*, where Holmes would be joined
by Brandeis in eviscerating the protections for free speech in the United
States. It would become the virtual mantra of the current anti–free speech
movement. While later set aside, the line (and its underlying fallacy) continues to be invoked by politicians and pundits alike to justify the limiting
of free speech. Even as the Supreme Court and commentators recognized
the failures of past periods, they rationalized these crackdowns as manifestations of periods of rage or fear. They focused on the catalyst but not
the cause of the speech erosion. Holmes is the perfect embodiment of
the intense conflict over the role and meaning of free speech in our society. His personal and intellectual struggle with natural or transcendent
rights would play out in a series of opinions on free speech. Finally, the
book turns to restoring this indispensable right by revisiting the question of what free speech is and why it is indispensable not for democracy
but humanity. It also explores legislative options for barring the government from supporting or funding censorship and blacklisting operations, and further proposes changes to restore a diversity of viewpoints

in higher education. The book ultimately suggests a final break with sedition crimes, the very concept discarded over two centuries ago after our founding. After centuries of rage followed by regret, we have to break our sedition addiction and finally put to rest what James Madison described as the "monster" lurking within our legal system.

Our history of the struggle for free speech is the story of extraordinary people, nonconformists who refused to yield to abusive authority. Our struggle with free speech is a mosaic of vivid characters and controversies, periods that spawned conspiracies and panic. From the Order of the Illuminati to the Copperheads to the Red Scare, our demons often reflected our own insecurities or prejudices as a nation. They were our excuses to deny this fundamental right to those with opposing views or values. In hindsight, these figures can seem largely harmless, even comically overblown. Yet, in any given period (including the current one), opposing voices seem existential threats. The cycle continues to repeat itself. We condemn earlier periods while replicating the same mistakes, even using the very same rhetoric from "false news" to "threats against democracy." Each of these periods shows not just rage rhetoric but state rage in the treatment of dissenting voices or political opponents. This pattern of speech suppression continued throughout our history in a failure of all three branches in the tripartite constitutional system. We are justifiably proud of our protection of free speech, particularly at a time when the right is in decline around the world. Yet our often mythic view of free speech ignores our systemic denial of this right. If we are to understand this right, we have to recognize our history through the figures and failures that shaped us. We have to ask difficult questions about the limits of our tolerance for the speech of others, including those who we view as hateful or harmful. We cannot focus on just the redemptive moments when our rage subsided and reason prevailed. We remain a nation grappling with what free speech means to us as a people. What follows is meant to be the unvarnished story of free speech in America. For better or worse, it is our story.

Part I

THE
INDISPENSABLE
RIGHT

One

FREE EXPRESSION AND THE HUMAN CONDITION

Free speech is a human right. It is the free expression of thought that is the essence of being human. As will be discussed in chapter 2, free speech is often justified in functionalist terms; it is protected because it is necessary for a democratic process and the protection of other rights. That is certainly true. Brandeis's view of the right's indispensability was due to the fact that most rights are realized through acts of expression, from the free press to association to religious exercise. However, it is more than the sum of its practical benefits. It is the natural condition of humans to speak. It is compelled silence or agreement that is unnatural. That is why it takes coercion or threats to compel silence from others.

We rarely teach the philosophy of free speech to young students. They largely learn a rote understanding of the First Amendment and a functionalist explanation on how the free speech right protects other rights. If students even receive civics lessons, there is little time or inclination to teach the relationship of speech to the essential qualities of being human. Natural and autonomous theories tie free speech to a preexistent or immutable status. As such, it is not the creation of the Constitution, but rather embodied in that document. There remains considerable debate over how natural rights theory motivated the Framers. What is clear is that these men were moved in the eighteenth century to create something that was a radical departure from what came before it. As historian Leonard Levy observed, "liberty of expression barely existed in principle and practice in the American colonies," let alone other nations around the world. What possessed James Madison to draft the First Amendment in absolutist terms was likely a mix of the experiential and the philosophical. The Framers had experienced the denial of free speech at the hands of the Crown, but it would have been an easy matter to expressly protect political speech. Rather than replicate what came before, the Framers spoke of protecting all speech from abridgment from the government. These were men who often spoke of the "unalienable" rights of humans in defining the role of the government. A transcendent right to free speech was consistent with the concepts of natural rights that emerged from the Enlightenment.

One of the most influential philosophers for the Framers (and a host of later philosophers like Voltaire) was John Locke. In 1689, Locke published his masterpiece, *Two Treatises of Government*, on the foundation for civil society and government. He described a "state of nature" and how God created the Earth with all that creation left in common for the use of mankind. Locke then presented his "labor theory" of property as a natural right that flowed from this divine gift. According to Locke, people have a right to property by removing something found in nature and mixing it with their labor. Through his labor, man becomes a creator by "join[ing] it to something that is his own." In other words, God gave Man the ability to create and claim the creations "mixed with his labor" as his own. What was left in common for the use of all was converted into private property through individual enterprise. Yet Locke added a "proviso" that you must still leave "enough and as good" for others. Many writers have explored both the labor theory and the proviso in defining the right to property, particularly against efforts of government to distribute wealth. It also raises a question of why God would leave everything in common and then allow Man to "make it his own property." The reason, I suggest, is that humans are themselves creators with a common need to express themselves in the world around them. Putting aside the desire to procreate as itself an act of creation, the desire to create objects or expressions is irresistible for most people, from the simple act of doodling to the construction of the Great Wall of China. It is seen from the drawings in the cave of Lascaux from 17,000 BCE to

the graffiti on walls in New York City in the twenty-first century. Creation is the expression of ourselves, the projection into the world of our values and visions.

Consider the center of Michelangelo's magnificent Sistine Chapel. People have debated for centuries of what the image of God touching Man was meant to depict. For many, the image is taken as giving life or an element of divinity. However, what is the divinity passed to Man? Perhaps that touch is not the act of creation but the power of creation. After all, the scriptures maintain that Man is both the creation of God but also made in the image of God. What is divine is the ability to change the world around us, to create. When Renaissance painter and writer Giorgio Vasari described Michelangelo, he used "the divine Michelangelo" to capture the provenance of his creations. The very terms *create* and *creation* are semantically and conceptually tied to the ultimate "Creator." To again bring in Locke, it is to use what is left in common to express ourselves in unique ways. Just as Man was created from clay, God left us clay to form our own creations from the state of nature.

To be human is to create, and these creations are a form of speech. Under this view, whether it is a column or a cake or a cathedral, creation is a quintessentially human act. Without such expression, we are human in form alone; realized clay, but clay alone, from the original act of creation.

What makes us human is obviously a subject heavily infused with subjectivity and religiosity. How one views the essential elements of humanity depends on how one views the potential and position of humans. Like other animals, we procreate; we experience pain and pleasure. We share chemical, muscular, and emotive impulses with other animals. There is even some evidence that other species have sentience. New studies indicate that other animals have an awareness of their existence and cognitive abilities long assumed to be uniquely human. We share 98.7 percent of our genetic sequencing with great apes like chimpanzees and bonobos. Does that make us more conversant, less hairy apes? We also share 80 percent with a cow, and 61 percent with a fruit fly. There is even a 60 percent overlap with a banana. The effort to distinguish a human from a banana is easy with comparisons from color to complexity. However, it is easier to explain why we are not a banana than it is to explain what makes us human beings.

Humans are more than talking bananas, despite our shared genetic sequencing. Whether that is due to the "divine touch" captured in the Sistine Chapel or some other element will continue to occupy philosophers and theologians for centuries to come. Yet understanding the essence of humanity is not entirely a debate over metaphysical points. There are some physical elements that distinguish humans in how we interact with the world around us. In her book *The Creative Brain*, neuroscientist Nancy Andreasen notes that the human brain is wired to all nonlinear thought and "when the brain/mind thinks in a free and unencumbered fashion, it uses its most human and complex parts."

Neurological studies suggest that the human brain is hardwired for expression. The evolution of innovative capabilities offered a survival advantage, including the ability to communicate and motivate through pictures and words. These include "basic biological needs in animals such as live-or-die (dire necessity), physical energy conservation, and survival through deception." This may have been responsible for creating the drive for innovation and expression in humans: "Given adaptive evolutionary processes, it is reasonable to assume that all of these have become interwoven into the underlying brain mechanisms of creativity in humans."

The frontal lobe was the last part of the human brain to evolve and addresses the complex cognitive functions that are closely associated with being human. The oldest part of the brain is often called the reptilian brain containing the brain stem and the cerebellum. Much as in other animals, it controls our bodily functions, from heart rate to balance. The limbic brain added key components for creative thought and high cognitive functioning. Containing the hippocampus, the amygdala, and the hypothalamus, the limbic brain gives us our powerful emotions and memories. Scientists have long identified the neocortex, including the frontal lobe, as affording humans higher capacities for language, imagination, and abstract thought. Neuroscientists believe that "subcortical brain circuits" evolved late in the development of "the forebrain bundle" and are the key to our curiosity and creativity.

Our early understanding of these physiological differences often came from intentional or accidental denials of stimulus or speech. It also came from the loss of the function of brain areas. Much of this early knowledge came from tragic stories like that of Phineas Gage and his tapping iron.

In September 1848, Gage, twenty-five, was working as a railroad foreman in Cavendish, Vermont. His crew was removing rock to lay track and, as the foreman, it fell to Gage to set the charge. A hole was drilled, and explosives stuffed into the bottom. The next step was to pack sand over the TNT using a tamping iron. The iron was 43 inches long, 1.25 inches in diameter, and weighed 13.25 pounds. Gage shoved it down the

hole but accidentally sparked the explosive. It was a nearly lethal mistake. Gage had built an effective cannon out of rock and was staring directly down the barrel. The rod shot straight out of the hole and entered Gage's left cheek and passed through the top of his skull. Brain matter and blood covered Gage as he was blown a fair distance from the hole. The crew was horrified.

They assumed Gage was

dead and were shocked when he regained consciousness and walked to a nearby oxcart to be taken to a doctor. In the cart, Gage was seen writing in his workbook, and he could recognize figures like Dr. John Martyn Harlow, who came to treat him. Despite Gage's extraordinary demeanor, Harlow expected his patient to die. That prognosis was understandable given the massive wound and the bleeding, which continued for two days. Gage then developed an infection that left him semiconscious for a month. His friends prepared a coffin for him. However, Gage did not die. The rod had blown away part of his brain's frontal lobe. Harlow recognized that this was a unique opportunity to better understand the function of that body part by observing changes after its removal. It was clearly not necessary for life, but it was necessary to being fully human. Even on the evening of the accident, Gage was conversant and could remember names and other details. After a month, Gage was able to travel to New Hampshire to continue his convalescence at his parents' home. Yet, more than just the loss of sight in one eye, Gage was an altogether changed man. He was more aggressive and had problems maintaining relationships. He became abusive and a heavy drinker. He had a hard time holding down a job. Despite being described as a model foreman, the mining company did not want him back. Gage would take various jobs including driving coaches in Chile and would even travel with his rod as a human curiosity with American showman P. T. Barnum. He would eventually die from what was described as epileptic seizures in 1860 at the age of thirty-six.

Some changes in Gage's personality were clearly related to the trauma of having a metal rod blown through his head. Moreover, some of the changes in Gage dissipated over time. Yet there remained lasting changes. His friends stated that his personality was different, and some described him as more impulsive, socially inappropriate, and as possessing what were described as "animal propensities." In his study, Dr. Harlow recounted how Gage's supervisors:

> regarded him as the most efficient and capable foreman . . . considered the change in his mind so marked that they could not give him his place again. . . . He is fitful, irreverent, indulging at times in the

grossest profanity (which was not previously his custom), manifest-
ing but little deference for his fellows, impatient of restraint or advice
when it conflicts with his desires. . . . A child in his intellectual capacity
and manifestations, he has the animal passions of a strong man. . . .
His mind was radically changed, so decidedly that his friends and ac-
quaintances said he was "no longer Gage."

Some of these changes have been tied to the loss of parts of the brain
connected to emotional processing. The tamping iron is now believed to
have destroyed roughly 11 percent of the white matter in Gage's frontal lobe
and 4 percent of his cerebral cortex. Later studies showed evidence of damage to the left and right prefrontal cortices. Studies of traumatic brain injury
(TBI) show how creativity can be lost with these areas of the brain. Gage's
wound not only removed part of the frontal lobe but caused traumatic injury to much of what remained after the rod was blown through his head.

Whether by divine creation or evolutionary change, humans are
creative beings. The loss of parts of the brain has been shown to have
profound impacts. Even in monkeys, the removal of prefrontal lobes produced changes in personality. However, for humans, the loss of areas of
the limbic and neocortex can limit those functions allowing for creative
expression—the very areas that distinguish humans from other primates.
Neuroscience studies have found that the "inordinate capacity for creativity [in humans] reflects the unique neurological organization of the
human brain." It was not just that Gage was viewed as having "animal
propensities," he lacked human characteristics. Creative thinking requires
the ability to project images; to apply concepts to new forms of application or expression. It necessitates "fundamental cognitive processes such
as working memory, attention, planning, cognitive flexibility, mentaliz-
ing, and abstract thinking." These are functions contained in prefrontal
areas of the brain. What Gage lost may have been not just part of his brain
but part of his essential humanity. Without the ability to be creative and
to express himself, the explosion was de-evolutionary, arguably returning
Gage to an earlier state of primate. He was still physiologically human but
lacked the full capacity for human expression.

That returns us to Michelangelo's touch. Some have noted the framing over the image of God is in the shape of the human brain. God's image appears over what can be interpreted as the limbic system, and his right arm extends to the prefrontal cortex, the areas that most distinguish human beings from other primates. Michelangelo was an anatomist who began dissecting corpses at age seventeen. In a 1990 paper published in the *Journal of the American Medical Association*, Dr. Frank Meshberger showed how the depiction in *The Creation of Adam* in the central panel appeared to be an anatomical cross section of the human brain. The anatomical overlay raises the question of what Michelangelo was trying to convey beyond a humanistic element. For example, by literally embedding the Almighty in the human brain, it could be viewed as bestowing the divine gift of creation and transcendent thought.

To be denied the gift of creation is to leave humans in a state far from divine. The Gage story allowed science to judge what happened to creativity and other human characteristics when an actual part of the human body was removed. The loss of certain environmental elements can produce similar effects on humans. As a lawyer that began his career working with prisoners, I have long observed the rapid decline of clients in segregation where inmates are cut off from most human contact or avenues for expression for prolonged periods of time. The impact of such isolation is often immediate and pronounced. Human beings are inherently social animals and require forms of expression or avenues of interaction. In one study of segregation, researchers found dramatically heightened levels of depression, anxiety, hallucinations, and other forms of mental illness. One common complaint is "a perceived loss of identity." It is a profound by-product of being deprived the interaction with others that we can lose our sense of ourselves, or self-identity. In a curious way, we need others to be ourselves.

Clearly, various elements are in play in segregated conditions that include sensory deprivation, monotonous routine, and strict confinement. However, studies show a need for inmates to be able to break from monotony and have exposure and interaction with different expressive elements. This is not simply psychological but physiological. One recent study looked at the impact of isolation of Antarctic expeditioners. These individuals could speak with each other and work on tasks associated with their expedition, including journals. But the range of intellectual stimulation and expression was sharply limited by the monotonous and confined conditions. Research found evidence of a shrinking hippocampus in the subjects. The seahorse-shaped region embedded in the temporal lobe of the brain is key to memory and creativity. In his work on creativity in the human brain, Dr. Roger Beaty noted that "memory, imagination, and creative thinking all activated the bilateral hippocampus." The studies on isolation suggest that humans forced into limiting or monotonous existences can experience actual physical losses affecting the capacity for creativity. They can lose their full potential for the range of human creative thought.

Isolation studies do not prove human nature or its essential elements. Yet the question remains: What is uniquely human? There exists a driving desire in humans to create, to express, to invent, and to build. While bees and termites can create intricate structures, humans constantly break from the status quo and seek new forms and concepts. It is not merely an effort to survive. Indeed, the iconic image of the starving artist attests to how this creative drive can be the denial of every other aspect of life. It is an irresistible, even involuntary impulse. Mozart, when once asked about his music composition, admitted "whence and how they come. I know not; nor can I force them." Nor can many deny them, from artistic to political expression—even at one's peril. As Dr. Andreasen noted, "[A]t the neural level associations begin to form where they did not previously exist, and some of these associations are perilously novel."

It is a drive that everyone exhibits in ways that can be grand or gross. Even neighbors who spend weeks creating elaborate Halloween or holiday displays seem to be fulfilling a deeper human impulse. As evidenced by the neurological studies, we are constructed for creative thought, for remembering and imagining, and for projecting thoughts into the future to create new realities. That process involves expression in myriad forms. It is an impulse that is irresistible for many. It is also an impulse that can threaten the status quo, which is why the earlier forms of government sought to control the expression of divergent thoughts.

Two

ANCIENT SPEECH AND
NATURAL LAW

The struggle of individuals against even tyrannical rule is a testament to this drive to think and speak freely. There is a compulsion to make actual what is conceptual or abstract. This includes adherence to a religious code that transcends immediate human needs or authority. The earliest philosophical works often addressed acts of free speech made in defiance of the government or the majority in a given society. *Antigone*, by Sophocles in 441 BCE, tells the story of the daughter of Oedipus, whose two brothers fought to the death for the throne of Thebes. The tyrant ruler Creon orders that one of the brothers be left where he fell on the field of battle while the other is buried with honors. The abandonment of her brother's corpse is a terrible offense, one that Antigone cannot abide. She disobeys her uncle Creon and buries her brother Polynices. Creon is outraged that his order was defied and has Antigone brought to him. His niece is unrepentant because she maintains that, despite his authority, it was an affront to God: "The unwritten laws of God that know not change. They are not of today nor yesterday." Her words send Creon into a full rage, and he orders Antigone to be walled off in a cave to die a slow death. When he finally sees that he has angered the Gods, he goes to the cave to free Antigone, only to find that she has hanged herself. The play is often discussed as one of the earliest works exploring the corruption of absolute power but also the existence of a natural law that goes beyond the power of the state. Antigone's offense was not simply her disobeying of the order but also her speech of defiance of the king of Thebes. She invoked laws that adhere to humans as human beings, not as the by-product of citizenship or by the allowance of rulers. Even though the play focuses on the superiority of moral tenets to secular rule, the moral tenets are only supported through acts of expression.

Other Greek accounts feature similar acts of defiance. The most famous is the death of Socrates. The ancient philosopher was convicted of corrupting the youth with his lessons and worshipping false gods (despite also being accused of being an atheist). Socrates remained defiant over his right to speak and think freely. Like Antigone, he invoked divine authority to be able to express his own truth: "I will obey the god rather than you and as long as I draw breath and am able, I shall not cease to practice philosophy, to exhort you." According to Plato's *Apology*, the jury in the trial was deeply divided. Had thirty voted to acquit, Socrates would have lived and continued to corrupt another day. If true, a jury of 501 had 221 jurors who agreed with the arguments of Socrates. The philosopher willingly

The Death of Socrates (1787) by Jacques-Louis David

took the hemlock cup rather than agree to be silent or to leave the city. The story of Socrates highlights another important element of free speech that reflects the different justifications of the right as a human right or a more limited functionalist right. The ancient Greeks captured this difference in two different terms for "the freedom of speech."

The Greeks used the terms *isegoria* and *parrhesia*. *Isegoria* described the equal right to participate in public debate in a democratic society, while *parrhesia* referred to the ability to speak freely, to speak one's mind. The Oxford political theorist Teresa Bejan has noted that *isegoria* is the older of the two concepts. It comes closest to the functionalist defense of free speech. However, there may be less to that than meets the eye. The first discussion of rights often follows its denial. Public debates or forums would likely be the first time that a fight over the right to speak would arise, or at least be recorded. *Isegoria* appears derived in part from *agora*, or the marketplace, where public debate often occurred in ancient Greece. During its periods of democratic rule, Athens was committed to the concept of *isegoria* to the point that the fourth-century orator and patriot Demosthenes complained about even slaves and foreigners having this right to speak publicly. Bejan notes "*isegoria* was fundamentally about equality, not freedom." Yet there was also *parrhesia*, which can be translated as "all saying," or speaking one's mind. It comes closest to the liberty defense of free speech. Great Greek playwrights like Sophocles and philosophers like Socrates were practitioners of *parrhesia*, confronting fellow citizens with often uncomfortable or unwelcomed views. The distinction between the functionalist and autonomous rationales would become more pronounced over time. Many theorists would frame their defenses of free speech in *isegoria* terms. However, philosophers such as Immanuel Kant spoke of "the freedom to make public use of one's reason." For those of us who favor *parrhesia*, the right to use one's reason extends beyond matters of public debate to a wide range of expression. It embodies the right for one's speech to follow where reason or creativity takes us.

Antigone and Socrates are early figures who died for their refusal to yield to the state or the views of the majority. Later works would tie the protection of speech to its place as "the cornerstone of democracy." This functionalist view of speech treats free expression as the means by which a democracy can fully function. From Plato to the poet Euripides, free speech was repeatedly connected to democratic guarantees. It would be a nexus that would become more and more prominent in the defense of free speech. By protecting free speech, you are protecting a right needed to fulfill the democratic process. It made for more informed and engaged citizens; it exposed bad ideas and policies in society. It is a highly effective defense against those who attacked speech as undermining good order. For much of human history, rulers sought to control speech and publications. The framing of speech protections as advancing good government was a radical view in these early works that served to expand liberty. Yet it also decoupled speech protections from a natural right or autonomous foundation for speech. When functionalist rationales achieved protections for free speech, they came at a considerable cost. It meant that speech was protected to the extent that it advanced that function. Speech that was not directed to matters of public concern or speech deemed to have little inherent value could be curtailed. In this way, a rationale that protected speech would over time become its nemesis.

There were early figures who were able to transcend the narrow framing of free speech theories. For example, in the seventeenth century, a philosopher named Baruch (Benedictus de) Spinoza emerged as one of the most intriguing and influential figures of the Dutch Golden Age. Raised in a Portuguese Jewish family, Spinoza had the unique ability to shed the assumptions and expectations of his age. He was unyielding in his quest for truth, even getting himself exiled from the Jewish community for questioning core religious dogma. Spinoza was influenced by writers like Thomas Hobbes, who wrote about the emergence of humanity from a state of nature to form organized societies. For Hobbes, the state of nature was a brutish, violent place that required a government Leviathan to protect citizens. What was different is that Spinoza did not view citizens as surrendering their natural freedom to all-powerful figures. Rather, he saw the creation of the state as a way for people to be fully human:

It is not, I say, the end of the state to change men from rational beings into beasts or automata, but the opposite, that their mind and body may perform their functions safely and that they may use this same reason freely, and that they should not quarrel in hatred, anger, or deceit, or hold unkind feelings toward one another. The end of the state, therefore, is really freedom.

For Spinoza, the state was created to guarantee the exercise of natural rights, not to limit them. By nature, man was meant "to think what he likes and say what he thinks." If one believes in the basic need for what Locke calls free thought, then figures like Spinoza would add it is impossible "to deprive men of the liberty of saying what they think."

Spinoza's theories were not without inherent contradictions. This included an exception for seditious speech. Once again, Spinoza believed in the concept of a social contract or covenant that created the civilized state out of the state of nature. Accordingly, citizens lose the right to challenge the authority of the state to be the state. He defined sedition as speech that "when accepted, immediately destroys the covenant whereby everyone surrendered the right to act as he pleased." Spinoza believed in a natural right to criticize the actions of the government, but not to deny the right of the government to act. While narrow, the sedition exception undermines the consistency and coherence of Spinoza's theory. Yet there is another aspect of Spinoza's writing that would prove particularly insightful and relevant in the United States. Spinoza believed that the government should focus on acts, not speech, in its enforcement efforts. In his view, the state "should merely have to do with actions [and] every man should think what he likes and say what he thinks."

Spinoza's natural rights theories are highly compelling for many of us. However, one can accept a natural rights view that is not dependent on a belief in a divine gift. Natural rights are often based on religious concepts of divinely imposed obligations and divinely granted entitlements. Yet speech is also discussed as a moral hazard in religious texts. Thus, as stated in Matthew 12:36, "That every idle word that men shall speak, they shall give account thereof in the day of judgment." Indeed, the Bible and other religious texts contain mixed views of free speech. The Bible and Torah often reaffirm the authority of both divine and terrestrial rulers and to protect them from contempt or insult. For example, Deuteronomy 17:12 states that "Now the man who acts presumptuously and will not heed the priest . . . or the judge, that man shall die. So you shall put away the evil from Israel." Exodus 22:28 states: "Thou shalt not revile the gods, nor curse the ruler of thy people." While a religious foundation for free speech can be maintained, it is not essential if one believes that certain rights are essential to being fully human, that all human beings require free speech as sentient, creative beings. It can also be based on a view of the inherent essentiality of free thought to being fully human. Nevertheless, some philosophers rejected natural rights as based on contrived or conclusory arguments. For example, the philosopher Jeremy Bentham declared, "Natural rights is simple nonsense: natural and imprescriptible rights, rhetorical nonsense,—nonsense upon stilts." But even Bentham believed strongly in the right to free expression and that it had to be protected absent overt acts against the government. In fact, he insisted that "malcontents may communicate their sentiments, concert their plans, and practice every mode of opposition short of actual revolt."

The danger of free speech from the perspective of government would only increase after the invention of the printing press and the means of mass communication. It would often be based on the view that speech is harmful or lacks value to the political system. This was most evident in Great Britain—a comparison that shows how the United States took a decidedly different path on free speech. The Framers generally liked English law. They simply felt it was arbitrarily applied and shielded a tyrant. Free speech is one area where the Framers took their own course in favor of a more protective rule for free thought and expression.

Three

THE BRITISH EXPERIENCE: THE STAR CHAMBER, BLACKSTONE, AND THE "NONCONFORMISTS"

T he modern concept of free speech was foreign to early English courts
and conspicuously absent in early statutes. This was evident in the
thirty-fourth chapter of the Statute of Westminster in 1275, which expressly stated that "from henceforth none be so hardy to tell or publish
any false news or tales, whereby discord, or occasion of discord or slander may grow between the King and his people, or the great men of the
realm." Those "so hardy to tell tales" would be subject to the severest punishment even when they did not specifically libel a person.

Starting in the thirteenth century, laws known as *De Scandalis Magnatum* prohibited "libels of peers" and any spreading of false rumors or
tales to cause public mischief. The Crown, going back to Henry II, sought
to prevent discord spread by "false bruits and rumors." These early accounts cover obvious rage rhetoric and heated hyperbole. For example,
Hugh of Crepping was charged for declaring that "the king had universally forbidden anyone to scythe meadows or to reap corn, and . . . that
war would come in a short time." It is the type of griping that is common
in a pub. Notably, the accused did not have to specifically libel a peer but
could be convicted for fueling public distrust or unrest. The *De Scandalis*

Magnatum would later give way to more defined libel actions that involved statements directed against a person, though the statutes would not be officially repealed until 1888.

There is one other aspect of the *De Scandalis Magnatum* that is particularly significant for later colonial trials: the statutes were most often used to prosecute criticism of highly ranked individuals. In a vicious circle, criticism of the very judges who enforced these statutes resulted in charges from the judges themselves. Later versions of the statutes listed the protected offices and expressly included judges: "prelates, dukes, earls, barons, and other nobles and great men of the realm, and also . . . the Chancellor, Treasurer, Clerk of the Privy Seal, Steward of the King's house, Justices of the one bench or of the other, and . . . other great officers of the realm." In the early seventeenth century, John Hudson wrote that "disgraceful words and speeches against eminent persons have been grievously punished in all ages." This would be a particular signature of early colonial prosecutions.

With the greater recognition of free speech values in later years, limits were tied closely to functionalist rationales. The Bill of Rights of 1689 protected speech not in public but in the Parliament. The protection was deemed essential for the Parliament to function. The same functionalist logic allowed the Crown to punish criticism of high-ranking officials and nobility as undermining the functioning of government. The English courts maintained a narrow view of free speech, one that had to exist in conformity with one's obligations to the state, including a duty of loyalty. Fights over free speech outside of the Parliament were largely focused on the freedom of the press, which was also sharply curtailed. The first seditious libel law was passed in 1275 and included the crime of what many today call "fake news." The law criminalized "any slanderous News . . . or false News or Tales where by discord or occasion of discord or slander may grow between the King and his people." The enactment of the sedition law sixty years after Magna Carta reflects the marginal importance given to free speech in that revered document. It also reflects one of the obvious purposes of this and later sedition laws. After Henry VII and his

Lancastrian forces defeated Richard III's Yorkist force at the Battle of Bosworth Field in 1485, the Tudors assumed the throne of a nation torn apart in the Wars of the Roses. Sedition prosecutions increased with Tudor insecurity and the advent of the printing press (Gutenberg used his press to print his first Bible in 1455). After deposing a Yorkist king, the Tudors would not brook criticism of their own authority.

Under the common law, libel was a private action as it is today under modern defamation law. However, in 1606, the infamous Star Chamber would hold the criminal *de Libellis Famosis* (or "of scandalous libels") trial. The defendants were accused of ridiculing high-ranking officials and clergy in England. The opinion of the court was striking in its absence of any cited authority. Lewis Pickering's offense was to have written a rhyme ridiculing Elizabeth I and Archbishop John Whitgift. Notably, both were dead. Under common law defamation, you "cannot defame the dead"— a rule effectively barring defamation actions on behalf of the reputation of a deceased person. However, like much else before the Star Chamber, such legal principles were immaterial to the need to punish miscreants disrespecting those in power. Chief Justice Coke simply declared that "although the private man or Magistrate be dead at the time of the making of the Libel . . . the Libeller doth traduce and slander the State and government, which dieth not." Coke suggested, again without cited authority, that the crime was well established in England and could be traced back to Roman law. He added that such disrespect must be punished as threatening the very existence of the state, "since what greater scandal of government can there be than to have corrupt or wicked Magistrates to be appointed and constituted by the King to govern his Subjects under him?"

The Crown also controlled what could be published or imported by imposing licensing systems and prior restraints. Errant publishers could have their ears clipped or chopped off. Notably, it was a punishment used for both publishers and Puritans. The ears of such figures were the entry points of prohibited views. In some cases, ears would be nailed to the pillory. In the case of Gilbert Pott, his seditious words against Queen Jane (known as the "Nine Day Queen," given her rapid deposition in favor of Queen Mary) resulted in both ears being nailed to the pillory, then cut off as his charges were read aloud. Seditious authors could also have their hands cut off. However, the expansion of printing presses made it increasingly difficult for the Crown to hold back corrupting ideas. Indeed, in 1671, the royal governor of Virginia, William Berkeley, wrote to businessmen in London, "I thank God there are no free schools nor printing [in the colonies], and I hope we shall not have [them] these hundred years, for learning has brought disobedience, and heresy, and sects into the world, and printing has divulged them, and libels against the best government."

One of the most famous such cases involved a remarkably stalwart figure named John Lilburne. Known as "Freeborn John" for his belief in "freeborn rights" like free speech, Lilburne was a "Leveller." (The name was given by their critics who portrayed the reformers as dangerous radicals who wanted to "level their estates.") Levellers believed in natural rights and spread their philosophy through pamphlets and other publications—putting them in the vanguard of press and speech rights. Lilburne was convicted of importing books that lacked licensing by the Stationers' Company, which held the monopoly on publishing in England. It used that power to

censor material opposed by the government or powerful interests. Lilburne was arrested and interrogated before the Star Chamber. Lilburne defied the Star Chamber's attempt to force him to give testimony to incriminate himself. It was not the attitude the abusive secret body was accustomed to. Yet Lilburne stood before them and declared, "I am unwilling to answer any impertinent questions, for fear that with my answer, I may do myself hurt. This is not the way to get to Liberty." For his insolence, he was not only fined £500 but sentenced to be whipped, pilloried, and imprisoned.

On April 18, 1638, Lilburne was tied to the back of an oxcart and
flogged from Fleet Prison to Palace Yard, at times being dragged as he was
subjected to a three-thonged whip as many as two hundred times. In the
Palace Yard, he was then pilloried, but still defied the authorities and used
his bloody appearance to lecture the crowd on the abuses of authoritarian
rule. He was then gagged, but continued to defy authority by stamping his
feet. They eventually relented and took him away to prison unbroken and
unrepentant. His case would rally many to the cause of free speech in the
right to publish without preapproval of the Crown. This early advocacy
was often expressed in terms of natural or autonomy-based rights. Figures like John Milton declared, "Give me the liberty to know, to utter, and
to argue freely according to conscience, above all liberties." In his work
defending free speech, *Areopagitica*, Milton saw censorship as a denial of
God's plan for humanity: "The light which we have gained was given us,
not to be ever staring on, but by it to discover onward things more remote
from our knowledge."

Speech prosecutions were often framed as sedition and tried before
the Star Chamber. Sedition was considered a type of "constructive treason"
without the predicate acts associated with that crime. Sir William Blackstone embraced the concept of seditious libel as a necessary precaution
against dangerous rhetoric or allegations from both the public and the
press. While there were protections from prior restraints, Blackstone reasoned that people could not demand immunity from the consequences of
spreading "blasphemous, immoral, treasonable, schismatical, seditious, or
scandalous libels." Thus, if an individual "publishes what is improper, mischievous, or illegal, he must take the consequences of his own temerity."
Speech is often "schismatical" in seeking to rally others to a cause, including a cause opposing government action. Yet divisive speech was viewed as
a danger to public order. That line between speech and sedition is precisely
why functionalist rationales for free speech are easily corrupted.

From its earliest records from the 1600s, the disparagement of the
Crown was viewed as an attack on its absolute authority and infallibility.
Yet these were not literal attacks on the Crown befitting treason prosecu-
tions, which "were too cumbersome to be used to suppress the fleabites

of political or religious pamphleteers." Nevertheless, punishments were severe and included whipping and body mutilation. Sedition allowed the avoidance of the regular courts, where treason was commonly tried based on overt acts. Even with the lower protections for speech in the country, English judges would balk at treason claims in conventional courts. Thus, in Pine's Case in 1629, the court was faced with a defendant who called Charles I "unwise" and "no more fit to be king than Hickwright." Since Hickwright was Pine's shepherd, it was insulting to the king, but the King's Bench still balked, since "the speaking of the words before-mentioned, though they were as wicked as might be, were not treason." Charging seditious libel meant that the matter could go before the Star Chamber and escape any demand for an overt act as opposed to pure speech as in Pine's Case. There was also the benefit of escaping the statute of limitations for treason offenses.

One of the most illustrative cases is that of Henry Redhead Yorke, which occurred around the time of the American Revolution. Yorke is an intriguing character. He was Anglo Creole born in Barbuda to an English father, Samuel Redhead (who was an attorney), and a mother, Sarah Bullock, who was a slave. He immigrated to England but found himself in Paris during the Revolution and quickly associated with radicals of the "British Club," where he would spend time discussing these rights with none other than Thomas Paine. Yorke, however, was disillusioned by their calls for overthrowing the Crown by force. It was in Paris where he encountered his first crackdown on free speech when a criminal complaint was sworn out against him. Back in England, Yorke again associated with reformers and radicals while studying at Cambridge. Yorke was an excellent writer with clear and penetrating

prose. Yorke would have the distinction of being the one source for a preserved Paine essay titled "On Forgetfulness." It appears as part of a letter in which Yorke notes that, as soon as he returned from Paris, he "was amongst the first on whom I called, and I have since been frequently in his company." He described Paine as not hard to find because "the name of Thomas Paine is now as odious in France as it is in England, perhaps more so." He noted that Paine was much altered in appearance after his constant pursuit in three countries for sedition and other crimes. He described the "dreadful ravages over his whole frame, and a settled melancholy."

Yorke lived with Joseph Gales, a journalist and the publisher of the *Sheffield Register*. Gales also was associated with Paine (who encouraged him to establish his newspaper) and would later flee to the United States from the threat of sedition prosecution. Yorke helped Gales assemble a very large gathering in 1794 billed as a "A Meeting of the Friends of Justice, Liberty, and Humanity." The thousands who attended were viewed as an immediate threat to the government as they rallied in favor of emancipation, universal suffrage, and natural rights. Yorke's speech mirrored the views of many in the United States. The speech spoke of "culture of reason" and "the foundations of all human polity." It was clearly a rejection of the status quo in favor of "something more natural" but did not call for violence:

> The government of Europe . . . present no delectable symmetry to the contemplation of the philosopher—no enjoyment to the satisfaction of the citizen. A vast and deformed cheerless structure, the frightful abortion of haste and usurpation, presents to the eye of the beholder no systematic arrangement, no harmonious organization of society. Chance, haste, faction, tyranny, rebellion, massacre, and the hot inclement action of human passions, have begotten them. Utility never has been the end of their institution, but partial interest has been its fruit. Such abominable and absurd forms, such jarring and dissonant principles, which change has scattered over the earth, cry aloud for something more natural, more pure, and more calculated to promote the happiness of mankind.

Yorke was first charged with treason in a case where the government alleged that he, Gales, and others encouraged followers to store pikes and other weapons. The failure to prove treason led the government to reach for seditious conspiracy. The charge laid bare the anti–free speech purpose of sedition prosecutions. He and his associates were accused of working to "seditiously combine, conspire, and confederate with each other, and with divers other disaffected and ill-disposed subjects . . . to break and disturb the peace and tranquility of the realm, and to rise and excite riots, commotions, and tumults therein," Yorke objected, stating that his words could not be criminalized due to the alleged actions of others:

> Did I stimulate them to arms? No . . . I never suggested the idea of arms . . . far from stimulating their passions against the government, my language was not only constantly peaceable, but specifically threatened them with the dangers which might arise from tumult and confusion; that the cause of reform could only go on with the cause of peace.

At the trial, the prosecution made clear that the seditious conspiracy was based entirely on Yorke's expression of his views on the government. The prosecutor told the court of "dangerous attempts that have been made, both from within and without, to undermine the government of the country, to spread disaffection and discontent among the minds of his majesty's subject, and particularly to draw into the disrespect of his majesty's subjects . . . the Commons House of Parliament." The prosecutors also argued that the assembly of thousands of supporters without sufficient preparation or housing evidenced an intent to cause disorder. Despite witnesses attesting to his peaceful views and lack of direct call for rebellion, Yorke was convicted and sentenced to two years imprisonment and fines.

The fate of Henry Redhead Yorke reflected the shallow view of free speech under English jurisprudence. Sir William Blackstone held a unique position in both England and the colonies due to his influential *Commentaries on the Laws of England*. His work often defended the rights of the public, but, on free speech, it was both highly functionalist and statist. Blackstone viewed free speech as a conditional right enjoyed at the sufferance of the government. Such speech was itself a danger to public order "by stirring up the objects ... to revenge, and perhaps to bloodshed." Blackstone supported these claims as the product of the common law. It is a telling rationalization. The common law tort of libel was a familiar civil action. However, claiming seditious libel as a product of that common law was dubious at best. There is little commonality between civil libel and criminal seditious libel. The first seeks damage for loss of reputation, while the latter seeks to punish criticism of the Crown. Indeed, the ratio- nalization captures the menacing aspects of the crime. It simply defines criticism of the government as a criminal form of defamation. Literally any political dissent could meet and satisfy that standard. Nevertheless, Blackstone seems to shift from analyst to apologist in presenting seditious libel as an extension of the tort common law. The claim that "the liberty of the press, properly understood, is by no means infringed or violated" is obviously absurd given the use of the Star Chamber and prosecutions to punish both publishers and dissenters. It is a matter of prior restraint over publications rather than the right to free thought and expression. Blackstone's rationalization would fool no one, least of all the Framers, who faced the threat of such "constructive treason" in their own advocacy for change. Anyone looking at the bloodied, pilloried, and gagged image of John Lilburne could see the folly in Blackstonian claims of uninfringed liberty.

The colonial records show that seditious libel was a well-known basis for prosecution in the colonies as well as in Great Britain. When licensing laws for publications were eventually relaxed, the slack of speech prosecu- tion was taken up by the sedition laws. The Star Chamber was dedicated to stamping out criticism of high officials, particularly royal judges, since there is no "greater scandal of government . . . than to have corrupt or wicked Magistrates." It was not the actual corruption but the declaration of corruption that was viewed as the greater threat. A couple of the Brit- ish sedition cases were well known and likely helped shape the views of the Framers. One of the most influential during the colonial period oc- curred in 1685 involving radical Whig and publisher John Tutchin, who wrote a series of poems that criticized the possible accession of James II.

He was tried and convicted of seditious libel in a trial in which Judge and 1st Baron George Jeffreys ridiculed him and sentenced him to not just seven years in prison and a fine but also to the annual punishment of being whipped through all the market towns of Devonshire. He appealed his sentence and would be later released. He was tried again for sedition in 1704. In that trial, Lord Chief Justice John Holt mocked the notion that speakers and writers "should not be called to account for possessing the people with an ill-opinion of the government." Otherwise, "no government can subsist. For it is very necessary for all governments that the people should have a good opinion of it." Holt's words reinforced the notion that, even if true, speech can be seditious. Indeed, true criticism of the Crown was viewed as potentially worse in terms of undermining the government.

Under the British approach, free speech was not just dispensable but dangerous. The English courts enforced a series of civil limitations on free speech under sedition, defamation, and blasphemy. There were those who challenged Blackstone at the time over his expansive view of criminalized speech. Appropriately, the greatest objections came from a group called the "nonconformists." This was a religious group that questioned the teachings of the Church of England and, despite a law called Act of Toleration protecting dissenters, Blackstone wrote in his *Commentaries* that they could still be prosecuted. Reverend Joseph Priestley, a leading nonconformist, published a blistering condemnation of Blackstone's view. In a unique response, Blackstone denied that he was a "bigotted High-Church-Man . . . of a persecuting Spirit." However, Blackstone revealed the intellectually dishonest premise of these speech crimes. While insisting that he and the law tolerated dissent, he affirmed that prosecutions were appropriate for "peevish or opinionated Men" and those who treated the Church "with Contempt and Rudeness" or expressed "Bitterness against the English Liturgy." He then added menacingly, "If Dr. Priestley is guilty of these Practices, he falls within the Danger of the Laws."

It was another nonconformist who leveled the strongest criticism of Blackstone's bad tendency rationale. Reverend Philip Furneaux's criticism in *The Palladium of Conscience* was published in Philadelphia in 1773, just three years before the Revolution. Like Spinoza, Furneaux tied any prosecution to overt acts and rejected the notion of prosecuting someone for speech alone: "the tendency of principles, though it be unfavorable, is not prejudicial to society, till it issues in some overt acts against the public peace and order; and when it does, then the magistrate's authority to punish commences; that is, he may punish the overt acts, but not the tendency." The act-speech dichotomy was dismissed in England, which continued to apply a fluid standard for the criminalization of speech. However, Furneaux's commentary on the eve of the American Revolution was a brilliant rejection of the "bad tendency" rationale for speech prosecutions that would later take hold in the new Republic.

The English view of free speech was shared by other European countries, as shown in Article 11 of the Declaration of the Rights of Man and the Citizen. The author of that article was another figure from the American Revolution, the Marquis de Lafayette, who embraced a fluid interpretation that limited the scope of free speech by demands of the state. The provision declared that "the free communication of ideas and opinions is one of the most precious of the rights of man. Every citizen may, accordingly, speak, write, and print with freedom, but shall be responsible for such abuses of this freedom as shall be defined by law." Where the First Amendment would effectively put a period after "freedom," the French made the grand statement of right to free expression conditional on the discretion of the government. If free speech is not a natural or personal right, the scope of speech can be limited at the point at which it is no longer viewed as serving a functional benefit or incurring a dysfunctional cost.

Four

THE AMERICAN REVOLUTION
AND MADISON'S MONSTER

Free speech for Blackstone and many of his contemporaries was alienable. That is why the First Amendment was a quantum shift in favor of the view of a natural right to free expression. Notably, despite his deep commitment to free speech, the author of the First Amendment did not believe that it was necessary. Madison agreed to the Bill of Rights as a compromise to secure the ratification of the Constitution. He was fearful that the articulation of some individual rights could be used to suggest that others were not protected. Madison had little faith in what he called "parchment barriers" in stopping government abuses. Yet when he put his shoulder to the wheel, Madison would embrace the Bill of Rights as a means to "expressly declare the great rights of Mankind secured under this Constitution." That would include the strongest protection for free speech in history.

Madison and philosophers such as Montesquieu believed that a constitutional system had to reflect and conform to human nature. As Montesquieu stated in his *Spirit of Laws*, "[O]ne must consider a man before the establishment of societies." Madison took the same view, particularly in his writings on the tendency of humans to form factions in political and social discourse. That approach is particularly important to understanding free speech where "one must consider a man" and the role speech plays in human associations. It is protected not to achieve the potential of the democratic system, but the fulfillment of one's own potential. Free speech remains one of humanity's most essential impulses, and the Constitution captured that essentiality in the First Amendment.

In the United States, it would come down to punctuation, a period where the French added a comma to the Declaration of the Rights of Man and the Citizen. The First Amendment states the right in absolute terms in declaring that "Congress shall make no law . . . abridging the freedom of speech." It is that clarity that led Justice Hugo Black to declare "I read 'no law . . . abridging' to mean no law abridging." It is a clarity that would quickly be abandoned by all three branches of the American constitutional system.

The new Republic offered the promise of liberty long denied by the Crown. The United States would be the culmination of what was viewed as a long human struggle for freedom against "ecclesiastical and civil" tyrannies. Adams insisted that the founding was not simply the result of religious persecution: "It was this great struggle, that peopled America. It was not religion alone, as is commonly supposed; but it was a love of universal Liberty, and a hatred, a dread, an horror of the infernal confederacy . . . that projected, conducted, and accomplished the settlement of America." That "universal liberty" transcended the prior government as it would the new government. It was universal to humankind. It was liberty founded in the natural rights of every individual. In a 1765 essay titled "A Dissertation on the Canon and Feudal Law," Adams references the divine gift of "the rights of mankind," including natural rights to "life," "property," "freedom," and "liberty." In this description of natural rights, Adams condemns efforts to limit the "press." Adams declared, "RIGHTS . . . undoubtedly, antecedent to all earthly government . . . cannot be repealed or restrained by human laws . . . derived from the great Legislator of the universe." It would prove a view that was tragically ironic for a president who would violate every aspect of those lofty sentiments.

Records of colonial trials are sketchy and often lack details on underlying offenses. There are exceptions like the account of the impressive criminal efforts of one Thomas Graunger, who was hanged "for buggery with a mare, a cow, two goats, diverse sheep, two calves, and a turkey."

The level of detail may have been the product of awe rather than accuracy. Most speech offenses were likely handled informally or without a formal record. Colonial laws banned a wide array of expression, from satire to dress. Some of these laws reflected the Puritanical mores of the time. In Massachusetts, Henry Sherlot was banished simply because he was "a dancing master and a person very insolent and of ill fame." Another, Nathaniel Washburn, was called to account for "wearing woman's apparel in a public meeting house . . . on the Lord's Day."

During the colonial period, one of the earliest British imports was sedition prosecutions. Before 1700, there were 1,244 recorded sedition trials in colonial courts. The English tradition of *De Scandalis Magnatum* was continued. Criticisms of high officials, including royal judges, were charged as seditious libel. This was long treated as a prerogative or entitlement of office, which some governors clearly relished. The case for such prosecution took on not just a classist but religious tenor. John Winthrop, the Puritan leader who led the "Winthrop Fleet" to Massachusetts in 1630, made a reference to this tradition in his famous "Model of Christian Charity" sermon that he gave in a Southampton church before the voyage. The future governor of Massachusetts spoke of the promise of a new land and a new American ethos. In his sermon, Winthrop referred to a new "city upon a hill"—a phrase later used by presidents such as Ronald Reagan to capture American exceptionalism. Yet the sermon also stressed that one must accept one's lot in life, including acceptance of their leaders as divinely directed: "God Almighty, in his most holy and wise providence, hath so disposed of the condition of mankind, as in all times some must be rich, some poor, some high and eminent in power and dignity, others mean and in subjection." It is a view that would reinforce the use of sedition laws to continue *De Scandalis Magnatum*. When he took the oath of office as governor, Winthrop made clear that this divine authority meant protection from criticism: "It is yourselves who have called us to this office, and being called by you, we have our authority from God." This authority meant that those guilty of "contempt and violation" of the office would be made "examples of divine vengeance." In Maryland, citizens could be arrested for uttering "scandalous or contemptuous words or writings to the dishonor of the Lord Proprietary or his Lieutenant Governor." In 1637, the second Lord Baltimore had the same message for the people of Maryland, ordering them to "honor, respect and obey him as they ought to do, upon pain or such punishment to be inflicted upon them, and every of them, as such high contempt shall deserve."

As historian Larry Eldridge noted in his detailed record of sedition cases in colonial America, "times of danger" led to increases in sedition charges. For example, before Virginians took up arms against Governor William Berkeley in Bacon's Rebellion, conditions in the colony had become increasingly dangerous with increasing prosecutions for dissenting speech. Nathaniel Bacon and his followers had long objected to Berkeley's appointments of cronies to key positions, his refusal to protect them from Indian attacks, and his being generally pro-Indian. The rebellion was crushed with the help of a couple British warships. After returning to his burned capital, Berkeley had twenty-three rebels hanged. However, after punishing those who were deemed traitors, Berkeley's next step was telling. His government ramped up sedition laws and declared "seditious and scandalous libels . . . the usual forerunners of tumult and rebellion." The pattern of these prosecutions also closely followed with British rule. Eldridge found that the half of all the sedition prosecutions in Maryland occurred after 1691, when the proprietary grant over Maryland of the Calverts (and the second Lord Baltimore) ended—converting the state to a royal colony.

These laws were meant to prevent even private disparagements of the Crown or government officials. Even Jonathan White, the speaker of the Pennsylvania House, was charged with sedition after observing to guests in his home that "the proposed laws were cursed laws" and then expressing his exasperation by exclaiming, "Hang it, damn them all."

The punishments were no less brutal than in England, including "bodily correction," which often involved public floggings. Eldridge's history is particularly replete with such examples. In Salem, later made infamous for the witch trials, Philip Ratcliff insulted officials and was fined, whipped, had both ears chopped off, and then banished. Another case concerning Edward Erbery in 1666 resulted in being tied to an apple tree and lashed thirty-nine times. Richard Barnes was accused of "base and distracting speeches." That was enough to justify having his arms broken, his tongue bored, and (with his broken arms dangling on his sides) being forced to run a gauntlet as men beat him with rifle butts. Tongue borings, nailing ears to the pillory, or the cutting off of ears were all common options. There could be variation in these horrific measures. For example, ear cutting could vary from "cropping" (removing the top of the ear) to cutting off the entire ear. Likewise, whipping was a common punishment, but courts would sometimes specify the force to be used in meting out the strokes. In sedition cases, it was not uncommon to expressly order vigorous strokes to be administered. For example, when Cornelius Jones gave what Maine magistrates described as "diverse, base, ignominious, vile, and reproachful speeches," he was sentenced to twenty-one "stripes on the bare skin, well laid on." In the case of Peter Bussaker, who was accused of "slighting the magistrates" in Massachusetts, the court ordered that his sedition be punished with twenty lashes "sharply inflicted." Other punishments were as creative as they were sadistic. Others were forced to ride the "wooden horse," a sharpened board elevated so the victim's feet would be left dangling. They could be left there for hours, as the pain became excruciating. In one sedition case of "slighting authority," William Warran was left for only an hour, but three heavy muskets were ordered to be tied to his legs.

Taken as a whole across the colonies, the punishments under sedition cases remained highly varied, discretionary, and at times improvisational. They could range from fines to shaming to mutilation. Some were remarkably mild and may have reflected the position of the accused. For example, Rhode Island president Benedict Arnold brought a seditious libel charge in 1662 against John Smith for "speaking words . . . [that] did absolutely tend to his disparagement in the execution of his office." The great-grandfather of the infamous traitor General Benedict Arnold was accused of ordering the arrest of a woman, Mrs. Ayres, and then warning her to facilitate her escape. For his punishment, Smith was forced to write out his confession and post it on the prison porch in Newport.

This history, however, also showed a different view emerging among colonists in the seventeenth century. Even with sharp limits on the role of the jury, colonial jurors engaged in jury nullification in free speech cases. Indeed, it was a matter of great chagrin among royal officials, who viewed seditious libel as a political entitlement. For example, when Lieutenant Governor and Massachusetts Chief Justice Thomas Hutchinson was aggrieved by the attacks of publishers Benjamin Edes and John Gill in their *Boston Gazette*, he went to the grand jury for relief from being "treated in the most abusive Manner, and vilified beyond all bounds." Hutchinson captured how the courts were composed of many political operatives with direct conflicts of interest in dealing with political speech cases. The grand jury refused to indict the men for criminal defamation.

In the colonies, it was the 1735 trial of John Peter Zenger that would bring the dangers of government censorship into full public view and debate. Zenger was the publisher of the *New York Weekly Journal*, and he quickly earned the ire of the newly installed British governor William Cosby, who was accurately described as "a petty, tyrannical sycophant." Appointed by George II as "Captain General & Governor in Chief of the Provinces of New York, New Jersey and Territories depending thereon in America," the former Irish soldier clearly viewed himself as more general than governor. Cosby personified the sense of privilege under the tradition

of *De Scandalis Magnatum* to be free of criticism and disparagement. In Cosby's case, even moderates chafed at his corrupt and autocratic tendencies. Cosby could be honestly described as a man born to excess. His family helped the Crown conquer Ireland and then jealously defended their privileges through the application of harsh penal laws. The family is described as having "all of the usual arrogance, avarice, and stupidity, vices that merely perverted a strong will and a certain resourcefulness in meeting obstacles." Cosby was a fawning aristocrat who used connections to advance his career despite repeated failures. He had a powerful patron in the Duke of Newcastle, and Cosby's wife had the fortune of being the sister of the Earl of Halifax. Indeed, he was known for primarily three overwhelming attributes: connections, conceit, and corruption. In his first governorship on the island of Minorca, the locals quickly complained of his high-handed and greedy practices. Cosby finally crossed the line when he seized the goods of a Spanish merchant and had them sold at auction. It created an international incident, and he was forced to give the money back and to give up his office. Yet he was able to secure new postings, including ultimately the office of the "Governor in Chief" in New York.

New York had all the temptations that played to Cosby's vices, particularly greed. The state was flush with money from the sugar trade with shipping, finance, and other flourishing enterprises. No sooner had he arrived than Cosby was demanding money. The assembly had provided him with an ample salary of £1,500 a year. Cosby demanded more and reminded the colonists that, while in England, he had helped scuttle a new tax on sugar. It was time to get his cut. While some questioned his actual role in stopping the tax, the assembly relented and agreed to pay him another £750. Cosby again raged at the amount and forced them to increase it to £1,000. He then demanded that he be paid for the year he stayed in London after his appointment. During his absence, Rip Van Dam had acted as governor and was paid for his service. Cosby now demanded half of Van Dam's salary. Van Dam had a devastating response: he would gradually hand over half of his salary if Cosby would give him half of the money and emoluments he received while in England. Cosby was enraged and arranged for his judicial allies to hear a case against Van Dam through a quickly assembled "court of equity." The problem is that the chief justice was Lewis Morris, who would not go along with the power grab. Morris declared that the court was invalid and then had his opinion published as a pamphlet. Cosby was furious, and his letter to the Duke of Newcastle on May 3, 1733, is invaluable as an insight into how sedition laws warped the perspective of English nobles:

> Things are now gone that length that I must either discipline Morris or suffer myself to be affronted or what is still worse, see the King's authority trampled on and disrespect and irreverence to it taught from the Bench to the people by him who, by his oath and his office, is obliged to support it. This is neither consistent with my duty nor my inclination to bear, and therefore when I return to New York I shall displace him and make Judge Delancey Chief Justice in his room.

The petulant tone captures the privilege that extended back to the *De Scandalis Magnatum*. Cosby refused to "suffer myself to be affronted" by criticism, even from the chief justice. Cosby proceeded to fire Morris. Yet the early controversies had made Cosby, once again, intensely unpopular. That was evident when Cosby and his cronies fought to rig an election to prevent Morris from becoming an assemblyman. After effectively barring his Quaker allies (by announcing that they would have to take an oath against their religious practices), Morris still won overwhelmingly.

The fight with Morris was just one of the petty squabbles that Cosby pursued with his signature utter abandon. Those who spoke or wrote against him were quickly seized upon as seditionists. One was John Peter Zenger, who detailed Cosby's many shady practices in New York and New Jersey, from stealing Indian lands to rigging elections to pilfering the Treasury. He also published Van Dam's accounts of how Cosby was trying to take half of his salary. The newspapers also heaped scorn and sarcasm on the notoriously thin-skinned governor: "A monkey . . . has lately broke his Chain, and run into the Country, where he has played many a Monkey Trick. . . . Whosoever shall take this little mischievous Animal, and send him back to his Master, so that he may be chained up again, shall have for his Reward a Thousand thanks." Cosby again wrote to England blaming his nemesis Morris and two others for the "false and scandalous libels printed in Zenger's Journal." He lamented how he could tolerate "all the insolent, false and scandalous aspersions that such bold and profligate wretches can invent."

Cosby ordered four editions of Zenger's *New York Weekly Journal* publicly burned and arrested Zenger. Cosby's ally Chief Justice James De Lancey set bail prohibitively high to keep Zenger in a virtual dungeon for nine months awaiting trial. (His wife would later publish at least one more edition of the newspaper with the help of his other associates.) Notably, when Cosby sought to have a grand jury indict Zenger, this body of colonials refused. He turned to the attorney general to prosecute on the basis of "information" that Zenger had published "scandalous, virulent, false and seditious reflections." He then left the matter to Chief Justice De Lancey, who proceeded not only to strike the defense lawyers from the case but also barred them from practicing in New York. De Lancey told the jury that Zenger was guilty of criminal libel if he was found to have published "words tended to beget an ill opinion of the government." That standard was easily met by these publications. However, Zenger's counsel, Andrew Hamilton, told the jury that the case was about more than the law of libel, but rather, the natural right to speak freely.

As in England, it was not a defense to prove a claim to be true. Moreover, the role of the jury was quite limited in such cases under the domination of royal judges. Faced with this stacked deck, Hamilton surprised many by admitting that Zenger was responsible for the publication. One of the best lawyers of his time, Hamilton was making a jury nullification argument, encouraging the jury to vote to acquit regardless of the evidence. He pleaded with the jury to stand with "that to which nature and the laws of our country have given us a right—both of exposing and opposing arbitrary power (in these parts of the world at least) by speaking and writing the truth." That was not a statement born from the English tradition but the writings of contemporary figures such as Locke and others. The jury acquitted Zenger. Despite a law and a judge that seemingly guaranteed conviction, the jurors defied Crown authority. When foreman Thomas

Hunt declared Zenger not guilty, the courtroom observers shouted three huzzahs. Where Cosby wanted to show that his authority could not be challenged, he succeeded in establishing the very opposite.

Andrew Hamilton's arguments can be viewed as referencing both the functional and autonomous basis for free speech. Free speech theories from this period would often interlace these rationales. This duality is captured in one of the most influential sources in the American Revolution, Cato's letters. British writers John Trenchard and Thomas Gordon adopted the pseudonym of the opponent to Julius Caesar to write about the rights of citizens. The letters would be read with great interest by those in the colonies, including the discussion of the right to free thought. Cato wrote, "Without Freedom of Thought, there can be no such Thing as wisdom; and no such thing as publick Liberty, without Freedom of Speech; which is the Right of every Man, as far as by it, he does not hurt and Control the right of another." The statement is notable in alluding to a type of harm principle (à la John Stuart Mill) as the measure of permissible government interference regarding the right to free speech.

Cato's reference to the necessity of free thought is strikingly Lockean. While Locke saw the necessity of citizens yielding freedoms as a condition of civilization, he also saw certain rights as elemental and inalienable, including the freedom of thought. Locke's views on free speech remain fiercely debated with some challenging the extension of his writing on freedom of thought to the specific protection of free speech. For some of us, freedom of thought necessarily embodies the freedom of speech. A freedom to think is a rather anemic right if it cannot be developed and articulated through speech. If free thought is inalienable, so must be freedom of speech. That critical nexus was emphasized in Cato's letters, which maintained that in a free society, you must be able to "think what you would, and speak what you thought." Cato amplified the importance of free speech as not just a protection of good government but the purpose of good government. His writings had an inescapable Lockean accent:

> By Liberty, I understand the Power which every Man has over his own Actions, and his Right to enjoy the Fruit of his Labour, Art, and

Industry, so far as by it he hurts not the Society, or any Members of it, by taking from any Member, or by hindering him from enjoying what he himself enjoys. . . .

The entering into political Society, is so far from a Departure from his natural Right, that to preserve it was the sole reason why Men did so; and mutual Protection and Assistance is the only reasonable Purpose of all reasonable Societies. . . .

True and impartial Liberty is therefore the Right of every Man to pursue the natural, reasonable and religious Dictates of his own Mind; to think what he will, and act as he thinks, provided he acts not to the Prejudice of another. . . .

This natural rights premise for government found expression in early American documents including the Virginia Declaration of Rights and the Declaration of Independence. It is also evident in a comparison of the Declaration of the Rights of Man and the Constitution on free speech. Finally, some Framers expressly noted that they wanted to break from what came before under British law. James Wilson denounced seditious libel as an "unwarrantable attempt made in the Star Chamber, to wrest the [private] law of libel to the purposes of ministers."

The Framers were not just familiar with these works and cases, but free speech was seen as a critical component in what historian R. R. Palmer called "the age of the democratic revolution." Indeed, Trenchard and Gordon were prominent among Whig theorists who argued that creation in the likeness of God bestowed a capacity and right to inquiry and reason. What emerges is a "natural religion" through which "[d]evotion [to] [God] requires . . . free, rational, and willing" inquiry. This also means that persecution for such inquiry and expression is "incompatible with true Religion, whether Natural or Revealed." Accordingly, the Whig philosophy contained not just a natural rights foundation for free speech but a well-articulated view of the illegitimacy of anti–free speech laws or "persecutions." The Whigs presented a fully formed and unqualified defense of an autonomous right to free expression.

The First Amendment is meant to protect citizens against state rage.

Yet our history is replete with such rage being expressed through speech prosecutions due to the very rationales used by the Crown against the colonists. A functionalist view of free speech emerged that allowed courts to curtail some speech while ostensibly protecting core speech linked to perfecting or protecting the democratic process. If speech was not centrally linked to that function, it was afforded less protection. That allowed for a sliding scale of speech that often left dissenting or minority voices in precarious positions. These functionalist rationales tend to narrow rather than expand protections. Even with regard to political speech, Justice Felix Frankfurter would later, in 1951, insist in an opinion that upholding the prosecution of communists is consistent with our history and values: "[T]he historic antecedents of the First Amendment preclude the notion that its purpose was to give unqualified immunity to every expression that touched on matters within the range of political interest." Of course, one can also look at that same history and see a paradigm shift away from such narrow functionalism.

Speech has another function for a democratic system that should militate in favor of broader protection. Free speech, even rage rhetoric, has a cathartic function for a political system. While rage is often blamed for violence, rage rhetoric also serves to express and release political pressure in a political system. Indeed, the suppression of speech in our history had tended only to produce greater isolation and violence. President John Quincy Adams remarked that his father's use of sedition prosecutions proved "an ineffectual attempt to extinguish the fire of defamation, but it operated like oil upon the flames."

It is tempting to adopt an idealized view of history where the American Revolution was the triumph of free speech advocates over those who opposed dissenting views and publications. The fact is that anti–free speech elements were not just present but prominent in many revolutionary groups. There were many Loyalist newspapers that were attacked by mobs. The hypocrisy was breathtaking in the Continental Congress in 1776 when, just after the Declaration of Independence to secure "unalienable Rights," representatives called on states to pass laws that punished dissenting views. The rationale was virtually identical to the Crown's defense of seditious libel law to protect the public from being "deceived and drawn into erroneous opinions respecting the American cause." Virginia criminalized "any word" supporting the king or doubting the Revolution. As law professor Stephen Solomon noted, "All of the states enacted laws punishing anti-patriot speech or requiring loyalty oaths, some focusing on derogatory comments about Congress, state legislatures, or the Continental currency." There were also still laws that barred blasphemy.

Despite the strong Lockean hold on many Framers, a natural rights basis for free speech had relatively little time to take hold in the colonies. The rapid move toward Revolution after the Boston Tea Party may have arrested efforts to finish this reframing of free speech. Given the low baseline of free speech protections in England, the writers were already arguing for a quantum shift in the balance between the citizen and the state. It is not surprising that many writers would make allowance for prosecutions in extreme cases. Such exceptions also likely made free speech arguments more politically or conceptually palatable at the time. Locke conceded that "no opinions contrary to human society or to those moral rules which are necessary to the preservation of civil society are to be tolerated by the magistrate." Other figures, even Paine, were primarily concerned with opposing prior restraints and the licensing of journals that characterized British rule. Paine often referred to "printing free from prior restraint" in discussing the freedom of the press, while noting that "the public at large—or in case of prosecution, a jury of the country—will be judges of the matter." Figures like Adams continued to view seditious libel as a means to punish critics of the government or ruling politicians. Some, such as historian Leonard Levy, have cited that history to challenge the view that the Framers exhibited a natural right or a libertarian view of free speech. They do not see the language of the First Amendment as an implied rejection of the Blackstonian approach, particularly since it refers to "Congress" not abridging free speech rather than the courts through the common law. That certainly may have been the view of some, while others followed a more cabined functionalist view of free speech. However, it is clear that others embraced the liberty rationale for free speech and rejected the criminalization of speech. Indeed, Madison discussed seditious libel authority as an example of how such abuses were barred constitutionally under the "actual meaning of the instrument."

The abridgment of free speech in the early years of the Republic would take hold of courts, which continued to afford considerable discretion to the government. That was also a by-product of British rule. As John Stuart Mill noted, free speech largely relied on the beneficent attitude of the government rather than the clear lines of protection and prohibitions:

> Though the law of England, on the subject of the press, is as servile to this day as it was in the time of the Tudors, there is little danger of its being actually put in force against political discussion, except during some temporary panic, when fear of insurrection drives ministers and judges from their propriety; and, speaking generally, it is not, in constitutional countries, to be apprehended.

That danger was realized in the United States in our periods of "temporary panic." Not surprisingly, the unfinished work with sedition continued to cause conflict from the very start of the Republic to the present day. Yet it is also important to recognize that the American Revolution was not uniformly viewed as a fight for free speech. Indeed, anti–free speech elements were present among patriots who denounced the Crown for abuses that they quickly replicated in the name of freedom. The debate can rage like a fever in society until it breaks. In a letter to Oliver Wendell Holmes, Judge Learned Hand would write about this fever and its impact on free speech: "[T]he merry spirit of Red-baiting goes on, and the pack gives tongue more and more shrilly. . . . I own a sense of dismay of the increase in all the symptoms of apparent panic."

As with the emphasis in England on the good intentions of the government, our history of speech prosecutions in the United States shows the same tragic reliance. It illustrates precisely what James Madison sought to avoid in a government that was dependent on good intentions. In Federalist 51, Madison famously declared, "If men were angels, no government would be necessary." He warned that citizens "must first enable the government to control the governed; and in the next place, oblige it to control itself." This was to be achieved not by trusting the government but

by controlling it, since "experience has taught mankind the necessity of auxiliary precautions."

The brilliance of the Madisonian system is found in the fact that it does not rely upon the good motivations of leaders for good government. "Auxiliary protections" would include devices like the separation of powers and the system of checks and balances. There is also a key protection under the First Amendment in exposing abuses and rallying opposition. Yet sedition prosecutions would allow for precisely the state rage that the Framers sought to prevent. Federalists would applaud the use of sedition prosecutions as a means for the government to use "in just display its power *in terrorem.*" Literally state terror. The fluid underlying interpretations would also leave speech dependent on the good intentions of the government, a reliance repeatedly shown to be dangerously misplaced. There are few angels in an age of rage, and even fewer rise to offices of authority in the politics associated with those periods.

The effort to deter public rage has often been an excuse for state rage. The government does not need to be protected against the rage of its citizens, only rageful acts. Moreover, in punishing rage rhetoric, it has suppressed other aspects of the Madisonian system. The Constitution was designed in part to direct pressures into protected forums where opposing views could be expressed and addressed. It is a model of democracy that encourages expression, deliberation, and compromise. The most obvious is the legislative process. Madison believed that the greatest danger to political systems was posed by factions. Countries tend to emphasize those values that unite a people, putting aspirational goals above actual divisions. Left unaddressed, such factions tended to become an increasingly unstable element due to pent-up pressures and unresolved grievances. Unexpressed grievances are more likely to fester and explode.

Free speech plays a key factor in forcing factional interests to the surface, where they can be addressed rather than remaining beneath the surface to fester and undermine the system as a whole. Where factional divisions would explode in other systems in the streets of Paris or Moscow, the Madisonian system forces them to implode toward the center of the legislative system. In this way, the First Amendment plays a critical role in defusing pressures even at the extremes of politics. It often seems counterintuitive how rage rhetoric may work toward resolution. However, by protecting speech, the Constitution allows intense passions and viewpoints to be expressed as part of a national dialogue, even through rage. It allows marginal voices to be heard and can even force change. When speech has been suppressed, rage rhetoric has at times become rageful acts, as shown in early conflicts like Shays' Rebellion and the Whiskey Rebellion. The "bad tendency" of rage rhetoric is often the justification for government limits rather than seeing the allowance of speech generally as a critical vent for the body politic. For Madison, free speech was an inalienable right and a human impulse that had to be expressed for the good of both the system and the individual.

While the courts showed little fealty to free speech, the public itself evidenced a broader understanding of the rights. Indeed, the abuses of the sedition prosecutions were considered a significant factor in Adams's loss in the 1800 election. Both Adams and Jefferson would later express regret over sedition prosecutions, including an effort by Adams to blame others for prosecutions that he clearly supported. He would adopt the same rationalization of others cracking down on speech that it was the times, not his view of free speech, that led to the abuses: "as they were then considered as war measures, and intended altogether against the advocates of the French and peace with France, I was apprehensive that a hurricane of clamor would be raised against them." Adams never questioned the underlying theory of free speech as yielding to such post hoc rationalizations. It was Madison who would remain faithful to the free speech principles that fueled the Revolution. Madison would emphasize as a member of Congress that "[o]pinions are not the objects of legislation, the censorial power is in the people over the Government, and not the Government over the people."

It was Madison's report on the Alien and Sedition Acts (also known as the "Report of 1800") that would redeem his generation of leaders in the cause of free speech. Madison not only destroyed the rationalizations of seditious prosecutions but spoke of expression as an essential human right and impulse. The report was ostensibly to support the Virginia Resolution of 1798, which Madison drafted to protect core rights, including the freedom of the press. However, it would prove far more for American law. It would become a touchstone for free speech values for centuries. Madison demolishes Blackstonian logic by noting that there is no comparison of the two nations. Where England was based on a monarchy, the United States is based on the view that "the people, not the government, possess the absolute sovereignty." Limiting free speech and the press was limiting the true sovereigns of this new nation. Our leaders are not selected by God but the people; "the executive magistrates are not held to be infallible, nor the legislatures to be omnipotent; and both being elective, are both responsible."

Unlike Jefferson, Madison condemned sedition laws on every level—federal or state—due to its "baneful tendency" to deny this core right. It was a characteristically brilliant case made for free speech. It also contained implied functionalist sentiments. Madison speaks of the need for free speech to guarantee good government, since "a government thus intrenched in penal statutes against the just and natural effects of a culpable administration will easily evade the responsibility which is essential to a faithful discharge of its duty." It would further establish this more limited rationale for free speech despite other writings by Madison speaking of free speech as a core liberty resting with individuals. Madison's view of the foundation for free speech remains uncertain. The Report of 1800 established a broad functionalist argument that Madison hoped would blunt the attack of seditious prosecutions. Madison argued that, given the benefits of free speech, some abuse must be expected and excused: "[I]t is better to leave a few of its noxious branches to their luxuriant growth, than, by pruning them away, to injure the vigor of those yielding the proper fruits." It was the most compelling argument that he could make in that age of rage—calling up citizens to consider how such sedition laws could protect corrupt governments in the future, including governments led by their opponents. Trial lawyers often select the argument that will secure a verdict, even if they believe that broader issues or arguments are more compelling. This was the argument for this jury at this time. It succeeded in securing a verdict of many against the abuse of the Adams administration and those eager to unleash what Madison called the "monster" of sedition.

Madison's monster was thought by many to have been finally chained, if not expelled from American society. In 1782, Junius Wilkes would write that even "false and groundless" speech must be protected in the new nation because free speech "produced the American struggle for liberty, and gave birth to our glorious independence!" He added that if patriots had been "intimidated from publishing their sentiments under an idea of 'transgressing the law,' and involving the Printer with prosecutions as a libeller, there is no doubt we should have sunk to the lowest class of slaves." Likewise, influential First Amendment writers in the early twentieth century such as Henry Schofield would develop their free speech theories based on the view that the American Revolution was fought in part "to get rid of the English common law on liberty of speech and of the press."

Some Framers clearly held a natural rights view of free speech, while others viewed it as essential to the functioning of the democratic system. All approved of language that was neither equivocal nor ambiguous. Free speech was not to be abridged by the government in the United States. It did not say good speech. It said simply speech will be protected. As Stephen Solomon noted in his work *Revolutionary Dissent*, they thought "they had severed ties to a legal system that punished criticism of the government." Yet, as discussed below, they were wrong. The scourge of sedition would quickly reassert itself as revolutionaries became governors in the new Republic.

Part II

THE AGES OF RAGE
AND THE CRUCIBLE
OF FREE SPEECH

The United States was born in rage. Violent speech has at times led to violent acts. There is no denying that speech can constitute incitement. There is no license in free speech to commit violent acts. Indeed, such acts are inimical to free expression by deterring or silencing others. If free expression is essential for human development and existence, people must feel safe in expressing their views, not just from threats from the government but from each other. The state can protect against those threats by focusing on overt acts rather than speech in prosecutions. However, the greatest danger shown through our history is rage rhetoric triggering state rage.

Extremist and inflammatory speech has been a common element to politics in the United States since the founding. Thomas Paine was the perfect voice for this age of rage. He famously observed that "he who dares not offend cannot be honest." Paine was all about giving offense and earned the distinction of alienating Royalists and Revolutionaries alike. He was one of the personalities who would test the principles of three countries: Britain, the United States, and France. All three would fail, and all three would accuse him of seditious speech during periods of state rage and speech crackdowns.

The three countries that would seek the arrest of Paine had one thing in common. The royals of Britain and even some of the revolutionaries of France and the United States lacked a clear and coherent view of free expression as a human right. The most surprising was the United States, which found such clarity in the First Amendment. James Madison originally wanted even more sweeping language: "the people shall not be deprived or abridged of their right to speak, to write, or to publish their sentiments; and the freedom of the press, as one of the great bulwarks of liberty, shall be inviolable." In a foreshadowing of what was to come, Jefferson and others balked at such language as too expansive. Yet the Framers still approved language to leave free speech unabridged by Congress.

Madison's original language would have been helpful in the years to come, as the country quickly fell victim to the same rationalizations for criminalized speech that had long plagued the colonies.

The United States would quickly face the very same causes for protest and the same natural rights arguments raised in the colonial cases preceding the Revolution. The opposition to taxes would become the flashpoint in the new republic as it was for the Revolution. Confiscatory taxes triggered demonstrations, and the colonial and postcolonial rationales for criminalizing such opposition were strikingly similar. For example, John Wise was a minister and respected elder in Ipswich, Massachusetts, when a meeting gathered on August 22, 1687, to discuss a new tax. The meeting foreshadowed the objections that would be heard roughly eighty years later in Boston. Governor Edmund Andros had imposed the tax unilaterally without any consultation with colonial representatives. Wise raised objections to the legitimacy of such taxation and the right of a people to be able to speak out on such actions. Notably, Wise relied heavily on views of natural law as the basis for the right of free speech and participatory government. He was immediately arrested. The charge alleged that Wise did "maliciously and seditiously say, publish and declare [that the tax] was not legal and to obey and comply with the same were to lose the liberty of freeborn English men." As was often the case, the trial was overseen by a judge closely associated with the governor. Judge Joseph Dudley directed the jury to convict the six defendants. Wise was hit with an onerous fine and then suspended from the ministry.

In less than ten years after the Revolution, the same objections—and prosecutions—would arise around new taxes and claims of confiscatory policies. The history below shows a persistent cycle of political unrest followed by speech crackdowns. To quote Jim Morrison of the Doors in his song "The End," time and again leaders would take "a face from the ancient gallery." While Morrison was referring to the face of Oedipus, the face from the ancient gallery was that of sedition. With it, some Framers became the very thing that they denounced in the British government. Not long after the Revolution, figures like Massachusetts representative (and future judge) Harrison Gray Otis would express "astonishment" over opposition to the Alien and Sedition Acts, since they merely replicated the British law under which they had all "been born and bred." Once the reins of power were held firmly by the Federalists, they set about limiting what Otis dismissed as this "darling privilege" of free speech.

Even the brief review of past periods of rage reveals a pattern of more than just periods of "panic politics," but instead a continual struggle with a right that was at the core of our founding. It also shows a gallery of intriguing characters from the left and the right: Americans who would shape our laws and politics by refusing to yield on their right to speak freely and boldly. From anarchists to feminists to zealots, they were nonconformists who held sharply different views of the ideal society but shared a core belief in speech as a right belonging to them as human beings. They are those "unreasonable" men and women who, as George Bernard Shaw noted, refused to adjust themselves to the world around them. They would bear the blunt of state rage, but test and retest the faith of a nation in this indispensable right.

Five

THE BOSTON TEA PARTY AND
AMERICA'S BIRTH IN RAGE

The Boston Tea Party remains one of the most celebrated moments in United States history, the breaking point where colonists started the transformation into revolutionaries. It also shows how rage rhetoric can become riotous action. On December 16, 1773, groups like the Sons of Liberty engaged in property damage as part of violent protest before seeking outright rebellion. However, most of those advocating action were not seeking an insurrection. In his book *Defiance of the Patriots*, the historian Benjamin Carp wrote that "the Boston Tea Party wasn't a rebellion, or even a protest against the king—but it set in motion a series of events that led to open revolt against the British Crown."

Tea was a commodity with enormous political and economic significance to both England and the colonies. While tea consumption was slow to take hold in the colonies, by the 1760s, Americans were drinking one million pounds of tea a year. Still others would put the figure at five times that estimate. The reason for the uncertainty is that much of the tea in the colonies was being imported illegally from Holland. The mechanics and economics of tea importation made smuggling a serious point of contention with England and the powerful East India Company. Merchants would bid on semiannual lot auctions. The tea had to be imported largely through Boston, New York, and Philadelphia. Given the heavy levy on importation, smugglers had a seller's market for their lower-priced tea.

The Crown and the East India Company reduced the levies to compete with the black market. The Townshend Act of 1767, however, added costs that were the source of renewed opposition in the colonies. The added costs would trigger boycotts of imported goods, which newspapers began to monitor.

The "party" had been brewing for months. On both sides of the pond, feelings were hardening. Prime Minister Lord North had been conciliatory toward the colonies in repealing the Stamp Act and eventually the Townshend Act. However, the riots and the declining revenues of the East India Company prompted him to take a harder line with the Tea Act. North reportedly declared that the tax would remain "until he saw America prostrate at his feet." He was facing the potential collapse of the East India Company with cascading implications for the country. The company had made a series of bad short gambles, including ill-timed dividend payments for shareholders that further depleted its reserves. Nevertheless, the conflict remained largely economic rather than political. Benjamin Franklin was confident that there could be reconciliation over the importation issues. There had been a period of relative calm before tensions returned when now governor Thomas Hutchinson drew up a list of civil officers who would be paid not through the assembly but through the receipts from the warehouses. Hutchinson's home was previously ransacked when he served as lieutenant governor during the Stamp Act protests. When the colonists rose up this time, Hutchinson put down the protest. The situation could not have been more volatile with intransigence in London and defiance in Boston. Pilots steering ships up the Delaware River were threatened with violence. The captain of the *Polly* was given unambiguous warnings about the perils of unloading tea in Boston: "What do you, Captain, of a Halter around your Neck, then Gallons of Liquid Tar decanted on your pate—with the Feathers of a dozen live Geese laid over that to enliven your Appearance."

The Boston Tea Party was organized by a variety of different groups who sought to end the Tea Tax, the remaining residue of the Townshend duties in 1767. These groups included not just the Sons of Liberty but the more mundane-sounding Boston Society for Encouraging Trade and

Commerce as well as the Loyal Nine and the Boston Caucus. In the meetings before the Tea Party, patriots opposed the unloading of tea from the *Dartmouth*, the *Eleanor*, and the *Beaver*. With British officials now being paid out of the duties collected, the tea became a type of self-sustaining suppression in the eyes of some colonials. Adding to the urgency was the fact that the unloading was expected to occur the next day. They believed that the minute the tea hit the dock, it would be subject to the Act. That belief was actually debatable. Indeed, a good colonial lawyer might have averted the destruction by clarifying the meaning of two words under the Act. The law specified a duty would be imposed upon "first entry" of the tea, not the unloading. Thus, the ship had already entered or "arrived" to satisfy the obligation of a duty to be paid within twenty days. Yet such legal niceties were lost with the arrival of the *Dartmouth*, *Eleanor*, and *Beaver*, each heavily laden with English tea. Moreover, it is likely that some of the Sons of Liberty would have still viewed the best place for the duty-laden tea to be at the bottom of the Boston Harbor.

Notably, even up to the very dumping of the tea, some moderates worked to defuse the situation. The patriots wanted the ships to turn around and return to England without unloading. Warnings were publicly proclaimed, including the threat that anyone unloading the tea would be treated "as Wretches unworthy to live and will be made the first victims of our just Resentment." Men were stationed on the docks to prevent unloading. However, the harbor was controlled by the Crown, and Governor Hutchinson refused to allow the captains to return to England without unloading. The captains were between a rock and a hard place. In this case, the hard place was the fortifications on nearby Castle Island and its thirty-two-pounders pointed at any ship attempting to leave Boston. Many viewed the situation as spiraling out of control and sought a face-saving alternative.

The owner of the *Dartmouth*, Francis Rotch, was called to one of the meetings and encouraged to speak with Hutchinson in Milton to reach a compromise. One private suggestion was a type of performative demonstration. A ship would try to leave Boston and then have cannon fire force it back into port. It would then be unloaded, since it was no fault of its own that it was trapped in the harbor. Ironically, this plan was hatched in consultation with Lord Dartmouth (the namesake for Dartmouth College), who supported the Coercive Acts against Boston. Rotch did not seem as eager to have the *Dartmouth* used, even for faux cannon fire, and doubted a crew would be any more game. He also feared that hotheads could punish him for his treachery. The plan came to nothing and Rotch returned to Boston, where he told the crowd that the governor declined to allow him to leave the harbor. The response was a cry for "A mob! A mob!"

In response, the Sons of Liberty and others sought to convert the rage into a riot. Samuel Adams declared that there was no choice now but to take action as some gave "war whoops" in the gallery of the Old South Meeting House. At the meeting, one voice was heard with an ominous appeal. It was John Hancock, who declared, "Let every man do what is right in his own eyes!" What was right in many minds was violence.

As the anger grew, some warned of the danger that speeches could be viewed as sedition. Figures like Josiah Quincy, Jr. (a patriot who would later represent soldiers in the Boston Massacre with John Adams) predicted that prosecutions would follow any violence and "whoever supposes that shouts and hosannas will terminate the trials of the day, entertains a childish fantasy." The colony's treasurer, Harrison Gray, was more direct, warning Quincy that he was engaging in potentially criminal speech and that the Crown would punish those causing unrest. Gray was a loyalist but also someone who maintained close ties with patriots. For some like Gray, the moment had come to pick sides, and he would ultimately stay a faithful subject, eventually joining expats in fleeing to Halifax and then London. For many others, it was time to join the patriots and for taking direct action. There sitting in the harbor were the *Dartmouth*, the *Beaver*, and the *Eleanor*, each with 114 chests of tea. This may sound like a modest amount of tea, but a typical shipment generally included just ten to twelve chests. Moreover, each of these lead-lined chests weighed 450 pounds and often contained 360 pounds of tea. The sheer amount of tea would prove a problem despite the careful planning of the rioters. It may have amounted to roughly 100,000 pounds of tea being dumped at low tide. The water was down to two or three feet in depth, and the tea was washing back on the ships. Men had to push away the thick, viscous slurry to dump more tea. On board, the release of the pent-up anger was exhilarating. A sixteen-year-old Joshua Wyeth would later remark, "[W]e were merry . . . at the idea of making so large a cup of tea for the fishes."

Most contemporary paintings of the famous protest show two things: the dumping of the tea and the support of a large crowd of citizens watching the destruction. This was a demonstrably criminal act, but one that was (and continues to be) celebrated in the United States as a righteous act.

The property destruction was denounced as "vandalism" by the Parliament. Governor Hutchinson called it "the boldest stroke that had been struck against British rule in America." The most interesting response came from John Adams (whose cousin Samuel Adams participated in the dumping). On December 17, 1773, Adams wrote this entry into his diary after witnessing the broken crates and globs of tea on his return to Boston:

> This is the most magnificent Movement of all. . . . There is a Dignity, a Majesty, a Sublimity in this last effort of the Patriots, that I greatly admire. The People should never rise, without doing something to be remembered—something notable. And striking. This Destruction of

the Tea is so bold, so daring, so firm, intrepid and inflexible, and it must have so important consequences, and so lasting, that I cant but consider it as an Epocha [*sic*] in History.

Ironically, it was John Hancock's ship the *Hawley* that brought the word of the destruction to England. The moment of rage left many patriots unnerved. One was Benjamin Franklin, who supported the protest but denounced the violent act of property destruction, even suggesting "reparations" for the company. In a letter on February 2, 1774, to figures including Samuel Adams and John Hancock, Franklin responded to an account of the dumping with consternation and contrition. He disagreed that "there should seem to any a Necessity for carrying Matters to such Extremity, as, in a Dispute about Publick Rights, to destroy private Property." While noting the provocation of the colonial government in preventing the "return of the tea," Franklin emphasized that "the India Company however are not our Adversaries" and encouraged "a Disposition to repair the Damage and make Compensation to the Company." Franklin feared that the destruction would alienate allies in London and compound problems for the colonies.

Franklin's concerns were well-founded. When word of the destruction reached London, the response was to treat the affair as treason and worthy of collective punishment for the city. The Boston Port Bill was introduced in Parliament to close the port until compensation was made to the East India Company. On March 14, 1774, Prime Minister Lord North declared that the government now had two imperatives: "to put an end to the present disturbances in America" and "to secure the just dependence of the colonies on the Crown of Great Britain." He told the Parliament that the destruction showed that "we are considered as two independent states" and that the issue was no longer whether they should tax colonists but "whether or not we have any authority." North and others wanted to make an example of Boston and defended collective punishment because Boston "has been the ringleader of all violence and opposition to the execution of the laws of this country. . . . Boston has not only therefore to answer for its own violence but for having incited other places to tumults."

The second of the "Coercive Acts" targeted the seditious elements further by curtailing the self-governance of the Massachusetts Colony and limiting public meetings.

Yet the crackdown only accelerated the conversion of many to the Revolutionary cause. In opposing draconian measures, Prime Minister William Pitt (known as Pitt the Elder to distinguish from his son William Pitt the Younger, who also served as prime minister) saw that danger and predicted that "if that mad and cruel measure should be pushed . . . England has seen her best days." Indeed, it had. Yet the Boston Tea Party was also an early test in distinguishing rage from rebellion, speech from sedition. The Boston Tea Party foreshadowed the difficult lines that would be drawn in later years between protected and criminalized speech. The nation was barely formed when roles would be reversed in a fight against taxes by the new government and ultimately violence not over tea but whiskey.

Six

SHAYS' REBELLION AND THE RISE OF AMERICAN SEDITION

The new faith in free speech would quickly be tested in the newly formed nation in 1786. In the immediate aftermath of the Revolution, the country faced war debt with no centralized government under the Articles of Confederation. Wealthy businessmen demanded payments for goods, which resulted in higher taxes. At the same time, veterans found their own promised pay delayed as their families struggled to find markets for their crops or goods. While the South had cash crops like tobacco, the situation in New England was more difficult for farmers. Currency was scarce, and the economy was largely based on barter outside of the wealthier areas along the coast. However, there was trouble even in the prosperous areas of Massachusetts Bay. European suppliers had become more skittish since the Revolution in extending credit and were demanding cash. Yet Congress was slow in printing money. These merchants in turn demanded cash from farmers, who had little available. In addition, the Treaty of Paris ending the war forced the assumption of debt by the United States as well as individual states. The state government largely supported the larger merchants and grew increasingly hostile to the farmers.

The Massachusetts Constitution of 1780, drafted by John Adams, only made things worse for poor farmers. As historian Leonard Richards observed, "The Constitution of 1780 undoubtedly consolidated power in the hands of the mercantile elite and the eastern part of the state. It shifted power from the rural backcountry to Boston, from the poor to the rich, and from town meetings to the state senate and governor's office." Courts refused to respond to the grievances of the farmers. It was a powder keg. After all, these men were rebels by definition. They had just defeated a world power. With the new state government refusing any assistance and supporting heavy-handed measures by debt holders, these farmers lashed out at the symbols of the debt system just as Bostonians lashed out at the symbols of the English tax system. They surrounded courthouses where their grievances were being dismissed and their homes confiscated.

The country was again facing an economic protest with rage rhetoric and violence. The mindset of these farmers was captured in the comments of an anonymous figure known only as "Plough Jogger," who wrote:

> I have been greatly abused, have been obligated to do more than my part in the war; been loaded with class rates, town rates, province rates, Continental rates, and all rates . . . been pulled and hauled by sheriffs, constables and collectors, and had my cattle sold for less than they were worth. I have been obligated to pay and nobody will pay me . . . the great men are going to get all we have, and I think it is time for us to rise and put a stop to it. . . . There will be no court until they have redress for their grievances.

Across the country, veterans and farmers grew more desperate and more confrontational. Well-regarded figures like James Warren, the president of the Massachusetts Provisional Congress and paymaster general for the Continental Army, grew alarmed over what they were witnessing. In a letter to John Adams on April 30, 1786, Warren warned that the scarcity of coin (or "specie") and rising taxes were breeding "confusion and anarchy." He added, "Every thing seems verging to Confusion, & anarchy, & certainly great Wisdom & Address are necessary to prevent it." Warren was no wide-eyed radical. He was a wealthy merchant himself, but he could see that these farmers were running out of options and patience.

Daniel Shays embodied many of his countrymen—and the concerns of Warren. A farmer from Pelham, Massachusetts, Shays was a natural leader who distinguished himself as a soldier in the Revolution. He joined the militia just before Yorktown, defending Boston as well as fighting at Bunker Hill. His calm and capable demeanor in battle led to field promotions to sergeant, then second lieutenant, and finally to captain. He fought at Saratoga and later battles. His wounds forced him to leave military service in 1780. After serving under the Marquis de Lafayette, he was given an ornamental sword. As a measure of how bad economic conditions were after the war, Shays sold the sword from Lafayette. Yet he was still called to court to answer for unpaid debts. It did not matter that his country had failed to pay its own debt to him for his military service.

At every turn, Massachusetts politics and policy fueled greater unrest. Massachusetts governor John Hancock was sympathetic to the plight of the farmers and veterans. For Hancock, it must have been eerily familiar. During the Boston Tea Party, he called on patriots to act as their consciences demanded. He was a wealthy merchant and shipper whose business ventures included the importation of tea. While he was initially supportive of the British authorities, he would join those opposing the taxes and the Crown. As the captain of the Corp of Cadets, he refused to heed the order of then governor Hutchinson to put his force into the field to quell any unrest over the unloading of the tea. He rejected "so extraordinary a Mandate." Now Hancock showed the same sympathy for farmers rising up against what they viewed as a confiscatory tax.

While he was unsuccessful in efforts to mediate and mollify, Hancock played a key role in resisting further escalation. That ended when Hancock's long-standing political rival, James Bowdoin (who is the namesake of the elite college), became governor. The two men could not have been more different in temperament and tenor. Closely associated with merchant interests, Bowdoin was both unsympathetic and unyielding. He ramped up property tax rates, tax collection, and debt enforcement. While these protests raged around local courthouses, protesters were primarily seeking some accommodation for their debts as well as printed money. In towns like Worcester, protesters confronted local jurists to demand relief. These were challenges to the taxes, not the Republic or even the state government. For example, on August 29, 1786, there was a riot in Northampton. Yet the protest was again confined to the courthouse, and the locals sought to prevent the holding of hearings on unpaid debts and confiscations. They were met with a stiff arm and threats of arrest. Bowdoin issued a proclamation denouncing "this high-handed offence . . . fraught with libel pernicious and fatal consequences." He ordered local governments and constables "to prevent and suppress all such violent and riotous proceedings."

These were farmers seeking to prevent the confiscation of their homes for want of coin and payment of their war salaries. Nevertheless, the governor rallied the people of the Commonwealth to the cause of "preventing and suppressing all such treasonable proceedings," including the arrest of all "ringleaders and abettors." There would be some riots worthy of criminal charges, but Bowdoin and Bostonian merchants quickly defined these incidents as treason and sedition—a continuation of the British approach to such unrest. On September 19, 1786, the Massachusetts Supreme Court gave Bowdoin what he wanted and set the course for a violent confrontation: it indicted eleven men as "disorderly, riotous, and seditious persons." Yet many did not see an actual rebellion in these protests. On October 21,

1786, there was an unsuccessful effort in Congress to raise half a million dollars for an army to defeat the Shaysites and their "dangerous insurrection." Whatever disorder was unfolding in Massachusetts, many in Congress did not view it as a threat to the nation.

The anger over taxes did manifest itself in occasional but localized violent acts. The first significant incident of violent opposition occurred in the fall of 1781. It was a confrontation over a pair of oxen. The town of Groton was compelled by the state to collect taxes from the locals. Constable William Nutting went to the farm of veteran Joseph Sheple who, like most in the area, lacked any coin for the tax. Nutting then "took a pair of oxen from Capt. Sheple for rates." The action showed locals that their protestations would be ignored and that enforcement had begun. A few days later, men led by Captain Job Shattuck took back the oxen and threatened Nutting that he should not come again. Like Shays, Shattuck personified the crisis. This was a patriot who, after serving as a colonial soldier for the British, fought for independence against the Crown. He was the largest landowner in Groton with hundreds of acres and an impressive home. Despite this relative wealth, he identified with the locals in their objections to the heavy-handed tax policies. For Shattuck and his confederates, the return of the oxen was likely viewed as maintaining the status quo rather than sedition. Yet he and his comrades would be arrested for his actions and charged as "willfully disposed licentious persons and unmindful of their duty to support and maintain the due administration of the government of the Commonwealth." They were accused of obstructing "the legal and regular collection of a tax . . . with force and arms, that is to say, with Staves and Clubbs." In 1786, Massachusetts treated such defiance as sedition. While they still were entirely focused on the debt actions, they were portrayed as being in open rebellion. On September 27, 1786, the *New-Haven Gazette* reported: "There are now assembled in this town about 2000 men, bearing arms: 1200 of which number appear disaffected to the present form of government; and threaten the annihilation of the court now sitting there, unless they acquiesce with their proposals, which they have sent them. The others are for supporting and protecting it."

Local accounts belie the notion that the farmers were at odds with "the present form of government." Even with a sizable force, these farmers were still seeking action from the court over the debt proceedings and forfeitures—not seeking rebellion.

As protests continued around courthouses to stop debt proceedings, there was still time to de-escalate the situation. Instead, Bowdoin raised a privately funded army with the help of merchants who held much of the debt. Citizen rage had triggered state rage. For Shays, the escalation by the government left no room for compromise, though he appeared eager for a nonviolent resolution. With General Benjamin Lincoln pursuing them with his large army, Shays told a friend that he "was sorry that he ever engaged in the scrape, but he had his hand to the plough and could not now look back." Pursued by troops and facing economic ruin, Shays and his followers decided to stand their ground and fight. These men could not have hoped to defeat Lincoln's army, let alone any federal army. However, they clearly hoped to force a resolution on the government by standing their ground.

The Shaysites had moved on to Springfield to halt court proceedings when they learned that Bowdoin's army was on the march. It was only then that they marched on the arsenal at Springfield to seize weapons. For many, it was a defensive move. The seizure of the arsenal would force the state to negotiate. Conversely, if they allowed those weapons to be used by Bowdoin's army, they would face overwhelming firepower. However, the locals miscalculated. Prior word of their move on the arsenal reached William Shepard, who was in charge of the defense of the fort. Shepard was an experienced veteran of the war and served with Washington at Valley Forge. There is evidence that he sought to avoid bloodshed and told his men to fire over the heads of the approaching forces. That did not stop these farmers, many of whom had seen combat only a few years before. That is when Shepard ordered a cannon to be loaded with lethal grapeshot and fired at waist height. Grapeshot turned these cannons into massive shotguns, firing canisters or canvas bags of small round shot to unleash a spread of projectiles. It cut down the vanguard, leaving two mortally wounded and at least twenty injured. It would earn Shepard the loathsome title of the "murderer of brethren," a reputation that would dog him for the rest of his life. However, it was effectively the end of the Shays' Rebellion. Notably, Bowdoin's actions were so resented by many citizens that he was roundly defeated in the next election.

As for the "rebels," many fled to Vermont (which was still not part of the Union) and Canada. Roughly four thousand locals admitted to playing a role in the rebellion and were largely granted amnesty. Hundreds were indicted, but only a few faced trial. Those tried included eighteen convicted ringleaders, but they were later freed after appeals or pardons. The only two defendants executed were John Bly and Charles Rose, who were accused of looting, theft, and other criminal acts. Shattuck was ultimately pardoned by Hancock in 1787 when he returned as governor. As for Shays, he made his way to Vermont but returned and, subsequently, was also pardoned in 1788.

The unnerving aspect of Shays' Rebellion is how quickly some of the figures associated with the Boston Tea Party adopted the same rhetoric and tactics as their British foes. Take Samuel Adams. This was the same man who enflamed public opinion against then lieutenant governor Thomas Hutchinson, whose home was ransacked as part of the Stamp Act riots. Adams threatened ship captains that they would be attacked if they tried to unload their goods. Much like the farmers of Massachusetts who blamed the Washington administration for refusing to listen to their grievances, Adams had blamed the British government for the property destruction, declaring, "I think we have put our Enemies in the wrong and they must in the Judgment of rational Men be answerable for the Destruction of the Tea, which their own Obstinacy rendered necessary."

Just a few years later, Samuel Adams, like his cousin John Adams, accused the farmers of being manipulated by foreign forces and called for the suspension of habeas corpus. This was one of the rallying points of the American Revolution. The ink on the Treaty of Paris was barely dry before this Son of Liberty was calling for the suspension of the "Great Writ." The hypocrisy was not lost on Samuel Adams, who insisted that "[i]n monarchy the crime of treason may admit of being pardoned or lightly punished, but the man who dares rebel against the laws of a republic ought to suffer death." The greatest irony is that the Massachusetts

General Court declared making or spreading statements against the government to be a crime.

Shays' Rebellion was chilling in that it occurred just ten years after the Declaration of Independence and just three years after the end of the War of Independence. Yet, upon assuming power, many of these Revolutionaries immediately picked up the very same bludgeon once yielded by the British. Just as the British saw their denial of rights as warranted given the protection of the greater good of the Empire, the new Americans saw their own revolution as self-authenticating to justify most any means of defense. The rebellion was largely addressed at the state and local levels. What made the next crisis notable was the test of federal authority and the response to violent protests. The Whiskey Rebellion not only involved federal authority but a wide array of key figures from the Revolution, from Washington to Hamilton. The division shown among those figures in how to address such dissent would only become more magnified in the two centuries that followed.

Seven

THE WHISKEY REBELLION
AND "HAMILTON'S
INSURRECTION"

The Whiskey Rebellion followed the same pattern of economic grievances escalating into protests, confrontations, and eventual military
action. The same elements continued to fuel the rage: worthless money,
unpaid war debts, farm seizures, and government crackdowns. Mob action
was common in defiance to excise taxes under the Crown, and colonials
used such protests to force the government to listen to their grievances.
However, there was one additional element. The fledging federal government under the influence of Secretary of Treasury Alexander Hamilton
had begun to raise revenue through a liquor tax to pay off its own war
debt. It was one of the nation's first "sin taxes." Indeed, the College of Phy-
sicians and Surgeons of Philadelphia had pushed for "heavy duties" on
"all distilled spirits . . . to restrain their intemperate use." The 1791 tax
legislation was titled "An Act Repealing, after the Last Day of June Next,
the Duties Heretofore Laid Upon Distilled Spirits Imported from Abroad,
and Laying Orders in their Stead, and Also upon Spirits Distilled with the
United States and for Appropriating the Same." That wonky bill no doubt
seemed innocuous to many in Congress, who saw it as an easy avenue for
relieving the dire financial situation of the government. Some were less
enthused. Southerners asked why Congress was not taxing beer or cider

popular in the East, while Georgia representative James Jackson even suggested taxing lawyers or salaries, while condemning those who would "squirt morality into the minds of the members."

Hamilton estimated that the tax could generate an additional $800,000 annually in revenue. Yet the excise tax had a particularly onerous impact on Pennsylvania farmers. The economy after the war remained a crude mix of worthless currency (including state currencies) and barter. For farmers, the costs of transporting grain consumed the marginal profits needed to sustain their families. Instead, many turned to distilling grain, and rye whiskey quickly became a viable form of currency. For these farmers, this was an illegal income tax.

The cost of hauling twenty-four bushels of milled rye over the Alleghenies to Eastern buyers would take a minimum of three pack animals, and transportation would leave only around $6 for the effort. Distilling the rye into two eight-gallon kegs of whiskey would reduce the transportation costs to one animal and result in roughly $16 in profit. Wheat or rye weighing 1,200 pounds could be distilled to just 160 pounds in the form of twenty gallons of whiskey. Moreover, whiskey held value better than paper currency in allowing farmers to trade for goods.

There was another punitive element to the excise tax. Eastern distillers were larger and were able to internalize the cost of the tax. Many supported the tax because it put them at an advantage over rural producers. Larger producers paid the tax based on their actual production of whiskey, since it was easier to regulate. For rural producers, the tax was based on the capacity of their stills and a projected production period of the full year. In reality, the rural producers operated on a shorter production schedule. Since the still-tax rate was based on the full year for the targeted nine-cents-a-gallon tax, the lower rural production rates meant that their tax was higher than nine cents. Conversely, the overall tax for Eastern or larger producers was about six cents per gallon.

The tax also had other regressive elements. First, the tax had to be paid in cash. Since rural producers and buyers engaged in trade and barter, cash was scarce. The irony was not lost on the farmers. They were forced to accept paper promises on payment for their war service, but the federal government was now demanding payment in coin. Second, the Eastern producers did not have the high transportation costs. The result was ruinous for the many small producers in Pennsylvania. Since whiskey was the most popular cottage industry and a source of a viable currency in trade, the federal tax had devastating effects. This new tax was combined with harsh enforcement by state officials, who tended to favor debt holders.

Rural Pennsylvania was a powder keg when the tax collectors arrived. Like the ships in Boston Harbor, the tax collectors personified everything that these farmers had come to despise in the corruption of the state capital, the unpaid salaries from the war, and the government's refusal to hear their grievances. As with the Sons of Liberty, some would even dress as Indians to carry out late-night vigilantism against the tax. They would meet in their own pubs like the Sign of the Green Tree on the Monongahela. Their own Thomas Paine was Herman Husband, an elderly Quaker who first came to the mountains to escape royal authority in North Carolina for violent agitation. The pamphleteer and pacifist was known as the "Philosopher of the Allegheny" and a correspondent with Benjamin Franklin. Much of these writings and meetings focused on the injustice of the excise tax. When Husband raised a flag in Somerset, Pennsylvania, it read "Liberty and No Excise."

Some locals expressed their anger in a horrific signature form: tarring and feathering. It was the same message given by patriots to captains who considered unloading tea in Boston. While sounding almost prankish, it was an excruciating and cruel act perfected by individuals like Daniel Hamilton, a small distiller and farmer who led a vigilante gang. The first appointed collector, Robert Johnson, provided a vivid example. Soon after his appointment, he was waylaid on the road by a curious-looking mob with black-painted faces, many of whom were wearing their wives' dresses. Johnson was stripped, and his hair painfully cut to the scalp with knives. Hamilton and others then poured the hot tar on his bare skin. They then threw chicken feathers over him and forced him to roll in the feathers on the ground. Afterward, they took his horse and left him in the forest. Johnson would survive and use grease and sand to remove the

hardened tar from his body. The attack would result in a clearly warranted criminal complaint. Hamilton and his mob had crossed from rage rhetoric to overt criminal acts. The question is whether the movement itself was truly a rebellion.

Even as figures like Daniel Hamilton engaged in violent forms of protest, there were continued efforts to address the excise tax peacefully. Well-known figures like wealthy distiller and shipping magnate David Bradford were no Revolutionaries but sought to gain redress for the taxes. Indeed, even the militia members associated with the Mingo Creek Association focused on the excise tax and the foreclosure of homes. These were farmers and small distillers who were opposing what they saw as a wholesale federal takeover of their communities.

For Alexander Hamilton, this was the test for a new emerging federal government. The excise whiskey tax of 1791 was the first such tax approved by the new national government. He wanted to make an example of farmers. The incident brought out the worst inclinations of Hamilton in seeking to crush the dissent—the rationale used against figures like Peter Zenger during colonial prosecutions. His tax favored the wealthy and further undermined the economic position of the lower classes. He also favored executive authority and was viewed by many as a closet monarchist. Notably, however, he did not refer to it initially as a rebellion. Hamilton wrote, "Beware my dear sir of employing an inadequate force to put down a riot. The government ought to inspire respect with a display of strength." It is striking how Hamilton's language is similar to the British governors' after the Boston Tea Party. At that time, General Thomas Gage, returning from his post as commander in chief in America, told George III that an example had to be made of the Bostonians or they would grow ever bolder: "They will be Lyons whilst we are Lambs, but if we take the resolute part, they will undoubtedly prove very meek."

Alexander Hamilton wanted the "riot" crushed and worked on Washington, who hesitated in the use of force. In the meantime, Hamilton sent George Clymer as a revenue inspector, a figure that historian William Hogeland described as "a crude caricature of their worst fears about the real nature of the Treasury Department, the federal government, and the east." He also assigned hard-edged general John Neville as the chief inspector of revenue. It was a deadly combination. Neville was hardly disinterested in the tax. He was one of the wealthiest figures in "the Forks" and operated the largest whiskey distillery. His largest customer was the army. Like other large distillers, he favored the tax as a way to force small competitors out of business. Hamilton had to know that Neville's appointment would be inflammatory and that Neville would be unrelentingly harsh on these farmers.

There were those close to Washington who pushed back against Hamilton's plan. The most prominent and active was Attorney General Edmund Randolph. The Virginian was made the nation's first attorney general after he distinguished himself at the Constitutional Convention as a member of the important Committee of Detail that drafted core provisions. While Randolph saw the need for a federal government, he would ultimately decline to sign the final version of the Constitution because he felt it lacked sufficient checks on federal authority. The Hamilton Plan likely confirmed his worst expectations. Hamilton cited a "convention" held in Pittsburgh as evidence of a growing rebellion. However, Randolph pointedly reminded Washington that they just fought for the right to assemble to seek policy change. Randolph acknowledged that the violence justified a response but counseled patience and caution. In the drafted proclamation of Washington on the violence, Randolph prevailed in a critical respect. He crossed out a line from Hamilton that threatened to send federal troops if the locals did not yield and restore order. Washington agreed to remove the line and held out for negotiations.

Locals attacked those who were viewed as assisting the federal government. Notably, when the militias had formed and were at their height, the calls remained focused on ending the tax and its collectors rather than the Republic. One man on horseback swinging a tomahawk declared, "It is not the excise law only that must go down. Your district and associated judges must go down, your high offices and salaries." Hamilton, however, continued to work toward a federal crackdown and turned to James Wilson to make the case. Wilson, a jurist and Federalist, compiled a list of the violence and unrest in the Forks. It was Randolph again who cautioned Washington that this was a time for restraint, not retribution, from the federal government. When Hamilton finally prevailed, his associates would unleash their pent-up anger, not on the militia but on those later captured. The federal force was massive, including a train of artillery with six-pounders and mortars. Yet locals ridiculed them as "the Watermelon Army" for their habit of stealing local produce. What followed was state rage. One of the first to be arrested was the elderly Herman Husband at his farm. The rapid arrest of Husband concerned Washington in how it would be taken locally. He was right. Many fled.

Neville and his associates searched for culprits. Their eagerness to make the case against some figures bordered on the ludicrous. For example, lawyer Hugh Henry Brackenridge was a moderating force in the protests, often steering others toward less violent or confrontational options. A close correspondent with Madison, Brackenridge was widely respected, even if some of the militants did not entirely trust his commitment to their cause. Neville and Hamilton sought to prosecute him and produced a letter to an associate from Brackenridge to one of the ringleaders, David Bradford, to prove a conspiratorial role. The associate, Senator James Ross, did in fact confirm to Hamilton that the chicken-scratch writing was undoubtedly that of Brackenridge. That moment of triumph, however, was short lived when Ross pointed out that the letter was addressed not to the rabble-rouser David Bradford but William Bradford, the head of the presidential commission. Hamilton, however, persisted in accusing Brackenridge and others of plotting rebellion.

For those arrested, the retribution was horrific and exceeded the violence meted out by the vigilantes. They were pulled from their beds late at night and forced in chains to walk through the snow, including some who were barefoot. In command was General Anthony "Blackbeard" White, a cruel and mentally unstable figure. White interrogated dozens of captives, who were forced into sitting positions in the icy mud of an unheated tavern cellar. Even the foot soldiers began to balk at the mistreatment, as the arrested men showed signs of serious physical deterioration. White was unrelenting, marching his prisoners for miles in the snow and denying them food and water.

In the end, it was all rage on both sides. Few were prosecuted and even fewer convicted. There was little evidence, and grand juries performed their role as a check on government abuse. They refused to indict even though judges demanded indictment and uniformly denied the accused basic information on their charges. Even with openly hostile judges toward the accused, only twelve cases went to trial and only two resulted in convictions. Those men, Philip Wigle and John Mitchell, clearly played roles in the violence. However, Washington remained cognizant of the need, as expressed by Randolph, to earn the trust of these mountain people. He pardoned both men. Wigle would ultimately have the most lasting revenge. A whiskey in Pennsylvania still bears his name.

The Whiskey Rebellion was an early test of how the government would respond to rage rhetoric and violent protests. Madison and Jefferson did not play a role in these discussions. They remained conspicuously silent in part due to an agreement with Hamilton to move the Capitol from Philadelphia to what is now Washington, DC. The excise tax would help pay for that move. Yet Jefferson blamed the government, not the locals, for the unrest. In a letter to Madison, Jefferson made clear his disagreement with the actions of Washington and Hamilton. He referred to the excise tax as "an infernal one" and stated: "The first error was to admit it by the constitution. The 2d. to act on that admission. The 3d. and last will be to make it the instrument of dismembering the Union, and setting us all afloat to chuse which part of it we will adhere to." Madison was also privately critical. The most damning comment came from Jefferson when, in another letter to Madison, he referred to what was being called "Hamilton's Insurrection." He declared, "The Incidents of Hamilton's insurrection is a curious work indeed. The hero of it exhibits himself in all the attitudes of a dexterous balance master."

Jefferson's views are often attributed by critics to his identification with the rabble or rebelliousness in general. However, Jefferson (and Madison) offered a more nuanced view of the "troubles" in recognizing the underlying economic and legal causes. Where figures like Hamilton and Adams saw such riots as rebellion, Jefferson saw these confrontations as part of a spectrum of political discord. Indeed, this was the impetus for Jefferson's famous line discussed at the start of this book: "I hold it that a little rebellion, now and then, is a good thing, and as necessary in the political world as storms in the physical."

Eight

FRIES AND THE FAUX REBELLION

While not as famous as the two earlier "rebellions," the Fries Rebellion is arguably the most illustrative of this period—and the most relevant to recent events. As in earlier protests against Federalist policies and the sedition laws, protests in Pennsylvania initially formed around a liberty pole. Shortly before Christmas in 1798, Henry and Peggy Hembolt and other locals in Montgomery County raised a pole with a French liberty cap, the tricolored cockade, and a sign that read "The Constitution Sacred, No Gagg Laws, Liberty or Death." It was a protest that began not just as an opposition to a confiscatory tax but in defense of the First Amendment, which was ratified only seven years earlier. They still believed that the First Amendment represented a break from the British traditions and sedition prosecutions. Indeed, the term used by these German immigrants for the Federalist accessors was equally telling: "Tories." The farmers saw the American officials as interchangeable with their monarch-loving predecessors.

The protest was triggered by two pieces of legislation signed by Adams on July 14, 1798: the Sedition Act and the Tax Act. This was only seven years after the passage of the 1791 Whiskey Act and just four years after the end of the Whiskey Rebellion. For Adams and figures like Hamilton, this "rebellion" would prove the lesson long sought for those challenging federal authority. The Constitution was newly ratified, and the federal government was now able to wield both an army and a new legal authority. After their hawkish response to the Whiskey Rebellion, there was little doubt how Adams and the Hamiltonian wing of the Federalist Party would respond to a new uprising in Pennsylvania a few years later. It did not matter that this was the same John Adams who insisted that the destruction of the tea in Boston just a few years earlier was "absolutely and indispensably" necessary to preserve American liberties.

With the rising costs of the Quasi-War with France, the Adams administration needed an infusion of cash and pushed through taxes on homes, real estates, and slaves. Pennsylvania farmers again rose up in anger. They believed that the tax was unconstitutional and were told that that they did not have to pay the tax. It was also punitive for those who had worked hard to pay for and to improve their lands. The undeveloped land of speculators was subject to less of a tax burden. Taxes were increased by factors like the number of windows in a dwelling. In a critical meeting, the Reverend Jacob Eyermann waved around what he (dubiously) claimed was a copy of the Constitution and federal laws and assured the farmers that the law was unconstitutional and unenforceable. He was asserting a strict construction of the Constitution and the right to nullify unconstitutional acts. Moreover, he warned them that, if they paid the tax, they would concede to new taxes to follow. The key congressional district at the center of the protests had recently switched parties from the Federalists to the Republicans. Since their representatives would not take office for months, they believed that they were entitled (as before the Revolution) to obstruct the direct tax until they could be heard in Congress.

When the tax collectors appeared, therefore, the farmers rose up. They were led by an extraordinary leader, John Fries. Like many in the prior "rebellions," Fries was a veteran of the Revolutionary War, where he commanded a company and served in engagements like White Marsh and Crooked Billet. (Indeed, of the 211 people eventually arrested in the "rebellion," roughly 40 percent were Revolutionary War veterans.) Fries was a member of the Bucks Associators under Captain Henry Huber. Ironically, Fries played a key role in the militia action against a royal foraging

light horse unit seizing livestock. In a moment reminiscent of the start of the Whiskey Rebellion, Fries alerted Huber, and the militia intercepted the British force—compelling them to release the livestock. The ultimate irony is that Fries later commanded a unit in crushing the Whiskey Rebellion. A bilingual public auctioneer who spoke both German and English, Fries was widely respected and believed honestly that the tax was unconstitutional and unfair.

The controversy came to a head when accessors, including Jacob Eyerle, appeared. The German population in the area was largely divided between the town-dwelling groups like the Moravians, Mennonites, and Schwenkfelders on one side and the rural Lutheran and German Reformed Kirchenleute, or Church People, on the other. The former groups tended to be less violent and less challenging of state and federal authority. Eyerle was a Moravian, while Eyermann was a Kirchenleute. The Kirchenleutes had just won the election in taking the district from the Federalists. Fries and others composed a paper explaining their opposition to the tax and demanding its repeal. Eyerle demanded that the local judge, William Henry, act to bring the resisters to the court. Eyerle and Henry were business partners. Henry's actions would escalate the matter even further in seeking federal intervention. When the farmers reaffirmed their opposition, U.S. district judge Richard Peters ordered their arrest, and U.S. Marshal William Nichols rounded up twenty resisters and held them in the Sun Tavern in Bethlehem, Pennsylvania. They were to be removed to Philadelphia, which outraged the locals, who feared summary justice once they were removed from the area. Yet they again held a meeting to discuss their constitutional rights to oppose the tax and to protect themselves from such injustice. They repeatedly invoked the First Amendment. They marched on the tavern to demand the resisters' release. The German farmers called the marshal "*Spitzbuben*," or rogue, and accused him of violating the constitution and thus acting without authority. This "rebellion" was composed of only 140 men and only around half were armed. Indeed, Fries dutifully paid a toll to cross into Bethlehem and marched peacefully to the tavern. They believed that they were acting within their rights, and Fries agreed to enter the tavern unarmed.

Throughout this brief standoff, Fries worked to make sure that the protest remained peaceful and lawful. He extolled the men, "Please, for God's sake, don't fire except we are fired on first." As the anger grew over the standoff, Fries pleaded with Nichols to see reason and release the men under bail. He made clear that they would not object to the trial of the men, but demanded that the trial be held locally. He offered to pay the bail for the men. Ultimately, Nichols relented, but he refused the bail and reported the men "stolen." Nichols would later portray his role as defying an armed rebellion and omitted the repeated assurances and actions of Fries to maintain the peace. In fact, Fries and others repeatedly stopped violence. The only real threat of lethal violence occurred when a militiaman pointed his musket at accessor Everard Foulke. However, as Fries and Huber interceded, the inebriated militiaman simply passed out (he was later found by Fries to have an unworkable musket after loading the ball before the powder). The entire group then dispersed without a single incidence of violence. Most assumed that the matter had been resolved and that trials would be held later on for the tax resistance.

On March 12, Adams ordered the "insurgents" to disperse despite their having dispersed a week earlier. Moreover, on March 15, a group of two hundred farmers (more than had actually participated in the protest) met at a tavern and, again, resolved to proceed lawfully. The group was told by an appointed committee "to desist from further opposition to the assessors and other officers in the execution of their duties and enjoined them to give due submission to the laws of their country." While there was a reported beating of assessor Stephen Balliott, there was general agreement not to confront or resist the government. The controversy had become a matter of rage—by the government. Adams sent in troops, which again faced no resistance as resisters were arrested. Fries was arrested at an auction, though it was his own dog who gave away his location when he hid in a forest grove. Associate Justice James Iredell arrived to preside as charges were brought for treason against Fries, Frederic Hearny, and Anthony Stahler. In the coming days, dozens more would be charged with "levying war against the United States" and other charges. It was utterly absurd, but a point was to be made. Those charges included counts under the newly minted Sedition Act.

The brutality of the crackdown was captured in the arrest of publisher Jacob Schneider, who published a critical article in his *Readinger Adler*. Schneider had already drawn the ire of figures like Timothy Pickering, who wanted him prosecuted for sedition for writings opposing the local Federalist candidate. Federalist representative Robert Goodloe Harper led a force to Schneider's home and demanded to know if he wrote the article. When Schnieder said that he had, his clothes were torn off, and he was dragged before the captain of the unit, who ordered him to be given twenty-five lashes with a knotted whip in the town square. The flogging was stopped only after the arrival of a mounted company from Philadelphia. The Federalist units attacked unarmed crowds, including innocent persons mistaken for "rebels." As historian Paul Douglas Newman noted, "in three weeks, they had spent $80,000 from the federal treasury, beat up one newspaper editor and inspired the thrashing of another, terrified women and children, killed a bull, nearly shot one man through the head and almost splayed another in two."

Fries was held in isolation and even denied visitation from his wife.

What was most striking is how the trial was based on the same claims used by the Crown to prosecute dissenters and political critics. Indeed, the cases pushed treason claims beyond what even the English court had been willing to accept. As discussed earlier, the Star Chamber was created in part because the Crown faced resistance from the English bench over charging treason without an overt act or based primarily on speech. Sedition was the solution, and the Star Chamber proceeded to make fast work of critics of the Crown. In the Fries cases, the Adams administration accused these farmers of treason despite their repeatedly affirming their desire to comply with constitutional standards, repeatedly being assured that this was an unconstitutional tax, and refraining from any violent acts as a group. To accuse John Fries of being a traitor was particularly dishonest and chilling. Fries had just led troops to crush the Whiskey Rebellion a few years prior and had served as a commander in combat to help win the Revolution. He consistently counseled against violence and played a key role in defusing the standoff at Sun Tavern without a single shot being fired. Nevertheless, the instruction of Iredell was so sweeping that it was hard to see room for acquittal. The jury was instructed that "the intention was to prevent by force of arms the execution of any act of the congress of the United States altogether. . . . [A]ny forcible opposition calculated to carry that intention into effect, was a levying of war against the United States." By the end of the trial, Iredell appeared to have his own doubts, but he emphasized to the jury that they would have to condemn Fries on the testimony of just two witnesses in contradiction to his other actions. Fries was found guilty after only three hours. Later, Iredell remorsefully wrote to his wife: "I could not bear to look upon the poor man, but, I am told, he fainted away. . . . I dread the task I have before me in pronouncing sentence on him." Nevertheless, he ordered the men hanged.

The trial then moved from the bizarre to the surreal. After the court learned that a juror had made biased comments about Fries, a new trial was ordered. This trial would involve Justice Samuel Chase, who had already shown his own bias in pursuing Jeffersonians under the sedition laws. Chase offered his own instruction that all but guaranteed conviction. He defined treasonously "levying war" as including "rising to resist or to prevent by force or violence, the execution of any statute of the United States." Furthermore, he stressed, the use of "military weapons" was not necessary for levying war, since "numbers may supply the want of military weapons." The defense declared that Chase's opinion left no defense and withdrew from representation in protest. Chase then made an extraordinary offer: come back and I will withdraw the opinion. The defense counsel knew that Chase did not need the opinion to enforce the standard and again demurred. Chase then declared that he would represent the defendants and be their judge. They were convicted and sentenced again to die.

In addition to Hamilton, Secretary of State Timothy Pickering was Adams's iron fist in pursuing critics under the sedition laws. He rejoiced in the convictions and death sentences, noting that Pennsylvania had to be brought to heel given the recent rebellions. Entirely detached from the gross injustice in the case, or its lethal effect, Pickering wrote to Adams that "an example or examples of conviction and punishment of such high-handed offenders were essential to ensure future obedience to the laws, or the exertions of our best citizens to suppress future insurrections." Adams, however, was warned by others that there was no real rebellion. Hanging these "high-handed offenders" would likely make them martyrs in a new cause.

There was a popular story of Adams signing the pardon when the wife of John Fries came to his office with a baby in her arms and kneeled before him. In reality, Adams had read accounts of the trial and reportedly came to view the men not as rebels but "miserable Germans . . . ignorant of our language as they were of our laws." That was hardly an apt description of the intelligent and bilingual Fries. Yet, either out of a political calculation or a sense of genuine sympathy, Adams issued a pardon for the "rebels" on May 21, 1800. It was only forty-eight hours before their execution. It was also less than a year before Adams would leave office. More important, the presidential election was to be held between October 31 and December 3, 1800. Adams was already being condemned for his actions against critics, and the issue would contribute to his defeat to Jefferson. The pardon may have been a calculated effort to blunt the impact of the overblown response of his administration.

Fries would return to his career as an auctioneer, but Adams would not be long in his own office.

Notably, Hamilton, Pickering, and other Hamiltonians were irate that Adams had spared these men from death. The same month that Adams pardoned the rebels, he would ask Pickering to resign. He refused, so Adams fired him. The Hamiltonian wing would abandon Adams and ironically help bring Jefferson to power.

The very framing of the Fries protests as a "rebellion" and its supporters as "insurgents" would follow a familiar pattern in our history. By declaring these patriots as "rebels," the early American government claimed sweeping powers to crush them in the name of the public good. Indeed, the incident showed how useful such alleged insurrections can be for people in power. Fries proves less of an emergency than an opportunity for those eager to expand federal authority in the nascent years of American governance.

Nine

ADAMS AND THE RETURN
OF "THE MONSTER"

A review of these historic events—the Boston Tea Party, Shays' Rebellion, the Whiskey Rebellion, and the Fries Rebellion—reveals striking similarities in how the country dealt with rage rhetoric in its formulative years. All four were propelled by economic distress and grievances. All four involved governments that were at best indifferent and at worst hostile to local populations. In three cases (with the exception of Fries), what began as protests became violent resistance. It was the first true age of rage for the new nation. The rage of the citizenry would be met by the rage of the government.

All these incidents involved governments that immediately treated violent rhetoric as sedition or treason, further pushing protesters toward violence. Where the first incident (the Boston Tea Party) was now celebrated as a triumph of democracy, the latter incidents (the Shays', Fries, Whiskey Rebellions) were treated as the triumph of authority over anarchy. Once again, rage is viewed differently depending on how one views the underlying cause. One riot is viewed as righteous, while the others are viewed as dangerous. For example, at the start of the Revolution, John Adams would call for the effigies of General William Howe and his officers to swing from the gallows. However, when Adams was burned in effigy at the College of William & Mary, it was viewed as seditious. The pro-Federalist writer William Cobbett would declare in his *Porcupine's*

Gazette that the college president was a "bitter, seditious, envious wretch" for allowing the display of this "rascally seditious crew."

Similarly, liberty poles (which go back to Roman times as a symbol of being freed from slavery) were widely used by Revolutionaries. On June 5, 1766, the Sons of Liberty erected a liberty pole on the Golden Hill in New York to celebrate the end of the Stamp Tax. It was the king's birthday, and a sign on the pole read "King, Pitt, and Liberty." While hardly revolutionary, the British considered it defiant and cut it down. The Sons of Liberty then erected a second pole. It was also cut down. They erected a third pole and finally, after the intervention of an exasperated colonial governor, it was left standing. Soon, liberty trees and liberty poles appeared as a protest against the Federalists and Presi-

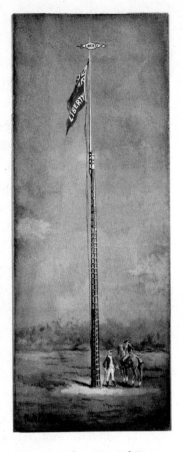

dent Adams. They were promptly declared seditious. When David Brown raised such a pole in Dedham, Massachusetts, he was arrested. Federalist representative Fisher Ames, a lawyer, declared Brown "a wandering apostle of sedition," and the newspapers called Liberty Poles "Jacobin Poles" that served as a "rallying point of insurrection and civil war." As done by the royal government, Brown's pole was cut down. Ames declared that an example must be made of Brown and "the government just display its power *in terrorem*." It was to be a display of state rage, and Brown was quickly found and convicted. Justice Chase was the willing vehicle of the state *"terrorem"* and sentenced Brown, who was known as a simple vagabond, to eighteen months in prison and a $450 fine (a considerable sum for the time).

For Federalists, the "rebellions" were an opportunity to establish national authority and reinstate sedition prosecutions. During the Shays' and Whiskey Rebellions, there was no Constitution and thus no federal courts to enforce federal laws. Congress passed laws but had little ability to enforce them without the cooperation of the states. In Shays' Rebellion, figures like Captain Shattuck were effectively charged with disturbing the peace in their resistance to tax collection, a local or state charge. More serious charges would follow, but the sedition charges against the eleven defendants in September 1786 were state charges. Of the handful of prosecutions that resulted from the Whiskey Rebellion, only two convictions could be secured. Most cases were declined by grand juries. The federal means to respond were as limited as the laws. When the Congress was worried about the Springfield arsenal falling into the hands of the Shaysites, it sought in October 1786 to raise $500,000 to quell the "dangerous insurrection." However, only one state (Virginia) agreed to supply funds and the effort failed. On November 30, 1786, Adams wrote Jefferson, "Dont be alarmed at the late Turbulence in New England, The Massachusetts assembly had in its Zeal to get the better of their Debt, laid on a Tax, rather heavier than the People could bear; but all will be well, and this Commotion will terminate in additional Strength to Government." In the end, the rebellions not only convinced many to abandon the Articles of Confederation but reinforced the view that the new Constitution should be based on representative democratic principles rather than direct democracy. The experiences in Massachusetts and Pennsylvania strongly counseled in favor of using buffers between the passions of the public and the business of government.

Jefferson called the actions of the farmers "absolutely unjustifiable," yet he also hoped "they will provoke no severities from their governments." That was not the attitude of John Adams, as he made clear to Jefferson: "I believe you never felt the Terrorism of Gallatins Insurrection in Pensilvania: you certainly never reallized the Terrorism of Fries's, most outragious Riot and Rescue, as I call it, Treason, Rebellion as the World and great Judges and two Juries pronounced it." The references are to Shays' Rebellion and the Whiskey Rebellion. The reference of Gallatin's

Insurrection (rather than "Hamilton's Insurrection") is particularly telling. Albert Gallatin, a Pennsylvanian who served as Jefferson's secretary of treasury, was a passionate voice for individual rights. He opposed the ratification of the Constitution not because he did not believe in a federal government but because he feared the lack of protections for individual rights. In the same way, Gallatin encouraged his fellow Pennsylvanians to yield to the taxation, but he opposed Hamilton's militarization of the conflict. He would also later oppose Adams as he sought to reinstate the criminalization of speech. There is good reason why Adams would loathe Gallatin. The Swiss immigrant was consistently a voice for individual rights, particularly one (free speech) that Adams would increasingly scorn.

For Adams, the Whiskey Rebellion was a tragedy not in the unrest or the crackdown but in the lack of any repercussions for what he saw as a rebellion. After the Whiskey Rebellion fizzled out, some in Congress still wanted a resolution of censure to denounce these groups in seditious terms. The resolution declared:

> [W]e cannot withhold our reprobation of the self-created societies, which have risen up in some parts of the Union, misrepresenting the conduct of the Government, and disturbing the operation of the laws, and which, by deceiving and inflaming the ignorant and the weak, may naturally be supposed to have stimulated and urged the insurrection.

Other members wisely recognized the anti–free speech implications of the legislation. Madison opposed passage while stressing that "opinions are not the objects of legislation." He added that "if we advert to the nature of Republican Government we shall find that the censorial power is in the people over the Government, and not in the government over the people." Others warned of the "hazard of interfering with the exercise and expression of opinion" and reminded colleagues that "the rights of opinion, or of thinking and speaking and publishing, are sacred." So, the new Congress refused to censure groups for the same underlying conduct.

Yet Adams and the Federalists would soon unleash sedition
prosecutions on the nation.

Even Abigail Adams would
call for sedition prosecutions,
writing in response to an article
by Benjamin Franklin Bache
in the *Aurora* that "I wish the
laws of our Country were com-
petent to punish the stirrer up
of sedition." She would get her
wish. Even before the law was
finally enacted, Bache would be
charged with sedition for insulting Adams. Bache, the grandson of Benjamin Franklin, was known for his unyielding writings, lashing out at the
pompous and the corrupt. Members called for his arrest from the floor.
Connecticut representative John Allen denounced him and the *Aurora*
as seeking "to overturn and ruin the Government by publishing the most
shameless falsehoods against the Representatives of the people of all denominations." He declared that the publication of such attacks was nothing less than "a conspiracy against the Constitution, the Government, the
peace and safety of this country." After his release on bail, Bache would
continue to publish his criticism, and ultimately he did, in a fashion, escape the wrath of Adams. Bache would die of yellow fever at the age of
twenty-nine. His wife (who would take over the publication of the *Aurora*) would describe him best as "a man inflexible in virtue, unappalled
by power or persecution."

Even Jefferson, who opposed the federal laws on sedition, would support the use of state sedition prosecutions of his opponents. He maintained
that even if the federal Sedition Acts are barred under the Constitution,
it did not:

remove all restraint from the overwhelming torrent of slander, which
is confounding all vice and virtue, all truth and falsehood, in the

United States. The power to do that is fully possessed by the several State legislatures. It was reserved to them, and was denied to the General Government, by the constitution, according to our construction of it.

Indeed, Jefferson remarked on one occasion that he "long thought that a few prosecutions of the most prominent offenders would have a wholesome effect in restoring the integrity of the presses." It was a striking contrast given Jefferson's view that "a little rebellion now and then" was a healthy thing for a republic. It would seem that Jefferson relished both a little rebellion and a little state suppression "now and then." For his part, Madison seemed to be conflicted in early comments on sedition. However, he would later become one of the fiercest critics of speech prosecutions. It was Adams who would become the face of American sedition abuse. Jeffersonians relished the opportunity to heap insults on the thin-skinned Adams. Franklin Bache used his *Aurora* newspaper to attack "the blind, bald, crippled, toothless, querulous ADAMS." Despite the abundance of pro-Federalist publications, figures like Bache outraged Adams and his allies.

One of the most curious allies was William Cobbett, who wrote in favor of reestablishing sedition prosecutions, writing, "Surely, we need a sedition law to keep our own rogues from cutting our throats, and an alien law to prevent the invasion by a host of foreign rogues to assist them." While he would become a major voice in favor of the Alien and Sedition Acts, Cobbett faced sedition charges not once but twice in Britain. His first trip to the United States was in flight from a possible arrest. Yet the former English soldier remained a fervent supporter of the Crown and became known as "Peter Porcupine" for his often caustic writings against abuses and hypocrisies in the new nation. He was an able writer who would eventually move back to England and run repeatedly for the House of Commons. His love for all things English did not wane after being repeatedly targeted by the quintessentially English charge of seditious libel. However, there was an admirable contrarianism to his conservatism. When he moved back to England in 1800 (after losing a civil defamation case), Cobbett proceeded to criticize the corruption in England. He would spend two years in jail after denouncing the flogging of militiamen who simply objected to cuts in their pay. Even though his publications on their behalf were deemed seditious, he continued to write such articles and again had to flee to the United States. And yet he would return again to England in later years, even succeed in becoming a member of the House of Commons. He remained wonderfully nonconformist. Indeed, he seemed in every other respect a true American in his irascible and irresistible impulse to challenge authority. In that sense, he was a conservative Thomas Paine. He would enrage even those he defended. For example, Cobbett supported reforms by the Whig Party even though he himself was no Whig. However, in 1831, Cobbett represented farmers who had rioted in protests against low wages. The Whig government viewed his arguments as seditious and once again moved for his arrest. Cobbett would not flee this time and successfully fought the charges. Despite this history, Cobbett, the Porcupine, remained a loyal Englishman and supported the use of sedition against those with errant thoughts. Yet Cobbett also held an intense love for America and would apply many of the lessons that he had learned in cities such as Philadelphia to the problems that persisted in his own country.

Adams displayed the same inherent contradiction in his own embracing of crackdowns on critics like Thomas Cooper. Adams was irate when Cooper alleged that the Federalists were trying "to stretch to the utmost the constitutional authority of our Executive, and to introduce the political evils of those European governments whose principles we have rejected." Adams notably embraced the cabined Blackstonian view of free speech to rationalize his sedition prosecutions: "As far as it alludes to me, I despise it; but I have no doubt it is a libel against the whole government, and as such ought to be prosecuted."

The Alien and Sedition Acts were the perfect vehicle for such partisan prosecutions. The sedition law seemed ripped from the Crown's seditious libel cases, making it a crime to "print, utter, or publish . . . any false, scandalous, and malicious writing or writings against the government of the United States, or either house of the Congress of the United States, or the President of the United States." Section Two of the Act expressly codified the common law rule and, in so doing, rejected the broader interpretation of free speech under the First Amendment. Members such as South Carolina representative Robert Goodloe Harper insisted that the objections to the law were misplaced because the First Amendment did not change the Blackstonian view of the right of the free press and only barred prior restraints as opposed to regulations of the press. There was one notable departure from early English sedition cases. Truth was a defense. This is a standard component of civil defamation law, but this was a law designed to criminally punish those speaking against government leaders and policies. Since most of the sedition cases involved opinion, the defense proved to be little use as a protection against abuse, particularly before a sympathetic Federalist jury. Once again, it was Albert Gallatin who cut through the false rationalizations and transparent excuses in defense of free speech. Gallatin chided the sponsors and said that the legislation "was intended to punish solely writings of a political nature, libels against the government." He asked, "How could the truth of opinions be proven by evidence?"

The passage of the Alien and Sedition Acts came in another period of "temporary panic." Indeed, the fear of French conspiracies has been described as "panic politics" used by Federalists to justify the wholesale crackdown on dissent. The law was used to target Jefferson's supporters, who Federalists denounced as the allies of the French. Each side portrayed the other as seeking forms of either monarchist or mob tyranny. The defense of the Acts echoed the British defense of seditious libel prosecutions, including direct reliance on Blackstone's views. Members including Representative Harrison Gray Otis dismissed the "certain and technical meaning" of the First Amendment and portrayed such prosecutions as long accepted as an essential tool of the government to protect public safety. He warned his colleagues that "the times are full of danger, and it would be the height of madness not to take every precaution in our power." There was also an underlying difference in what free speech represented in the new nation. As law professor Geoffrey Stone observed, "[T]he Federalists had little faith in free and open debate" and even less faith in the common man's ability to sort out the truth. Even Federalist newspapers warned of the dangers of free speech given the vulnerability of "the weak" and "foolish" to spread alarm like "a contagious disease." Violence was rampant throughout the United States, and eventually the rage extended to Congress, as shown in the cartoon on page 113 depicting a fight on the House floor between Democratic-Republican representative Matthew Lyon and Federalist representative Roger Griswold.

As if to prove the characterization of Adams as a thin-skinned despot, Lyon was prosecuted for criticizing Adams's "unbounded thirst for ridiculous pomp, foolish adulation, and selfish avarice." He was convicted and sentenced to four months in prison and a fine. Twenty-five leading Republicans were arrested, including journalists, and many others were threatened with arrest if they uttered similar thoughts. Lyon was the prototypical figure in free speech fights: a loud, irascible Irishman who resisted authority. He came from Ireland in 1764 as an indentured servant but was soon released after "throwing a mallet at the head of his master." He would take his wife to the Green Mountains and would fight with Ethan Allen's legendary Green Mountain Boys, including in the attack on Fort Ticonderoga. He would flourish in Vermont as a businessman and campaigned unsuccessfully as a Republican until his election in 1797. Once in Congress, he attacked the Federalists and denounced Alexander Hamilton for "screwing the hard-earnings out of the poor people's pockets"—a view that would also be heard among the farmers in the Whiskey Rebellion. However, what most earned the ire of the Federalists was Lyon's position as the publisher of a Vermont newspaper.

The Lyon trial was a Federalist farce with a mob denouncing the "Vermont Beast" and a band playing "Rogue's March" as he arrived at the courthouse. Lyon was unrepentant and published a letter reaffirming his objections to the "principle of Presidential infallibility." As in other trials, the presiding judge was openly biased. In this case, it was United States associate justice William Paterson, a die-hard Federalist who would later try individuals charged in the Whiskey Rebellion. Paterson's charge to the grand jury was a caricature of legal process. He told them that they should remain vigilant against "the seditious attempts of disaffected persons to

disturb the government." If there were any doubt that the message was received, the grand jury responded with an indictment and the statement, "[W]e solemnly feel what the Honorable Judge has so powerfully expressed, that licentiousness more endangers the liberties and independence of a free Government than hosts of invading foes." It was enough to make a Tudor blush, but Paterson was pleased with an indictment that accused Lyon of maliciously seeking to bring the President and government of the United States into contempt and such offenses as accusing the Adams administration of "ridiculous pomp, foolish adulation, and selfish avarice." Lyon represented himself, but Paterson informed the jury that they had to "render a verdict of guilty." They quickly followed his lead and convicted. Paterson was not satisfied by railroading Lyon into the conviction. He denounced him for his "mischiefs" in his "unlicensed abuse of government." He asked the virtually destitute defendant how much he could possibly raise in a fine. Lyon responded that he could conceivably raise $200. Paterson promptly set the fine at five times that amount and ordered him jailed for four months. He added that, until Lyon could pay the fine of $1,000, he would stay in jail beyond the four months. He was then handed over to the marshal, Jabez Fitch, to serve as his jailer—a man who was one of his most outspoken critics and "seized every opportunity to add to the prisoner's misery."

When others came to the aid of Lyon, they were also accused of sedition. Another Revolutionary War veteran, Anthony Haswell, tried to have a lottery to raise money for his release, which he called a "ransom" to save him from "the oppressive hand of usurped power." Fitch went to his home and dragged him out of bed in the dead of night. Haswell had previously published criticism of Fitch for his treatment of Lyon. Fitch threw him into a filthy cell. He was later charged and brought before Paterson, who instructed the jury that they had to protect the nation "from the malicious attacks of unprincipled sedition." Given Paterson's prior abusive trials, it is clear that Haswell would not have fared better with "principled sedition," but conviction was quickly secured. Paterson sent Haswell to join Lyon for two months and imposed a $200 fine.

Others charged were Thomas Adams, editor of Boston's *Independent Chronicle*, and William Durrell, editor of the *Mount-Pleasant Register* in New York, as well as lesser figures including tavern critics. The support for sedition prosecutions was particularly evident in one case that jumped from the federal courts to the Senate. William Duane, the publisher of a Republican newspaper, printed the text of a Federalist bill that he charged would give the reigning party the ability to review and possibly reject state electoral votes—a controversy that would foreshadow the controversy on January 6, 2021, following the Biden election. True to form, the Federalists charged Duane with sedition, but juries acquitted him twice. His critics were undeterred. Duane was then summoned to the Senate for trial and, when he did not appear, the Senate found him in contempt and issued a warrant for his arrest. The warrant was issued by the vice president presiding over the Senate: Thomas Jefferson. While Duane was not prosecuted, the case laid bare the use of the law to punish core, protected speech under the First Amendment.

Jefferson would join Madison in denouncing the sedition prosecutions. Jefferson complained that "our general government has, in the rapid course of [nine] or [ten] years, become more arbitrary and has swallowed more of the public liberty than even that of England." Jefferson ran against the use of the laws in 1800. Jefferson now declared, "[i]f there be any among us who would wish to dissolve this Union or to change its republican form, let them stand undisturbed as monuments of the safety with which error of opinion may be tolerated, where reason is left free to combat it." However, others continued to equivocate. When asked to intervene with Adams to pardon publisher James Callender, John Marshall responded: "The unconstitutionality of the law, cannot be urgd to the President because he does not think it so. . . . [His] opinion is confirmed by the judgement of the courts & is supported by as wise & virtuous men as any in the Union."

The future chief justice was not alone in this view. The judiciary joined the legislative and executive branches in the headlong plunge into speech prosecutions. The most disgraceful example was Justice Samuel Chase, a notoriously partisan jurist who actively participated in the crackdown on political dissent. Indeed, "Chase turned his circuit ride into a search and destroy mission for sedition," including the notorious actions against Thomas Cooper of the *Northumberland Gazette* and James T. Callender due to his book *The Prospect Before Us*. Critics would call it "Chase's Bloody Circuit." Chase was particularly committed to stamping out "the licentiousness of the press," which he viewed as threatening the "destruction" of the government. Chase initiated the arrest of Callender after reading his writings and then sat in judgment of him.

Callender was truly a man of his times. Self-educated, he would personify the rage of the early Republic. He was someone who would vent his anger on Federalists and then on Jeffersonians. He would turn on his political sponsors in both Scotland and the United States in one of the most colorful careers of this period. Born in Scotland, Callender showed an early penchant for challenging and enraging authority. While working in Edinburgh, he started his career as a pamphleteer targeting the wealthy and the privileged. He would earn the support of Francis Garden, Lord Gardenstone, and became increasingly bold in challenging the government. In 1792, he published the anonymous *The Political Progress of Britain*, a condemnation of British imperialism. He had finally run out his string with Scotland, and a warrant was sworn out for his arrest. There was a falling-out with Lord Gardenstone, who reportedly revealed Callender as the author, and Callender then implicated Lord Gardenstone as his sponsor. Callender fled to the United States to avoid arrest for sedition.

Callender was repugnant on many levels, from his filthy and often drunken appearance to his questionable finances and associations. He would make enemies of even those who paid him, defended him, and represented him. His own lawyer, George Hay, beat him with a stick when he threatened to attack him in print and later had him arrested for libel.

In Philadelphia, Callender leveled broadsides against Washington, Adams, and Hamilton through newspapers like *Aurora*. In one of those publications, Callender exposed Hamilton's affair with the married Maria Reynolds. He eventually found a new patron in Thomas Jefferson, who was drawn to Callender's attacks on Federalists and his advocacy for the rights of the impoverished. Callender saved some of his most vituperative work for *The Prospect Before Us*. Jefferson was rumored to be his financial supporter and correspondent. The publication railed against the Federalists for corruption and authoritarian impulses. Callender took a particular delight in goading Adams, whom he called "a repulsive hypocrite" and a "hoary headed incendiary." He rallied citizens to support Jefferson and to oppose Adams, whom he described as a "man whose hands are reeking with the blood of the poor." Writers such as William Cobbett responded in kind by targeting Callender. In the meantime, Adams's secretary of state and chief sedition hunter, Timothy Pickering, was fast on Callender's trail as one of his top targets. On July 13, 1798, the day before Adams signed the Alien and Sedition Acts, Callender fled to Virginia.

Once in Virginia, Callender returned to taunting the Federalists, including a prophetic offer: "If the author has afforded room for an action, do prosecute him. But do not take such pitiful behind the door measures in order to stop the circulation of truth." It was taken as much as an invitation as a declaration. When Chase was on a circuit trip between courts, his friend and fellow Federalist Maryland attorney general Luther Martin gave him a copy of *The Prospect Before Us* to "amuse himself with it on the road, and after-wards make what use of it he pleased." Chase was not amused. He diverted to Virginia, pledging to teach Callender a lesson.

Near Richmond, a fellow passenger on a stage coach, James Triplett, told Chase that Callender had been arrested in Virginia as a vagrant. Chase replied that it was a pity that they had not hanged him outright. He pushed forward with the grand jury to arrest Callender for sedition, publicly expressing his concern that they would not be able to find Callender "to get the damned rascal in this court."

With the prosecution, Adams and his allies succeeded in proving Callender's claim that the "grand object of [the Adams] administration has been to exasperate the rage of contending parties, to calumniate and destroy every man who differs from his opinions." Callender was arrested and his counsel, George Hay, offered an unenviable defense that it is ridiculous to claim that Adams's reputation and standing could ever be undermined by such "an obscure and friendless foreigner." That was his own counsel. For his part, Samuel Chase proved himself to be every inch a partisan in the trial over what were clearly political statements. When Hay argued that this was merely one loathsome person's opinion, Chase dropped any pretense of neutrality and declared his writings to be clear expressions of fact. There were allegations that Chase struck all Jeffersonians from the jury. Whether by design or happenstance, Callender would be tried by a Federalist judge before a Federalist jury for insulting a Federalist president. The farcical quality of Chase's ruling was evident in the opening arguments of the prosecution by Thomas Nelson, who read the first charge based on Callender's statement that "the reign of Mr. Adams has been one continued tempest of malignant passions." Nelson asked the jury, "Is this true? What evidence is there of its truth? If not true, with what intention has he published it? Was it not to excite the contempt and hatred of the people against him?"

Presiding over the trial of a man he personally targeted, Chase left virtually no room for acquittal. He regularly interrupted Hay to prevent him from asking exculpatory questions. Hay finally removed himself from the case, since he was prevented from defending his client. Callender went to the jury in the end as an undefended defendant. When the jury quickly returned a guilty verdict in less than two hours, Chase expressed that the verdict was "pleasing to him." He sentenced Callender to nine months in jail, assessing a $200 fine. Callender would remain in jail until the law and the Adams administration came to an end.

Jefferson would pardon Callender. However, in true form, Callender would then turn on Jefferson. Callender wanted an appointment as postmaster in Richmond, but Jefferson balked at making such a controversial appointment. Given Callender's history of debt and drunkenness, few would view him as an ideal choice, even discounting his past writings. In what Jefferson would describe as "human nature in a hideous form," Callender supplied a political example of the old adage "scratch a lover, find a foe." Callender had previously described Jefferson as a man "un-spotted by crime" and the embodiment of "peace and competency." He now joined a Federalist paper and started to attack all things Jeffersonian. The muckraker who revealed the Hamilton-Reynolds affair wrote about Jefferson's relationship with his slave Sally Hemings. He would also be sought by Federalists to testify for the defense in sedition trials. One such trial was in progress when Callender was found drowned in the James River on July 17, 1803, almost on the anniversary of the signing of the Alien and Sedition Acts. He was spotted near the river in his usual intoxicated state, so the drowning was declared an accident despite the shallow water. Others believed it was murder given his many enemies and the pending trials. (That was the view taken by William Safire in his novel *Scandalmonger*.)

The Callender trial showed the purpose of sedition laws: to punish speech and to chill political opponents. The trial bore striking resemblance to the previously mentioned trial of David Brown that truly captures the vicious quality of Chase's judicial work. Chase was an actual former member of the Sons of Liberty, which used liberty trees as a form of protest against British rule. Yet he went after Brown with an utter abandon. Even though Brown was neither a publisher nor a political leader, Chase hammered him with eighteen months in jail and a crippling fine of $400. When Brown wrote to Adams to seek mercy or clemency, Adams refused.

These early cases showed that the English view of free speech was embedded deeply in the nascent country and had not been excised by the First Amendment. The most chilling language may have come in the prosecution of Thomas Cooper, who had merely published a one-page handbill criticizing Adams. Again, Chase presided and made clear that such attacks could not be tolerated. Indeed, he described free speech and the free press as existential threats to society:

> Since ours is a government founded on the opinions and confidence of the people, if a man attempts to destroy the confidence of the people in their officers, their supreme magistrate, and their legislature, he effectually saps the foundation of their government. A republican government can only be destroyed in two ways; the introduction of luxury, or the licentiousness of the press. This latter is the more slow but most sure and certain means of bringing about the destruction of the government. The legislature of this country knowing this maxim, has thought proper to pass a law to check this licentiousness of the press.

It was a statement that could have come directly out of the proceedings of the Star Chamber and restated the premise of the *De Scandalis Magnatum* statutes in prosecuting those who undermined the reputations of government officials.

The passage of the Sedition Act was one of the first tests of constitutional principles faced by the new republic, and it failed in spectacular fashion. John Adams, who declared that the destruction of the tea in Boston was "absolutely and indispensably" necessary, found free speech entirely dispensable when it insulted or challenged his rule. Fries was an example of state rage, unalterable and unyielding, in crushing dissent.

Both Madison and Jefferson were alarmed by the return of sedition prosecutions under the Adams administration. In perhaps the most chilling measure of this period, both men indicated that they were concerned that they could be charged under these laws, even avoiding mail during some periods as a precaution. They even would occasionally employ codes. As the Adams administration was pushing to pass the Alien Act, Madison wrote to Jefferson on May 20, 1798, to warn that the law was "a monster that must forever disgrace its parents." He added that, while one house could take leave of its senses, he never thought that it could "possibly be fathered by both."

Ten

JEFFERSON AND *THE WASP*

E ven after the close of the Adams administration, the use of seditious libel did not end. While the convicted would later be pardoned by President Jefferson, the Sedition Act was never found unconstitutional. Allies like Madison had every reason to hope for a new era of speech protection under Jefferson, the author of the Declaration of Independence defending "unalienable rights." He was also the man who wrote that "[t]he people are the only censors of their governors; and even their errors will tend to keep these to the true principle of their institution. To punish these errors too severely would be to suppress the only safeguard of the public liberty." Yet Jefferson proved an unreliable ally for free speech after he assumed office. As with Adams, the temptation to silence critics proved too much for Jefferson, though his failures paled in comparison to those of his predecessor. In hindsight, there were indications before his administration that Jefferson's commitment to free speech was not as deep or principled as Madison's. When he was still in Paris in 1788 as the minister to France, Jefferson sent Madison a lukewarm response to the First Amendment draft as something "I like as far as it goes." He then indicated that he wanted to retain some ability for prosecution for "false facts affecting the peace of the confederacy with foreign nations." That residual interest in speech prosecutions would prove a blindside for Jefferson as president.

The Jeffersonians often resorted to violence, and just as often, targeted Federalists. One of the leading (and most disturbing) cases of seditious libel occurred during the Jefferson administration. In *People v. Croswell*, Harry Croswell was accused of libeling President Jefferson, who he alleged paid publisher James Callender to spread vicious and derogatory statements against George Washington and John Adams. It was a case that put the political use of sedition into sharp relief. Callender was previously declared a seditionist after he called Washington and Adams "poltroons" and "venal" and accused Adams of being a habitual liar whose administration was a "scene of profligacy and . . . usury." Now it was the Jeffersonians who would accuse Callender's accuser of sedition.

Croswell was a highly educated minister and an ardent Federalist with a gift for stinging satire and commentary. He created his publication *The Wasp* as a counterfoil to the Jeffersonian newspaper *The Bee*. Croswell found that his pointed prose could have direct and personal consequences. One story tells of how he wrote about a prominent judge who refused to pay a tavern after a night spent gorging himself with food and drink. Croswell recalled how, soon after publication, a local justice of the peace saw him on the street and leaped off his wagon. The man is described as large in stature and shaking his horsewhip in Croswell's face while promising to get his revenge on the spot. Croswell recounted how "I had no cane or other means of defense. But . . . stood erect and . . . in the most cool and collected manner apprised him that . . . neither he nor any other man could ever whip me and it was a mistake for him to talk so loud about it." The brute finally, "in a tempest of oaths, turned shortly on his heel, mounted his wagon and drove off at a furious pace, his poor horse having received the rash intended for me." It was then that

Croswell noticed a fellow Federalist laughing from a doorway. The man asked, "Harry Croswell, how could you be so sure that he would not whip you?" "Mainly," Croswell replied, "because I planned to run away if he had attempted it."

There would be nowhere to run after Croswell published his account of the Jefferson-Callender connection. The indictment by Attorney General Ambrose Spencer, a Democratic-Republican allied with Jefferson, was right out of the old English tradition of *De Scandalis Magnatum*, accusing Croswell of

> [b]eing a malicious and seditious man, of a depraved mind and wicked and diabolical disposition, and also deceitfully, wickedly, and maliciously devising, contriving and intending to detract from, scandalize, traduce, vilify, and to represent [President Thomas Jefferson] . . . as unworthy the confidence, respect, and attachment of the people of the said United States, and to alienate and withdraw from the . . . President as aforesaid, the obedience, fidelity, and allegiance of the citizens . . . [and] wickedly and seditiously to disturb the peace and tranquility, as well of the people of the state of New York, as of the United States.

New York's law incorporated the English rule that truth was no defense to sedition. That rule was enforced by the trial judge, Chief Justice Morgan Lewis, a Democratic-Republican who would soon after the trial be elected governor as a Jeffersonian candidate. The trial would be a launching pad for Lewis, and his rulings worked to protect Jefferson from public embarrassment given evidence of his rumor campaign against these and other Federalist leaders. Lewis barred every attempt of Croswell to show the basis for the article, including a motion to call Callender himself as a defense witness. Conviction was all but certain.

On appeal, a curious representative stepped forward: Alexander Hamilton. After calling for the crushing of sedition in the prior "rebellions" and opposing the leniency for figures like John Fries, Hamilton took the Croswell case and offered a brilliant defense of why truth must be allowed as a defense to sedition. Coming less than a year before his death in the duel with Aaron Burr, it was Hamilton at his best in defending rather than denigrating free speech. Despite Hamilton's brilliant six-hour argument, the divided appellate court decision allowed the conviction to stand. Yet Justice James Kent would write a powerful opinion on the need for the truth defense. Kent framed the opinion by emphasizing the central importance of free speech and the free press, declaring that "the people of this country have always classed the freedom of the press among their fundamental rights." Notably, as Madison did in his condemnation of sedition laws, Kent stressed that there was a fundamental difference with the English, who "have never taken notice of the press in any parliamentary recognition of the principles of the government, or of the rights of the subject." However, despite being celebrated for his protection of free speech, Kent reflected the same cabined view of free speech as Hamilton and others. He did not embrace Madison's view of the fundamental conflict between seditious libel and free speech. Instead, he offered a defense of free speech when exercised with good motives. Truth must be a defense because of "the right to publish, with impunity, truth, *with good motives, and for justifiable ends*, whether it respects government, magistracy, or individuals"; by this definition, it would be possible to be convicted for libel for truthful statements made "with bad motives." Kent offered support only for "libels founded in truth and dictated by worthy motives."

The appeal, however, would have yet one more wicked twist. Chief Justice Lewis sat with the other judges in the review of his own decisions. Yet Kent seemed to win the day when the other two justices, Justice Smith Thompson and Justice Henry Brockholst Livingston, voted for Croswell. However, Lewis immediately adjourned the proceedings and went into conferral with his colleagues. When he returned, Livingston switched his vote, leaving a tie—and the conviction standing. To make the optics worse, Livingston was later put on the Supreme Court . . . by Jefferson. Despite its conceptual limitations, the opinion had a lasting impact and, while the conviction was upheld, New York amended the law to allow for truth as a defense. As for Croswell, the government never moved for sentencing, and a new trial was eventually ordered. However, it was simply dropped. It was perhaps the understanding during the adjournment that the deadlock would leave both the conviction and the status of the defendant unchanged. Croswell would return to writing and face new battles over his views in newspapers like *The Balance*. He eventually grew tired of the rage politics, would take Episcopal orders, and serve as a cofounder to Trinity College.

Another illustrative sedition trial during the Jefferson presidency involved Federalist publisher Samuel Freer, who published a criticism of the Croswell charges. He was charged with contempt rather than seditious libel by a court with a majority of Jeffersonian judges. He was also represented by Hamilton and, in 1804, Judge James Kent imposed a fine of $10 for Freer's contempt of the court. The result is striking because in both cases the focus of the court was not on the right to free speech as much as the right to prove the truth of the alleged libel. Indeed, the token fine against Freer carried far greater weight as a judicial rejection of the right of this publisher to write freely on the Croswell case, even in response to a rival newspaper's claims.

For Jefferson, sedition would prove just another level of self-contradiction. Blazingly brilliant and intellectually insatiable, Jefferson remains one of the greatest political minds in American history. Yet the man who wanted to denounce slavery in the Declaration of Independence would continue to enslave people at Monticello. The man who wrote passionately about the freedom of the press would reserve the right to try others for sedition. Joseph Ellis captured this complex figure in his aptly titled book *American Sphinx*. Centuries after Jefferson's death, we are all still struggling to understand the core values of this extraordinary man. He was at times a great civil libertarian and at others an enslaver; he was a man motivated by the highest principles who would stoop to rumor-mongering and rage politics. On free speech and sedition, Jefferson may be easier to understand in reaching a damning conclusion. Jefferson did understand the value of free speech, but, like Adams, he allowed his personal sensitivities and political ambitions to embrace speech prosecutions. That betrayal of his own values was captured in a letter to ally and governor of Pennsylvania Thomas McKean. He told McKean that "[the] press ought to be restored to its credibility if possible" and that "I have therefore long thought that a few prosecutions of the most prominent of-fenders would have a wholesome effect. . . . Not a general prosecution, for that would look like persecution: but a selected one." Jefferson did not want to look like he was persecuting the press, but he was not above persecuting a few writers as an example to others. He was openly seeking to restore the chilling effect of sedition prosecutions for the "wholesome effect" of deterring critics. While Jefferson would not engage in the level of sedition prosecutions under Adams, it was a distinction in degree as opposed to principle. In this area, like so many others, both men would be eclipsed by the man who Jefferson helped enter politics and then nurtured as a friend and colleague: James Madison.

Eleven

JACKSON AND THE "LURKING TRAITORS" AMONG US

In 1833, the caricature of President Andrew Jackson as "King Andrew the First" captured the view of Jackson as a type of democratically elected despot, an imperial president who often acted unilaterally regardless of the constitutional or statutory restraints. While the artist is now unknown, the image was used widely by Jackson's opponents and featured him holding a vetoed bill to capture his stubborn intransigence. When it came to free speech, the caricature proved dangerously apt. Despite his legal training, Jackson would show the same intolerance as his predecessor John Adams for opposing views. However, Jackson's greatest attack on free speech occurred before his presidency with the all-too-familiar rationale of wartime necessity during the War of 1812. It would be a prelude to the deprivations in the Civil War.

BORN TO COMMAND.

OF VETO MEMORY.

HAD I BEEN CONSULTED.

KING ANDREW THE FIRST.

In the winter of 1812, Jackson was facing an existential threat not just for himself but for his country. The British taking New Orleans would give them control over the vital Mississippi, cutting off the key avenue for the transportation of trade and resources. The British were descending upon New Orleans with a larger battle-tested force. Militarily, Jackson was the right man at the right time. Experienced and charismatic, he was a born leader. His value as a commander, however, reflected a certain dog-headedness that often became arrogance and intolerance. He was single-minded and self-assured in wielding his authority. That would become an asset on the battlefield and an ordeal in the city itself. Morale was low in a city awaiting the ravages of war, and his ragtag band of volunteers, pirates, and regular soldiers offered little promise of success. The man called "Old Hickory" quickly imposed martial law—the first such declaration in the history of the young nation.

Jackson suspended both civil authority and civil liberties in what has been described as "lunatic militarism," where "Jackson established a police state with no other authority but his own." Jackson proclaimed, "[T]hose who are not for us are against us, and will be dealt with accordingly." Mass arrests followed and many were held without charge.

Magnifying the abuses by Jackson was his refusal to lift martial law after the battle. In reality, the battle was entirely unnecessary, since the war effectively ended with the Treaty of Ghent on December 24, 1814. However, Jackson was unaware of the treaty when he engaged the British on January 8, 1815. Even when informed of the treaty, however, Jackson refused to yield his absolute power over the city. Again, a great American dissenter would step forward. His name was Louis Louaillier, a naturalized Frenchman who was both a state senator and a well-known patriot fighting the British. It was Louaillier who chaired the committee that secured most of the resources used by Jackson to defend the city. It was also Louaillier who helped rally the city to support Jackson. However, as time went on, Louaillier became concerned that he and others had fought an imperial army only to empower an imperial military governor. Jackson refused repeated calls to lift martial law and to release the militia.

Rumors of a peace fueled questions over the necessity of continuing martial law and specifically Jackson's iron-fisted governance. Then, on February 21, the *Louisiana Gazette* declared that a peace agreement had been reached for the cessation of all hostilities. Jackson was irate and ordered the censorship of the article. Even when Jackson was informed of the Treaty of Ghent by then secretary of war (and future president) James Monroe, he refused to accept it. In a message dated February 14, 1815, Monroe told Jackson:

> It is with great satisfaction I inform you that a Treaty of peace was concluded between the United States and Great Britain at Ghent on the 24th day of December last. A copy of this Treaty was received to day by Mr. Carroll; has been examined by the President, and will I have no doubt be ratified. I give you this information that hostilities may immediately cease between our troops and those of Great Britain.

Jackson demanded proof of ratification and refused to accept Monroe's notice. He enforced a prior restraint order on any articles, particularly those disclosing the treaty details. The editor of the *Louisiana Gazette* was irate and published the order and wrote: "Every man may read for himself, and think for himself; (Thank God! our thoughts are as yet unshackled!!) but as we have been officially informed that the city of New-Orleans is a camp, our readers must not expect us to take the liberty of expressing our opinion as we might in a free city."

It was an all too familiar pattern for those who remembered British rule. On March 3, an anonymous letter written in French then appeared in the *Louisiana Courier* calling for the restoration of civil authority and civil liberties. The writer praised Jackson for his preservation of the city and the defeat of the British. However, that sense of indebtedness did not include the loss of the freedoms for which they fought:

> We do not feel much inclined, through gratitude, to sacrifice any of our privileges, and, less than any other, that of expressing our opinion of the acts of his administration; that it is time the citizens accused

of any crime should be rendered to their natural judges, and cease to be brought before special or military tribunals, a kind of institution held in abhorrence, even in absolute governments; that, after having done enough for glory, the moment of moderation has arrived; and, finally, that the acts of authority which the invasion of our country and our safety may have rendered necessary are, since the evacuation of it by the enemy, no longer compatible with our dignity and our oath of making the Constitution respected.

Jackson was not in the mood for a "moment of moderation" and forced the editor to reveal the identity of the author, who had signed the letter only as "A Citizen of Louisiana of French Origin." It was his own ally, Louaillier. He used the same wartime rationale to justify Louaillier's arrest, a ridiculous claim that the state senator was a "lurking" spy found "in or about the fortifications or encampments of the armies of the United States."

Even for Jackson, it was a breathtaking move and galvanized the opposition to the martial law. Attorney Pierre Louis Morel went to federal judge Dominic A. Hall, who issued a writ of habeas corpus. Jackson then ordered the arrest of Judge Hall and anyone who attempted to serve the writ. He ordered the arrest of all those opposing martial law as engaging in "sedition." He declared expressing opposition to his rule as per se rebellion, stating that the city

shall be protected against every design of the enemy, in what manner soever he may shape his attack, whether it be made by the known and declared foe, or by the pretended and deceitful friend. . . . The lurking traitor is now laboring to feed fresh fuel, a spirit of discontent, disobedience and mutiny, too long secretly fomenting.

Hall was arrested as was civilian James Hollander for insubordination and mutiny in camp after voicing his support for Louaillier. When federal district attorney John Dick sought to get state judge Joshua Lewis to intervene to release these men, Jackson ordered both Dick and Lewis also arrested (but later withdrew the order). Even as Jackson finally relented to the news of the peace by relaxing martial law, he still had Louaillier stand trial in military court. Louaillier refused to recognize the jurisdiction of the court. After all, Louaillier never served in the militia and was a purely political figure. General Edmund P. Gaines presided and rejected the threshold claim but reduced the charges to solely that of insubordination despite the fact that this was a state senator and not a militiaman. Louaillier was then acquitted in a one-day trial. Nevertheless, Jackson still held him in jail, as was his prerogative as the reigning military authority. He insisted that war "makes every man a soldier" and, if dissenters are freed, "disaffection and disobedience, anarchy and confusion, must take the place of order and subordination—defeat and shame, of victory and triumph."

Before finally lifting martial law on March 13 (with final proof of the treaty), Jackson banished Hall from the city. Hall, however, returned and commenced proceedings against Jackson. Hall imposed severe restrictions on Jackson's counsel in arguing his case—destroying the moral and legal high ground for the court. Jackson was found guilty and fined $1,000. Citizens were still thankful to Jackson for his brave defense of the city and raised the fine from donations. However, Jackson suggested that the money should go to the children and widows of the fallen. He paid the fine out of his own funds. Notably, in 1844, Congress ordered that the fine should be repaid with interest. The $2,700 was sent to Jackson a year before his death.

As president, Jackson would continue to show little tolerance for opposing views from the courts or critics. The infamous "Trail of Tears"— the forced removal of the Cherokee, Muscogee (Creek), Seminole, Chickasaw, and Choctaw peoples from their ancestral homelands—will forever stain his legacy. The discovery of gold in Georgia and a land rush led to the Cherokee removal in 1838, and that resulted in many deaths as members were marched in winter to Oklahoma. Indian removal was a priority for the Jackson administration. It remains a policy denounced by many as ethnic cleansing. Yet when the Supreme Court ruled in favor of the Cherokees in *Worcester v. Georgia* (1832), Jackson remained defiant.

There is no evidence that Jackson actually said the oft-attributed line of "John Marshall has made his decision; now let him enforce it!" However, he did write his fellow comrade in arms John Coffee that "the decision of the Supreme Court has fell still born, and they find that they cannot coerce Georgia to yield to its mandate."

If Jackson was intransigent toward the Court, he was openly intolerant toward critics. Among those was John Ross, the principal chief of the Cherokee Nation. The son of a Scottish trader and a Cherokee mother, Ross would adopt a Cherokee name, Kooweskoowe, and became a fierce defender of his people. He had one particular weapon. He had a newspaper, the *Cherokee Phoenix*. He used the newspaper to lay bare the greed and cruelty of the Indian removal policies. That was halted when Jackson's supporters learned that the newspaper was relocating from Georgia to Tennessee. They waylaid the wagons and destroyed the printing presses. Some have alleged that Jackson supported the action.

Jackson pushed for censorship of opposing views on the Indian removals as well as slavery in the United States mails. His arguments were chillingly similar to those used in New Orleans in seeking to prevent views that would inflame the public. In 1835, his administration censored a mail campaign by the American Anti-Slavery Society. Postmaster General Amos Kendall justified the actions as an effort to prevent abolitionists from inciting violence and rebellion by mailing "newspapers, pamphlets, tracts, and almanacs, containing exaggerated, and in some instances, false accounts of the treatment of slaves." A slave owner himself, Jackson saw abolitionists as provocateurs in the same way that he saw lawyers as spreading dangerous dissension. He called on Congress to pass laws mandating such censorship of antislavery views as "destructive of the harmony and peace of the country"—a virtual verbatim repetition of the British rationale for speech regulations and criminalization. Jackson described the role of the post office as "to foster an amicable intercourse and correspondence between all the members of the Confederacy" and denounced the use of the mails (and, by extension, free speech) "from being used as an instrument of an opposite character." Of course, the government would determine what viewpoints turned the mails into "an instrument of an opposite character."

Jackson remains a maddening figure. Brave yet brutal, he was a lawyer who became a virtual tyrant in his lawless conduct. However, his view of martial law would later be replicated by military governors during the Civil War. Once again, the first right to fall in this time of panic was free speech, which was often treated as seditious and rebellious. Jackson showed, again, how the suspension of such rights led to exponentially expanding abuses. Dissent itself was disloyalty even in the form of lawyers and judges raising constitutional objections. Notably, these were not cases of rage rhetoric but reasoned viewpoints that were met by state rage.

Twelve

LINCOLN AND THE COPPERHEADS

The Sedition Act fittingly expired with the Adams administration in 1801. However, the attacks on dissenting political views would continue in the nineteenth century. The most extensive attacks were implemented by President Abraham Lincoln. Like Adams, Lincoln moved against free speech when it was expedient to do so. Both were presidents at perilous times of instability who saw threats from without and within. Other figures such as Andrew Jackson showed the same intolerance for dissent or even debate. They all betrayed core values of free speech. In some ways, the sense of betrayal was deepest with Adams and Lincoln. These historical icons articulated core principles and embodied the essence of the American Republic. Lincoln was perhaps the deepest cut of all because he was a man of great sensitivity to constitutional values, but he abandoned them out of necessity. This was the president who stood before the nation in his first inaugural address and declared that the country should "[c]ontinue to execute all the express provisions of our national Constitution, and the Union will endure forever." That promise was more honored in the breach once hostilities broke out between the states, including Lincoln's clearly unconstitutional suspension of habeas corpus. Yet before the suspension in April 1861, Lincoln's administration had already gone constitutionally rogue. After various newspapers denounced the war, the Union army shut down publications, censored articles, and even arrested writers.

Like Adams, Lincoln reverted to Blackstonian principles of seditious speech. What followed was a crackdown on dissent through Secretary of State William Seward, who supervised a network of agents and police in arresting war critics, including public officials, newspaper editors, and "Copperheads." Copperheads like Representative Clement Vallandigham opposed the war for various reasons. While critics gave them the label to suggest that they were akin to venomous snakes without a nation, many "Peace Democrats" embraced the label as a reference to the head of Liberty on coins. The prosecution of these figures showed that the expiration of the Sedition Act would not be the end of sedition or speech prosecutions in the United States.

A former Ohio congressman, Vallandigham made a series of speeches that denounced the war and emancipation in 1863. At that time, Ohio was under the command of General Ambrose Everett Burnside, a commander remembered for primarily two things: incompetent military leadership and the source of the term "sideburns." In Ohio, he added facial attacks on free speech. He was himself a rather blunt instrument so, when faced with dissent over the war, Burnside turned to blunt

force. He imposed martial law with an order that included a warning that the "habit of declaring sympathies for the enemy will not be allowed in this Department." Among other measures, he ordered the arrest of Vallandigham, who was tried for "declaring disloyal sentiments and opinions with the object and purpose of weakening the power of the government." Burnside insisted that citizens and politicians must use "a proper tone" in discussing the war and that Vallandigham had opted for "intemperate discussion."

Vallandigham was indeed intemperate, but he was also entirely within his rights to be so in discussing a war that he despised. He was a congressman who was wedded to Jefferson's views of a limited federal government and did not believe that Congress should meddle with slavery issues in circumvention of the states. He wrote his wife: "When the secession has taken place, I shall do all in my power first to restore the Union, if it be possible; and failing in that, then to mitigate the evils of disruption." He blamed Lincoln and Congress for forcing the South to arms and opposed the Emancipation Proclamation. He was on the wrong side of history and humanity with the exception of maintaining his right to espouse unpopular views. While referring to "the sin and barbarism of African slavery," he still defended the states in preserving it and said "slavery in the South is a question, not of morals, or religion, or humanity, but a form of labor, perfectly compatible with the dignity of free white labor in the same community, and with national vigor, power, and prosperity." In his farewell address to the House, he accused the Republicans of fighting for abolition over the Union. He asked them what they had accomplished and then answered the question himself with "Let the dead at Fredericksburg and Vicksburg answer."

The trial was an utter travesty. When he filed a challenge based on Lincoln's clearly unconstitutional suspension of habeas corpus, he appeared before a judge with little more faith in the Constitution than did Burnside. Judge Humphrey H. Leavitt immediately disavowed any meaningful judicial role in checking executive abuse. He declared that "self-preservation is a paramount law." He dismissed as absurd the notion that "anyone connected with the judicial department" should take any action that would "embarrass or thwart the executive in his efforts to deliver the country from the danger which press[es] heavily upon it." As with the judges in the sedition trials during the Adams administration, Leavitt exuded bias and hostility, including for free speech values. The judge denounced Vallandigham as one of the "class of mischievous politicians [who] had succeeded in poisoning the minds of a portion of the community with the rankest feelings of disloyalty. Artful men, disguising their latent treason under hollow pretentions of devotion to the Union, were striving to disseminate their pestilent heresies among the masses of the people."

Vallandigham was sentenced to be incarcerated for the duration of the war, a sentence that Lincoln commuted to banishment to the confederacy. When taken to the enemy lines, he walked across the no-man's-land until he met a confederate soldier on picket duty and asked to be arrested. One can only imagine the surprise of some lone sentry faced with this former congressman declaring, "I am a citizen of Ohio, and of the United States. I am here within your lines by force, and against my will. I therefore surrender myself to you as a prisoner of war." Ultimately, after the war, Vallandigham would return to Ohio and run unsuccessfully for office and resume the practice of law. He would die at fifty with the tragically ironic words "I have foolishly shot myself." It was a literal statement. Vallandigham was defending a man for murder and wanted to show that the victim likely shot himself when pulling out his pistol during a brawl. In an early use of forensic evidence, he had previously performed powder-burn tests with a pistol, which still had live rounds. After he returned to the hotel room, the actual unloaded weapon in the case was brought to him to examine and placed next to the loaded gun on a table. Vallandigham mistakenly grabbed the loaded gun and then lethally proved his point: he pulled it and shot himself in the abdomen. He died the next day after reminding his wife of "that good old Presbyterian doctrine of predestination." If so, it was his destiny to lay bare the continued hypocrisy of our treatment of free speech.

For his part, Burnside showed little concern for the suppression of speech and seemed to channel Blackstone in his sense of license of others in censoring speech deemed demoralizing. He explained that he would hang those seeking to "demoralize" his troops and asked, "Why should such speeches from our own public men be allowed?" The question for Burnside was what speech should be tolerated as opposed to what limits are permitted under the First Amendment. Not surprisingly, once they crossed again the Rubicon of speech criminalization, it became a rout. Just a month after the conviction of Vallandigham, Burnside would shut down the *Chicago Times*, which opposed the war and the Emancipation

Proclamation. It denounced Burnside for the arrest of Vallandigham as "the funeral of civil liberty." Many of the statements of the newspaper were deeply offensive. Yet, again, these racist and rageful words should have been protected political speech under the First Amendment even under narrower functionalist theories.

Notably, even in his act of leniency toward Vallandigham, Lincoln amplified the anti–free speech purpose of the prosecution by noting that banishment would prevent his views from influencing others in the Union. Lincoln adopted an artificial and illusory distinction in later insisting that the case was not a crackdown on critics of his administration or policies, but rather punishment for "laboring, with some effect, to prevent the raising of troops, to encourage desertions from the army; and to have the Rebellion without an adequate military force to suppress it." Lincoln's rationalization would foreshadow the very logic used by the Supreme Court in the crackdown on war dissent in the twentieth century.

Thirteen

THE GILDED AGE AND THE MOBBING OF "FREE SPEECH"

With Reconstruction came prolonged martial law in Southern states, where free speech continued to be abridged by military governors. Yet the return to civilian authority only magnified the rage and anti–free speech measures. As the Gilded Age expanded with new industries and monopolies, the federal government gradually left the South (and its emancipated slaves) to local control and violence. The vacuum left by the withdrawal of federal authority was quickly filled by vigilantes and racist mobs, including the rise of the Ku Klux Klan. Local police often rioted with white vigilantes. There was little tolerance for opposing views amid the violence against Black citizens and their supporters. In cities such as Memphis, dozens died. In New Orleans, desperate Blacks and sympathetic whites sought to convene a state constitutional convention to seek political reform. Local newspapers labeled the participants "insurrectionists" and encouraged a crackdown to protect society. Thirty-eight were killed in the riots of 1866, including thirty-four Black citizens. Once again, a combination of the government and an enabling media painted the dissenters as rebels to justify a lethal crackdown.

Like other ages of rage, there were profiles of courage in the face of terrifying oppression and violence. One of the greatest of these figures was Ida B. Wells-Barnett, a journalist and activist. Ida Bell Wells was born into slavery in Holly Springs, Mississippi, on July 16, 1862. Her parents,

James Madison Wells and Elizabeth "Lizzie" Wells, valued education. James Wells would help found Shaw University, which was later renamed Rust College. Wells used her family's savings to attend Rust College. She would not spare allies or enemies from the penetrating criticism of her columns. Like many of the American dissenters discussed earlier, she showed a certain predisposition for defiance in the face of orthodoxy and authority. That became clear early in college when she was expelled for a

dispute that she had with the college president. When the yellow fever epidemic of 1878 took her parents and a sibling, she was only sixteen, but claimed to be eighteen to secure a job teaching to support her family. She would later continue her education at Fisk University when she had an incident that was strikingly similar to the experience of Gandhi that led him to a life of activism. In 1893, Gandhi was removed from a whites-only train—seventy-one years before the famous stand taken by Rosa Parks on a bus in Montgomery, Alabama. Gandhi had purchased a first-class ticket as a young attorney and refused to give up his seat. Nine years before Gandhi's train encounter, Wells-Barnett was barred from a first-class car in 1884 despite buying a ticket for the seat. Many African American women wanted to sit in "ladies cars" by purchasing first-class tickets. These cars were reserved for women and men traveling in their company. Under a state law, these separate cars were not only required for women, but it was also expressly mandated that "all colored passengers who shall pay first-class rates of fare may have the privilege to enter." She sued and won $500, but the Tennessee Supreme Court ruled against her. Referring to Wells as a "mulatto passenger" who purchased the ticket "in error," Chief Justice

Peter Turney applied an early separate-but-equal rationale. The Court ruled that "we know of no rule that requires railroad companies to yield to the disposition of passengers to arbitrarily determine as to the coach that they take passage." Turney would later be propelled into the governor's mansion. Wells was now set on a course of fearless advocacy against segregation and all forms of sexual and racial discrimination.

Wells later became part-owner in the *Memphis Free Speech and Headlight*, showing her signature fearlessness in taking on not just the white establishment but also leaders in the Black community. The *Memphis Free Speech* was arguably the leading African American source for news and commentary. Wells lashed out at a Black minister for an affair, the low quality of teaching in Black schools, and even criticized towering figures such as Isaiah Montgomery and Booker T. Washington.

Lynchings were on the rise, and Wells became a leading voice against the murders. One of the most infamous lynchings occurred in Memphis in 1892. Thomas Moss, a postal worker, created a grocery store for the Black community at what was known as "the curve," where the streetcar made a turn at what is now Mississippi Boulevard and Walker Avenue. It was a prime location and a success. A white competitor, William Barrett, hounded the business and was accused by William Stewart, a grocery worker, of assault. He appeared with the police to demand the location of Stewart, and when fellow worker Calvin McDowell refused to give his location, Barrett pistol-whipped him. In the process, he lost control of the gun and McDowell grabbed it and fired a shot. McDowell said it was self-defense and "[b]eing the stronger, I got the best of the scrimmage." A judge then deputized Barrett to lead a mob back to the grocery store to make arrests. The local community gathered to defend the grocery, and a gunfight ensued. Politicians and press portrayed the men as part of an insurgency pushing a race war. Moss, McDowell, and Stewart eventually turned themselves in. Later, security at the jail was reduced, a mob took over the jail, kidnapped the men, and took them a mile away to be beaten and killed. On March 9, 1892, the *Memphis Appeal-Avalanche* praised the decency of the killings, conducted without being loud or "boisterous": "[T]he vengeance was sharp, swift, and sure but administered with due regard due to the fact that people were asleep all around the jail." Barrett later reportedly bought the grocery at a fraction of its original value.

Wells wrote a column denouncing the lynching of three of her friends, who were accused of the rape of a white woman. Wells suggested that the claims of rape were in reality common misrepresentations of consensual relations with white women. She kept writing about white vigilantism. On May 21, 1892, she wrote:

> Eight Negroes lynched since last issue of the *Free Speech*. Three were charged with killing white men, and five with raping white women. Nobody in this section believes the old threadbare lie that Negro men assault white women. If southern white men are not careful, a conclusion will be reached which will be very damaging to the moral reputation of their women.

It was a breathtaking level of honesty and defiance in a column, and it enraged many whites. She was called a "black wench" fueling an uprising. She persisted and published her research in her famous pamphlet *Southern Horrors: Lynch Law in All Its Phases*. Her friend Frederick Douglass wrote the introduction. The offices of the *Memphis Free Speech* were destroyed by a mob as police did nothing. Once again many in the media joined the mob. The *Columbia Herald* ran a racist attack on the "wench" Wells and those "thin-legged scholars and glassy-eyed females . . . worshipping at the flat feet of Ida B. Wells and . . . crowning her kinks with flowers from the conservatories of the elite." Wells was denounced peddling "obscene filth." Yet Wells was undeterred and continued to write on racism, lynchings, and the denial of equal rights.

Wells would end up in Chicago and then New York and write for newspapers, including the one owned by her husband. As the *Appeal* (Saint Paul, Minnesota) observed at the time:

> We cannot see what the "good" citizens of Memphis gained by suppressing the Free Speech. They stopped his papers of a few hundreds of subscribers and drove Miss Ida B. Wells to New York, and now she

is telling the story to the hundreds of thousands of readers of the Independent and the papers that copy from it. Free Speech is not so easily suppressed as The Free Speech.

The Gilded Age was marked by broad corruption, political violence, and highly biased courts. Often the targets of such attacks were called insurrectionists or rebels by an enabling media. Attacks were often carried out with the imprimatur of local judges or police. Yet, as noted by the *Appeal*, free speech also showed its own resilience. Wells continued unabated and unbowed in calling society to account for its hate and hypocrisy.

Fourteen

COMSTOCK AND THE
OBSCENITY OF DISSENT

The history of speech crackdowns often focuses on dissenting political viewpoints of wars and presidents. This is understandable given the functionalist rationalizations for protecting speech. However, it also involves speech deemed immoral or corrupting for the mores of the nation. The Civil War would produce a critical schism in the free speech community when libertarians would break away from civil libertarians over the meaning of free speech, including on the matter of speech deemed immoral. The nomenclature is telling. "Civil" libertarians, associated with groups such as the ACLU, emphasized narrower, functionalist views of free speech tied to democratic theories. Libertarian groups such as the Free Speech League adopted a more sweeping protection. That division would become more pronounced in controversies over obscene speech. One of the figures most associated with the crackdown on corruption of societal values was Anthony Comstock, a postmaster and foe to all things wicked or obscene.

Comstock was raised as one of ten children in a deeply religious Calvinist farming family in New Canaan, Connecticut. As a soldier in the Civil War, Comstock was known for assuming the role of the monitor of the virtue and values in others, even denouncing other soldiers for the use of profanity. He was uncompromising and, with many, unpopular. In her book *The Man Who Hated Women*, the journalist and novelist Amy Sohn has this account of Comstock's attitude and reputation:

> While crossing the street in New York one day, [Comstock] was nearly run over by a mail wagon. He shook his badge at the horse and cried, "Don't you know who I am? I'm Anthony Comstock!" A reporter once called his office and asked an assistant whether Comstock had been punched in the face that morning. The answer was concise: "Probably."

Anarchist writer Emma Goldman called him the "moral eunuch," opposing Comstock using his position as an inspector of the U.S. mails for "weeding in God's garden."

After the war, Comstock became an opponent of everything from contraception to masturbation to obscenity. Where Madison called speech prosecutions the "monster" lurking in our society, Comstock saw a horde of monsters—from racy literature to over-the-counter medicines—threatening our existence. He rallied against the "sin and wickedness" that

ST. ANTHONY COMSTOCK. THE VILLAGE NUISANCE.

he saw in every quarter of society. The most "monstrous evil" of all appeared to be obscenity, a term that encompassed a wide array of values different from his own. This included blasphemy and the writings of "infidels" and "free lusters." The founder of the New York Society for the Suppression of Vice, Comstock set about his work of "saving the young from contamination" and "Devil traps." Cartoons like the one on page 144 by L. M. Glackens captured the range of Comstock's rage, including against figures like Victoria Claflin Woodhull as free lovers inviting debauchery and drunkenness.

For Anthony Comstock, nothing was more obscene than the very existence of Woodhull and her sister, Tennessee "Tennie" Claflin. They were born into a rough life in Ohio with a one-eyed snake oil salesman father and a religious fanatic mother. Claflin would practice as a faith healer, and Woodhull believed that she communicated regularly with the spirit of Demosthenes, who told them that their fortunes awaited them in New York City. Their wacky spiritualist views found an early ally and financial supporter in Cornelius Vanderbilt. The "old goat," as Woodhull called him, would ultimately set the sisters up as a brokerage house, Woodhull, Claflin & Co. They had immediate success, though it is not clear if that was more due to the influence of Demosthenes or Vanderbilt. At this point, the sisters had attracted the ire of Comstock. It is hard to imagine two women who would more drive Comstock to a sputtering rage. Woodhull was divorced, worked as a medium, and advocated socialism and free love. In 1872, she even announced herself as a candidate for president on the Equal Rights ticket.

The sisters then created a newspaper called the *Woodhull & Claflin's Weekly*. It was a shocking tabloid for the times, featuring stories on women's rights, sexual freedom, and socialism. In a rigidly conservative society, it must have been a thrill for some and a shock for most New Yorkers. For Comstock, it became a mission after the women ran a story on the sexual escapades of Reverend Henry Ward Beecher, pastor of Brooklyn's Plymouth Congregational Church and the son of Calvinist theologian Lyman Beecher (and brother of author Harriet Beecher Stowe). They also published the account of an alleged rape of a teenage girl by another prominent New Yorker, Luther Challis, at a masquerade ball. Rather than be outraged by the allegations of sexual assaults and immorality, Comstock was outraged that these two libertine women would accuse respected men of the community, including a man of God.

Comstock arranged for the women to be arrested on obscenity charges. Police confiscated newspapers, destroyed furniture, and tossed about the type used for printing. After their release on bail pending trial, the women defiantly continued to publish. Then Comstock did something that captured the depths of his rage. He went to Connecticut and mailed copies of the paper to an alias. He then had the sisters rearrested for a federal misdemeanor for the interstate mailing. When supporters again paid their bail, they were arrested for a third time. Comstock then convinced Challis to file a criminal libel charge, and they were again arrested. It was a notable use of the same charge utilized by the Crown against dissenting colonists. The women would ultimately win their federal case, but only because the federal law did not apply to newspapers. The state libel allegations also collapsed after witnesses supported the newspaper account. Nevertheless, the women were ruined financially, particularly after the Panic of 1873. The sisters ultimately had to go to England, an ironic destination given its history with seditious libel. There Claflin would marry Francis Cook, the wealthy businessman and Viscount of Monserrate. With the later creation of the Cook Baronetcy under Queen Victoria, Claflin became Lady Cook and the Viscountess of Monserrate. It must have been a maddening turn of events for Comstock to see the radical libertine and feminist become a leading figure in English society.

For Comstock, the loss of the cases only brought him greater support and backing by many in society. Vice is the one thing that politicians privately relish but publicly abhor. The same year that he established his suppression society, Comstock was able to get Congress to pass the Comstock Act prohibiting the mailing or transport of "obscene, lewd, or lascivious" material. He would assume the role of special agent of the United States Post Office while continuing to serve as the secretary for the New York Society for the Suppression of Vice—the ultimate merging of public authority and public rage.

Comstock triggered a debate over censorship in the cause of virtue. After Comstock targeted George Bernard Shaw's play *Mrs. Warren's Profession*, about a former prostitute and madam of a brothel, the author coined the term "Comstockery" to capture the "the world's standing joke at the expense of the United States" as "a provincial place, a second-rate country-town civilization after all." Before his death in 1915, Comstock would reportedly boast that he had seized one hundred fifty tons of books. He also claimed credit for four thousand arrests and driving fifteen people to suicide.

Fifteen

"WOBBLIES" AND
WORLD WAR I

"Panic politics" would again demand sedition prosecutions in the early twentieth century with crackdowns on socialists, anarchists, unionists, and antiwar activists. In 1886, the Haymarket Riot is a vivid example of rage rhetoric triggering state rage. The speeches leading up to the riot concerned social and political reforms. They bore striking resemblance to the address of Henry Redhead Yorke before his own prosecution by the British Crown. The speeches in Haymarket Square of Chicago included calls for strikes by the Workingmen's Party. The night before the riot, police fired into a crowd of striking workers, killing and wounding protesters. That led to further protests on May 4 in the square, when editor and anarchist August Spies spoke to the crowd. He notably called for peaceful protest, and the crowd appeared to heed that advice. That changed when an unknown person threw a bomb into a line of police officers. The police responded by firing indiscriminately into the crowd, a clearly unrestrained and unjustified act. Many were killed and wounded. Notably, every wounded officer was shot by other officers. Spies was among the eight individuals charged. They also included Louis Lingg, who was an accused bomb maker. All were convicted in trials that focused on their views and public statements. The judge left little question that these men were to be punished for their beliefs rather than their actions. Judge Joseph Easton Gary used their own words to condemn them: "'the people whom they

loved' they deceived, deluded, and endeavored to convert into murderers; the 'cause they died in' was rebellion, to prosecute which they taught and instigated murder; their 'heroic deeds' were causeless, wanton murders done." All but one of the eight convicted would be sentenced to death. However, only four would hang, including Spies. (Two were commuted to life, and one, Lingg, blew his own head off with a smuggled blasting cap that he set off in his mouth.)

Haymarket Square followed a familiar pattern of extremists triggering extreme reactions from the state. The police killed protesters, and then protests turned violent in a cascading failure.

A similar fact pattern played out in the so-called Wheatland Hop Riot. The conflict began when a hops grower named Ralph H. Durst offered jobs to any laborers who came to his 641-acre ranch farm in Yuba County, California. With jobs scarce, almost three thousand workers showed up. Durst promptly slashed their pay. Despite appalling living conditions, Durst made them pay seventy-five cents a week to live in tents. To make matters worse, with temperatures often surpassing 100 degrees Fahrenheit, Durst barred commercial trucks from offering food or water. Instead, with workers only making $1.50 for twelve-hour workdays, he sold his workers lemonade at an obscene rate of five cents a cup. To prevent workers from quitting, Durst held back 10 percent of their wages until they finished the picking. One worker had already died in the heat, and others were sick. The workers had had enough. A group of "Wobblies" with the Industrial Workers of the World helped to organize a strike. Their spokesperson, Richard "Blackie" Ford, an unemployed boilermaker and labor organizer, demanded modest improvements in pay as well as labor and living conditions. While Durst conceded on a couple of points, like allowing water to be brought to the laborers, he refused other concessions including $1.25 per one hundred pounds picked for laborers.

When the organizers called for a mass meeting, Durst called in Yuba County district attorney Edward Manwell, Marysville sheriff George Voss, and his deputies. Manwell also happened to be the private counsel for Durst. When Ford rose to speak, they moved in to arrest him. In the chaos, a platform railing collapsed, and the crowd surged to protect Ford. Voss said that he was knocked down after announcing that there would be order, and "[w]hen I came to, both my billy club and my pistol were gone." A deputy fired his shotgun into the air as a warning shot to "sober the mob." It had the opposite effect. There is no evidence that the laborers were armed, but they struggled with the deputies and disarmed some of them. One worker ran from a tent, grabbed a deputy's weapon, and fired. Shots rang out and, after less than a minute, Manwell, Deputy Sheriff Eugene Reardon, and two pickers lay dead or dying. One hundred workers were arrested in the subsequent sweep by authorities.

Ford was not just unarmed, but he was an advocate of nonviolence. Nevertheless, a coroner's jury found that he deserved arrest for the death of Manwell because a "gunshot wound inflicted by a gun in the hands of rioters incited to murderous anger by IWW leaders and agitators." Also arrested was Wobbly leader Herman Suhr, who was not even present at the riot. Some workers were tortured by police to force confessions. Ford and others were charged. The defense asked for a change of venue, but the court refused. Judge E. P. McDaniel was a personal friend of Manwell, and most of the jury was composed of farmers. Despite the lack of evidence against Ford and Suhr, they were both found guilty of second-degree murder and given life sentences. Two others were acquitted.

There was violence during this period that offered the government cover for these crackdowns, including the assassination of President William McKinley in 1901. Most did not engage in such overt acts, but the government still sought to prosecute those who were seen as radicalizing others. Spurning hierarchical structure, the very philosophy of anarchists made them difficult to track and, as a result, particularly sinister and threatening for the public and officials. Individual acts of violence without a central leadership were an extension of an anarchist creed: "Only unorganized individuals . . . were safe from coercion and domination and thus capable of remaining true to the ideals of anarchism." The assassination of McKinley captured those elements. McKinley's assassin, Leon Czolgosz, was an anarchist and disciple of Emma Goldman. He acted alone but notably said that Goldman's words set him "on fire."

Anarchists were a diverse group divided between what has been called "philosophical" anarchists and violent anarchists. There were anarchists who demanded the destruction of the state. For example, Alexander Berkman was a Russian émigré from a wealthy family who declared that "when the time comes we will not stop short of bloodshed to gain our ends." He proved his point by attempting to assassinate the chairman of the Carnegie Steel Company, Henry Clay Frick, in New York. Berkman's own account captured the almost cartoonist image of these anarchists, who struggled unsuccessfully to build a bomb as they spurred each other on with proletariat platitudes. (They were later crushed to learn that "workingmen" had felled Berkman after he shot the businessman three times.) It was an act of violence that was rationalized in his mind despite his view that "violence is the method of ignorance, the weapon of the weak." He would spend fourteen years in prison for the crime.

Berkman's lover was Emma Goldman. Known as "Red Emma," Goldman had a far greater following among radicals. Like many anti–free speech figures today, Goldman viewed opposing views or institutions as violent and harmful—thus justifying extreme countermeasures. She

defined the movement broadly as following "the philosophy of a new social order based on liberty unrestricted by man-made law; the theory that
all forms of government rest on violence, and are therefore wrong and
harmful, as well as unnecessary." The rhetoric of the anarchists was often
one of rage, and Goldman was the face of righteous rage for many in the
movement. Overheated rhetoric was the norm, though actual violence
remained relatively rare. For example, after the McKinley assassination,
New York police arrested Johann Most, the well-known anarchist writer
and editor of the German anarchist newspaper *Freiheit* (Freedom). In its
September issue, *Freiheit* ran excerpts from the essay *"Mord contra Mord"*
("Murder versus Murder") by a German revolutionary writer. It included
that statement that "[d]espots are outlaws . . . to spare them is a crime. . . .
We say murder the murderers. Save humanity through blood and iron,
poison and dynamite." After news of the assassination reached Most, he
pulled the edition, but some copies were released. He then was arrested
and convicted for disturbing the peace. The Most case was an example of
advocating for but not acting in rebellion. Yet the words were viewed as
fueling the well-publicized violence. It was a case built on Blackstonian
principles of bad-tendency speech. Indeed, the public tended to view all
anarchists as violent due to the bombing and assassination attempts by a
minority within the movement. President Theodore Roosevelt captured
that view by declaring anarchism "a crime against the whole human race,
and all mankind should band against the anarchist."

The appellate court upholding the conviction was not concerned
about the obvious implications in denying political speech. Instead, it was
aggrieved that the government had not gone far enough. The court asked
why Goldman was allowed to escape punishment for inflaming such followers: "The evil is untouched if we stop there. In this class of cases the
courts and the public have too long overlooked the fact that crimes and
offenses are committed by written or spoken words. . . . It is the power of
words that is the potent force to commit crimes and offenses in certain
cases." That admonishment would not be lost on others who sought to
blunt "the power of words" by cracking down on radical speakers.

President Woodrow Wilson would show the same troubling pattern of a president who abandoned prior free speech views to crack down on his critics. As a well-known academic, it was particularly shocking to see the transformation in Wilson, who declared that "if there should be disloyalty, it will be dealt with a firm hand of stern repression." Just years earlier, as president of Princeton, Wilson defended rage rhetoric—which he called agitation, in his work *Constitutional Government in the United States*:

> We are so accustomed to agitation, to absolutely free, outspoken argument for change, to an unrestrained criticism of men and measures carried almost to the point of license, that to us it seems a normal, harmless part of the familiar processes of popular government. We have learned that it is pent-up feelings that are dangerous, whispered purposes that are revolutionary, covert follies that warp and poison the mind. . . . Agitation is certainly of the essence of a constitutional system, but those who exercise authority under a non-constitutional system fear its impact with a constant dread and try by every possible means to check and kill it, partly no doubt because they know that agitation is dangerous to arrangements which are unreasonable.

Wilson correctly treated rage as the expression of political disassociation and condemned the use of government power to suppress it as the greater danger. Indeed, he added that the United States had nothing to fear from agitation, which "is unquestionably very dangerous in countries where there are no institutions—no parliaments, councils, occasional assemblies even—in which opinion may legitimately and with the sanction of law transmute itself into action."

Wilson would abandon those principles as president, as would his party. The anti–free speech push started before Wilson's presidency with a Democratic Party that denounced any groups for views that undermined national unity. In a Flag Day speech, he promised to be unrelenting in his pursuit of anyone who attempted to "inject the poison of disloyalty into our most critical affairs." His support for the Espionage Act of 1917 was based on a chilling claim that disloyal citizens "sacrificed their right to civil liberties." Much like today's government, which funds offices and projects to police social media to target dissenting viewpoints, Wilson's government established a Committee on Public Information (CPI) to identify those espousing dangerous thoughts. Wilson's towering hypocrisy was evident in a visit he made to France in 1919, where he declared himself a defender of free speech, saying: "I have always been among those who believed that the greatest freedom of speech was the greatest safety, because if a man is a fool, the best thing to do is to encourage him to advertise the fact by speaking."

As with the earlier periods, the courts turned a blind eye to the First Amendment protections and focused on the harmful messages being espoused by dissenters. During World War I, one such voice was Frank Shaffer, who sent out copies of *The Finished Mystery* by mail. The book declared, "The war itself is wrong. Its prosecution will be a crime. There is not a question raised, an issue involved, a cause at stake, which is worth the life of one blue-jacket on the sea or one khaki-coat in the trenches." In holding his conviction, the United States Court of Appeals for the Ninth Circuit dismissed any protection afforded to this clearly political speech. It was deemed sufficient that the speech had the "natural and probable tendency" to undermine public support for the war: "To teach that patriotism is murder and the spirit of the devil, and that the war against Germany was wrong and its prosecution a crime, is to weaken patriotism and the purpose to enlist or to render military service in the war." The opinion vividly illustrates the slippery slope of the Blackstonian view of speech limits. The speech is unlawful because some might find it convincing and, if enough are convinced, it could weaken the objectives of the government.

As shown by the Whitney, Haymarket, and Wheatland Hop trials, the advocacy of radical change was interpreted as a call for unrest and violence. Anarchists were treated as demonstrably and inherently violent—presenting immediate threats due to their underlying philosophy. One defender of free speech at the time was Moses Harman, editor of the newspaper *Lucifer: The Light-Bearer*, which advocated not just principles of free speech but also free love. His defense resonated with views of many free speech advocates supporting the Haymarket defendants: "[W]ords are not deeds, and it is not the province of civil law to take preventive measures against remote or possible consequences of words, no matter how violent or 'incendiary.'" That view was again rejected. By 1920, thirty-two states passed anti-sedition and anti-anarchy laws to make the utterance of such views a crime. For example, New York passed a law in 1902 making it a felony to "advocate" anarchism. Publishing or distributing anarchist literature was likewise a felony. With the Communist takeover in Russia, Communists soon became the focus of a new and similar crackdown, including the infamous Palmer raids. Again, many Communists advocated radical change and even revolution. Most did not take violent steps to achieve such goals, but their philosophy was treated as an imminent and violent threat. Attorney General A. Mitchell Palmer declared that "like a prairie fire, the blaze of revolution was sweeping over every American institution of law and order." Thousands were arrested. The government was indiscriminate in arresting everyone in "radical hangouts." On one day, January 2, 1920, more than four thousand were arrested in thirty-three cities.

During World War I, the crackdown on political dissent became raw and repressive. One judge described how many "harmless working people, many of them not long ago Russian peasants, were handcuffed in pairs, and then, for the purpose of transfer on trains and through the streets of Boston, chained together . . . exposed to newspaper photographers." These repellent scenes were played out in front of Americans, who were blinded by panic and anger. Ironically, while using foreign Communist movements as threatening American values, its citizens embraced the very intolerance and abuse associated with those movements. Take anarchist Mollie Steimer. She was repeatedly arrested but defied the government. Eventually she was deported back to Russia for her views. Once in Russia, the Communists could not tolerate her views, either, and deported her. Thus, Steimer held the distinction of being deported by both the United States and Russia for engaging in free speech.

By this point, all three branches supported the suppression of speech with the same relish as the John Adams administration. Rage rhetoric from dissenters was often matched by rage rhetoric from officials. Attorney General Thomas Gregory promised vengeful justice for those who disagreed with the war: "May God have mercy on them, for they need expect none from an outraged people and an avenging government." These crackdowns only affirmed to marginal groups that there was no recourse for those who challenged the government. The prosecutions succeeded in chilling the speech of many, but also pushed others toward more radical views.

This period of speech suppression is also notable in the position of civil libertarians and how free speech was defended. After World War I, free speech advocates often reaffirmed the view of free speech as a functionalist right tied to the democratic system, as opposed to a broader individual right. Even the American Civil Liberties Union (ACLU), which was founded on free speech values, insisted that it would challenge only regulations or rules "relied upon to punish persons for their political views." This meant the continuation of the British approach to censoring immoral and corrupting works.

While we often discuss the use of "bad tendency" rationales as a vehicle for political suppression, it was still embraced by many civil libertarians outside of the democratic process. Thus, American courts long accepted the test of Lord Chief Justice Alexander Cockburn in *Regina v. Hicklin* to allow the censorship of material with the "tendency . . . to deprave and corrupt those whose minds are open to such immoral influences, and into whose hands a publication of this sort may fall." That would include the censorship of pamphlets arguing for the legalization of prostitution and other social reforms. The Comstock Act barring "obscene material" continued to be enforced against advocates of contraception and other causes. In 1923, the ACLU refused to defend a play about prostitution that was closed under New York's obscenity law. The ACLU would adopt a broader view of free speech protections in later years, including the successful defense of Mary Ware Dennett after the government prevented the mailing of copies of her sex education pamphlet, *The Sex Side of Life: An Explanation for Young People*. Nevertheless, the ACLU has been criticized in recent years for rolling back on such protections in combating disinformation, hate speech, and other social ills. Thus, even civil libertarian groups have experienced the seesawing of speech protection due to the uncertainty underlying what this right means outside of the political process. In his book *Transforming Free Speech*, government professor Mark Graber explores the schism within the free speech community between libertarians and civil libertarians. Libertarians embraced the individual right of free speech while civil libertarians doubled down on the view of free speech as based on the social interest in promoting civil discourse. The civil libertarian view would dominate with the ascendence of the functionalist view of free speech. The most notable group of dissenters was the Free Speech League, founded by libertarians such as Theodore Schroeder who committed themselves to fighting for all viewpoints, from Emma Goldman's to Margaret Sanger's. They would be part of a "Libertarian radicalist" movement that rejected any tethering of speech protections to maintaining civil or democratic discourse or, for that matter, social harmony. However, with civil libertarians embracing the more limited foundation for free speech, the government could continue to limit speech in the balance against countervailing interests.

Sixteen

THE BUND AND THE BIDDLE: SEDITION IN WORLD WAR II

The abuses of speech suppression during World War I were recognized as the United States geared up for a new global conflict. There were even voices warning not to let history repeat itself with the targeting of dissenting voices. Yet, as law professor Geoffrey Stone has noted, the same voices were quickly heard to round up those deemed disloyal. In one meeting, President Franklin Delano Roosevelt would ask his attorney general with some exasperation, "[W]hen are you going to indict the seditionists?" Like a dormant virus resting in the body politic, the intolerance for free speech quickly manifested itself in Congress and even in the press.

One of the early focuses of this backlash was the American Bund. The large German population in the United States became a breeding ground for pro-Nazi, anti-Semitic groups. The Bund required members to pledge that they were not just Aryans but also "free of Jewish or colored racial traces." One of the most central missions of the Bund was its outreach to youth, who were invited to summer camps. The strong reaction to the Bund rallies was due to large gatherings appearing around the country. On February 20, 1939, the Bund held a rally in New York at Madison Square Garden that was replete with anti-Semitic tropes. It took more than fifteen hundred New York police officers to hold back the sizable number of protesters. For most of us, the images of Bund camps with the American flag waving over brown-shirted, Nazi-saluting teenagers is haunting. However, the Bund was not accused of systemic or widespread violent acts but of spreading vile fascist and racist views. Thus, when a House committee in 1935 proposed a law to criminalize speech spreading dissension and discord, it was defeated. Yet as hostilities increased in Europe, the defense of free speech again seemed to recede in Congress.

Nothing captures the fleeting fealty for free speech as much as the speech given by Attorney General Frank Murphy in September 1939. Murphy would later join the Supreme Court and assure that there would be no repeat of the roundups from the prior years. However, his speech was laced with ominous language foreshadowing what was to come. He said that, while he would not be a tyrant, he would also not allow "laxity" in the face of subversion. Murphy promised Roosevelt that he would not allow these subversive elements to make the United States look like "a soft, pudgy democracy." Murphy would green-light prosecutions of various groups based on their radical viewpoints. Murphy would be replaced as attorney general by another future justice, Robert Jackson, who also inherited speech prosecutions against the left, including those affiliated with the Abraham Lincoln Brigade that was fighting fascists in Spain. Jackson was dismissive of the case as an "embarrassment." He began his tenure as attorney general with a full-throated endorsement of the protection of free speech and the need to prosecute "only overt acts, not the expression of opinion."

Jackson embodied the intellectual conflict for many of his generation in recognizing the abuses of past crackdowns while yielding to the temptation of speech criminalization. As a justice, he would quickly adopt the fluid relativism of functionalists. It would be Jackson who would write a line that (like Holmes's "shouting fire" line) would be used as a rationalization for speech limits and other government abuses: declaring that the Constitution is no "suicide pact." The line would come in dissent to the Court overturning the conviction of Father Arthur Terminiello, a Catholic priest who supported the fascist leader Gerald L. K. Smith. Terminiello was accused of encouraging a mob to confront his critics and condemned "atheistic, communistic . . . or Zionist Jews." Jackson would denounce the overturning of the conviction with the ultimate example of speech relativism. He reminded his colleagues of the old proverb to be practical, "lest we 'walk into a well from looking at the stars.'" He then added: "The choice is not between order and liberty. It is between liberty with order and anarchy without either. There is danger that, if the Court does not temper its doctrinaire logic with a little practical wisdom, it will convert the constitutional Bill of Rights into a suicide pact."

It is precisely the rationale long used by other "practical" jurists in allowing "bad tendency" speech to be criminalized. The ravings of this racist, anti-Semitic priest were enough to satisfy Jackson that later property damage was incited by his remarks and thus constituted a threat to public order.

The immediate impact of Jackson's elevation to the Court was that the office of attorney general passed to a man who would show little tolerance for free speech: Francis Biddle. Biddle became the fifty-seventh attorney general in 1941—almost exactly one hundred and fifty years after his great-great-grandfather Edmund Randolph took the oath as the first attorney general. Tragically, Biddle was no Edmund Randolph. It was Randolph who counseled against the harsh measures pushed by Hamilton in the face of the Whiskey Rebellion. Biddle showed no such restraint or patience. He would pledge to rid the nation of ninety-five "vermin publications" and pursued political dissenters with an abandon that was reminiscent of English sedition trials. As Stone noted, it was a reversal of fortunes for civil libertarians, who expected more from a man who was a card-carrying ACLU member and previously declared, "We do not lose our right to condemn either measures or men because the country is at war." Biddle would use the Smith Act to pursue dissenters, particularly those opposing the war. Roosevelt's Smith Act was a nightmare for free speech, rivaling Adams's Alien and Sedition Acts. Sections 1 and 2 of the act made spreading dissension a crime. It would be another trifecta of failure of all three branches in protecting free speech. Biddle used the act as a cudgel against minority viewpoints. That included his green-lighting the abusive prosecution of twenty-nine leaders of the Socialist Workers Party (SWP) in Minneapolis. The SWP was active in labor strikes and was charged for engaging in what should have been clearly protected speech. The SWP engaged in inflammatory speech in opposing the war and declared a "war can be won only if it is fought against the capitalist class and its chief executive in Washington." That was enough for Biddle to allege a conspiracy to overthrow the country and led to the conviction of eighteen of the leaders. Later, Biddle would admit that the indictment was a "stretch" and that the defendants merely engaged "in the time-honored Marxist lingo."

Roosevelt pressed Biddle and Hoover to sweep away dissenters in a call reminiscent of the Palmer raids. For example, in January 1942, he demanded to know why a fascist named William Dudley Pelley had not been arrested for his viewpoints. Pelley was a chilling figure of hate and rage. He recounted how he had a transformative experience in his cabin during which he "plunged down into a mystic depth of cool, blue space." It appears that the "mystic" novelist, former journalist, and screenwriter came up from his plunge as a virulent, hate-spewing Nazi. Pelley adored Adolf Hitler and wanted to pursue a "Christian Economics in the United

States." With his pince-nez glasses and goatee, Pelley perfected the faux scientific pitch so popular with Nazis. The depths of Pelley's rage were captured in a Christmas card that he wanted to send to Jews reading:

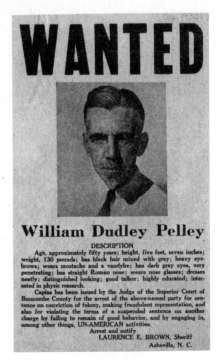

> *Dear Shylock, in this season*
> *When we're all bereft of reason,*
> *As upon my rent you gloat,*
> *I would like to cut your throat.*

Under his twisted vision, all property would be owned by the state and white citizens would receive "shares" based on their loyalty. African Americans would be re-enslaved and Jews deported. In 1936, Pelley ran for president and claimed one hundred thousand followers in his "Silver Legion." Yet he appeared on only one ballot (Wisconsin) and received only 1,598 votes. His writings and "Silver shirt" followers were hateful and fascistic, but Pelley had not actually committed any overt acts of violence. Nevertheless, Roosevelt insisted that his speeches came "pretty close to being seditious." It was the next statement that captured the collapse of any pretext of constitutional faith. Roosevelt stated, "[I]t looks like a good chance to clean up a number of these vile publications." Biddle admitted in his autobiography that Roosevelt "was not much interested in the theory of sedition, or in the constitutional right to criticize the government in wartime. He wanted this anti-war talk stopped."

Pelley was arrested and convicted on eleven charges. The evidence of his crimes under the Espionage Act of 1917 was more of an indictment of Biddle and the government. He was charged for clearly political views, including statements that Pearl Harbor might have been avoided and that "[t]here is not the slightest enthusiasm anywhere in all America for this war—with the sole exception of the Jewish ghetto sections of our swollen cities. And those ghettos will not fight. Gentile boys from factory and farm must do the fighting." On the basis of these statements, Pelley would be sentenced to fifteen years and sent to the federal penitentiary in Terre Haute, Indiana. The United States Court of Appeals for the Seventh Circuit upheld the sentence. After concluding that Pelley's "evil intent" was obvious, the court stressed that he could not make statements as if they were facts: "It is urged that 'The publications . . . are not upon their faces seditious, for they consist of opinions, criticisms, arguments and loose talk.' The trouble with this position is that the readers of *The Galilean* magazine were not so candidly informed of the true character and value of the statements made. . . . Further quotation of these statements is unnecessary to prove they were announced as definite or inevitable facts, not the personal 'opinions' or loose talk of the author." The court does not explain how a speaker is to make sure that followers do not take his words seriously as facts. However, this was obviously not a standard applied to those making pro-government or pro-war statements.

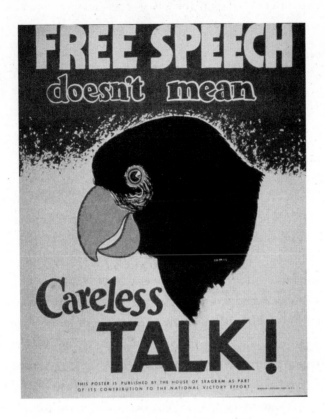

Roosevelt, Jackson, and Biddle follow a pattern reminiscent of Adams and figures associated with progressive views who embrace repressive policies and practices. What is striking is that, even though Biddle would later regret some of these cases, he blamed them on the misuse of discretion rather than the underlying concept of free speech. They all descended along a slippery slope of functionalism where free speech was traded off against security interests. The view of free speech that emerged from World War II was captured on a popular Seagram's wartime poster that simply read: "Free Speech Doesn't Mean Careless Talk!"

Seventeen

McCARTHY AND
THE RED SCARE

Crackdowns would continue in periods of "temporary panic." The next major resurgence would come with the Cold War and "Red Scare." As federal officials arrested suspected Communists, Congress enacted new powers under the Internal Security Act of 1950 to allow the mass detention of dissidents. The Justice Department used the grand jury process to target political dissidents and coerce their associates. The work of the committees on "Un-American Activities" took the Blackstonian model to its natural and grotesque conclusion. The very belief in socialism or communism was treated as a threat to public safety. That view received the support of intellectuals such as law professor Carl Auerbach, who maintained that allowing constitutional protections for speech was itself a threat to the Constitution. Free speech was defined in strictly functionalist terms to support the constitutional system and, accordingly, the First Amendment could not have been interpreted in a way that undermines the stability of the system. In this way, the government had full authority "to curb the power of Congress to exclude from the political struggle those groups which, if victorious, would crush democracy and impose totalitarianism."

The panic politics of the 1950s were based on the earlier fear of Communists but multiplied by the threat of new technology from Sputnik to the atomic bomb. As is often the case, politicians such as Joe McCarthy fed on fears, and few were willing to defy them, including President Harry Truman. This popular effort prompted not only attorney Roy Cohn to join McCarthy's staff but also figures including Robert Kennedy. Truman found himself in a precarious spot politically, and Michigan senator Arthur Vandenberg warned him that, if he wanted to survive politically, he would have to "scare the hell" out of the voters. The Truman administration unleashed a familiar crackdown on political dissidents, including an executive order banning "disloyal" Americans from federal positions. The bar included not just membership but "affiliation with or sympathetic association" with any group deemed by the attorney general to be "communist, or subversive." As law professor Geoffrey Stone has noted, the Communist Party never counted more than a hundred thousand members and was effectively irrelevant. However, a great number of groups shared common agendas on labor and political reforms. As in past crackdowns, this was no time for fine distinctions. Soon, the attorney general assembled a list of 250 groups deemed disloyal.

There were some who pushed back on McCarthy and his allies, including Senator Millard Tydings, a conservative Maryland Democrat who

demanded proof of McCarthy's sweeping claims of Communist infiltration in government. McCarthy soon painted them all as "parlor pinks and parlor punks." Riding a wave of anti-Communist rage, McCarthy attacked anyone who did not yield. In one famous confrontation, he even denounced Major General Ralph Wise Zwicker, a war hero who landed ahead of the first wave at Omaha Beach in Normandy in World War II. Zwicker defied McCarthy's effort to punish a young soldier who took the Fifth on questions about his background by granting him an honorable discharge. McCarthy publicly lashed Zwicker as having the "brain of a five-year-old child" and being unfit to wear his uniform. When fellow senators later denounced him, McCarthy insisted that there was a Communist alliance that "has now extended its tentacles to . . . the United States Senate."

The widest impact of McCarthyism came from the blacklisting carried out by the government through private companies, including Hollywood studios and publishers. It was not until 1956 that Truman had had enough. He attacked McCarthyism as a "horrible cancer [that] is eating at the vitals of America." Yet thousands were fired and prosecuted; "'scaremongers' had generated such a wave of fear that their attacks on civil liberties now went 'almost unchallenged.'" It would be television and a little-known lawyer that would finally prove McCarthy's undoing. Joseph Welch was a lawyer (and later an actor) who knew the value of a perfectly delivered line. His most famous moment would come at the Army-McCarthy hearings when McCarthy attacked one of Welch's young associates, Fred Fisher. McCarthy asked Welch about "a young man named Fisher . . . who has been for a number of years a member of an organization which was named, oh, years and years ago, as the legal bulwark of the Communist Party." Welch pounced: "Until this moment, Senator, I think I never really gaged [sic] your cruelty or your recklessness. . . . Let us not assassinate this lad further, Senator. You have done enough. Have you no sense of decency, sir, at long last? Have you left no sense of decency?" Welch then rose in defiance and walked out to the applause of the room. McCarthy was done. One's own rage is often considered justified. Rage in others can be frightening. What the public saw was state rage and the target was a young lawyer who simply belonged to a legal advocacy group.

This period also continued the type of attacks under the Comstock Act in the name of protecting public mores and values. History has shown that speech regulation creates an insatiable appetite for greater and greater limits. Once speech prosecutions are allowed in one area, it is easier (and even irresistible) in other areas. In the second half of the twentieth century, there was an increase in crackdowns on social and religious dissenters, including noncrimi-

nal sanctions. One of the most notable was Bertrand Russell. A brilliant writer and philosopher, Russell was also an atheist. The crackdown on Russell vividly shows the elasticity of views of harm from free speech. He was a contrarian who showed the same defiance as Thomas Paine in resisting the orthodoxies and expectations of his time. He was an anti-imperialist at a time of empires, an atheist at a time of faith. He believed in sexual freedom at a time of rigid sexual mores and laws. He would go to jail for his antiwar advocacy during World War I. He would eventually receive the Nobel Prize for literature in recognition of his contributions to humanity.

Russell was heavily influenced by Mill, who was asked to be his godfather by his equally contrarian and libertine parents. (Mill was the first child of James Mill, secretary to the great philosopher and father of utilitarianism Jeremy Bentham, who took a role in helping design his course of education. So, for some of us who are fans of all three philosophers, there is a type of intellectual *lignée royale* running from Bentham to Mill to Russell.) In a work on his godfather, Russell wrote that "I think [Mill] is entirely right in emphasizing the importance of the individual in so far as values are concerned."

In 1940, a board unanimously appointed Russell to teach philosophy at the City College of New York. His appointment caused a public outcry due to his writings on religion and sexual freedom. Since CCNY was a public university, Mayor Fiorello La Guardia announced that he would delete the provision in the city budget supporting Russell's professorship. The board was forced to reconsider the appointment but courageously voted again to support it. The matter was then taken to court by Jean Kay, who claimed standing on the basis that her daughter would be morally harmed by taking a class with Russell. The court ignored that it was a purely speculative danger, since CCNY was then a male-only school. The case went before Judge John E. McGeehan, who ruled against Russell. Besides declaring Russell ineligible for a city teaching position due to his foreign nationality and lack of a qualification examination, McGeehan agreed that Russell's immoral views made him a risk to students. It was a modern replay of Socrates's conviction for corrupting the young. La Guardia then made good on his threat and removed funding for Russell's position. The appellate courts upheld the lower court. In the end, the greatest defense would come from Albert Einstein, who wrote Raphael Cohen in defense of Russell's appointment on March 19, 1940:

"Great spirits have always encountered violent opposition from mediocre minds. The mediocre mind is incapable of understanding the man who refuses to bow blindly to conventional prejudices and chooses instead to express his opinions courageously and honestly."

Many academics remained silent as politicians, religious leaders, and newspapers blocked Russell from teaching due to the danger of exposing college students to his ideas. Fortunately, a Nobel Prize rather than a cup of hemlock awaited Russell, but the shame of his case would stain academia for years to come.

Eighteen

DAYS OF RAGE: RACE, RHETORIC, AND REBELLION IN THE 1960S

Extreme social, economic, and political conditions continued to fuel rage and extremist rhetoric in the 1960s. Those conditions magnified long-standing racist, anti-Semitic, and other hateful elements in American society. White supremacist groups from the KKK to neo-Nazi groups have long called for racial cleansing. Revolution was a familiar call on the left. Malcom X famously asked, "Whoever heard of a revolution where they lock arms . . . singing 'We Shall Overcome'? Just tell me. You don't do that in a revolution. You don't do any singing; you're too busy swinging." While a minority of members of these groups turned to violent acts, these groups were accused of fueling violence through hateful messages on the right and on the left. In the 1960s, racial divisions prompted groups such as the Black Panthers and others to call for arming followers. A good example is the October 1969 aftermath of the "Summer of Rage" in Chicago, where some, including the Weather Underground, pushed for direct action beyond the mere protests of other groups such as the Students for a Democratic Society (SDS). Far-left groups like SDS were portrayed as feckless or naïve by those pushing for violent change.

The government again responded to rage rhetoric with a crackdown on a wide array of advocacy groups. As was the case in the eighteenth

century, it was common for rioters to target government property associated with the FBI and other symbols of authority. One such act occurred
on March 8, 1971, when a cabdriver, a day care provider, and two professors broke into an FBI office in Media, Pennsylvania. They were part of
the Citizens' Commission to Investigate the FBI and had waited for the
night of the boxing match between Muhammad Ali and Joe Frazier. They
knew that agents, like most everyone else, would be watching or listening to the "Fight of the Century." They proceeded to steal more than one
thousand classified documents, including material on the FBI's Counter
Intelligence Program (COINTELPRO), which they then mailed anonymously to several U.S. newspapers. It revealed an extensive effort to sur-
veil, infiltrate, and disrupt left-wing groups, particularly antiwar groups.
The FBI's targeting of figures such as Reverend Dr. Martin Luther King
enraged many groups.

While many Black Panthers brandished arms, relatively few were accused of violent acts despite crackdowns in various states. Black Panther
and writer Stokely Carmichael spoke in terms of self-defense that were
interpreted as calls for violent action:

> Those of us who advocate Black Power are quite clear in our own
> minds that a "non-violent" approach to civil rights is an approach
> black people cannot afford and a luxury white people do not deserve.
> It is crystal clear to us—and it must become so with the white soci-
> ety—that there can be no social order without social justice. White
> people must be made to understand that they must stop messing with
> black people, or the blacks will fight back!

Malcolm X is a fascinating example of rage rhetoric. He intentionally
goaded the white community with veiled threats, but he remained nonviolent. However, a rageful righteousness was his signature. On December
10, 1963, in a speech in Detroit, Malcolm X declared:

> You don't have a peaceful revolution. You don't have a turn-the-other-
> cheek revolution. There's no such thing as a nonviolent revolution.

. . . [R]evolution is bloody. Revolution is hostile. Revolution knows no compromise. Revolution overturns and destroys everything that gets in its way. And you, sitting around here like a knot on the wall, saying, "I'm going to love these folks no matter how much they hate me." No, you need a revolution.

Again, this type of rage rhetoric was treated as a sufficient basis for criminal investigation and arrests. Yet the common call for Blacks to engage in "self-defense" and to arm themselves was present not only in the Black community but in the white community, too. The rhetoric, however, served to draw even greater efforts from the FBI and local law enforcement to target organizations like the Black Panthers. Once again, the rhetoric within the Black community was not taken as a call to actual violence by many. For Malcolm X, the language of self-defense was commonly used by whites but denied to Blacks. As theologian James Cone noted, "Malcolm regarded nonviolence as a ridiculous philosophy, one that whites would never embrace as their own." Malcolm X often discussed virtually identical language used by figures like Patrick Henry and asked why such rhetoric was deemed hateful and violent when uttered by Blacks. Yet calls for "self-defense" were widely reported or interpreted as a call to armed rebellion. As journalist Bryan Burrough observed in his book *Days of Rage*, this familiar phrase for the Black community struck "a generation of wary whites [that] saw [it] simply as a call to violence, to shotgun blasts in the night, to rioting, to black men rampaging through the streets of burning white homes and businesses." The result was that the violent rhetoric led to greater surveillance and arrests. That in turn led to further radicalization and, in some cases, violence.

One example is Robert F. Williams, who headed the NAACP chapter in Monroe, North Carolina. Williams organized a chapter of the National Rifle Association for Black citizens and was placed under close surveillance by federal and state authorities. His rhetoric shifted from nonviolence to "self-defense" as tensions rose in his town. During one night of racial violence, a white couple was surrounded in his neighborhood and taken to Williams's home. While the facts were murky, Williams said he was trying to protect the couple and prevented them from leaving for their own protection. The FBI and local police reportedly convinced the white couple to accuse Williams of kidnapping. While claiming innocence, Williams fled to Cuba (and later China). During this exile, he wrote anti-American and extremist articles as well as his well-known work *Negroes with Guns*. Williams is an example of how the government's response to rage rhetoric resulted in such rhetoric becoming more violent and rebellious.

Malcolm X's rhetoric stood in contrast to his own actions. However, while there were many calls for Malcolm X to be arrested, he was not charged with incitement or sedition. His only arrests and prison stints came in his early years as Malcolm Little, including an eight-to-ten-year sentence for various felonies in Massachusetts. Others, however, were prosecuted for their violent rhetoric. Michael X, a Black revolutionary in Britain, was charged with inciting racial hatred under the country's Race Relations Act, the first Black person to be so charged. Stokely Carmichael was convicted of inciting a riot in 1966 in Selma, Alabama, as was Stuart House, the local Student Nonviolent Coordinating Committee (SNCC) secretary. Leading up to Carmichael's arrest was an FBI report that showed how his inflammatory rhetoric was being treated as a possible crime. Indeed, much like the prosecutions of figures such as Eugene Debs for opposing the draft in 1918, the FBI cited Carmichael's opposition to the Vietnam draft. The report on September 7, 1966, titled "Student Nonviolent Coordinating Committee Stokely Carmichael" detailed an array of criminal charges after an antiwar protest targeting the Twelfth Corps Headquarters, including "destruction of Government property and possible violations of the Selective Service Act of 1948." Carmichael was cited for his rhetoric that encouraged others to defy the draft or cause property damage. The crackdown served only to confirm the narrative of others who directly participated in violent acts.

An example of the violent rhetoric leading to actual violence is found in a speech in the town of Cambridge, Maryland, by H. Rap Brown, who declared, "This ain't no riot, brother! This is a rebellion, and we got 400 years of reasons to tear this town apart! . . . In a town this size, three men can burn it down. That's what they call guerrilla warfare. . . . Don't love him to death! Shoot him to death!" He later proclaimed, "[V]iolence is necessary, it is as American as cherry pie." Fires broke out in the town, and seventeen buildings were destroyed. There was an exchange of gunfire in which an officer and Brown were wounded. Brown was charged with inciting a riot. Later, the Cambridge courthouse was bombed. Brown then disappeared but was rearrested after an attempted robbery and another shootout. After serving time at Attica, Brown (now going by the name Jamil Abdullah al-Amin) would appear to turn his life around. However, he would later go to prison for life after killing a police officer.

Like Brown, there were groups who hoped to trigger revolutionary change through social unrest. They were largely motivated by anti-racism and anti-capitalism views. The Symbionese Liberation Army (SLA) and the Black Liberation Army (BLA) are other examples of the move of some from violent speech to violent action. As Bryan Burrough noted, the United States had seen political violence throughout its history. However, "[a]cts of political terrorism . . . have been comparably rare." It was not until the 1970s that the country "spawned any kind of true underground movement committed to terrorist acts." What is notable is that the FBI made no significant distinction between these violent groups and civil rights and political groups engaging in inflammatory speech. The government launched criminal investigations into groups from the Southern Christian Leadership Conference (SCLC) to the Weather Underground. The result was to push some into more radical and violent action. At the same time, the crackdown in Chicago during the Days of Rage protests confirmed for some that they were now enemies of the state. Weatherman activist Russell Neufeld later said, "The decision to go underground was largely a function of what happened to us in Chicago, the violence, the brutality. Things like getting a gun put in your mouth, it convinced a lot of us we really were living in a police state. [Going underground] seemed the logical next step."

It was during this period that the courts were forced to deal with the protections of rage rhetoric. One of the most significant incidents arose after Paul Robert Cohen appeared in the Los Angeles County Courthouse wearing a jacket on which was written "F**k the Draft." It was April 1968, when antiwar protests were raging on campuses. Cohen was arrested and convicted of "maliciously and willfully disturb[ing] the peace or quiet . . . by . . . offensive conduct." The case would make its way to the Supreme Court in *Cohen v. California*. Notably, Chief Justice Warren Burger made clear that he did not want "that word" uttered in oral argument, since if it were it "would be the end of the Court." It did not matter. In answering the first question, Cohen's counsel, Melville Nimmer, used the word and reportedly sent marshals into a frenzy. Justice John M. Harlan would write for a slim five-justice majority in favor of Cohen, noting that "[w]hile the particular four-letter word being litigated here is perhaps more distasteful than most others of its genre, it is nevertheless often true that one man's vulgarity is another's lyric." If so, rage lyrism did not appeal to four justices, including surprisingly Justice Hugo Black, who was a great advocate of free speech. One of his clerks would later recount how Black could not get beyond the thought that his wife might have seen such a jacket while visiting the Supreme Court. In his dissent, Justice Harry Blackmun wrote that Cohen was not prosecuted for his speech but for his conduct. It is a reframing of the speech question that is popular today, as will be discussed later in this book. In *Cohen*, the majority wisely rejected the convenient logic and held that the "conviction quite clearly rests upon the asserted offensiveness of the words Cohen used to convey his message to the public. The only 'conduct' which the State sought to punish is the fact of communication." The case would offer a clarity that would soon be lost again in the Court's struggle with the meaning and limits of free speech.

Nineteen

ANTIFA, MAGA, AND THE AGE OF RAGE

In 2016, I referred to our current period as an "Age of Rage." With the election of Donald Trump, rage supplanted reason, contorting the analysis of ethical and legal issues. While the expression caught on, it was not meant to be an exclusive term given earlier periods of rage politics. The rage rhetoric in prior periods is strikingly familiar to that of violent groups like Antifa on the left to the Proud Boys on the right. However, that rage has also extended to mainstream figures and the media. At the same time, we have seen the return of the government to both sedition prosecutions and a degree of state rage in dealing with those who challenged the system. Members of Congress have again called for censorship and speech prosecutions. Indeed, some politicians are expressly running on the promise of greater censorship. Most importantly, many citizens have lost interest in dialogue and now enjoy a sense of release that comes from rage on the internet and in the streets. We have a rage addiction that has swept the nation and it now threatens, again, our core values.

For many, the face of rage politics is Donald Trump. Trump's Make America Great Again (MAGA) movement transformed politics in the United States. Trump would harness rage politics to an extent not seen in this country since the eighteenth century. He was the very vehicle of the rage that many felt toward the establishment, the media, and other elements of modern society. In some ways, Trump would tar and

feather the system as a whole. Many did not particularly like him, but they saw him as a type of human Molotov cocktail that they could throw into the very center of the nation's governing elite, the heart of the "deep state."

Many of us criticized Trump's personal attacks on opponents, judges, and others. He also used violent rhetoric that recklessly fueled the rage of the period, including labeling critics and reporters "traitors" and "enemies of the state." In 2018, Trump praised Montana's then-representative Greg Gianforte (R) after he assaulted a reporter, saying, "Any guy that can do a body slam, he is my type!" When violent protests arose around the country after the death of George Floyd, Trump did not attempt to mollify or mediate. He tweeted in May 2020, "When the looting starts, the shooting starts." Trump's language was inflammatory by design. For some citizens, he was a departure from the scripted establishment figures that preceded him. He channeled their feelings of isolation and, yes, rage.

A wealthy businessman with a successful television reality show, Trump measured public response to products on a daily basis. He sensed a deep and growing anger among many Americans—a growing isolation of conservative and religious citizens in the country. Call it retail rage. Trump knew how to tap into it, package it, and sell it. While figures such as populist Louisiana governor Huey Long succeeded on the state level by marshaling economic and social forces of discontent in the early 1930s, no president since Jackson has put together a more spontaneous populist alliance. In some ways, Trump approached politics the same way he did his reality show, *The Apprentice*. He knew his audience. He kept his message simple, accessible, and immediate. It was impulse-buy politics. From the outset, Trump used social media to vent against the media, judges, and the "deep state." While the left has long used rage politics in declaring "no justice, no peace," Trump was offering conservatives the same righteous license to be angry . . . very angry.

For Trump, it was all smashmouth politics where you said things that other politicians might think but never utter. There was a rage wave, and Trump caught it and rode it like a Level 4 surfer. While Trump harnessed these political forces, there had long been anger building in American politics on the left and the right. What followed Trump's election was pure, unadulterated, and uninhibited rage from the left. Democratic members opposed the certification of Trump's election despite the lack of any serious election controversies.

The Trump inauguration sparked riots in Washington. At the center of these riots was Antifa, an organization that bills itself as pure, uncorrupted rage in the same way as did groups like the Weather Underground. Many engage in rage politics, but Antifa rejects the politics for the rage. The group traces its origins in European anarchist movements and is arguably the most anti–free speech movement in modern United States history. Antifa originated with European anarchist and Marxist groups from the 1920s, particularly Antifaschistische Aktion, a Communist group from the Weimar Republic before World War II. Its name resulted from the shortening of the German word *antifaschistisch*. In the United States, the modern movement emerged through the Anti-Racist Action (ARA) groups, which were dominated by anarchists and Marxists. It has an association with the anarchist organization Love and Rage, which was founded by former Trotsky and Marxist followers, as well as offshoots like Mexico's Amor Y Rabia. The oldest U.S. group is likely the Rose City Antifa (RCA) in Portland, Oregon, which would become the center of violent riots during the Trump years. The anarchist roots of the group give it the same organizational profile as such groups in the early twentieth century with uncertain leadership and undefined structures.

Antifa has a long and well-documented history of such violence in acting against journalists, protesters, and speakers. Like the Black Panthers and other groups, Antifa rationalizes its violence as an act of self-defense. The group treats free speech as harmful. In his book *Antifa: The Anti-Fascist Handbook*, Rutgers history professor Mark Bray defends Antifa as "social revolutionary self-defense," "pan-left radical politics uniting communists, socialists, anarchists." However, he notes that "[a]t the heart of the anti-fascist outlook is a rejection of the classical liberal phrase that says, 'I disapprove of what you say but I will defend to the death your right to say it.'"

Antifa continues the same amorphous organization, making it difficult to track with an array of associated groups, including the Chelsea East Boston Antifascist Coalition (CEBAC), Smash Racism DC, and others. The signature violence is justified as preventing the harm of "fascism." For example, Bray explained that, when Antifa and its allies sought to disrupt the Trump inauguration, anyone celebrating the inauguration became a per se "fascist." The goal was to destroy "iconic" corporate images. He described the targeting of "fascists in tuxes . . . [and] how corporate enterprises [like] the glass storefronts of Starbucks and Bank of America were rapidly demolished, similar destruction forced a McDonald's to shut down and ATMs and other corporate property spray-painted or destroyed." Indeed, "the most iconic moment of the day may have been when a limousine was set ablaze."

Violent protests would grow over the next four years. The property damage would reach the billions with deaths across the country during protests. "No justice, no peace" would often be chanted during the day with more violent calls and actions following each night. Police stations and city halls were burned or occupied. A federal courthouse in Portland was attacked over the course of many days. The White House itself was the target of a violent protest that led to President Trump and the First Lady being removed to a secure room. In addition to two historic structures being burned, more than one hundred federal officers were injured. The Park Police alone have asserted that "51 members of the USPP were injured; of those, 11 were transported to the hospital and released and three were admitted." The violence of many Antifa supporters did not diminish the support or tolerance of some in politics, academia, and the media. On December 21, 2020, Antifa member Thomas "Tas" Alexander Starks, thirty-one, of Lisbon, North Dakota, took an axe to the office of Senator John Hoeven in Fargo; in 2021, he was convicted. While federal sentencing guidelines suggested ten to sixteen months in prison, he was sentenced only to probation and fined $2,784 for restitution after various people declared him a hero and Democratic politicians pitched in for his legal defense. He never apologized for his attack and publicly declared, "I am ANTIFA. I will always attack fascists, racial superiority complexes built around nationalism that promotes genocide to fuel a war machine is the worst humanity has to offer." He was then given back his axe by the FBI.

In the *Washington Post*, Bray warned that public condemnations of Antifa could serve to "delegitimiz[e] militant protest," but admitted that

> it's true that most, if not all, members do wholeheartedly support militant self-defense against the police and the targeted destruction of police and capitalist property that has accompanied it this week. I'm also confident that some members of antifa groups have participated in a variety of forms of resistance during this dramatic rebellion.

In 2020, the federal government arrested George Washington University student Jason Charter as the alleged "ringleader" who led efforts to topple statues in Washington, DC. Charter has been an active Antifa member for years, and after his arrest, reportedly proclaimed, "The Movement is winning."

Despite this violent history, politicians and pundits have supported the group while Trump has been accused of supporting right-wing groups known for violence. At one point, Trump even told the Proud Boys in a presidential debate to "stand by." Conversely, in Minnesota, where riots led to massive property damage, former Democratic National Committee deputy chair Keith Ellison, now the Minnesota attorney general, said Antifa would "strike fear in the heart" of Trump. His son, Minneapolis City Council member Jeremiah Ellison, declared his allegiance to Antifa in the heat of summer protests. Likewise, MSNBC's Joy Reid defended Antifa on the air, reminding people that Antifa is "literally" short for antifascist. She added that "[i]f you're constantly yelling 'Antifa!'—which literally is short for 'anti-fascists,' ding-ding-ding! . . . you might be the fascist they're focused on." It is all rage rhetoric being used as a means for political ends. However, as we have seen, rage can be an end to itself.

Twenty

JANUARY 6TH AND
THE REVIVAL OF
AMERICAN SEDITION

For many of us, the image of rioters scaling the walls of the Capitol and storming over barricades will remain painfully embedded in our memories. As someone who first worked in Congress as a young House page in the 1970s, I was speechless as the mob charged the building. I had just participated in the coverage of Trump's speech on the Ellipse and criticized his words while he was still speaking on that day. I specifically objected to Trump's claims that Vice President Pence could stop the certification and his continued claim that the election was stolen. However, nothing had prepared most of us for what followed. Despite the long notice of the massive demonstration, no additional fencing or barriers were installed and there was no deployment of the National Guard. The violent riot at the White House had recently resulted in historic buildings being torched and a large number of officers injured. Despite that recent history, the Capitol was left protected by a thin line of under-equipped Capitol police.

The attack on the Capitol was a disgrace. No matter how vicious our politics have become, citizens share a common article of faith in the Constitution. The peaceful transfer of power is the unbroken realization of that promise. In the end, the system prevailed. The vice president did as many of us said he was bound to do under the law. After the riot was quelled, he reassembled with our elected representatives, and they certified the election of Joseph Biden as the forty-sixth president of the United States.

Every tragedy, however, offers an opportunity. January 6th was no exception. No sooner had the certification occurred than the media and Democrats insisted that the attack be called an "insurrection." Within days, there were calls for treason and sedition prosecutions, and anyone calling this a "riot" was labeled an "apologist" or "sympathizer." The morning after the riot, I wrote that it was a desecration of our constitutional process. However, it was not an insurrection. Thousands of Trump supporters marched to the Capitol that day. The vast majority did not enter the Capitol or engage in any violence. Most who entered the Capitol did so through the open doors after the breach. Indeed, after a massive crackdown and investigation, the FBI admitted that it found "scant evidence" of any "organized plot," and one agent explained that "ninety to ninety-five percent of these are one-off cases." Acknowledging those facts does not diminish what occurred. There were violent individuals who came prepared for a riot with mace, ropes, and weapons. However, it was clearly a protest that became a riot after a breach of security. Most of us called for those rioters to be arrested and punished severely for their attack on our Capitol. Yet this proved to be no more of an insurrection than it was a peaceful demonstration.

Democratic leaders such as Representative Bill Pascrell (D-N.J.) demanded the disqualification of the 120 House Republicans—including House Minority Leader Kevin McCarthy (R-Calif.). The argument under the long-dormant provision in Section 3 of the Fourteenth Amendment—the "disqualification clause"—was an argument that was not just unfounded but dangerous. Yet it was still supported by many legal experts. Written in the late nineteenth century to disqualify anyone who took an oath of federal office but later "engaged in insurrection or rebellion," the clause was drafted after a real civil war in which over 750,000 people died in combat. The Confederacy formed a government, an army, a currency, and carried out diplomatic missions. These members were calling for the provision to be applied to a protest that became a riot.

The calls for widespread arrests and electoral disqualifications raised again the selectivity of speech crackdowns. To criminalize inflammatory political rhetoric would invite the type of retaliatory measures used by the Federalists and Jeffersonians in the early Republic. For example, as criminal threats were being directed at justices, Chicago mayor Lori Lightfoot made a "call to arms" after the *Dobbs* decision. Representative Jamie Raskin (D-Md.), the leading impeachment manager, called on supporters to "fight like hell" in a 2019 interview with the *Atlantic*—the very words used by Trump in his January 6th speech. Representative Maxine Waters (D-Calif.) called on people to confront Republicans in public. Representative Ayanna Pressley (D-Mass.) insisted during 2020's violent protests that "there needs to be unrest in the streets." Then-senator Kamala Harris (D-Calif.) declared "protesters should not let up" even as many protests turned violent or deadly. House Speaker Nancy Pelosi (D-Calif.) condemned fellow members as effectively traitors and the "enemy within." In the midst of violent protests, Pelosi also declared, "I just don't know why there aren't uprisings all over the country. Maybe there will be."

Moreover, Democrats had used the same law to oppose the certification of Republican presidents, including citing voting irregularities. In January 2005, Senator Barbara Boxer joined former Representative Stephanie Tubbs Jones to challenge George W. Bush's victory over Democratic challenger John Kerry in the state of Ohio. At the time, I was working for CBS, and many of us looked into allegations of voting irregularities but failed to see anything sufficient to change the outcome. Nevertheless, Boxer argued that Republicans had engaged in voter suppression that contributed to Bush's victory. There was no hue and cry in the media over an attack on democracy, and Speaker Nancy Pelosi praised the challenge as "witnessing Democracy at work." Senator Dick Durbin took to the Senate floor to praise Boxer. He declared, "[S]ome may criticize our colleague from California for bringing us here for this brief debate. I thank her for doing that because it gives members an opportunity once again on a bipartisan basis to look at a challenge that we face not just in the last election in one State but in many States." Indeed, the January 6th Committee included Chairman Bennie Thompson (D-Miss.), who voted to object to

the counting of the electoral votes in President George W. Bush's 2004 re-election. Likewise, Jamie Raskin challenged Trump's certification in 2016. These same members went on to denounce those voting to challenge the certification of Biden as part of the insurrection. The question is where to draw the line for the disqualification of members.

When past riots or inflammatory language are raised, politicians and pundits often end any discussion by saying that it is all "whataboutism," the favorite rationale today for avoiding difficult questions. So, what about whataboutism? The measure of history and the test of principle is often comparative. The danger of ambiguous or subjective standards is that they are used selectively. Indeed, the foregoing history shows how biased the application of standards like the "clear and present danger" proved to be. It is the comparison—the whataboutism—that exposes the hypocrisy and abuse. Yet even judges engage in this evasion.

In the one direct ruling on the Trump speech in a civil case, Judge Amit Mehta ruled that Trump could be forced into a trial (despite dismissing some of the speakers as defendants). When Trump's lawyers noted that his language was largely indistinguishable from that of many Democrats like Maxine Waters, Mehta chided them for playing "a game of what-aboutism." Yet the Court proceeded to engage in the same question-able line-drawing comparison with others on that day. In his 112-page opinion, Mehta has no difficulty in dismissing claims against Giuliani and Donald Trump Jr. He noted that Giuliani's declaration—"Let's have trial by combat"—"were not likely" to cause a riot. Likewise, he found that the statement of Representative Brooks that Trump's supporters should "start taking names and kicking ass" was not inciteful. Nor were Trump Jr.'s inflammatory comments. However, Trump's statements were found potentially inciteful even though Judge Mehta acknowledged that Trump told the crowd that "everyone here will soon be marching over to the Capitol building to peacefully and patriotically make your voices heard." It did not matter that his comments were consistent with a protest in saying that "are going to cheer on our brave senators and congressmen and women. It also did not matter that these comments were virtually identical what other politicians had been saying at other protests. After dismiss

the other defendants, Mehta simply declared Trump a "unique case" and avoided the clearly protected speech at the Ellipse.

The ultimate whataboutism is called precedent. Even under the functionalist construct of past cases, this was protected speech going to the core of the democratic process. While many of us believe that Trump was wrong on the law and reckless in his rhetoric, he was espousing a view shared by many about the election. To maintain a criminal charge, the Court would need to reverse decades of precedent involving inflammatory speeches to potentially violent groups. In *Brandenburg*, the Supreme Court ruled that a Ku Klux Klan leader calling for violence is protected under the First Amendment. Yet it also found that it was not a threat of "imminent lawless action [nor] likely to incite or produce such action." In *Hess v. Indiana*, the court rejected the prosecution of a protester declaring an intention to take over the streets because "at worst, [the words] amounted to nothing more than advocacy of illegal action at some indefinite future time." In *NAACP v. Claiborne Hardware Co.*, the Court overturned a judgment against the National Association for the Advancement of Colored People after one of its officials promised to break the necks of opponents.

As shown from prior periods, violent protests are hardly unique. They were often called "rebellions" and "insurrections" by those who wanted to crack down on opponents or justify draconian legal measures. While the storming of the Capitol was a terrible act, it is not uncommon for protesters to go to legislatures to oppose or support measures being considered inside. As a page in the 1970s, I witnessed protesting truckers break through police lines and storm into the Capitol. State and federal capitol buildings have always been targeted for such demonstrations, particularly when considering controversial measures. For example, in May 2023, multiple protesters were arrested in Nebraska trying to stop a vote on abortion and transgender legislation, including one who assaulted an officer. Likewise, the attack on the White House (which injured a greater number of officers than on January 6th and involved multiple arsons) was characterized by many Democrats as a "peaceful protest." What is a riot to some is a rebellion to others. Yet polls show that, despite the media

reinforcing the characterization of an "insurrection," the public saw the riot for what it was. The public denounced the violence but, according to a 2022 Harvard poll, overwhelmingly saw the protesters as motivated by their loyalty for Trump rather than any insurrection. Likewise, a 2022 CBS poll shows that the public viewed the attack as a riot and not an insurrection. ·

The characterization of the riot as an insurrection was used to justify calls for not only decertification but arrests. Harvard law professor Laurence Tribe insisted that Trump should be charged with criminal incitement for an insurrection as well as other crimes. Tribe declared that "without any doubt, beyond a reasonable doubt, beyond any doubt, and the crimes are obvious," including a charge of the attempted murder of Pence. The fact is that such a prosecution based on the Trump speech would require the Court to gut *Brandenburg* and return to the oppressive precedent surrounding the *Schenck* decision. Indeed, many members and professors have made this argument while citing Holmes's theater analogy. Figures like District of Columbia attorney general Karl Racine received overwhelmingly favorable press in declaring, soon after the riot, that he was investigating Trump for criminal charges of incitement. Then, nothing happened. The reason is likely that Racine discovered, as some of us noted at the time, that existing precedent barred such charges. The January 6th Committee failed to uncover clear evidence that Trump conspired to cause the riot. Tellingly, despite objections, the committee routinely edited out part of a quote where Trump told his supporters to protest "peacefully." Absent evidence of a conspiracy to commit specific criminal acts, the criminalization of his speech would convert every election into Schenckian "crowded theater" for the purposes of prosecution.

January 6th resulted in a revival of American sedition. As will be discussed later in chapter 29, a small number of seditious conspiracy charges were added on to other crimes against members of the Proud Boys and the Oath Keepers. Again, most of us agree that those who planned for and carried out violence should be facing stiff sentences. However, there remains the question over the necessity of a resurgence of sedition charges even in these relatively few cases.

For the remainder of the roughly seven hundred people arrested, they faced relatively minor charges but extremely heavy-handed measures. Many were kept unnecessarily in jail, including long periods in segregation. The Justice Department seemed to be channeling the state rage from earlier periods as when Attorney General Thomas Watt Gregory in 1917 promised vengeful justice for those protesting World War I: "May God have mercy on them, for they need expect none from an outraged people and an avenging government." In 2021, federal prosecutor Michael Sherwin proudly declared in a television interview that "our office wanted to ensure that there was shock and awe. . . . It worked because we saw through media posts that people were afraid to come back to DC because they're like, 'If we go there, we're gonna get charged.'" For some, the "shock and awe" looked a lot like state rage with unusually long sentencing demands and pretrial conditions. Indeed, Sherwin's interview seemed ripped from the pages of past speech crackdowns. One could hear echoes of Fisher Ames defending the use of the sedition laws under the Adams administration for "the government just display its power *in terrorem.*" Likewise, there was a whisper of the words of John Lord O'Brian (who headed the Justice Department's War Emergency Division one hundred years earlier) when he admitted that prosecutors were pressured to launch "indiscriminate prosecutions" and the "wholesale repression and restraint of public opinion."

Sherwin's intent to cause "shock and awe" resulted in a massive dragnet to investigate anyone who went to the protest or supported the challenge on January 6th. Courts showed the same punitive impulse in refusing to release hundreds of those charged for long periods of pretrial incarceration. However, judges treated their danger as spreading election denial. While some of these defendants expressed violent intentions and could reasonably be viewed as a threat, Judge Amy Berman Jackson added the danger of spreading false rumors as a basis for the denial of bail. In one such case, she noted, "[T]he canard that the election was stolen is being repeated daily on major news outlets and from the corridors of power in state and federal government, not to mention in the near-daily fulminations of the former President." Thus, she reasoned, bail could be denied because defendants could repeat these lies. Another judge echoed that

rationale. Again, the defendant was accused of engaging in violence, but the court cited Jackson in also claiming that bail would be inappropriate because the defendant might spread dangerous lies that "could give rise to another protest." Yet spreading lies was not charged, and the Supreme Court has correctly ruled that even lies can be constitutionally protected in its striking down of the Stolen Valor Act in *United States v. Alvarez*.

The most iconic image of the riot may have been the "QAnon Shaman." Bare-chested and wearing an animal headdress, horns, and red-white-and-blue face paint, Jake Angeli Chansley became indelibly linked to the attack. His case would become a microcosm of the January 6th prosecutions from the justified anger over his role to concerns about the heavy-handed measures of the government.

Chansley's road to the Senate floor provides insight into a segment of American society that is largely unknown to most Americans. He went to Moon Valley High School in 2005, where his yearbook showed a typical American kid with his arm around his half brother and pictures as a member of the debate and math clubs. He was also a member of the "Rocket Town" cultural diversity program and described his time with students of color as "like being with my family." Chansley, however, took a dramatic change when he served in the Navy and became increasingly immersed in the internet labyrinth of conspiracy theories, New Age concepts, and a twisted form of spiritualism. After leaving the Navy, he struggled to find work as an actor and could not pay the $900 rent on his apartment. In his bio for acting positions, there was a notable entry where he billed himself as "a highly talented actor, voiceover artist and singer . . . capable of performing over 30 different voices and numerous different accents." He then added this line: "I am also very skilled at embodying characters and expressing emotions in a way that causes people to become captivated and entranced." It would prove disturbingly prophetic.

Chansley would return to living with his mother, Martha, in her modest home in Glendale, Arizona. Around this time, he began to wear his signature horned Shaman outfit around the neighborhood. He would rave at rallies about pedophiles and secret codes embedded in signs. He raged against the COVID "globalist propaganda hoax." He wrote two self-published books, including one titled *One Mind at a Time: A Deep State of Illusion*. The book is an amalgamation of conspiracy theories. In a classic reference stretching back to the Fries Rebellion, even the Illuminati are raised by Chansley as one of the sinister forces that have shaped our society. The book shows the thin line between the rhetoric of conventional and conspiracy politics. Chansley begins his book with a quote from John F. Kennedy, who declared, "For we are opposed around the world by a monolithic and ruthless conspiracy that relies primarily on covert means for expanding its sphere of influence." For Chansley, that was a historical reveal hidden among such speeches, an early recognition of a deep state at work in our country. In late 2020, he found himself drawn to "Stop the Steal" rallies. For Chansley, the Trump claims of a stolen election pushed every button on his conspiracist and activist impulses. It also gave him an audience for his Shaman performance art shtick.

This self-created, cartoonish persona seemed both intentional and irresistible for Chansley. He was consumed by conspiracies and tapped into an internet space with millions of like-minded people. When Trump summoned followers to Washington, it was one engagement that the QAnon Shaman would not miss. Videotapes showed him thanking officers on the Senate floor, and a court found that his flagpole was not a dangerous weapon. For Chansley, his conduct appeared part protest and part performance art. He had long trafficked in conspiracy theories and was a favorite on the QAnon site. Indeed, he would show up at Trump rallies with a sign reading "Q Sent Me." He was a weird mix of a climate activist, conspiracist, and actor. Some called him an "ecofascist." Others referred to Chansley as part of a movement of people practicing "[c]onspirituality . . . the overlap between New Age/wellness culture and conspiracy culture." After leaving the Navy, Chansley experimented in psychedelic drugs, including mushrooms and peyote, as part of self-elevating mystic ceremonies. He would incorporate cultural and movie images into his wacky New Age conspirituality, including organizing "red pill" parties (named after the red pill/blue pill choice of consciousness in the movie *The Matrix*). He used names like Yellowstone Wolf and spoke of how he "defeated dark demonic forces, held sacred ceremonies, cleansed ecosystems and liberated minds." His Facebook account captured a New Age mysticism that bordered on outright madness:

> Jake Angeli is a Self Initiated Shaman, Energetic Healer, Ordained Minister, Public Speaker & Published Author. He is native to the Valley of the Sun and has worked in the behavioral health field for over 6 years and has walked the Shamanic path for over a decade. During his Shamanic path, he underwent over ninety hours worth of tattooing, wrote several books, influenced hundreds of lives and spent endless hours in deep trance states and meditation. He is a metaphysical warrior, a compassionate healer and a servant of the Divine Creator God.

The one thing that he never personally embraced was violence. He did use inflammatory language including calling former vice president Mike Pence a "f—ing traitor" and leaving a note on January 6th that read "It's Only a Matter of Time. Justice Is Coming!" Nevertheless, the government imposed the harshest possible conditions on Chansley in jail, including a long stint in segregation that appeared entirely gratuitous, and opposed every effort to release him on bail. Rather than argue that he was violent, the government insisted he was simply a "dangerous man obstructing the normal functioning of the United States government." Even Judge Royce Lamberth admitted that Chansley was being treated more harshly due to his fame: "He made himself the image of the riot, didn't he? For good or bad, he made himself the very image of this whole event."

In seeking a long sentence of incarceration, federal prosecutor Kimberly Paschall dismissed arguments that Chansley was nonviolent. At his sentencing, she played videos showing Chansley yelling along with the crowd and insisted "that is not peaceful." In a rambling statement to the court, Chansley apologized for "a lot of bad juju that I never meant to create." Lamberth hit Chansley with a heavy forty-one-month sentence for "obstructing a federal proceeding." It was an excessively harsh sentence for a first-time, nonviolent offender. Chansley, and the others on the floor, deserved incarceration for obstructing the certification and parading around on the Senate floor. However, concerns over the sentencing were magnified by videotapes showing that Chansley walked through one of the doors with hundreds of others after the breach. He walked by groups of Capitol police officers and was even led through the Capitol by officers. While he was charged with obstruction, he was assisted by officers in gaining entry to the empty Senate floor. The videotape was known to the January 6th Committee but never shared with the public.

The government insisted that Chansley waive an appeal of the plea agreement as a condition for his plea agreement. Once again, none of this means that Chansley or others were wrongly arrested or wrongly punished. Rather, the importance of Chansley as an example to others in the "shock and awe" campaign seemed to drive the demand for the harsh sentencing more than the evidence of his conduct did.

Roughly a dozen defendants among the hundreds of cases were charged with sedition. They are worthy of more serious charges, but the use of sedition laws will be discussed in chapter 29. Notably, some of these sedition defendants discussed a fringe theory that President Trump would invoke the Insurrection Act of 1807, a possibility that mainstream media like National Public Radio explored. The law allowed the president "to call forth the militia for the purpose of suppressing such insurrection, or of causing the laws to be duly executed." Under their twisted view, Trump would invoke the act and deputize militia members to prevent the stealing of the election. In other words, Trump would stop the insurrection of the Democrats. The theory spread across the internet and, according to the "militia" members, led them to bring weapons and store them near the Capitol. It was the perfect pitch for conspiracists with Trump projected at the head of a citizen army arresting insurrectionist Democrats.

The Insurrection Act theory and the election fraud claims before the riot are analogous to the false constitutional claims that fueled the Fries Rebellion. In that uprising, farmers were told by the Reverend Jacob Eyermann that the underlying tax was unconstitutional and invalid. He even waved around what he claimed was a copy of the Constitution and federal laws to assure the farmers that they were acting in support of rule of law. The Fries Rebellion in retrospect was clearly no rebellion despite convictions for treason. Today, the claims of the Adams administration are shocking and even laughable that this protest against a tax was an insurrection. That is the benefit of the separation of time. Watching the rage of others lacks that distance and perspective. In the case of January 6th, the actions of violent groups like the Proud Boys and the Oath Keepers are more serious than those of the Fries "rebels." Questioning the framing of their actions as an actual insurrection does not lessen their culpability or punishment. However, for the thousands of others on that day, they do share a common element with the Fries farmers. They believed the election fraud claims of the president and a host of lawyers, who assured them not only of the factual basis for the fraud claims but of their right to stop the certification. Even if one accepts that a dozen individuals engaged in a seditious conspiracy, the charges indicate that over 99 percent of those who participated in the protest and the riot were not found to have such an intent. The cases support the public view that this was a protest that became a riot over support for Trump rather than any desire for rebellion.

Notably, Special Counsel Jack Smith brought charges in 2023 against Trump in two separate cases, including one based on charges linked to the 2020 election and the January 6th riot. The second indictment does raise some of these same free speech issues, but Smith notably did not find sufficient evidence to charge Trump with any sedition charge or either insurrection or incitement. That did not stop an array of legal actions designed to bar Trump from the 2024 ballots under Section 3 of the

Fourteenth Amendment. It is arguably one of the most dangerous arguments to emerge in decades based on a disqualification for those who "engaged in insurrection or rebellion against the same." It then adds that that disqualification can extend to those who have "given aid or comfort to the enemies thereof." Despite an earlier court ruling that this provision requires action from Congress, proponents argue that any state can unilaterally bar anyone based on this rationale.

As noted above, Democratic politicians have called for the disqualification of not only Trump but 120 Republican members of Congress under the theory that they gave aid and comfort to the "January 6 insurrection." By simply declaring the riot to be an actual rebellion or insurrection, advocates claim the right to bar one of the leading candidates for the presidency on a state-by-state basis. Not only would such an argument allow both parties to engage in opportunistic disqualifications, but it ignores the clear language of the amendment. January 6 was many things, but it was not a rebellion or an insurrection. Only a small number of individuals were charged with seditious conspiracy, which entails the effort to disrupt official proceedings. No politicians were charged with incitement or insurrection or conspiracy to commit those offenses. While a criminal charge is not a prerequisite under the amendment, a riot seems a far cry from a civil war that costs hundreds of thousands of lives.

The impetus for constitutional provision came in the 39th Congress in December 1865 when members were shocked to see Alexander Stephens, the Confederate vice president, waiting to take a seat with other former Confederate senators and military officers. Justice Edwin Reade of the North Carolina Supreme Court explained, "The idea [was] that one who had taken an oath to support the Constitution and violated it, ought to be excluded from taking it again." Advocates insist that "insurrection or rebellion" can be read broadly to include any effort to obstruct a constitutional function. In the case of Trump, that claim still relies on his continued assertion of unfounded legal theories and factual claims as well as his January 6th speech. The problem again is any limiting principle. It ignores the clear textual limitation to cases involving a prior "insurrection or rebellion." When figures such as Representative Jamie Raskin challenged Trump's certification in 2016, they also lacked a legal or factual basis. There were also riots occurring after the election. Under this theory, Raskin and Democrats could be barred from ballots in endless tit-for-tat actions carried out on a state-by-state basis.

Notably, the first court to adopt this reasoning to bar a politician from a ballot based on January 6th was New Mexico state judge Francis Mathew in 2022. The opinion disqualifying a local politician named Couy Griffin was conclusory and poorly supported. It notably began with a long quotation of the charge given by Illinois judge Peter Stenger Grosscup in a case in 1894 on insurrectionists. It was a telling choice. The "insurgents" denounced by Grosscup were union organizers that the court sought to strip of both their free speech and freedom for protesting work conditions. Grosscup is quoted by Mathew for declaring that "every person who knowingly incites, aids, or abets them, no matter what his motives may be, is likewise an insurgent." Grosscup called for federal troops to put down union organizers and is associated with the abuses of the period. The reliance on Grosscup's analysis is a chilling return to the use of sedition to punish viewpoints deemed dangerous or inflammatory.

The January 6th riot seemed to bring us back to where we began in the early Republic with cries of oppression on one side and insurrection on the other. This history shows a recurring cycle of panic politics and speech suppression in the United States. It is an intriguing contradiction for a country founded on a revolutionary view of free speech. The U.S. remains the world's leading protector of free speech even as our closest allies roll back this indispensable right. Yet our pendulous history of crackdowns on free speech is the result of the reembracing of Blackstonian views of free speech and sedition that took place soon after the revolution. That wrong turn by the Adams administration was quickly reenforced by the courts, which began decades of struggle over the meaning of free speech in the United States.

Part III

HOLMES AND
DOUSING THE FIRE
OF FREE SPEECH

Twenty-One

HOLMES AND THE
"ROUTE TO HELL"

The history of free speech in the United States was shaped by periods of rage. However, free speech itself was not the product of such rage. It is a right that can transcend the rage by binding a people to a core, defining value of human expression. In that sense, these periods were catalytic but not the cause for the erosion of free speech. The cause was a weakening of free speech by courts and intellectuals who saw it as much as a destabilizing element as a defining right in our system. History reveals a nation founded on a revolutionary vision of free speech that many saw as a natural right. Almost immediately after ratifying a sweeping expression of this right under the First Amendment, the same Blackstonian view from the British tradition reasserted itself through judicial decisions. It was that judicial regression that not only would curtail the scope of the right but also foster later anti-speech policies and prosecutions. After all, political figures such as John Adams were able to criminalize free speech only because they were enabled by a host of judicial figures.

Before we can restore this right, it is essential to understand the theoretical foundation for the qualification of this right over two centuries. It is a functionalist view of free speech that allowed endless trade-offs and concessions in the protection of political and social minority viewpoints. No single figure was more influential in this functional view than Oliver Wendell Holmes. Moreover, no figure more personifies the struggle of American thought over free speech. Holmes's story encapsulates how the promise of free speech was lost on later generations of intellectuals in America. Understanding Holmes goes a long way to understanding the intellectual and social forces behind the revision of the right after the Revolution. The underlying positivist and functionalist views that shaped Holmes's approach to free speech still hold sway with many in our society. If one wants to find a new path for free speech, one should start where Oliver Wendell Holmes lost his way.

Holmes famously observed, "The life of the law has not been logic, it has been experience." The observation laid the foundation for Holmes's masterful writings on the common law, the evolution of law from cases over time. It also may have captured Holmes's own experiential knowledge and perspective. He was a jurist who would write some of the most farsighted opinions in the history of the Court, breaking away from decades of calcified precedent. Holmes was a man who had learned to trust his instincts and his pragmatic perspective. That background would have a pronounced impact on how Holmes viewed natural law and "transcendental" truths. It would lead him to some of his worst and most damaging mistakes as a jurist.

Holmes was more than the author of some of the most important cases limiting free speech. He embodied the deep divisions over the foundations and the functions of free speech that have raged since our founding. Like the analogy to fire that Holmes repeatedly used to describe free speech, it is a right that he viewed as both an essential element of and an existential threat to democracy. It could produce the energy for our system *and* engulf that system in a conflagration of

dissent. Holmes would seek to cut off "the breath" that feeds the "flame" of dissenting free speech. That is why Holmes remains such an enormously complex and enigmatic figure. He could articulate liberating principles in one opinion only to become the voice of oppression in the next. There was no one more patriotic or courageous. Holmes proved that in the war. However, he was a man at war with himself on the basis for free speech and, more generally, the use of natural law.

From college to the Court, Holmes exhibited an admirable skepticism; a willingness to challenge fixed assumptions and seek new understandings of the world around us. He wrote that "to have doubted one's own first principles is the mark of a civilized man." The question is what principles Holmes ultimately embraced, particularly in the area of free speech, where his skepticism would lead to the wrong side of sedition. He was described as possessing a "certain severity of . . . character" and a "chastity [of] intellectual style." The biographer Stephen Budiansky would later note that "it was chastity not in the sense of moral innocence, but in a kind of austere purity and rigor about the process of thought itself." That chastity and austerity in thought could produce opinions devoid of empathy or lenity.

Holmes was capable of opinions that could be poetic or horrific, depending on which Holmes was dominant at the moment. In *Buck v. Bell*, the Court considered the case of Carrie Buck, twenty-one, a woman who was raped and became pregnant at seventeen. After she gave birth, she was committed to the Virginia State Colony for Epileptics and Feebleminded. It was the very institution where her mother, Emma Buck, was sent on the same grounds of being "feebleminded." Dr. Albert S. Priddy designated Buck as the first person to be sterilized under a new state law after concluding that she is "unfit to exercise the proper duties of motherhood" due to her "anti-social conduct and mental defectiveness." The case would come before the two icons of American law, Holmes and Brandeis, who would sign off on the constitutionality of the horrific law. Holmes wrote the opinion, declaring (with only one dissent) that "three generations of imbeciles are enough." With other notorious decisions such as *Dred Scott* and *Korematsu*, *Buck* abandoned the fundamental guarantees of our constitutional system and yielded to our worse prejudices. Indeed, Holmes's opinion would be later cited as authority by the Nazis in Germany for their own eugenic sterilization laws. Holmes's cold and callous views were evident in his private correspondence, where he sounded like a Boston Brahman with a Malthusian fetish. He wrote to a close friend that the right to life was a social construction: "Most of the great things have been done with thin populations, and as I am not a Catholic, I take no joy in increased members of ordinary ugly people."

Holmes would show the same disregard for free speech. Both as a member of the Massachusetts Supreme Court and as a Supreme Court justice, he routinely saw speech as a space defined by the law rather than any abstract principle. In 1915, Holmes would write the opinion in *Fox v. Washington* to uphold the conviction of Jay Fox, an anarchist who was criminally charged for writing a single article on a case involving nude swimming. The article was in defense of Stella Thornhill, who said that she liked to swim naked because it helped her rheumatism. The problem was that the good people of Pierce County, Washington, were likely anti-rheumatism but decidedly more anti–nude sunbathing. Fox wrote an article titled "The Nude and the Prudes" defending Thornhill and denouncing her prosecution. He praised the small "Home" community of anarchists as "a community of free spirits, who came out into the woods to escape the polluted atmosphere of priest-ridden, conventional society." He insisted that "one of the liberties enjoyed by the Homeites was the privilege to bathe in evening dress, or with merely the clothes nature gave them, just as they chose." While Thornhill was merely fined $65, Fox was sent to prison for two months under a clearly unconstitutional state law prohibiting any publication "advocating, encouraging or inciting, or having a tendency to encourage or incite the commission of any crime, breach of the peace, or act of violence, or which shall tend to encourage or advocate disrespect for law or for any court or courts of justice."

Holmes was unmoved. What is most striking is his tortured logic to avoid the constitutional question. Despite the obvious use of the statute to punish an opposing view, Holmes declared, "[I]t does not appear and is not likely that the statute will be construed to prevent publications merely because they tend to produce unfavorable opinions of a particular statute or of law in general." He then cavalierly added the following mind bender: "[T]he disrespect for law that was encouraged was disregard of it, an overt breach and technically criminal act. It would be in accord with the usages of English to interpret disrespect as manifested disrespect, as active disregard going beyond the line drawn by the law."

Holmes was a positivist who believed that the legitimacy and authority of a law came from its creation through a proper legislative process. His rejection of natural law, particularly in the early twentieth century, was not unique. This was the time of the rise of legal positivism and continued embrace of utilitarianism. The father of utilitarianism, Jeremy Bentham, called natural law "nonsense on stilts." In the early 1900s, figures such as Roscoe Pound were writing for a type of "sociological jurisprudence" that sought greater social justice and the balancing of social interests. Free speech was just one of those social interests to be balanced, and Pound rejected the individualistic view of the right. He noted, "[T]he individual gets so much fair play, that the public gets very little." Yet natural law arguments during this period were also taught as a type of orthodoxy in many schools, an overarching and unquestioned view that would clearly trigger the skeptical and freethinking Holmes.

The most striking aspect of Holmes's writings was not that he was a critic of natural law theories but that he was so vehement in that criticism. To Holmes, claims of natural rights were little more than a pretense or mythology used to avoid tough choices; "the jurist's search for criteria of universal validity." Again, the validity of a law for Holmes was found in the fact that a majority properly enacted a legislative choice. His clinical detachment was on display in a letter after his ruling in *Buck* when he told a friend, "I wrote and delivered a decision upholding the constitutionality of a state law for sterilizing imbeciles the other day— and felt that I was getting near to the first principle of real reform. I say merely getting near. I don't mean that the surgeon's knife is the ultimate symbol."

There is nothing nuanced about Holmes's dismissal of arguments for natural rights as merely an example of how a "dog will fight for his bone."

In a letter to English political theorist Harold Laski, Holmes seems to channel the rejection of natural law by philosophers such as David Hume as a bunch of conversation-stopping "oughts." Hume famously expressed his frustration over how his arguments asserting what "*is*, and *is not*" were often met with "an *ought*, or an *ought not*." Natural law arguments, for Hume, were a type of intellectual cheat to cut off further need for discussion or defense. In his letter, Holmes similarly mocked natural rights arguments as conclusory; "the values [that] are simply generalizations emotionally expressed." He tells Laski, "If as I sometimes suspect, you believe in some transcendental sanction, I don't."

It is a telling statement from a man who was raised by two abolitionists in Boston, was himself an ardent abolitionist, and would fight to free African Americans. That fight was presumably based (at least for his parents) on something more than the shifting preferences of the majority in a democratic society. It was based on concepts of the natural right of humanity to be free. The Holmeses were supporters of Frederick Douglass, who wrote about the "moral government of the universe" and "inexorable moral laws." Douglass declared "that the universe is governed by laws which are unchangeable and eternal." Even one of Holmes's most influential contemporaries, Ralph Waldo Emerson, wrote about how "All things are moral. . . . Justice is not postponed." Holmes believed in a war to set men free but seemed to avoid the natural law rationales for that freedom that were so central to the war.

There were strong intellectual currents pushing Holmes toward positivism and away from natural rights. Even as a college student, he questioned religious orthodoxy. Holmes's first publication occurred in December 1858 when he was seventeen years old in *Harvard Magazine*. In what became known as his "Books" column, he railed against organized religion and challenged his fellow classmates to think for themselves:

> A hundred years ago we burnt men's bodies for not agreeing with
> our religious tenets; we still burn their souls. And now some begin
> to say, Why is this so? Is it true that such ideas as this come from
> God? . . . And when these questions are asked around us,—when we,

almost the first of young men who have been brought up in an atmosphere of investigation, instead of having every doubt answered, It is written,—when we begin to enter the fight, can we help feeling it is a tragedy? Can we help going to our rooms and crying that we might not think? . . . Read no books of an agitating tendency; you will have enough by and by to distress you.

The column "Books" is revealing in not just the rejection of religious orthodoxy but the mocking of those who would limit books due to their "agitating tendency." Decades later, Holmes would be faced with "bad tendency" rationales for criminalizing speech. He would arguably become what he despised in cases like *Schenck*.

Holmes was a man with the unique ability to transcend his times, but he was also a man of his times. In that sense, the impact of the Civil War on Holmes can be easily overlooked in his intellectual evolution. His incredible experiences left him with a hardened resolve and cold pragmaticism. However, it may have had a far more profound impact on Holmes in his view of the absence of "transcendental" rights. Holmes would not be the first to be stripped of such faith in the face of the horrors of war, but his skepticism of religious dogma would grow more intense during the war. Before the war, Holmes was a restless youth. His father, Oliver Wendell Holmes Sr., taught medicine at Harvard and was a widely respected poet. Both father and son possessed brilliant minds, but Dr. Holmes lacked his son's rigidity and chastity of thought. Dr. Holmes actually started his career in law school but eventually switched over to medicine. Despite his obvious skills as a doctor, it would also fail to satisfy the creative impulse within him. He would later write that "I did not like one and I do not like the other." Where his son was a freethinker, Dr. Holmes was a free liver. He was quick with a witty retort and had a teasing quality that sometimes irritated his son. Holmes chastised his father for his faithful attendance of church and observed, "[L]ike other lax Unitarians there were questions that he didn't like to have asked."

While attending Harvard, Oliver Wendell Holmes Jr. was drawn to Socrates and his advocacy of "keen and caustic spirit of enquiry." It is an ironic choice, since the philosopher chose to die rather than yield his right to free thought and speech to the state. Yet Socratic skepticism found an eager disciple in Holmes. He was also greatly influenced by Emerson. Holmes was given a collection of Emerson's work by his parents, which he devoured. One can see why Emerson would appeal to the young Holmes: "Whoso would be a man, must be a nonconformist." Holmes's "Books" column also reflected a struggle against orthodoxy at Harvard and other schools. Charles Darwin had just published *On the Origin of Species* in 1859, and it was widely denounced by the faculty as dangerous and immoral. Holmes rebelled against such orthodoxy. He was intellectually restless and frustrated with the rigidity and narrowness of many faculty members. He was also now what he would later describe as a "pretty convinced abolitionist."

It was in the midst of this internal debate that Holmes was pulled into the conflagration of civil war. Like most of his friends, Holmes was eager to join the fight to preserve the Union and free the slaves. A regiment was to be formed at Harvard and would become the famed 20th Regiment, also known as the "Harvard Regiment" (though many of the enlisted men were from the German and Irish working class). What they lacked in combat experience, they made up in social connections. Stephen Budiansky described the list of officers as reading like "a page from Boston's social register with members of the Revere, Cabot, Putnam and other leading families." At one point, Holmes spotted Colonel Harry Lee Jr. walking across Harvard Yard. Lee was not just Holmes's cousin

but also the governor's aide-de-camp. Holmes asked him to speak to the governor about giving him a commission as an officer with the regiment. Lee's response was telling. He would later admit to Holmes that he had a feeling of "pity for your youth and delicacy." The Harvard regiment, including the officers, fought with great courage and would lose more men than all but four other regiments. Indeed, it would lose so many officers and men that it became known as "the Bloody Twentieth."

Holmes would eventually reach the rank of lieutenant colonel—a remarkable accomplishment, as Holmes seemed to virtually attract lead shot. His first major battle was Ball's Bluff, a disastrous engagement that illustrated the poor leadership of the Union army. The Union troops were placed on a bluff with a river to their backs and a massive Confederate force secreted in the woods. Holmes was first hit below the rib cage by what appeared a spent round. It knocked him down, and his commander told him to move to the rear. Instead, Holmes grabbed his sword and yelled for his men to follow him. He was then hit again, this time in the chest, with a minié ball, a newly invented hollow round that was heavier and hit with greater velocity than the old musket balls. Notably, Holmes eschewed religion even at this time of mortal danger. He later recounted:

> Of course when I thought I was dying the reflection that the majority vote of the civilized world declared that with my opinions I was en route for Hell came up with painful distinctions.—Perhaps the first impulse was tremulous—but then I said—by Jove, I die like a soldier anyhow . . . I am proud—then I thought I couldn't be guilty of a death-bed recantation—father and I had talked of that and were agreed that it generally meant nothing but a cowardly giving way to fear—Besides . . . has the approach of death changed my beliefs much? & to this I answered—No—Then came in my Philosophy—I am to take a leap in that dark—but now as ever I believe that whatsoever shall happen is best.

It is notable that Holmes believed his "opinions" committed him to Hell. Neither his contemplation of suicide nor the need for final confessions

weighed heavily on the young soldier. It suggests that Holmes was knowingly or effectively an atheist. Rather than religious faith, Holmes turned
to his "philosophy" for solace at death.

The wound came close to ending the career of Oliver Wendell Holmes
before it began. The doctors gave him even odds to survive. However,
it was common for men to linger in pain in field hospitals under triage
protocols. Holmes came prepared. His father had given him a bottle of
laudanum for if he were ever wounded. Holmes was resolved to take a
lethal dose. However, after pulling out the bottle, he passed out. When
he woke, someone had taken his bottle. There would be no suicide or
"route for Hell." Instead, Holmes was later put on a train in Philadelphia,
where his father suddenly appeared to take him home to Boston under
his care. Notably, Holmes was critical of his father's emotions in finding
him in the train car and criticized "his lack of restraint."

Dr. Holmes nursed his son back to health over the next six months,
but, as soon as Holmes could travel, he rejoined his unit just in time for
the Battle of Glendale. As the battle began, Holmes would look down the
line of infantry and spot a close cousin. They exchanged a wave between
them just before the cousin was obliterated by enemy shot. Later, Holmes
was a captain when Antietam became the bloodiest battle in United States
history up to that time. He was in command in the West Woods when the
20th Massachusetts was hit by an overwhelming Confederate counterat-
tack. This time Holmes was shot in the throat. He was left for dead, but
later was found staggering around the corpse-strewn field.

On the night of September 17, 1862, Dr. Holmes received the
dreaded news in the form of a telegram from a William G. LeDuc saying that his son was "shot through the neck thought not mortal" and
nothing more. A brilliant physician, Dr. Holmes knew quite well that
major wounds in the Civil War were often lethal. The war came just before major medical breakthroughs such as improvements in anesthesia
and basic understanding of germs. As a result, more soldiers died from
disease and dysentery than wounds. His mind careened with the maddening ambiguity of the message: "Through the neck,—no bullet left in
wound. Windpipe, food-pipe, carotid, jugular, half a dozen smaller, but

still formidable vessels, a great braid of nerves, each as big as a lamp-wick, spinal cord,—ought to kill at once, if at all. Thought not mortal, or not thought mortal,—which was it?" He immediately set out to make the long journey to the Virginia battlefield. He would later write a moving account in the December 1862 edition of the *Atlantic* titled "My Hunt After 'the Captain,'" a vivid account of searching among the thousands of wounded and killed for his son.

Dr. Holmes described as best he could the indescribable; how "the battle-field sucks everything into its red vortex" of piles of broken bodies, broken equipment, broken homes. Even the living left a haunting picture: "Delicate boys, with more spirit than strength, flushed with fever or pale with exhaustion or haggard with suffering, dragged their weary limbs along as if each step would exhaust their slender store of strength." He re-coiled at "something repulsive about the trodden and stained relics of the stale battle-field. It was like the table of some hideous orgy left uncleared, and one turned away disgusted from its broken fragments and muddy heeltaps." He passed through this wasteland to find his son and bring him home to recover. While his father was celebrated by critics, Holmes was angry with him and resented his article.

Once again, Holmes took months to recover and then, again, insisted on returning to his regiment. He arrived in Virginia just in time for the Battle of Chancellorsville, where he was wounded for a third time. This time, he was hit in the ankle by shrapnel and beat the odds again by not experiencing the common use of amputation for such wounds. After this wound, Holmes forbade his father from coming to his side and said that he did not "wish to meet any affectionate parent half way" on his return to Massachusetts. When the wounds did not kill him, dysentery almost suc-ceeded. Notably, Holmes wrote a note so that he could be identified in case he died in the field hospital. It simply read: "I am Capt. O.W. Holmes 20th Mass. Son of Oliver Wendell Holmes M.D. Boston." The note summed up the two most influential elements in his life: the war and his father. In the former, he would find clarity while, regarding the latter, he would remain conflicted.

Yet Holmes again did not find himself "en route for Hell" unless his return to his family home qualified. His recovery would spare him from the bloody fields of Gettysburg, where the 20th Massachusetts Infantry Regiment would again be devastated after taking the full brunt of General Pickett's charge. In one letter to his parents, Holmes described how "the dead of both sides lay piled in trenches 5 or 6 deep—wounded often writhing under superincumbent dead." Holmes had seen the horrors of war but would still write romantically of his experience. He insisted that "through our great good fortune, in our youth our hearts were touched with fire," which set veterans "apart by our experience."

That fire would burn Holmes to the core. He would write, "I am not the same man. [I] may not have the same ideas . . . & certainly am not so elastic as I was." What idealism was present in the student seemed to disappear in the man. He would lash out at the "Jingo spirit" used in war. He would reflect an almost visceral rejection of "transcendent" values. Holmes speaks almost clinically of "Man [as] an idealizing animal." Even his opinions distinguished the common law from some "brooding omnipresence in the sky." Rather than relying on some divine authority, "the common law in his view is rooted in the articulate voice of some sovereign or quasi-sovereign that can be identified." The brute force he saw on the battlefield seemed to leave him with a brute faith in government: "The law does not mean sympathetic advice [that] you may neglect if you choose, but stern monition that the club and bayonet are at hand ready to drive you to prison or the rope if you go beyond the established lines."

Holmes left something on the battlefields of Virginia, something buried beneath the bodies of friends and the wreckage of war. He had lost his faith in anything other than what law professor Albert Alschuler described as a "power-focused philosophy." When cases later came before him (for example, *Buck* and *Schenck)* demanding the recognition of an autonomy-based right, Holmes is dismissive to the point of mockery. He could no more see a transcendent right than he could a transcendent truth. He would write to diplomat Lewis Einstein in 1905, "I mean by truth simply what I can't help accepting. . . . Therefore I know nothing about absolute truth." He was a romantic who described his heart as touched by fire but could not, it seems, rekindle a faith in transcendent rights.

In all the accounts of Holmes's Civil War experiences, one reference stands out. After he was deployed with the Harvard Regiment, he brought with him a couple books, including Hobbes's *Leviathan*. This young officer sat in his tent reading Hobbes after his first encounter with the horrors of battle. Hobbes described the social contract that removed humans from the senseless violence of the state of Nature, where men lived in "continual fear, and danger of violent death; and the life of man, solitary, poor, nasty, brutish, and short." He is widely viewed as an early positivist, even though his writings referred to divine authority. For Hobbes, society was a human creation to escape the dystopian realities of Nature. In doing so, citizens gave up the freedoms they enjoyed in the state of Nature:

> This is more than consent, or concord; it is a real unity of them all in one and the same person, made by covenant of every man with every man, in such manner as if every man should say to every man: I authorise and give up my right of governing myself to this man, and authorise all his actions in like manner. . . . This is the generation of that great LEVIATHAN, or rather, to speak more reverently, of that mortal god to which we owe, under the immortal God, our peace and defence.

There was Holmes reading of the senseless violence of the state of Nature, surrounded by scenes that must have seemed like the return to that primitive state. He wrote of the horror of seeing a "carpet of blue-clad corpses strewn across the fields" and the "carpet of butternut and gray-clad corpses in the appropriately named Blood Lane." There were also glimpses of Holmes's detached and almost clinical view of the necessary evolution of the species. While telling his parents that they were overly optimistic about the war "because (excuse me) you are ignorant" of the Southern resolve, he looked on the bright side that civilization and progress might "conquer in the long run and will stand a better chance in the proper province." Professor Ronald Collins has noted how the letter "smacked of Darwinism."

It was a mosaic of the madness of mankind. Holmes marveled at "how immense the butcher's bill has been" in sadly reporting how "nearly every Regimental officer I knew or cared for is dead or wounded." In a passage that is reminiscent of his decision in *Buck*, Holmes later defended his callous disregard for any natural rights with reference to the carnage of war: "[T]he right to life—is sacrificed without a scruple not only in war, but whenever the interest of society, that is, of the predominant power in the community, is thought to demand it." Such rights, in his view, would rise and fall with Hobbes's "mortal God" of government.

Where previously discussed philosophers like Spinoza shared Holmes's interest in Hobbes, they came to a different conclusion about natural rights. Spinoza saw the creation of the state as a way for people to be fully human. For Holmes, it was safety, not natural rights, that was guaranteed by the state. The depth of these feelings was also revealed years later in a response of Holmes after he was given a few book suggestions from a close friend that included natural rights theories. Holmes admitted that this suggested reading left him in "a kind of rage." He seemed to harken back to his college and war years when he said, "[A]ll my life I have sneered at the natural rights of man." In his "rage," he would proceed to write his famous *Harvard Law Review* article on "Natural Law." It was a blistering rejection of natural law principles, including the declaration that "the jurists who believe in natural law seem to me to be in that naïve state of mind that accepts what has been familiar and accepted by them and their neighbors as something that must be accepted by all men everywhere."

Whatever the reason for his fervent rejection of natural rights, it would become manifest when faced with dissidents claiming the right to speak without fear of arrest. In some ways, these cases were the perfect storm of "the Captain." Holmes's love of the military and his positivist rejection of natural rights would prove controlling once again when faced with those seeking to undermine an even larger war. This was the jurist who wrote, "If conscripts are necessary for its army, it seizes them, and marches them, with bayonets in their rear, to death." He would have little sympathy for those accused and little interest in their broad notions of free expression. Those earlier voices in his life would be silenced, at least for now.

One such voice was that of his father in his last poem, which ironically dealt with the Boston Tea Party and heralded those who defied the government. The poem, "The Last Leaf," was inspired by a participant in the Tea Party who came from their area in Boston, Thomas Melville. The grandfather of *Moby-Dick* author Herman Melville, this Son of Liberty was at the center of the destruction, even later finding tea in his shoes. Dr. Holmes describes watching Melville, now an elderly man in his out-of-style "three-cornered hat," left as a humorous and incongruous object for the young:

> *But now he walks the streets,*
> *And looks at all he meets*
> *Sad and wan,*
> *And he shakes his feeble head,*
> *That it seems as if he said,*
> *"They are gone."*

The one man remained, Dr. Holmes noted, like "The last leaf upon the tree / In the spring." The poem captured how men but not memories fade with time. This "last leaf" reminded Dr. Holmes of a time of rebellion, of a defiance of a government viewed as denying their inalienable rights. His son would later sit in judgment of the "new leaves" from the same tree—with a far less charitable view of their dissent.

Twenty-Two

HOLMES AND SCHENCK: THE SOCIALIST IN A CROWDED THEATER

Holmes was a curious mix of the intellectual and the instinctual. The closest that Holmes would come to a transcendent belief was his fealty to democracy. It was not natural rights but the democratic process that gave the law its authority under his positivist perspective. Holmes once remarked, "If my fellow citizens want to go to Hell I will help them. It's my job." From the perspective of free speech advocates, that is precisely where he would send them in a case called *Schenck*.

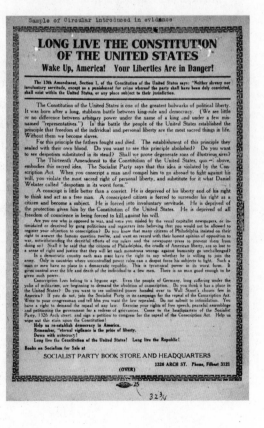

Sample of Circular introduced in evidence

LONG LIVE THE CONSTITUTION OF THE UNITED STATES
Wake Up, America!   Your Liberties Are in Danger!

The 13th Amendment, Section 1, of the Constitution of the United States says: "Neither slavery nor involuntary servitude, except as a punishment for crime whereof the party shall have been duly convicted, shall exist within the United States, or any place subject to their jurisdiction."

The Constitution of the United States is one of the greatest bulwarks of political liberty. It was born after a long, stubborn battle between king-rule and democracy. (We see little or no difference between arbitrary power under the name of a king and under a few misnamed "representatives.") In this battle the people of the United States established the principle that freedom of the individual and personal liberty are the most sacred things in life. Without them we become slaves.

For this principle the fathers fought and died. The establishment of this principle they sealed with their own blood. Do you want to see this principle abolished? Do you want to see despotism substituted in its stead? Shall we prove degenerate sons of illustrious sires?

The Thirteenth Amendment to the Constitution of the United States, quo—¹ above, embodies this sacred idea. The Socialist Party says that this idea is violated by the Conscription Act. When you conscript a man and compel him to go abroad to fight against his will, you violate the most sacred right of personal liberty, and substitute for it what Daniel Webster called "despotism in its worst form."

A conscript is little better than a convict. He is deprived of his liberty and of his right to think and act as a free man. A conscripted citizen is forced to surrender his right as a citizen and become a subject. He is forced into involuntary servitude. He is deprived of the protection given him by the Constitution of the United States. He is deprived of all freedom of conscience in being forced to kill against his will.

Are you one who is opposed to war, and were you misled by the venal capitalist newspapers, or intimidated or deceived by gang politicians and registrars into believing that you would not be allowed to register your objection to conscription? Do you know that many citizens of Philadelphia insisted on their right to answer the famous question twelve, and went on record with their honest opinion of opposition to war, notwithstanding the deceitful efforts of our rulers and the newspaper press to prevent them from doing so? Shall it be said that the citizens of Philadelphia, the cradle of American liberty, are so lost to a sense of right and justice that they will let such monstrous wrongs against humanity go unchallenged?

In a democratic country each man must have the right to say whether he is willing to join the army. Only in countries where uncontrolled power rules can a despot force his subjects to fight. Such a man or men have no place in a democratic republic. This is tyrannical power in its worst form. It gives control over the life and death of the individual to a few men. There is no man good enough to be given such power.

Conscription laws belong to a bygone age. Even the people of Germany, long suffering under the yoke of militarism, are beginning to demand the abolition of conscription. Do you think it has a place in the United States? Do you want to see unlimited power handed over to Wall Street's chosen few in America? If you do not, join the Socialist Party in its campaign for the repeal of the Conscription Act. Write to your congressman and tell him you want the law repealed. Do not submit to intimidation. You have a right to demand the repeal of any law. Exercise your rights of free speech, peaceful assemblage and petitioning the government for a redress of grievances. Come to the headquarters of the Socialist Party, 1326 Arch street, and sign a petition to congress for the repeal of the Conscription Act. Help us wipe out this stain upon the Constitution!

Help us re-establish democracy in America.
Remember, "eternal vigilance is the price of liberty.
Down with autocracy!
Long live the Constitution of the United States! Long live the Republic!

Books on Socialism for Sale at
SOCIALIST PARTY BOOK STORE AND HEADQUARTERS
1326 ARCH ST. Phone, Filbert 3121

(OVER)

25

32 3/4

212

Not much is known about Charles T. Schenck other than his political views and his position as general secretary of the U.S. Socialist Party. Schenck was against World War I and was joined by a mix of socialists and pacifists in opposing the draft. To that end, they used the names and addresses of draftees published in Philadelphia's *Bulletin* to encourage them to resist conscription. The socialists printed fifteen thousand copies of a circular and mailed some of them to draftees. One side was titled "Assert Your Rights," and the other side was titled "Long Live the Constitution of the United States." The circular asserted that the Selective Service Act was unconstitutional under the First and Ninth Amendments as denying religious convictions and impinging on rights retained of both citizens and states. Postmaster General Albert Burleson quickly banned the Philadelphia Socialist Party newspaper from being sent through the mail. The government noted that Schenck in particular had "continually harangued American militarism and American czardom . . . but [had] never had a word to say against German militarism or ruthlessness, not even at the time of the sinking of the Lusitania."

On August 28, 1917, armed agents with the Justice Department and the post office inspector raided the offices of the Socialist Party, looking for Schenck to arrest him for "a well-organized plot to foment sedition among men selected for the National Army." When they arrived, they did not find Schenck but a young store clerk named Clara Abramowitz and a group of men in a back room. They seized sixteen thousand circulars, books, and other papers including the "minute book" of the organization. When Schenck arrived, he was arrested with Abramowitz, Edward H. Wanamacher, and Alexander MacLeod for violating the Espionage Act. When Abramowitz secured bail, she reportedly told police, "Oh thanks. I will be back to work in the morning." The next day, the socialists put up a sign across the bookstore window reading "The Peoples Press, Suppressed by the Post Office, Help Us in Our Fight, Subscribe Here Now." It had the opposite effect. Hundreds of demonstrators appeared to "clean out the vipers," and a riot was only avoided by the last-minute arrival of the police.

The trial served only to highlight the lunacy of trying to kill ideas through the incarceration of individuals. Five defendants were each charged with the same three counts under the Espionage Act: Schenck, Charles Sehl, Elizabeth Baer, Jacob H. Root, and William J. Higgins. Baer was charged because she took the minutes of the socialist meetings. The government called eleven draftees who received the circular, but all eleven testified that it had no impact on them. Nevertheless, the government argued that the circular could only harm the war effort. In another such prosecution of socialists for handing out the circular, Charles E. Bartlett, the assistant district attorney, insisted that such literature could cause doubts in the minds of "lukewarm citizens." The government in the *Schenck* trial presented little evidence beyond the seized circulars, minutes, and recipients. It was enough. While Judge J. Whitaker Thompson ordered the jury to return not-guilty verdicts for the other three defendants for lack of evidence, Schenck and Baer were found guilty on all three counts. Yet the jury called for mercy and their attorney, Henry Nelson, said that the Philadelphia Socialist Party had agreed to censor itself and would not distribute any anti-draft literature for the duration of the war. Judge Thompson declared that the true culprits were the authors, who had escaped the government dragnet. That resulted in a relatively lenient sentence of six months for Schenck and ninety days for Baer.

In *Schenck v. United States*, the echo of early sedition cases resonated in Holmes's articulation of the "clear and present danger" test. Holmes declared, "It well may be that the prohibition of laws abridging the freedom of speech is not confined to previous restraints, although to prevent them may have been the main purpose." While Holmes sought to carve out a uniquely American approach to sedition, he was channeling Blackstone. Indeed, in a later letter from Harvard philosophy professor Zechariah Chafee Jr., Holmes was asked whether this opinion "was at all suggested to you by any writers on the subject or was the result entirely of reflections." Holmes responded that "I had taken [William] Blackstone and [Isaac] Parker of Mass. as unrefuted, wrongly." It was a shocking admission that suggested that, at the time of the opinion, Holmes was unaware or uninterested in the countervailing evidence of a broader intent behind the First Amendment. The reference to Judge Parker was equally chilling. In the 1825 case of *Commonwealth v. Blanding*, Parker handed down one

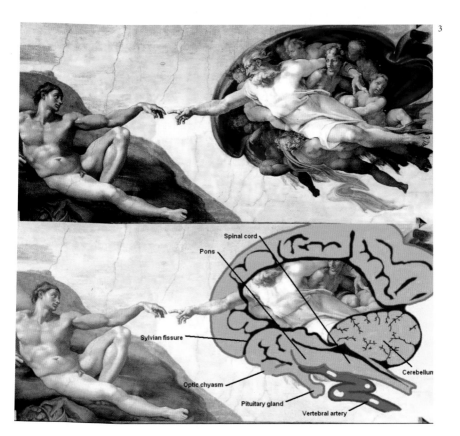

The Sistine Chapel and human brain.

1

Socialist Charlotte Anita Whitney remained defiant in speaking her mind, even refusing to ask for a pardon because, she said, "I've done nothing wrong."

2

Social reformer turned Supreme Court justice Louis Brandeis, who declared free speech "the indispensable right."

James Madison broke from his contemporaries in his sweeping defense of free speech and condemnation of the "monster" of sedition.

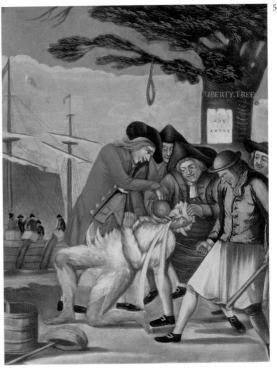

Tarring and feathering, used both in the American Revolution and later "rebellions" against tax collectors and government officials.

The Boston Tea Party was described by John Adams as displaying "a Dignity, a Majesty, a Sublimity" in the patriotic cause.

John Adams, who celebrated the Boston Tea Party, would become one of the most anti–free speech presidents in history.

Born into slavery, Ida Bell Wells would later defy lynchers and prosecutors to advocate for racial equality.

Cartoons were often used by Federalists and Jeffersonians to attack each other as traitors, such as this British cartoon showing Lady Liberty being ravaged by the French.

Victoria Claflin Woodhull, journalist, spiritualist, and reformer, challenged a host of sexual and political norms in American society.

Supreme Court associate justice Oliver Wendell Holmes would become the intellectual force behind restrictive views of free speech, as captured by his famous "shouting fire in a crowded theater" rationale for speech limitations.

12

Mug shot of former president Donald Trump, the first such presidential mug shot in history.

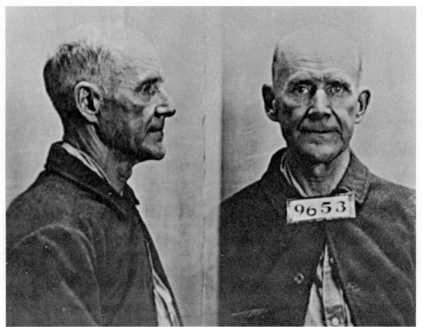

Socialist Eugene
Debs, who ran for
president from
prison, was jailed
for his exercise
of free speech.

Norman Rockwell's
penetrating clarity
was called "spurious"
by critics, but it
captured a certain
transcendent truth
about America.

Rockwell's *Freedom of Speech* painting captured a moment
where a Vermont selectman stood up to address
the financing of the building of a new school.

Rockwell's *The Connoisseur* was depicted in a Jackson Pollack style and would later prompt Willem de Kooning to declare, "It's better than Jackson!"

1873 caricature of John Stuart Mill, who articulated a harm principle that could be the foundation for a revival of free speech in the United States.

of the most anti–free speech and anti–free press rulings in history. The case involved James Blanding, who was a farmer and the city clerk. He wrote an article accusing an innkeeper of causing the death of a customer through alcohol poisoning. Parker adopted the narrow Blackstonian view of free speech as well as the rejection of truth as a defense. He called such writings the work of "private intermeddlers" that could lead to "duels and assassinations." He dismissed the arguments over "the *liberty* of the press" as nothing more than "the *licentiousness* of the press."

Holmes adeptly framed the issue in the same narrow terms of prior restraint, noting that it may not have been the sole focus of the First Amendment, but it "may have been the main purpose." Holmes clearly saw the inherent conflict with the free speech values protected under the First Amendment and the danger presented by sedition prosecution. He addressed that disconnect by focusing not on the speech but on the inchoate crime. Under this construct, speech is converted into an attempt to commit the criminal offense depending on the circumstances and time of expression. Thus, speech can be criminal or noncriminal depending on the audience and the context if the words "are used in such circumstances and are of such a nature as to create a clear and present danger that they will bring about" a crime like obstructing the draft. The test was subjective and malleable as shown in Schenck's conviction for making arguments in opposing conscription.

The comparison to the early English cases is tragically ironic. The Framers sought to break from a system that allowed for the prosecution of Henry Redhead Yorke, for working to "combine . . . disaffected and ill-disposed subjects . . . to break and disturb the peace and tranquility of the realm, and to rise and excite riots, commotions, and tumults therein." Like Schenck, Yorke was attempting to rally fellow citizens in support of core legal values. He could not be tried for treason, so he was tried for a speech crime. Yorke represented a clear and present danger of causing unrest or opposition to Crown authority. The "clear and present danger" test simply cloaked the same speech crime with a patina of legal process. The danger was that Schenck might bring about a change in the views of others: to rally the public against the war.

The fluidity of Holmes's test was perfectly nightmarish for free speech. For a right demanding bright lines, Holmes described a right that was dependent on the context on whether it would be tolerated or sanctioned—the judicial embodiment of "panic politics" into panic precedent. That path took Holmes to arguably the single most damaging line on free speech in the Court's history:

> We admit that in many places and in ordinary times the defendants
> in saying all that was said in the circular would have been in their
> constitutional rights. But the character of every act depends on the
> circumstances in which it is done. The most stringent protection of
> free speech would not protect a man in falsely shouting fire in a the-
> ater and causing a panic. . . . The question in every case is whether the
> words used are used in such circumstances and are of such a nature
> as to create a clear and present danger that they will bring about the
> substantiative evils that congress has a right to prevent.

The line had an immediate intuitive appeal as a judicial sound bite rivaling other notable "one liners" like "the Fourth Amendment protects people, not places." However, unlike *Katz v. United States*, it was the place that drove the decision in *Schenck*. Where *Katz* expanded privacy protections for Americans, Holmes's line would prove a virtual license for judges and legislators to limit free speech. At the time, University of Chicago law professor Ernst Freund responded to Holmes's analogy by denouncing it as cloaking the same intolerance of an "unsafe doctrine" with a catchy phrase.

"Shouting fire in a crowded theater" quickly became a mantra for every effort to curtail free speech. The fact that Holmes actually wrote "falsely shouting fire in a theater and causing panic" is long forgotten. Yet the new rendition is telling in a number of respects. First, Holmes referred to "falsely" shouting fire. This may seem obvious since you could not be punished for crying fire when there was a fire. However, as discussed above, the English and some early American cases maintained that true statements could indeed be seditious or criminal. The common rendition also omits the added condition of "causing panic." From these two omissions, it would appear that a person can be held liable for making the statement (regardless of intent) and without regard to how it is received. That broader meaning would be in line with past sedition and speech prosecutions. Indeed, the evidence in *Schenck* did not support the claim that the circular actually caused panic, or draft dodging. Finally, the common rendition adds the qualifier that this alarm was raised not just in a theater but a "crowded" theater. It is notable that the condition that the statement was false would be removed, but the condition of congestion would be added. A "crowded theater" captured more of the imminent danger of panic to justify the censorship. Thus, when Justice William Douglas (who replaced Brandeis on the Court) would write a concurrence in *Brandenburg* to adopt a more protective standard than *Schenck*, he would refer to shouting in a "crowded theater" to emphasize that it was speech "brigaded with action." The line would quickly take hold not just of public parlance but decisions. Dozens of decisions. The line would be used to curtail the scope of free speech protections in cases dealing with conflicts from indecency to noise regulations. It would even take hold in society. Holmes's words would be repeated by figures such as Mike Tyson, who once responded to critics by noting, "It's not like I yelled fire in a theater or something."

The rewording of the Holmes line captures the central problem with it. It effectively cast Schenck's free speech claim as absolutist and absurdist. Rather than deal with Schenck's obvious political speech (including ironically the discussion of constitutional rights), Holmes offered an analogy that became the more appealing framework for the case. The tremendous penetration of the line masked the shallow depth in its underlying premise. It is the classic dichotomy of speech and harm: the balancing of the abstract benefits of free expression against the real costs of its use. The analogy was immediately challenged, including Chafee's observation that Schenck was much more like a "man who gets up in a theater between the acts and informs the audience honestly but perhaps mistakenly that the fire exits are too few or locked."

Twenty-Three

HOLMES AND THE "DEBS REBELLION"

The full impact of Holmes's functionalism would become clear in two other cases decided shortly after *Schenck*. Indeed, one of those cases (*Debs*) may have been the actual origin of the Holmes theater analogy. The first of the rulings came in *Frohwerk v. United States*. Writing for the Court, Holmes again upheld a conviction under the Espionage Act of 1917 for the exercise of free speech. In this case, the punishment would be breathtaking: a ten-year sentence. Again, Brandeis would join Holmes with a unanimous court.

Jacob Frohwerk was the editor of a German-language newspaper in Kansas City, the *Missouri Staats Zeitung*. He was against the war; he believed that Germany was not the instigator of the war and that our intervention was unwarranted. He published thirteen antiwar articles between July and December 1917. Notably, none of these publications expressly opposed the draft, and none was shown to have been sent directly to draftees. It was an even more extreme version of *Schenck*, where the witnesses testified that the anti-draft circular had no impact on them. Here Frohwerk was opposing the war, not the draft, and did not target draftees. Holmes, however, wrote an opinion upholding the conviction on the presumptive bad tendency of the political views. Holmes recognized that "[i]t may be that all this might be said or written even in time of war in circumstances that would not make it a crime. We do not lose our right to condemn either measures or men because the country is at war." He then proceeded to gut that fundamental principle by just presuming the worst:

> But we must take the case on the record as it is, and, on that record, it is impossible to say that it might not have been found that the circulation of the paper was in quarters where a little breath would be enough to kindle a flame, and that the fact was known and relied upon by those who sent the paper out.

Where *Schenck* was intellectually ill-informed, *Frohwerk* was intellectually lazy. Holmes seems to begrudgingly recognize the need to protect free speech in times of war, but dismisses it in the next breath by saying that the mere potential of harm was sufficient to criminalize speech. Of course, such harm would come only from others agreeing with the factual and legal arguments made by Frohwerk, so his views would have to be silenced.

If Holmes wanted to build to a crescendo in this terrifying trifecta, he succeeded with *Debs v. United States*. As noted by Professor Carlton F. W. Larson, the case came before the Court with *Schenck* and the record included the argument of United States attorney Edwin Wertz to the jury that "a man in a crowded auditorium, or any theatre, who yells 'fire' and there is no fire, and a panic ensues and someone is trampled to death, may be rightfully indicted and charged with murder." Notably, Wertz's rendition comes closer to the common rewording of Holmes's analogy. It includes the adjective "crowded" and omits the condition that it is a false alarm. The man who was risking panic was Eugene Debs.

Eugene Victor Debs was a high school dropout who would become one of the most important political leaders in our history. Debs worked various jobs while taking classes at night, starting work at fourteen years of age cleaning grease from truck engines. He showed an early interest in politics and union organizing. He would help lead the Pullman Strike in 1894, which, notably, was quickly called "Debs Rebellion." Due to his involvement, the *New York Times* declared Debs "a lawbreaker at large,

an enemy of the human race." After securing an injunction to end the strike, President Grover Cleveland sent in federal troops and arrested Debs. As a result, workers were blacklisted and roughly thirty were killed in the crackdown. While in prison, Debs would be given a copy of *Das Kapital*. He would emerge from prison a dedicated socialist and would run for president five times, including one campaign while in prison.

The *Debs* case began with a speech in Canton, Ohio. The government had agents in the crowd as well as a stenographer to write down every word. Notably, unlike figures like Frohwerk, Debs had no love for Germany, which he denounced for its militarism and the arrest of socialists. He primarily opposed the war as an outgrowth of the capitalist system in which the "master class" declared wars and the "subject class" died in them. With only one direct reference to the war, Debs warned that "[t]he master class has had all to gain and nothing to lose, while the subject class has had nothing to gain and all to lose—especially their lives." He largely spoke generally and historically:

> They have always taught and trained you to believe it to be your patriotic duty to go to war and to have yourselves slaughtered at their command. . . . But in all the history of the world you, the people, have never had a voice in declaring war, and strange as it certainly appears, no war by any nation in any age has ever been declared by the people.

It was political speech in its purest form. Just as John Peter Zenger had railed against the corruption of the Crown, Debs rallied against what he saw as the corruption of capitalism. For that he was arrested.

In a repeat from *Schenck*, prosecutor Edwin Wertz called various young men subject to the draft, but they said that the speech did not discourage them from registering. Moreover, the stenographer that he used turned out to be a used-car salesman who admitted that he did not write down a complete or verbatim account. Only one witness would appear for the defense: Debs. He spoke directly to the jury for two hours and refused to yield in his views in opposition to "the present government" and "social system":

> Your honor, I ask no mercy, I plead for no immunity. I realize that finally the right must prevail. I never more fully comprehended than now the great struggle between the powers of greed on the one hand and upon the other the rising hosts of freedom. I can see the dawn of a better day for humanity. The people are awakening. In due course of time they will come into their own.

He then declared to the jury: "What you may choose to do to me will be of small consequence after all. I am not on trial here. There is an infinitely greater issue that is being tried in this court today. American institutions are on trial before a court of American citizens. Time will tell." He was right about the real issue before the court. Our system was on trial, and it failed utterly and completely. He was sentenced to three concurrent sentences of ten years in prison.

This is a record that should have been condemned by the entire Court. Instead, they settled the "great issue" against free speech. Writing for a unanimous Court, Holmes ruled for the government, stating that these words had the "natural tendency and reasonably probable effect" of deterring people from supporting or enlisting in the war. Putting aside the fact that Debs should be allowed to speak against the war and the draft, Holmes again simply disregarded the lack of any clear call to avoid conscription:

> The statement was not necessary to warrant the jury in finding that one purpose of the speech, whether incidental or not does not matter,

was to oppose not only war in general but this war, and that the opposition was so expressed that its natural and intended effect would be
to obstruct recruiting.

Again, Holmes engages in embarrassingly biased and shallow analysis. Since the speech would not support conviction, Holmes declared Debs
could be convicted by his associations. Holmes pointed out that Debs expressed support for an "Anti-War Proclamation and Program" and that
this proclamation promoted antiwar protests. The opinion borders on the
incoherent:

> Evidence that the defendant accepted this view and this declaration
> of his duties at the time that he made his speech is evidence that if in
> that speech he used words tending to obstruct the recruiting service
> he meant that they should have that effect. The principle is too well es-
> tablished and too manifestly good sense to need citation of the books.

It is never a good sign when jurists dismiss the need for citations in
claiming guilt from uncharged statements. Holmes explains that a statement that Debs supported in St. Louis was ample reason to conclude that
"the words [Debs] used had as their natural tendency and reasonably
probable effect to" commit the underlying crime. That is, a speech that
did not call for opposition to the draft had the "natural tendency and reasonably probable effect" to obstruct the draft because of statements that
he supported previously in a proclamation used hundreds of miles away.
In other words, if you have supported a cause previously, you would be
guilty of a crime regardless of if your speech actually calls for a prohibited
act. Under this logic, Debs could not speak against war generally unless
he denounced the earlier proclamation or expressly supported the war. It
is not reason but rage. State rage reinforced by the courts.

In 1921, Debs would be released from jail by Warren Harding. However, Harding did not give him a pardon, only a commutation. Indeed,
Harding emphasized that Debs remained a dangerous man and "there is
no question of his guilt." He remained dangerous because of his ideas and

oratory skills: "He is an old man, not strong physically. He is a man of much personal charm and impressive personality, which qualifications make him a dangerous man calculated to mislead the unthinking and affording excuse for those with criminal intent." After developing health problems in jail, Debs died not long after his release.

During this period, Holmes was privately challenged in his views by both fellow judges and academics. One of those was a judge who equaled Holmes in stature and intellect, Judge Learned Hand. The New York judge is a legal icon for his brilliant opinions, particularly in his articulation of a test for negligence in torts. In *Masses Publishing Co. v. Patten*, Hand ruled against a New York City postmaster in the use of the Espionage Act of 1917 to prevent the mailing of antiwar material. It is celebrated as one of the most powerful decisions in favor of free speech—rejecting the very basis of cases like *Schenck*. However, beneath its endorsement of speech tolerance, *Masses* reveals the same conceptual flaw of functionalism. After finding that the Espionage Act was not intended to target "the spreading of false rumors which may embarrass the military," Hand rejected the "bad tendency" rationale. Even though he accepted that the antiwar material had "a tendency to arouse emulation in others," he ruled that was not enough to justify the censorship of speakers. It was an important break with Blackstone, and Hand was justifiably heralded by academics as unrecognized for his free speech jurisprudence. Yet Hand was not interpreting the First Amendment broadly but the statute narrowly. In so doing, he adopted an artificial construct that Congress would never have intended such a draconian, anti–free speech measure. In reality, it appears precisely what some had in mind. The Espionage Act was an act of state rage against dissenters, not just a measure against spies. Instead, in a letter to Holmes, Hand explained that he was demanding tolerance:

> Here I take my stand. Opinions are at best provisional hypotheses, incompletely tested. The more they are tested, after the tests are well scrutinized, the more assurance we may assume, but they are never absolutes. So we must be tolerant of opposite opinions or varying opinions by the very fact of our incredulity of our own.

For Hand, the tolerance for free speech was a recognition that you or others could be wrong. Both Holmes and Hand had read John Stuart Mill and his view that one must accept that fallibility of man in advancing "wrong opinions and practices." Hand would prove more faithful to that precept, but only up to a point. Hand's narrow functionalist view of free speech would lead him to uphold the convictions of Eugene Dennis and other Communists for sedition under the Smith Act of 1940. Hand applied the same functionalist rationalizations, though in fairness he was bound to some extent by prior precedent. Indeed, Hand seemed to merge his famous "Hand formula" of negligence into constitutional law. He defined negligence as a formula of B<PL, or the relationship of the "burden of precaution" balanced against the probability of a loss and the cost of the loss. In *Dennis v. United States*, he seemed to adopt a type of negligence standard for speech prosecutions, declaring that a court must weigh the "gravity of the evil, discounted by its improbability." For Hand, like Holmes, this was a legislative determination, and it meant that Congress could use the courts to make the practical decisions between repression and liberty.

Debs was arguably the lowest point for Holmes the judicial nihilist. Having forsaken transcendent truths, Holmes found himself channeling the worst impulses of speech control. He had finally hit rock bottom in affirming the incarceration of a political figure for sharing his historical and legal opinions. While he would not change his relativistic view of free speech, Holmes did appear to regret the practical effects of his rulings. He would make a surprising turn in *Abrams v. United States*, where he would file a dissent in support of free speech. The dissent revealed the inherent struggle within Holmes. It left us with two Holmeses: the civil libertarian willing to stand up for the least popular in our society and his evil twin, who saw dissent as a clear and present danger to that society.

Twenty-Four

THE GOOD HOLMES AND THE ABANDONMENT OF *SCHENCK*

The "good Holmes" emerged from the wreckage of *Schenck*. In 1919, in *Schenck*, he used his renowned intellect to deliver a body blow to free speech. In one line about shouting fire in a theater, Holmes would snuff out calls for broader protections of free speech. Yet, ten years later, in *United States v. Schwimmer*, Holmes would sound almost Lockean as he declared that "[i]f there is any principle of the Constitution that more imperatively calls for attachment than any other it is the principle of free thought—not free thought for those who agree with us but freedom for the thought that we hate."

It appears that this shift in Holmes was not sudden but may have been building even before *Schenck*. In one case in 1918, *Baltzer v. United States*, Louis Brandeis went to his chambers to ask Holmes to write what he describes as "another dissent on burning themes." At issue were a group of farmers who signed a petition objecting to the number of draftees being taken from their area and demanding a uniform number be set for all districts. They were promptly arrested and sentenced to up to five years in prison. It was too much, even for Holmes. He wrote a draft dissent that he circulated to colleagues:

Real obstructions of the law, giving real aid and comfort to the enemy, I should have been glad to see punished more summarily and severely than they sometimes were. But I think that our intention to put out all our powers in aid of success in war should not hurry us into intolerance of opinions and speech that could not be imagined to do harm, although opposed to our own. It is better for those who have unquestioned and almost unlimited power in their hands to err on the side of freedom.

Notably, that was weeks before the argument in *Schenck*, and Chief Justice White was sufficiently alarmed by the departure from prior cases that he delayed the opinion. Then, after possibly being told of the dissent, the Justice Department withdrew the challenge.

It was an obvious shift of Holmes from his prior strident rhetoric. However, he would still go on to write *Schenck*. Holmes remained as dogmatic in his rejection of natural law on the bench as he was in his youth. Indeed, his self-described "rage" against natural law seemed to extend to free speech. In a letter to Harold Laski, Holmes responded to past efforts to get him to moderate his views. He exhibited the same cold certainty: "[W]e should deal with the act of speech as we deal with another overt act that we don't like." It was a telling dismissal of the distinction between speech and overt acts—a view that laid the foundation for early English sedition law. Moreover, Holmes's views in *Baltzer* indicated that he would be "glad" to see more punishment for those opposing the draft and simply voted in dissent because he failed to see how these farmers could do real harm. He only supports defendants who, in a given context, express "opinions and speech that could not be imagined to do harm." However, it would foreshadow Holmes's shift one year later in another free speech case.

Abrams involved speech that was virtually the same as that in *Frohwerk*, *Schenck*, and *Debs*. The case began with a meeting of anarchists and socialists in Harlem. In the summer of 1918, Jacob Abrams, Hyman Lachowsky, Samuel Lipman, Jacob Schwartz, and Mollie Steimer gathered to discuss the class struggle around the world. They were workers—three bookbinders (Abrams, Lachowsky, and Schwartz) a furrier (Lipman), and a shirtwaist factory worker (Steimer). They were all supporters of the

Bolshevik Revolution and opposed the decision of President Woodrow Wilson to send U.S. troops to Vladivostok, Russia, as a bulwark against the Russian Revolution. The group printed leaflets in English and in Yiddish calling on workers to support their counterparts in Russia: "The Russian Revolution cries: Workers of the World! Awake! Rise! Put down your enemy and mine! Yes! friends, there is only one enemy of the workers of the world and that is CAPITALISM." They denounced the "coward" Wilson and his capitalist "robberish aims" and allies by opposing liberty loans. There was the usual hyperbolic language of the time, telling workers that they "must now throw away all confidence, must spit in the face the false, hypocritic, military propaganda which has fooled you so relentlessly, calling forth your sympathy, your help, to the prosecution of the war." However, there were also specific calls for strikes and a specific plea to "[w]orkers in the ammunition factories" that they were creating the very weapons being used to "murder . . . your dearest, best, who are in Russia and are fighting for freedom." They added, "Do not let the Government scare you with their wild punishment in prisons, hanging and shooting. We must not and will not betray the splendid fighters of Russia. Workers, up to fight." It was signed "the Rebels," and thousands of the pamphlets were distributed.

Congress had enacted the sedition provisions to the Espionage Act, including the criminalization of calling for the "curtailment of production in this country" of anything "necessary . . . to the prosecution of the war . . . with intent by such curtailment to cripple or hinder the United States in the prosecution of the war." The group was quickly charged and tried (with an associate named Hyman Rosansky) under the Espionage Act. The exception was Schwartz, who became ill while being held in the Tombs in New York. His supporters claimed that he was beaten in custody and was listed as dying from the Spanish flu. The trial was short and predictable with convictions across the board. Their counsel, Harry Weinberger, was associated with the Free Speech League and sought to show that the deployment of the troops was in fact in support of the counter-revolutionaries. Judge Henry DeLamar Clayton Jr. barred such arguments from being made. Clayton conducted the trial much like Chase did in the Adams administration: with mocking disregard for the defendants and their rights. He was described by the *New York Times* as conducting "a cross-examination of his own." Clayton also made prejudicial statements to the jury about the defendants' presumed guilt. They all were quickly convicted with less than an hour of deliberation by the jury. Rosansky cooperated with the government in identifying his codefendants and was given three years. The rest received twenty years, except for Steimer, who appears to have been given fifteen years due to her gender.

This should have been an easy case under the prior opinions for Holmes. After all, Debs had not even expressly called for resistance to the draft, but he was still treated as a clear and present danger to the security of the nation. Here the leaflets presented direct challenges to the war and direct pleas to munitions workers. Yet Holmes would dissent from the opinion of Associate Justice John Clarke and the rest of the Court (other than Brandeis). Clarke methodically went through the leaflets line by line, noting that the statements clearly "avowed the purpose to throw the country into a state of revolution, if possible, and to thereby frustrate the military program of the Government." The Court recognized that the "immediate" reason for the speech may have been "resentment caused by our Government sending troops into Russia," but declared that "the plain purpose of their propaganda was to excite, at the supreme crisis of the war, disaffection, sedition, riots, and, as they hoped, revolution, in this country." In a convoluted concluding paragraph, the Court noted that such language can mean different things, but "it is not necessary to a decision of this case to consider whether [there is] such distinction" because "the language of these circulars was obviously intended to provoke and to encourage resistance to the United States in the war . . . and advocated a resort to a general strike of workers in ammunition factories."

Holmes dissented and noted that, while some counts charge an intent to overthrow the United States, the leaflets "in no way attack the form of government of the United States." He then states that this is a denial of an essential right and a return to an earlier dark era:

"I wholly disagree with the argument of the Government that the First Amendment left the common law as to seditious libel in force. I had conceived that the United States through many years had shown its repentance for the Sedition Act of 1798, by repaying fines that it imposed."

It is an extraordinary statement from the man who wrote the earlier opinions punishing political speech. Yet Holmes goes further and states:

[W]hen men have realized that time has upset many fighting faiths, they may come to believe even more than they believe the very foundations of their own conduct that the ultimate good desired is better reached by free trade in ideas—that the best test of truth is the power of the thought to get itself accepted in the competition of the market, and that truth is the only ground upon which their wishes safely can be carried out. That at any rate is the theory of our Constitution. It is an experiment, as all life is an experiment. Every year, if not every day, we have to wager our salvation upon some prophecy based upon imperfect knowledge. While that experiment is part of our system I think that we should be eternally vigilant against attempts to check the expression of opinions that we loathe and believe to be fraught with death, unless they so imminently threaten immediate interference with the lawful and pressing purposes of the law that an immediate check is required to save the country.

The dissent would lay the foundation for the break from *Schenck* and the "clear and present danger" test. Holmes may have been influenced by criticism of his decisions and the views of Zechariah Chafee, who had written a brilliant *Harvard Law Review* article on how the Framers sought to "make further prosecution for criticism of the government . . . forever impossible in the United States of America." Yet, despite the celebration of Holmes's redemptive moment, the dissent still has echoes from his earlier opinions including a threshold statement that

> I never have seen any reason to doubt that the questions of law that alone were before this Court in the cases of Schenck, Frohwerk and Debs . . . were rightly decided . . . [T]he United States constitutionally may punish speech that produces or is intended to produce a clear and imminent danger that it will bring about forthwith certain substantive evils that the United States constitutionally may seek to prevent. The power undoubtedly is greater in time of war than in time of peace because war opens dangers that do not exist at other times.

Thus, Holmes still rejected a broader view of free speech, and his functionalism still allowed for a sliding scale of speech, permitting government censorship and criminalization under vague contextual standards. His continued endorsement of the trilogy of cases leaves his dissent in a muddle. Holmes seems to struggle to find a principled path out of the morass of the case trilogy while preserving their hideous holdings. He does so with shallow distinctions. He notes that this case is merely "the surreptitious publishing of a silly leaflet by an unknown man," presumably to distinguish figures like Debs. He suggests that speech could be criminalized based on the level of influence of the speaker in producing "immediate danger that its opinions would hinder the success of the government arms or have any appreciable tendency to do so." In this way, the dissent is more of a view that free speech may have added benefits to the system; "to the ultimate good desired is better reached by free trade in ideas." His dissent would serve as the foundation for the "marketplace of ideas" rationale for raising the tolerance for opposing or dissenting speech.

The struggle over foundation for free speech would continue to surface as the Court struggled to draw lines between criminal and noncriminal speech. That was most evident in *Dennis v. United States*, where a plurality applied a slightly augmented "clear and present danger" standard. An exchange between Justices Felix Frankfurter and William Douglas returned to the ongoing debate over whether the Framers intended to break with or build on the Blackstonian view of free speech. Frankfurter latched onto Jefferson's allowance for state sedition laws and other sources to rebut broader interpretations of the First Amendment. Rather, he viewed this history as showing that "free speech is subject to prohibition of those abuses of expression which a civilized society may forbid." Nothing in the amendment, Frankfurter reasoned, "impairs its usefulness nor compels its paralysis as a living instrument." Of course, this "living instrument" allows not only for society to forbid speech but to define abuses in the exercise of this right. In reaching this conclusion, Frankfurter was transparently selective in such sources. Moreover, even if Jefferson remained supportive of state sedition laws as a matter of federalism, it did not alter his view of the First Amendment itself. The opposing view of free speech was presented by Douglas, who argued for the same distinction between speech and acts voiced by Montesquieu. He offered an alternative Jefferson: "The First Amendment reflects the philosophy of Jefferson 'that it is time enough for the rightful purposes of civil government, for its officers to interfere when principles break out into overt acts against peace and good order.'"

Ultimately, decades later, in 1969, the Supreme Court would adopt a more protective standard in *Brandenburg v. Ohio*. At the center of the case was a vile figure named Clarence Brandenburg, an Ohio Ku Klux Klan leader. Brandenburg vented his racist views at a televised rally in which he declared, "We're not a revengent [*sic*] organization, but if our president, our Congress, our Supreme Court, continues to suppress the white, Caucasian race, it's possible that there might have to be some re-vengance [sic] taken." He called for the sending of Blacks to Africa and Jews to Israel. Local authorities proceeded to arrest him under an Ohio law criminalizing the advocacy of crime or violence or to assemble with a group for that purpose. The Court unanimously declared the law uncon-stitutional in seeking to criminalize the "advocacy of the use of force or of law violation."

With *Brandenburg*, criminal liability must be premised on speech that is "directed to inciting or producing imminent lawless action and is likely to incite or produce such action." It broke cleanly from Holmes's "clear and present danger" standard to remove any question about criminalizing the mere advocacy of future unlawful acts. Building on Holmes's dissent, the Court added the requirement of imminency to further narrow the permissible range of criminality that existed under the "clear and present danger" standard. The result was a tighter nexus that made criminaliza-tion of speech far more difficult. There would remain, however, a linger-ing uncertainty over what constitutes "imminent lawless action" and the requisite showing for incitement to such action.

Despite Holmes's tacking back on *Schenck* and the rejection of the "clear and present danger" standard, his theater analogy would remain arguably his most well-known and most quoted line. Indeed, the most unnerving aspect of Holmes's opinion and analogy is that it is making a comeback with some on the left to justify censorship of anything deemed hateful or "disinformation." In 2019, Christopher Finan wrote a piece ti-tled "Was Oliver Wendell Holmes Right About Free Speech?" The answer should be clearly no, but "dark Holmes" has come back into vogue as a retort to those claiming free speech rights. For that reason, it is important for us to understand why he remains all the rage with anti–free speech advocates.

In February 2023, the House of Representatives began to hold hear-ings on the government's various efforts to target and censor citizens and groups on social media. I testified at the first hearing and was alarmed to see the impassioned defense of blacklisting and censorship. Yet it was the repeated invocation of the Holmes theater analogy that was most jarring.

Despite the origins in a case justifying the arrest of socialists due to their political views, Democrats recited the line over and over in the hearings. When Representative Dan Goldman (D-NY) invoked the line to me in the hearing as a justification for censorship, I started to point out that the line came from an abusive case long abandoned by the Court, when Goldman shot back, "We don't need a law class here." It is an analogy that continues to be used for its most superficial purpose of silencing others. Even when the line is used to justify censorship, countervailing arguments are dismissed as legalistic or dangerous. While members prefer to use terms like "disinformation" rather than "sedition," the result is the same. Opposing views are now the "fire," and the internet is a crowded theater.

Part IV

RESTORING THE INDISPENSABLE RIGHT

Twenty-Five

ROCKWELLIAN FREE SPEECH

In 1941, artist Norman Rockwell was moved to paint his Four Freedoms series after listening to President Franklin Delano Roosevelt's famed speech of that name on January 6, 1941. Roosevelt declared, "The first is freedom of speech and expression—everywhere in the world." Rockwell decided to capture the meaning of this indispensable right. His inspiration for the painting would come not from Roosevelt but instead from his neighbor, a young selectman in Vermont named Jim Edgerton. Rockwell

was struck by the power of the moment when this young man rose in a town meeting to address the financing of the construction of a replacement for a school that burned down. Edgerton's singular voice on that day proved persuasive to many in town in approving a new school construction plan. Rockwell's image was so penetrating and powerful that it was adopted by the government as part of its war bond campaign. This simple act of

free speech embodied not just the American constitution but the American character. It was not our wealth, land, or our power that citizens would rally around to defeat the Axis powers during World War II. It was the freedom of speech that defined us and distinguished us from our enemies.

Rockwell's painting captures the essence of this right to our nation. Yet, for many, it remains a quaint, if not campy, reference. For some, Rockwell was simply not as sophisticated as a cubist or abstract painter. Indeed, there is a striking parallel to the interpretative perspectives in the art and legal fields. Like the criticism of Rockwell's work, the natural right or autonomous view of free speech is dismissed as simplistic or even jingoistic. The world and art, critics suggest, must be recognized as more complex and nuanced.

While Rockwell studied at some of the leading art schools in America, including the National Academy of Design and the Art Students League, he was drawn to realism. Art critic Clement Greenberg (who is credited as the intellectual force behind abstract expressionism) denounced his realist art as popular kitsch: "the epitome of all that is spurious in the life of our times." He railed against anyone who liked Rockwell (which clearly included most of America), describing him as an artist who "chose not to be serious." Rockwell's popularity baffled and irritated Greenberg, who was unrelenting in his criticism.

Rockwell responded to such criticism with his work *The Connoisseur* depicting a man staring at an abstract piece of art. The large abstract piece in the background was done in the style of Jackson Pollock, who Greenberg had championed as the future of art. Rockwell's abstract rendition was surprisingly good. Willem de Kooning, one of the leading abstract expressionist painters, loved *The Connoisseur* and declared, "Square inch by square inch, it's better than Jackson!" (De Kooning even once forced a critic to closely examine Rockwell's "drip" painting with a magnifying glass and called it "Abstract expressionism!") Yet *The Connoisseur* remained part of Rockwell's signature narrative style with a man seemingly searching the picture for meaning. The man's posture and folded hands leave the impression of someone who has been staring at the piece for an extended time. Though we cannot see the man's face, he appears affluent in his neat suit and shiny shoes as he clutches his copy of the *Art Gallery Guide*. He seems to wait patiently for meaning to emerge from the paint drips.

I happen to like modern art. However, when it comes to constitutional law, I am unapologetically Rockwellian. The Constitution resonates with first principles that are profound and defining values of a free people. Once again, there has long been a rejection of classic free speech views as unsophisticated and lacking proper nuance. Once free speech becomes more of an abstraction, it can be balanced against other interests and confined to achieve other goals. It is more Rothko than Rockwell, leaving greater room for the interpretation by the beholder. In constitutional law, the criticism of figures such as Greenberg are strikingly familiar. Many law professors brush off natural or autonomy-based interpretations of the First Amendment as not "serious" and lacking a certain discernment. Free speech is one of the paint drops in an abstract constitutional work in which the meaning comes from a functionalist whole. As we have seen, this untethering of interpretation from the text proved to be little more than a constitutional conceit. It can render meaning so fluid as to become entirely situational or subjective. Pollock once advised observers that, if they wanted to truly enjoy his work, they should stop looking for objective meaning. That is a dangerous practice when applied to the interpretation of a constitutional right.

The problem with the First Amendment is not that it is abstract, but that many academics do not like the seemingly clear and transcendent meaning. They are constitutional connoisseurs looking at a Rockwell and seeing a Pollock. It is not what many of us see in the First Amendment—a bold statement of an indispensable and largely indivisible right. We are left in the same position of Rockwell, who once explained, "I was showing the America I knew and observed to others who might not have noticed." Of course, many notice a broader meaning of free speech but simply reject it as untenable or implausible. That rejection is often coupled with a view that robust interpretations of free speech can limit the achievement of other political and social goals. Again, there is a parallel to the same dismissal of objective meaning in the arts. In his 1939 essay "Avant-Garde and Kitsch," Greenberg explained that the rejection of realism coincided with the embrace of radical political movements like Marxism. In both art and politics, he saw a "superior consciousness of history . . . the appearance of a new kind of criticism of society" that broke away from "our present bourgeois social order." Earlier realism or literalism was denounced as furthering the status quo and thus "was shown to be, not an eternal, 'natural' condition of life, but simply the latest term in a succession of social orders."

Immediacy and clarity of meaning reduces the power of interpretation in both art and the law. Rockwell's paintings drew out intense feelings through the representational depictions in works like *Freedom of Speech* and *The Connoisseur*. However, that meaning was found beyond the immediate realism. It was accessible and allowed the public to contemplate the implications of the images as they related to their own lives and surroundings. *The Connoisseur* captured the searching for meaning through abstract imagery. In her essay on Rockwell and "ways of seeing," Professor Wanda Corn explored the disconnection of many with modern art with a Barney Tobey cartoon of two tired women sitting in front of an abstract painting in an art museum and one woman lamenting, "I wish this bench was in front of something I understood." The First Amendment was a work that people could understand without the assistance of interpretative agents to explain that the world is too complex for univocal meanings or simplistic depictions. For "unsophisticated" viewers like Justice Hugo Black, the concept of free speech is immense, but the protection was clearly depicted: "I take no law abridging to mean no law abridging."

I do not view Rockwell's paintings as "simple" depictions. However, simple truths, like simple pictures, can hold profound meaning. The First Amendment's clarity was not due to a lack of sophistication but an embodiment of an essential element to a new American vision. Free speech may be fairly univocal as a protection of a human right of expression, but that human need is itself complex. It is a meaning that many Americans hold instinctively. Law professors today often sound like constitutional connoisseurs defining the complexities of free speech to justify limitations on this right. Yet what if the First Amendment is a realist depiction of free speech, both literal and profound?

It is a question that is unlikely to receive more than passing or perfunctory consideration in today's law schools. Indeed, one of the problems that artists like Rockwell faced was what author Tom Wolfe called the "Cultureburg" in his book *The Painted Word*, a reference to Greenberg and two other critics who effectively controlled art theory and the valuation of artists. These dominant critics left little room for alternative visions and artists. Wolfe criticized the new "religious" view of art where "the artist is viewed as a holy beast who . . . receives flashes from the godhead." Notably, one of the two original covers for Wolfe's book featured *The Connoisseur*, and Wolfe spoke of Rockwell as the master not of the simplistic but the "super perspective." In today's academic echo chamber, there is a similar domination of constitutional critics who tend to reject a natural rights or autonomous basis for constitutional rights like free speech. As discussed in chapter 28, most law schools have largely purged their faculties of conservative or libertarian professors. Natural law or autonomous theories are considered passé. Young faculty embracing such views are at risk of being dismissed as "cho[osing] not to be serious," and any works are likely to be met with Greenbergian harrumphs that they are little more than constitutional kitsch.

In law schools, many professors have railed against what they call "rights talk," or the affirmation of rights over social reforms. Law professor Mark Tushnet declared, "We must insist on preserving real experiences rather than abstracting general rights. . . . The language of rights should be abandoned to the very great extent that it takes as a goal the realization of the reified abstraction 'rights' rather than the experiences of solidarity and individuality." Mary Ann Glendon, another law professor, warned that "our rights talk, in its absoluteness, promotes unrealistic expectations, heightens social conflict, and inhibits dialogue that might lead toward consensus, accommodation, or at least the discovery of common ground." Much like their counterparts in art, these professors insist that true meaning is derived from one's experiences and expectations. In particular, the facial meaning of the First Amendment creates a barrier to silencing those views deemed harmful. For example, in her work *Feminism Unmodified*, feminist legal scholar Catharine MacKinnon denounced free speech rights talk as harmful to achieving gender equality: "In a society of gender inequality, the speech of the powerful impresses its view upon the world, concealing the truth of powerlessness under that despairing acquiescence that provides the appearance of consent. . . . Liberalism has never understood that the free speech of men silences the free speech of women."

The rejection of "rights talk" coincides with a broader movement in academia against the notion of objectivity, even in disciplines once closely tied to that value. In journalism schools, professors now denounce objectivity's place as the "supreme deity" of American journalism. Professors such as Stanford's Ted Glasser have called for an end of objectivity in journalism as too constraining for reporters in seeking "social justice." This cause has been adopted by mainstream media figures. Reporters must serve as active interpreters in framing the news to convey what they view as the truth, including the suppression of opposing views on issues like climate change, the pandemic, or gender identity. In 2023, former *Washington Post* executive editor Leonard Downie Jr. and former CBS News president Andrew Heyward released the results of their interviews with over seventy-five media leaders and concluded that objectivity is now considered reactionary and harmful. Emilio Garcia-Ruiz, editor in chief at the *San Francisco Chronicle*, said it plainly: "Objectivity has got to go." Likewise, some law professors have railed against neutral concepts of interpretation, including "dominant legal claims of neutrality, objectivity, color blindness, and meritocracy." Rather than textual or historical interpretations that were once the foundation of legal analysis, critical legal and feminist scholars have argued for the use of new forms of interpretation based on "experiential knowledge of people of color . . . personal histories, parables, chronicles, dreams, stories, poetry, fiction and revisionist histories."

Law professors have imported theories from philosophy and English departments to supplant traditional legal interpretations. Many have incorporated the new theories of meaning from the study of hermeneutics to challenge objectivity in the law. Theoreticians like Hans-Georg Gadamer emphasize interpretation and the dialectic over objectivity and neutrality. Gadamer posited that "a law does not exist in order to be understood historically, but to be concretized in its legal validity by being interpreted." More generally, professors have eschewed textual meaning for more fluid interpretations allowing for greater adherence to social and political context. Critical legal studies scholars have also focused on deconstructing language by borrowing concepts of interpretation from literature. Deconstructionists work with the "open-ended play of meaning" and "celebrate the indeterminacy of texts as an opportunity for joy, freedom, and play."

These new interpretive approaches followed years of functionalist theories and have allowed even greater reductions in free speech to achieve political and social agendas. Once decoupled for a natural rights or autonomous basis for free speech, the debate could focus more freely on the balancing of competing values. Over decades, the natural rights foundation for free speech waned with the greater adherence to utilitarianism and positivism in legal theory. The latter movement spawned figures who rejected the natural rights views of Locke and others. For Holmes, rights like free expression were separate from "the rights of man in a moral sense." Advocates for free speech shifted toward defending free speech in terms of its value to the democratic process and balanced that value against what Roscoe Pound called other "public interests." Free speech was necessary for the maintenance of the marketplace of ideas—a value of "social interests" as opposed to "the individual interest." The resulting balancing allowed for trade-offs with state interests. Under this framing, free speech "may so affect the activities of the state necessary to its preservation as to outweigh the individual interest or even the social interest in free belief and free speech." Once unmoored from a natural rights foundation, free speech becomes a socially defined and socially tolerated right, often balanced against countervailing interests like combatting hate speech.

Despite the strong Lockean hold on many Framers, a natural rights basis for free speech had relatively little time to take hold in the colonies. The historian Leonard Levy would challenge the view that the Framers of the First Amendment evidenced a natural rights or autonomous view of free speech. The history of sedition prosecutions was used as evidence that "[t]he security of the state against libelous advocacy or attack was always regarded as outweighing any social interest in open expression." The import of this abridged view was not lost on the Supreme Court. Justice Hugo Black denounced Levy's interpretation as "probably one of the most devastating blows that has been delivered against civil liberty in America in a long time." Yet this Blackstonian view of free speech has found even greater allies in the United States in the "postmodern" period.

One of the interesting elements of Rockwell's free speech depiction is that it perfectly captured a theoretical divide over free speech that must be addressed if we are going to restore this right. Edgerton was rising to speak his peace about a matter of public interest in the rebuilding of a school. For functionalists, this is the core meaning of free speech and the type of expression that warrants the greatest protection. Around the time that Rockwell was painting his vision of free speech, philosopher Alexander Meiklejohn was penning a famous work on free speech, *Free Speech and Its Relation to Self-Government* (1948). It was the ultimate functionalist theory that saw little protection beyond the scene captured at the Vermont town meeting. This type of political speech, he maintained, should be protected, while other types of speech lacked the democratic function and therefore the constitutional protection:

In the town meeting the people of a community assemble to discuss and to act upon matters of public interest—roads, schools, poorhouses, health, external defense, and the like. Every man is free to come. They meet as political equals. Each has a right and duty to think his own thoughts, to express them, and to listen to the arguments of others. The basic principle is that the freedom of speech shall be unabridged. . . . As the self-governing community seeks, by the method of voting, to gain wisdom in action, it can find it only in the minds of its individual citizens. If they fail, it fails. That is why freedom of discussion for those minds may not be abridged.

Meiklejohn rightfully condemned Holmes's "clear and present danger" standard, but his fierce defense of political speech was matched by his adamant dismissal of the protection of other types of speech.

The emphasis on political speech, however, was both artificial and superficial. To continue the art analogy, Rockwell's painting clearly contained a political message, as did paintings such as Picasso's antiwar *Guernica*. Yet artists have the same essential impulse of expression on less political subjects from *Whistler's Mother* to Coolidge's *Dogs Playing Poker*. Many are statements of society that are every bit as profound as Warhol's *Campbell's Soup Cans*. All these artists are speaking to the world around them. They can take comfort in the fact that the Framers barred the abridgment of "speech," not just "political speech." The desire to add a conditional qualification for constitutional protection is obviously appealing. It avoids drawing difficult lines or more extensive limits for government regulation of speech. However, it also creates its own internal inconsistencies. Though the Court has long maintained that it would not allow a "free-floating test for First Amendment coverage . . . [based on] an ad hoc balancing of relative social costs and benefits," it has excluded low-value speech from the same protections based on nebulous and ill-defined categories like "fighting words." That has led to precisely the type of ad hoc balancing repudiated by the Court.

Take, for example, the Court's statement in *Gertz v. Robert Welch, Inc.*, where the Court explored the constitutional limitations on civil liability in defamation cases: "We begin with the common ground. Under the First Amendment, there is no such thing as a false idea. However pernicious an opinion may seem, we depend for its correction not on the conscience of judges and juries but on the competition of other ideas. But there is no constitutional value in false statements of fact."

Those three lines are both profound and problematic. Indeed, it is true that there are no false ideas under the First Amendment. However, the question is why. It is "speech," not good or bad speech, that is protected. Moreover, even from a narrower functionalist approach, choosing between good and bad ideas is heavily laden with subjectivity and dangers. It is inimical to the democratic process for the government to sort out ideas according to their inherent worth. Yet it does not fully answer why bad ideas are protected. Why should bad ideas or bad speech be protected to the same degree? The most that the Court can say is that the marketplace of ideas will take care of bad ideas. That, however, is not necessarily true.

While many of us have great faith in the classic assumption that the best response to bad speech is good speech, one has to recognize that bad ideas are never truly eliminated. Racism, anti-Semitism, sexism, and other prejudices continue to rage on the internet and in society. If the marketplace does not eliminate bad ideas (or if bad ideas become majoritarian views), does that mean that the First Amendment is a failure? For some, the answer is clearly yes. Some have called the Constitution "trash" that should be discarded. Others believe that the First Amendment should be fundamentally reframed in an "equality-based" approach that allows for sweeping censorship of speech that "harms" other groups by replicating racist or marginalizing ideas.

Ultimately, functionalist and autonomy-based theorists agree that, regardless of the success of the marketplace in eliminating bad ideas, there is a greater danger in the government becoming the arbiter of what is good or bad, permissible or impermissible in the exercise of free speech. As law professor Harry Kalven once declared, "Freedom of speech is indivisible; unless we protect it for all, we will have it for none." Specifically, he maintained that "the First Amendment . . . was designed to preclude courts as well as legislatures from weighing the values of speech against silence." Yet this argument (which I believe is historically self-evident) avoids the most elemental question on why bad speech or rage rhetoric should be protected other than the potential collateral costs incurred by combating it. After all, many insist that certain speech is divisible and suppressible as harmful without risking tyrannical or authoritarian applications. Functionalist theories have only led to questions of why we should protect ideas that are inimical to society or groups. Law professor Mary Ellen Gale has asked why "we all must acquiesce in suffering the harms that free expression may inflict as the cost of ensuring the continuing vitality, not of self-government itself, but of individual freedom and self-expression as fundamental principles of our national democratic experiment."

The autonomy-based view of free speech offers a different reason why "under the First Amendment, there is no such thing as a false idea." If free speech is a right that adheres to the individual as opposed to the state or the democratic process, ideas are how people project themselves into the world around—for better or worse. Saying that there are "no bad ideas" does not mean that all ideas are equal on their merits. Rather, there is a no-threshold criteria for being able to speak. Edgerton would still be protected stating his view on the financing of a new school. However, he would also be protected in espousing his views on art or athletics. This broader view of free speech also addresses how private institutions and individuals should treat this right. Even for institutions that are free from the limits of the First Amendment, an autonomy-based understanding of free speech conflicts with trade-offs that often occur under functionalist approaches of the courts.

The bifurcated view of free speech under functionalism avoids more difficult questions. To his credit, Kalven lambasted the bifurcation and the Supreme Court's separation of low-value speech from protection under the theory that there is some speech that is "apparently so worthless as not to require any extensive judicial effort to determine whether they can be prohibited." It can also justify censorship by raising the countervailing costs of free speech. In her recent book *Attack from Within: How Disinformation is Sabotaging America*, Michigan law professor and MSNBC legal analyst Barbara McQuade describes how the First Amendment protects disinformation despite its danger to democracy. Given that existential threat, Professor McQuade has called the First Amendment the "Achilles heel" of the nation when citizens are exposed to information she deems harmful or untrue. There are obvious echoes of the arguments previously used to justify censorship of dissents or extremists as undermining our political, moral, or legal values. It seems entirely sensible until your own views are deemed false or harmful. For McQuade, disinformation includes anything that she or others consider to be "the deliberate use of lies to manipulate people . . . to advance a political agenda."

Like racism, disinformation has always and will always plague this nation. It is certainly true that free speech will not eradicate bad ideas any more than practicing democracy will eradicate the impulse for authoritarianism. It is also true that the ability to remove false ideas is enhanced without free speech or a reduced version of its protections. Yet, historically, the greatest threat to citizens has come not from those who state falsehoods but those who claim the right to regulate what is true and false. To use Professor McQuade's analogy, the First Amendment certainly exposes the body politic to harmful views at the extremes, but it does protect the rest of the body from the greater threats of censorship and the criminalization of speech. To toy with the scourge of public or private censorship to combat false views is the classic example of making the perfect the enemy of the good. The natural right or autonomous view of free speech treats the right to express one's view as inherently worthy of protection, regardless of the objective worth of the speech itself. Once we start to protect those deemed by McQuade to be "dupes," the education of America can easily become its indoctrination.

That brings us to the third line from the *Gertz* quote: "[T]here is no constitutional value in false statements of fact." In the case, the Court was referring to libel actions. When someone makes a false statement about an individual, it is a direct and real harm to their reputation. However, the Constitution does protect false statements as shown by the Court in reviewing "stolen valor" claims in *United States v. Alvarez*. In that case, the Supreme Court (correctly) struck down a statute criminalizing false claims of military honors. The Court declared, "[T]hough few might find [Alvarez's] statements anything but contemptible, his right to make those statements is protected by the Constitution's guarantee of freedom of speech and expression." Yet the reason for this conclusion is more muddled due to a lack of clarity as to why such false statements are protected. The Court retreats to the safety of relying on the marketplace to declare that "remedy for speech that is false is speech that is true." Moreover, it stated:

> The Government points to no evidence to support its claim that the public's general perception of military awards is diluted by false claims such as those made by Alvarez. [Furthermore, the] Government has not shown, and cannot show, why counterspeech would not suffice to achieve its interest. The facts of this case indicate that the dynamics of free speech, of counterspeech, of refutation, can overcome the lie.

So, there are constitutional protections for false statements, but it is not clear why. What if there was damage to the "public's general perception"? Would it then be unprotected? Even Geoffrey Stone, a great defender of free speech and political dissent, could be equivocal on the value and protection of such speech. He noted that "false statements of fact are not the sort of expression the First Amendment was meant to promote . . . [A]lthough it may be appropriate to protect false statements of fact because 'erroneous statement is inevitable in free debate,' there is no reason to protect them because they are valuable in their own right."

As with racist speech, it is hard to find value in the speech of Xavier Alvarez, who was criminally convicted for lying about a military record. For most, his lies about receiving military honors are not just valueless but also demean the honors that were so costly won by others. He built lies upon lies, including claiming that he played hockey for the Detroit Red Wings and that he was married to a Mexican television star. Under a functionalist theory, one could safely say that the value of his speech to society at large is at or near zero. Accordingly, many felt the narrowly defined crime of lying about military honors is constitutional as low-value speech. That is not the case under an autonomy-based right. Alvarez was living a lie in creating a false persona of a hero, athlete, and celebrity. It is a sad statement about his life and perhaps our celebrity-driven society. However, he has every right to live that lie and project that alter ego into society so long as he does not harm others, including engaging in fraud (like raising money off his honors or any alleged military wounds). In the free speech community, we are often compelled to defend what is vile in society to protect the value of free speech. Brandenburg, Alvarez, and others are the price we pay for free speech under both functionalist and autonomy theories. But their right to speak is not bestowed by society. It is a right that cannot be abridged without a showing of concrete harm, as discussed in the next chapter.

Even when the Supreme Court rejected harm-based claims for limiting free speech, the Court would draw the same threadbare public-private distinction. Thus, in *Snyder v. Phelps*, the Court rejected the use of common-law tort actions against the infamous Westboro Baptist Church, which picketed the funerals of dead soldiers to spew hateful, antihomosexual viewpoints. For the grieving families, these deranged protests were horrific, and they sued the church for the infliction of emotional distress. The Court refused to allow such a curtailment of free speech, but it did so with a familiar rationalization: "Whether the First Amendment prohibits holding Westboro liable for its speech in this case turns largely on whether that speech is of public or private concern, as determined by all the circumstances of the case." In this case, Westboro was found on the right side of that line as having value as political speech.

The ripple effect of the functionalist framework grew with time until it became the current tsunami of speech limitations in various areas. For example, if free speech is primarily protected for political expression, it can be disassociated from academic freedom—allowing greater flexibility in barring certain views. A natural rights or liberty-based theory encourages institutions and companies to strive for neutrality to allow individuals to reach their own conclusions and their own truth on political, social, religious, and economic issues. If free speech is viewed as part of an essential process of individual thought, expression, and resolution, major institutions facilitate that process by striving to maximize the spaces for individual inquiry and expression.

Twenty-Six

FINDING THE FORTY-
TWO OF FREE SPEECH

In Douglas Adams's 1979 science-fiction novel *The Hitchhiker's Guide to the Galaxy*, a lingering mystery runs through a series of five books as Deep Thought, a supercomputer, is asked to answer "the Ultimate Question of Life, the Universe and Everything." After 7.5 million years of calculations, Deep Thought finally reveals the answer to the meaning of life: forty-two. Deep Thought's answer was a brilliant commentary on macro theories that seek to explain life's mysteries and our tendency to search for a single unifying answer to complex questions.

For American Revolutionaries, the numerical reduction of their struggle was reduced to forty-five—a number that featured greatly in early free speech protests. That was the number of the edition of a publication that became the focus of the sedition prosecution of John Wilkes. Wilkes, a publisher and member of Parliament, became a cause célèbre when he was charged over his political views. Those views were printed in issue 45 of the *North Briton* that criticized George III. Wilkes fled to France, but was charged in absentia. Citizens opposed such prosecutions and reelected him to Parliament. Yet upon his return, he was thrown into irons and spent two years in jail. The resulting demonstrations featured the number 45 as the symbol of free speech and the free press. The answer to the meaning of free speech has often been reduced to insular fights over publication rights or prior restraint. However, the

failure to establish a deeper understanding of free speech is due to the failure to look beyond these immediate conflicts and instead to examine the underlying view of free speech.

Free speech itself is both simple and complex. In the act of free speech, nothing is more straightforward. Likewise, the denial of free speech is often as plain as a gag or ban. However, free speech is more than the act of speech, and its denial is more than the act of an arrest. If free speech is a human right, the exercise or abridgment of that right transcends the specific message or context of expression. At the risk of being trite, free speech is not about perfecting democracy; it is about perfecting ourselves. It is part of an individual's interaction with the world and other people. It is what Immanuel Kant called "the freedom to make public use of one's reason." It is part of not just formation of political views but also artistic, religious, and social values. It is often both explorative and expressive. It is part of the dynamic process that includes the interaction with others. While functionalists often focus on how speech impacts others, they rarely consider how the right (or denial) of expression impacts the individual. Speech is transformative, as one uses reason and observations to make sense of the world around us. It allows us to create new realities and concepts for ourselves or others. It can take the form of not just written or oral expression. In the *Masterpiece Cakeshop* case, it was a cake and, in the *303 Creative* case, it was a website design. Each of those expressions involve a host of antecedent acts and conceptual stages linked to the freedom of thought. It is a process of exploration, engagement, and expression.

The restoration of free speech values will require a clarity and conviction that has long evaded our country. At the founding, many were drawn to a natural rights basis for free speech in the writings of John Locke, who stressed inalienable rights that included the freedom of thought. Figures such as Madison referenced free speech as one of the inalienable rights of all humans. If so, the right could not be deemed as surrendered as the price for leaving the state of nature for a civilized state. While it is not an absolute right, the securing of inalienable rights was the purpose of the establishment of the state to protect not just safety but freedom. Likewise, Milton defined the very legitimacy of the state in terms of protecting free thought and free debate: "Where there is much desire to learn, there of necessity will be much arguing, much writing, many opinions; for opinion in good men is but knowledge in the making." There was also a contemporary distinction drawn between words and action that help define when the government may legitimately act. The French philosopher Montesquieu believed in the distinction between speech and overt action. In *The Spirit of the Laws*, he stressed that "[t]he laws do not take upon them to punish any other than overt acts. . . . Words do not constitute an overt act; they remain only an idea."

Despite these philosophical foundations, functionalist rationales soon overwhelmed liberty conceptions of free speech. As noted above, the Supreme Court has held that the level of protection differs depending on the importance of the speech: "[S]peech on public issues occupies the highest rung of the heirarchy [*sic*] of First Amendment values, and is entitled to special protection." Accordingly, the courts look to the "content, form, and context of a given statement" with greatest concern for "any matter of political, social, or other concern to the community." In 2023, the Court issued a powerful free speech decision in *303 Creative* that protected the rights of a web designer in refusing to create a website for a same-sex wedding. Justice Neil Gorsuch wrote that "the freedom to think and speak is among our inalienable human rights." However, he also added that the right was "indispensable" as a "means . . . to the discovery and spread of political truth." While the decision has a mix of rationales, Gorsuch does state that "the framers designed the Free Speech Clause of the First Amendment to protect the 'freedom to think as you will and to speak as you think.' . . . They did so because they saw the freedom of speech 'both as an end and as a means.' . . . An end because the freedom to think and speak is among our inalienable human rights." Despite the Court's reference to free speech as a human right, there remains an uncertainty as the Court vacillates between the natural and the functionalist rationales.

A natural or liberty-based right avoids the sand trap of functionalism where speech becomes less protected depending on its inherent contribution to participatory or democratic values. It is important to perfect democracy, but so, too, can be combating disinformation or creating a nonthreatening space for political or social or educational activities. Under this paradigm, political speech is given the greatest protection on a sliding scale of speech. For some, the bottom of that scale is commercial speech, disinformation, and hateful speech. The trade-offs become greater the further you move away from speech used to advance political change or causes. This also can lead to greater content-based judgments on what speech should be favored or disfavored. If speech is a means for achieving political dialogue, bad speech becomes inimical to that objective. As seen with social media companies, the effort to remove harmful or false speech is often justified as protecting democracy. Conversely, allowing more free speech is often attacked as endangering society by undermining the government and "experts" who are trying to advance beneficial policies.

Even with the changes proposed in the final four chapters, the erosion of free speech will continue unless citizens embrace an autonomy-based concept. While it is a bit much to claim an answer as succinct or complete as "forty-two," it is possible to define the outer limits or framing of the answer for this quintessential right. Free speech demands bright lines.

Ambiguity and uncertainty are its death knells. The absence of clarity on the use of the right is what drives the chilling effect where citizens self-censor rather than risk sanctions for speech. That clarity is offered in the harm principle of John Stuart Mill, who articulated a limited view of government action. The harm principle is arguably the single most influential theory in protecting individual rights from majoritarian controls.

Mill identified "one very simple principle [as] entitled to govern absolutely the dealings of society with the individual in the way of compulsion and control." The principle is that "the sole end for . . . interfering with the liberty of action of any of their number, is . . . to prevent harm to others." The natural default under Millian theory is the rights of the individual to speak, to live, to associate. Mill defined the legitimate scope of governmental power as protecting citizens from the harm of others; conduct that externalizes or imposes costs on our neighbors. It flips the assumption of many advocates today that the government is meant to permeate and shape aspects of our lives, including what we read or discuss. For Mill, the government's core function is to protect us from harm of others while maximizing individual rights.

The meaning of harm is clearly the key element to this theory and many in the anti–free speech movement have used their own harm principle to justify sweeping limits on individual rights. Figures such as media commentator and former CNN host Brian Stelter have called censorship a "harm reduction model" in journalism. Mill anticipated that his principle could be misused since "no person is an entirely isolated being; it is impossible for a person to do anything seriously or permanently hurtful to himself without mischief reaching at least his near connections, and often far beyond them." Yet Mill adopted a narrow view of harm under his theory to maximize individual choice and expression. The thrust of his work was to insulate individual rights by minimizing the range of government action. His writings include statements supporting the essentiality of free speech "being almost of as much importance as the liberty of thought itself, and resting in great part on the same reasons, is practically inseparable from it." For those who view free speech as a natural right, we tend to take a categorical view of harm as excluding speech that does not fall into a narrow category of crimes like conspiracy. Mill clearly was influenced by such views. Thus, in his writings, Mill touched upon the two critical elements for those who seek to protect free speech as a human or autonomous right: the broad protection of free thought and a narrow harm-based justification for the regulation of speech.

Mill offers a critical foundation for restoring free speech values in the United States. Yet Mill's writings also illustrate that this country helped develop these foundational concepts but elected to abandon them in favor of more functionalist concepts. Mill looked to the United States in formulating his early concepts on free speech. He was particularly influenced by Josiah Warren, whom Mill described in *On Liberty* as "a remarkable American." The influence of Warren is telling. He was an anarchist who held a fierce sense of individualism against the state.

A musician and an inventor, Warren was an early adherent of Robert Owen, an industrialist who favored communal ownership and sought to create the perfect society. Owen believed that collectivism was "universally admitted to be far superior to the individual selfish system." To that end, Warren joined a commune in New Harmony, Indiana, in 1826. It was meant to be a collectivist utopia, but Warren quickly became disillusioned with the communal life. The commune lasted only two years and was beset by divisions over the use of resources and the need for labor. It turned out that the intellectuals drawn to New Harmony were not eager to work when they saw others spending their time and efforts on contemplative matters. Owen's own son observed that the town was a combination of idealists, "lazy theorists," and "a sprinkling of unprincipled sharpers."

For Warren, the undoing of New Harmony was its failure to recognize human nature. He observed that New Harmony exhibited a tendency to yield to groupthink and orthodoxy: the "difference of opinion increased just in proportion to the demand for conformity." The commune failed in his view because it denied something essential in being human. In his publication *Periodical Letter*, Warren observed that "[i]t appeared that it was nature's own inherent law of diversity that had conquered us . . . our 'united interests' were directly at war with the individualities of persons

and circumstances and the instinct
of self-preservation." For Warren,
social harmony was possible only
if society recognized the need for
individual thought and expression.
He then stressed that "[S]ociety
must be so converted as to preserve
the SOVEREIGNTY OF EVERY
INDIVIDUAL inviolate. That it
must avoid all combinations and
connections of persons and interests, and all other arrangements

which will not leave every individual at all times at liberty to dispose of
his or her person, and time, and property in any manner in which his
or her feelings or judgment may dictate, WITHOUT INVOLVING THE
PERSONS OR INTERESTS OF OTHERS." That language should be strikingly familiar to anyone familiar with Mill, who wrote "over himself, over
his own body and mind, the individual is sovereign."

The failure of New Harmony is a poignant reminder of how great enterprises without a true foundation or connection to basic human qualities can be undone. Montesquieu, Madison, and others warned that no
government could be sustained without an understanding of what it is
to be human. The harmony missing in New Harmony was its failure to
recognize the basic human needs and impulses. That same is true with
efforts to construct a legal system without first understanding the human
need for expression.

This understanding moves beyond Mill's own writings. Mill was in
the end a utilitarian who incorporated rights into his view of what is best
"for all concerned." Mill is such a touchstone for libertarian and civil libertarian writing that we often overlook his own inherent contradictions.
In works like *On Liberty*, Mill was ambiguous on the limits of free speech.
Yet some of his observations could be used to support a type of Holmesian "clear and present danger" test. He defended his right to espouse
views that could amount to "tyrannicide" but stressed that punishment

is appropriate "only if an overt act has followed, and at least a probable connection can be established between the act and the instigation." He also acknowledged that such "immunity" can be lost in "circumstances in which they are expressed are such as to constitute their expression a positive instigation to some mischievous act." That includes inflammatory statements "delivered orally to an excited mob assembled before the house of a corn dealer, or when handed about among the same mob in the form of a placard." As someone who often identifies as a Millian, it is one of the few passages that I truly abhor. Mill set the horizon for this emerging right at a considerable distance from many of his predecessors and contemporaries (including Blackstone) but, in my view, not far enough to achieve consistency and coherence with his harm principle.

Mill's harm principle can be read as part of a general utilitarian philosophy where utility favors functionalist limits on free speech and other values. At its most extreme, the harm principle can be reduced to a simple threshold exclusion for entirely harmless acts or views. Under that approach, once harm is found, the issue becomes not harm but expediency. Writers such as Gerald Dworkin have stressed that it "is clear that the [harm] principle is supposed to settle the issue of the state's jurisdiction, not the question of when the state should exercise its power." The danger of this jurisdictional, as opposed to categorical, approach is evident in the slippery slope of speech prosecutions discussed throughout our history. Mill offered a more nuanced view between these extremes. He was admittedly more utilitarian than categorical in his discussion on free speech. He also rebuffed orthodoxy and embraced heterodoxy as a vital element of the advancement of thought. Mill saw the need for free thought to allow ideas to be tested, supplying a range of options for society to choose from.

The discussion of the practicality or utility of free speech expressed in Mill's writings should not take away from his overall philosophy of maximizing individual freedom and confining state action. He started with the view that "all restraint, *qua* restraint, is evil." Mill viewed free speech as "the necessity to the mental well-being of mankind (on which all their other well-being depends) of freedom of opinion, and freedom of the expression of opinion." Mill clearly rejected the notion of insults or offense as harms that crossed the threshold for coercive actions. While he acknowledged that lines must be drawn, he argued that those lines ought to be as far removed from limitations on the freedom of thought as possible:

> That there is, or ought to be, some space in human existence thus entrenched around, and sacred from authoritative intrusion, no one who professes the smallest regard to human freedom or dignity will call in question: the point to be determined is, where the limit should be placed; how large a province of human life this reserved territory should include. I apprehend that it ought to include all that part which concerns only the life, whether inward or outward, of the individual, and does not affect the interests of others, or affects them only through the moral influence of example.

Mill was the ultimate believer in heterodoxy, as was Jeremy Bentham. While Mill tended to defend values like free speech in classic utilitarian terms, his very work, particularly *On Liberty*, was a testament to his faith in the freedom of thought. Free speech allowed both individuals and society at large to transcend calcified or orthodox values.

Today's debates over free speech would have seemed all too familiar to Mill, who was attacked in his life with some of the same arguments. Many today are adopting arguments used by critics of Mill in favor of morality laws and reactionary social measures seen in the nineteenth century. One such figure was the English judge Patrick Devlin, who used his Maccabean Lecture at the British Academy in 1959 to argue that immorality was a social harm that justified coercive government measures. That fluid concept of harm is the basis for a variety of laws and theories that would curtail free speech, including Catharine MacKinnon's effort to ban "pornography" or the common arguments for censoring "harmful" views deemed misinformation, disinformation, or malinformation. These are the same voices heard in Mill's time that certain views were unhealthy or harmful. The importance that Mill placed on free speech was reflected in the second chapter of *On Liberty*, titled "Of the Liberty of Thought and Discussion." Then, as now, the view of speech as harm allowed for the expansion of speech regulation. Yet Mill emphasized how free thought and expression belonged to one's internal "domain":

> With respect to the domain of the inward consciousness, the thoughts and feelings, and as much of external conduct as is personal only, involving no consequences, none at least of a painful or injurious kind, to other people: I hold that it is allowable in all, and in the more thoughtful and cultivated often a duty, to assert and promulgate, with all the force they are capable of, their opinion of what is good or bad, admirable or contemptible, but not to compel others to conform to that opinion; whether the force used is that of extralegal coercion, or exerts itself by means of the law.

Today's advocates of harm-based speech controls flip this concept on its head in treating censorship as a type of self-defense. That is the flawed logic behind the now common position on campuses, that blocking or interrupting speakers is itself a form of free speech. Such private action, while not the focus of Mill's writings, contradicts his defense of "the freedom of discussion." Mill was not assuming that all public advocacy would be a "discussion" of rivaling viewpoints. Protests are not particularly dialogic for the opposing sides, but they are part of a larger dialogue in articulating positions and viewpoints. However, many protests today focus on stopping speech by entering speaking areas to scream or shout out speakers. It also occurs when protesters block entrances to speaking areas. That is certainly a form of protest, but it is also designed to stop speech. Without the freedom to debate these questions, "the meaning of the doctrine itself will be in danger of being lost, or enfeebled, and deprived of its vital effect on the character and conduct." Mill considered speech regulation as inimical to both individual and societal growth because true knowledge for the individual cannot come in the vacuum of speech control. As Mill noted, "He who knows only his own side of the case, knows little of that." In that sense, Mill saw the denial of free speech as not only a denial of

"domain" of every person over their own values but a denial of a critical
element of discourse for a healthy society:

> The peculiar evil of silencing the expression of an opinion is, that it
> is robbing the human race; posterity as well as the existing genera-
> tion; those who dissent from the opinion, still more than those who
> hold it. If the opinion is right, they are deprived of the opportunity of
> exchanging error for truth: if wrong, they lose, what is almost as great
> a benefit, the clearer perception and livelier impression of truth, pro-
> duced by its collision with error.

Thus, in his writings, Mill touched upon the two critical elements for
those who seek to protect free speech as a human or autonomous right:
the broad protection of free thought and a narrow harm-based justification for the regulation of speech.

A harm principle for free speech can offer the clarity missing in functionalist approaches. It also allows adherents to both functionalist and
autonomy-based views to support a broader scope of free speech protections. Even for functionalists eager to protect speech as a component of
the democratic society, the harm principle curtails the role of the government as an arbiter of speech and the dangers inherent in that role. Once
you eliminate the concept of harm from the exposure to opposing views
or values, the remaining harm falls in a narrow category of speech that
is closely tied to overt acts or crimes like fraud or conspiracy. It would
not include sedition or the notion of harming the authority of the state
through divisive or disrespectful commentary. It cannot be emotive or
offensive injury to a listener or reader. The "harm" from such views is precisely what Mill rejected as the basis for state action. As the legal scholar
Jeremy Waldron noted, moral distress is not part of the balance of liberty
and harm under Mill's approach. To the contrary, moral distress, "far from
being a legitimate ground for interference . . . is a positive and healthy
sign that the processes of ethical confrontation that Mill called for are
actually taking place." It would serve to protect core political expression
that functionalists often emphasize but would not be as susceptible to the

trade-offs and ambiguity of functionalist theories. It would go beyond speech tied to the democratic process and reach speech protected under natural or liberty-based views.

That does not mean that there are no limits. For example, critics of the "self-fulfillment" or autonomy notion of free speech often cite defamation as an example of a limit on speech that is not tied to an overt act. It is a reputational harm that penalizes the free speech of others. However, even the functionalist Supreme Court limited this tort to protect free speech values. In *New York Times v. Sullivan*, Justice William Brennan actually cited Mill as part of the justification for extending First Amendment protections to defamation cases. Brennan notably focused on free speech, not as a natural right, but as a right that was instrumental or important to the democratic process. He quoted Mill to reaffirm that "even a false statement may be deemed to make a valuable contribution to public debate, since it brings about 'the clearer perception and livelier impression of truth, produced by its collision with error.'"

The *Sullivan* decision was a great advance for the protection of free speech and the free press. However, it also tied the right to a functionalist rationale. Defamation is consistent with a natural or liberty-based right in combination with the Millian harm principle. A person has a right to speak against others in both public and private forums. However, to the extent that the right is used to harm others by making false statements that damage a person's reputation, it can be curtailed. Indeed, defamation holds a strikingly Millian character. It protects opinion and requires that a statement be both false and injurious.

The harm principle is also consistent with other limitations placed on speech. For example, corporations have free speech rights as recognized in *Citizens United v. Federal Election Commission*. The limitations on those rights are fiduciary or economically driven by the corporation. Shareholders can object that they are being harmed from controversial campaigns or products. It is a matter of consent and contract. Moreover, corporations can limit the speech of employees to avoid harm to their business or values when employees violate rules against political statements or symbols at work. Such advocacy has a direct impact on sales and customer relations. Likewise, universities are harmed when protesters prevent opposing views from being heard on campus. A content-neutral rule barring the disruption of speakers or events is designed to prevent the harm caused to others in the denial of free expression in education. As discussed earlier, these efforts at "deplatforming" may not violate a functionalist view of free speech, but they violate an autonomous view of free speech.

Under this approach, a harm principle would not extend to harm from ideas. Mill was right to tie speech sanctions closely to overt acts and to build his own view from the intense individualism of Josiah Warren. Even in the absence of overt acts, there can be prosecutions of some narrow categories of speech. They must satisfy the elements (including intent) for crimes like fraud or conspiracy to commit specific criminal acts. "True threats" and "attempts" have also been long recognized as legitimate criminal charges if they evidence "an intent to commit an act of unlawful violence to a particular individual or group of individuals." This excludes rage rhetoric used in the political context. It is the antithesis of the emerging "speech-as-harm" rationales sweeping across campuses, media, and corporations.

Natural law or autonomous-based models of free speech offer a brighter line of free speech protection. Free speech demands such clarity and space to fully function. It is also clear that, with the triumvirate limiting speech, we cannot rely on a cultural shift in all these fields. It took years for a new generation of academics, journalists, and corporate officers to steer these institutions in a new direction. It will take years to reverse that trend. Moreover, history has shown that governments—both democratic and authoritarian—tend to gravitate toward greater speech controls over time. As discussed below, the autonomy-based view of free speech removes the ambiguities used to justify censorship and blacklisting by the government, corporations, and academia.

Twenty-Seven

"FALSE NEWS" AND CENSORSHIP BY SURROGATE

The use of misinformation, disinformation, or malinformation is a modern conceit used to protect the sensibilities and self-image of those denying free speech. As with "content moderation," these terms allow advocates to avoid terms like *censorship* that still come with a stigma in polite circles. One term, however, is a direct import from the earliest days of speech criminalization: *fake news*. In the first sedition law in 1275, the English Parliament declared that "from henceforth none be so hardy to cite or publish any false news or tales whereby discord or occasion of discord or slander may grow between the king and his people or the great men of the realm."

The punishment of "false or fake news" would be imported in both treason and sedition trials during the colonial period to prosecute political dissidents. For example, in 1677, opposition was rising to the feckless rule of the eight "lord proprietors" appointed by England in North Carolina. Parliament had passed the Navigation Acts to force goods to pass through England and to tax the transportation of goods within the colonies. While North Carolina was exempt for seven years to encourage settlers, the law was ultimately imposed on colonists who resented not just the tax but these wealthy rulers who did little to protect them from Indian raids or represent their interests. Three leaders emerged to make the case for the colonists—John Culpeper, John Jenkins, and George Durant.

They found some support in Governor Peter Carteret, who argued for the suspension of the tax. However, the proprietors responded by appointing a new governor. In the meantime, the proprietors relied on two allies in the colony, Thomas Miller and Thomas Eastchurch, who pushed the new governor to enforce the taxes. Miller was arrested and charged with treason of the colony. He would escape and make it to England to tell the proprietors of a loss of authority and control. He was then sent back as the tax collector. Given his arrest and treatment by the locals, Miller set about his task with a certain abandon, applying heavy-handed measures to those who previously sent him packing. He later declared himself the interim governor and was so unpopular that he traveled with security guards. It didn't help. The locals again arrested him. Miller then, again, escaped and fled to England. The colonists elected Culpeper as governor, and he went to England to plead the case for the colony. The proprietors clapped him in irons and charged him with treason. It would become known as Culpeper's Rebellion. While Culpeper would ultimately escape conviction, he would languish for five months in prison. The basis for his treason is all too familiar today. He allegedly spread "false news" that served to incite and agitate the population. The proprietors charged that Culpeper used such false news in his "poisoning the people's ears, unsettling and disquieting their minds, by diffusing abroad by their agents false and dangerous reports."

President Donald Trump would latch on to the term *fake news* in his criticism of the mainstream press. It became a signature of his political antiestablishment repertoire, particularly as it related to the Russia investigation and other allegations of wrongdoing. However, it is the use of fake news to justify censorship that has had the most lasting and damaging impact. Notably, disinformation is used in the same way that "false news or reports" were used by the Crown at the height of its crackdown on free speech. As the Center for Information Technology and Society at the University of California, Santa Barbara, explains: "Fake news—news articles that are intentionally and verifiably false designed to manipulate people's perceptions of reality—has been used to influence politics and promote advertising. But it has also become a method to stir up and intensify social conflict." In recent years, academic groups have worked with the government and social media companies to isolate and silence those deemed to be spreaders of disinformation and, to use their English predecessors, from "poisoning the minds" of citizens.

The use of fake news and disinformation rationales from the thirteenth to the twenty-first century is no coincidence. Once you protect free speech to advance democratic processes, you can just as easily limit free speech if it is interpreted as inimical to the free speech of others. While the rationale has not changed, the ability to control speech has been greatly enhanced with the concentration of speech along channels like social media, which constitute choke points, or gateways, subject to "content moderation," the new term for censorship. It further allows for government, corporate, and academic actors to rationalize censorship, blacklisting, and banning dissenting voices.

The reappearance of blacklisting efforts is also all too familiar in our history. Speech crackdowns historically often involved such blacklists. For example, during the Fries Rebellion, lists were drawn up of people suspected of being part of a conspiracy of an "Order of the Illuminati" associated with France. Figures such as Reverend Jedidiah Morse waved around a list that he said contained a hundred such confirmed members in league with "the Grand Orient of FRANCE." The same type of lists of those conspiring or undermining the country would be waved around by Senator Joe McCarthy and others throughout our history. Today, lists of dissenters or controversial speakers or groups are banned on social media and their financial support targeted in the name of combating disinformation.

The censorship on social media also shows another continuation from the early Republic in the lack of faith in ordinary citizens to make their own decisions on what is true and what is not. Many of those demanding bans and blacklisting to stop the spread of disinformation today sound strikingly similar to figures like Federalist Fisher Ames, who warned that "rabble" would spread "false stories" to undermine the next election and "spread the infection" of what we now call disinformation. Underlying this view was an utter contempt for the intelligence and the ability of average citizens. As Ames argued in the eighteenth century, they simply cannot rely on the "political discernment of its citizens, to discover and repel the danger to its liberty and independence." Likewise, Adams viewed those arrested in the Fries Rebellion as "pitiful puppets danced upon the wires of jugglers." Federalists had little faith in the masses to be able to discern truth or falsity in the popular press. In the same way, anti–free speech figures today argue for the use of algorithms and blacklisting to shield citizens or "nudge" them into more reliable sources of information.

The result has been the establishment of the largest censorship system in history through an alliance of this triumvirate of forces. This effort was directed at those with dissenting views on subjects ranging from COVID to climate change to transgender issues. This was all done with the support of an eager, even evangelizing, media. Recent years have shown, once again, how censorship creates an insatiable appetite for greater and greater speech regulation. It also showed the high costs of censorship as scientists were silenced in raising objections later found to be valid on pandemic policies. For example, early in the pandemic, leading scientists signed the Great Barrington Declaration warning that the government and academia were joining in ill-advised policies in dealing with COVID-19. Figures such as Sunetra Gupta of Oxford University, Jay Bhattacharya of Stanford University, and Martin Kulldorff of Harvard University wrote that past pandemics offered important lessons on how to deal with COVID-19 and argued against the wholesale shutting down of businesses, schools, and other parts of the society. Instead, they argued that the government should focus on the most at-risk population. Many now believe that they were correct and that the national shutdown was a mistake, particularly in the closure of schools. Other nations kept their schools open and avoided our later drops in testing scores and rise in mental illness among the young. Yet these scientists and others were banned from social media, denounced by their universities, and stripped of academic or professional associations. The same is true for those questioning the efficacy of masks or arguing that natural immunities from prior illnesses were as effective against retransmission as the vaccine. Both viewpoints were later established as well-founded, but scientists and commentators were widely banned or canceled. Likewise, some scientists believed that COVID-19

originated in the Chinese biolab in Wuhan, China, due not just to its location at the outbreak but curious genetic code elements that suggested
human engineering. It was suggested that the accidental release was due
to "gain-of-function" testing of the virus. Those views were denounced
and banned as conspiratorial and racist. Even in 2021, long after most
media acknowledged that the virus could have originated in the lab, the
science and health reporter for the *New York Times*, Apoorva Mandavilli,
was warning other journalists not to write about the theory, which she
called "racist."

While leaders including President Biden declared that the failure of
social media companies to engage in greater censorship was "killing people," the opposite may be true. For years, any debate that might have influenced policies (like keeping schools open for children) were effectively
blocked by the government and the media. While there are good-faith
arguments on both sides of theories in these areas, only one side was allowed to be widely heard, as dissenting voices were declared public health
dangers and actively suppressed in public discussions. Censorship lost its
stigma. It was now considered noble to actively regulate viewpoints. Former Twitter CEO Parag Agrawal pledged to "focus less on thinking about
free speech" and more on "who can be heard."

The coordination of censorship and blacklisting of dissenting voices
in recent years raises the concern over the establishment of a de facto
state media. While the First Amendment was designed to prevent state
control over media through prior restraint and direct regulation, it is
possible to have a state media by consent rather than coercion. The government found willing allies in media and social media companies for a
system of censorship and blacklisting. Some of these censorship efforts
were directed at political stories impacting elections, the very core of the
functionalist theories. For example, just before the 2020 election, the *New
York Post* ran a story on the laptop of Hunter Biden that was abandoned at
a computer repair shop. The laptop contained not only images of the use
of unlawful drugs and prostitutes by Hunter but also detailed emails on
millions of dollars secured from foreign interests through alleged influence peddling. The Biden family had long been criticized for influence

peddling, and these emails showed money transfers from figures closely associated with foreign intelligence. Twitter blocked discussion of the story, and the media ran with a false claim that the laptop was likely "Russian disinformation."

Twitter eventually reversed its decision, but the story was blocked until after the election. In a later hearing, tech CEOs appeared before the Senate to discuss censorship programs. Twitter CEO Jack Dorsey apologized for censoring the Hunter Biden laptop story but then pledged to censor more people in defense of "electoral integrity." That did not sit well with Delaware Senator Chris Coons, who warned Dorsey and the other executives that their censorship efforts were not broad enough. While admitting that it was hard to define "misleading information," he insisted that the companies had to impose a sweeping system to combat the "harm" of misinformation on climate change as well as other areas. "The pandemic and misinformation about COVID-19, manipulated media also cause harm," Coons said. "But I'd urge you to reconsider that because helping to disseminate climate denialism, in my view, further facilitates and accelerates one of the greatest existential threats to our world." Connecticut senator Richard Blumenthal also warned that he and his colleagues would not tolerate any "backsliding or retrenching" by "failing to take action against dangerous disinformation." He demanded "the same kind of robust content modification" from the companies. Companies were also warned by figures like Representative Adam Schiff (D-Calif.) that they had to expand their censorship efforts or face possible congressional backlash.

For years, there was no serious threat of investigation or disclosure on the federal censorship program. Free speech advocates faced a near total blackout from social media companies, Congress, and the media. In that vacuum, the censorship efforts expanded exponentially out of the public eye. That all changed in 2022 when billionaire Elon Musk purchased Twitter and pledged to open the files showing the prior censorship partnership with the government. Musk was one of the few individuals on earth who could take on the government, corporate, and media establishment over free speech. While this triumvirate would launch a concerted (and successful) effort to get General Motors, Apple, Chipotle, and other companies to boycott the company, Musk could take a financial hit that would ruin most other businessmen. It was the ultimate unstoppable force meeting the immovable object. The Twitter Files laid bare a censorship operation that shocked even those of us who have long warned about the effort.

The Twitter Files revealed a host of federal agencies working with social media companies to target and ban individuals and groups. The back-channel communications with the FBI continued to expand to the point that one Twitter executive complained that the FBI was "probing & pushing everywhere." There was also a revolving door between the FBI and the company with Twitter hiring dozens of ex-FBI employees, including former FBI general counsel James Baker. There were so many FBI employees that they set up a private Slack channel and a crib sheet to allow them to translate FBI terms into Twitter terms more easily. The government would send the names and accounts of targeted persons, and Twitter ultimately banned many of them. Thousands were targeted, with dozens of agents working on the censorship program with Twitter.

The FBI was not alone among the federal agencies in systemically targeting posters for censorship. Indeed, emails reveal FBI figures, like San Francisco assistant special agent in charge Elvis Chan, asking Twitter executives to "invite an OGA" (or "Other Government Organization") to an upcoming meeting. A week later, Stacia Cardille, a senior Twitter legal executive, indicated that the OGA was the CIA, an agency under strict limits regarding domestic activities. Much of this work apparently was done through the multiagency Foreign Influence Task Force (FITF), which operated secretly to censor citizens. Cardille discussed her regular ninety-minute meetings with FBI, DOJ, DHS, ODNI (Office of the Director of National Intelligence), and industry peers. She referenced long lists of tasks sent by government officials. The censorship efforts included warnings to social media companies about a "hack-and-leak operation" by state actors targeting the 2020 presidential election. That occurred just before the *New York Post* story on Hunter Biden's laptop was published and then blocked by Twitter and other social media platforms like Facebook.

The files show a staggering size of government searches and demands on Twitter, including the use of key word searches to flag large numbers of postings for referrals to Twitter. To better facilitate such back-channel communication, Chan even offered to grant temporary top secret clearance to Twitter executives to facilitate greater communications and integration into the government network. The FBI used the company's broadly defined terms of service to target a wide array of postings and posters for suspensions and deletions. On November 3, 2020, Cardille told Baker that the FBI has "some folks in the Baltimore field office and at HQ that are just doing keyword searches for violations. This is probably the 10th request I have dealt with in the last 5 days." This close working relationship also allowed the government use of accounts covertly, reportedly with the knowledge of Twitter. One 2017 email sent by an official from United States Central Command (CENTCOM) requested that Twitter "whitelist" Arabic-language Twitter accounts that the government was using to "amplify certain messages." The government also asked that these accounts be granted the "verified" blue check mark.

The range of available evidence on government coordination with censorship extends beyond the Twitter Files and involves other agencies. For example, litigation brought by various states over social media censorship revealed a back-channel exchange between defendant Carol Crawford, the CDC's chief of digital media, and a Twitter executive. The timing of the request for the meeting was made on March 18, 2021. Twitter senior manager for public policy Todd O'Boyle asked Crawford to help identify tweets to be censored and emphasized that the company was "looking forward to setting up regular chats." However, Crawford said that the timing that week was "tricky." Dorsey and other CEOs were to appear at a House hearing to discuss "misinformation" on social media and their "content moderation" policies. I had just testified on private censorship in circumventing the First Amendment as a type of censorship by surrogate. Dorsey and the other CEOs were asked at the March 25, 2021, hearing about my warning of a "little brother problem, a problem which private entities do for the government which it cannot legally do for itself." Dorsey insisted that there was no such censorship office or program. He also denied shadow banning, which would later be revealed by the Twitter Files.

What is chilling is that these files only addressed the censorship partnership with Twitter. Despite Twitter having hundreds of millions of active users, it was ranked fifteenth in the number of users, after companies such as Facebook, Instagram, TikTok, Snapchat, and Pinterest. The other companies have resisted efforts to reveal their own records on censorship efforts in conjunction with the government. What we learned from Twitter, however, showed how censorship became the natural default for employees who followed the lead of Agrawal that they had the power and privilege to determine "who can be heard." At one hearing, former Twitter executive Anika Collier Navaroli testified on what she called the "nuanced" standard on censorship, including their effort to eliminate anything that they considered "dog whistles" and "coded" messaging for racist, offensive, or intolerant speech. She explained that they balanced free speech against safety and that they sought a different approach:

"Instead of asking just free speech versus safety to say free speech for whom and public safety for whom. So, whose free expression are we protecting at the expense of whose safety and whose safety are we willing to allow to go the winds so that people can speak freely?"

Representative Melanie Stansbury (D-NM) responded to this chilling statement of censorship with total agreement. This fluid standard allowed for a maximal effort with government agencies who flagged certain viewers or posters as dangerous, including some posters who merely made jokes about contemporary issues.

The Twitter Files revealed that the government actively sought to support a system of blacklisting and censorship while concealing the full extent of its operations. When these efforts became known, the reaction was overwhelming from the public, which continues to viscerally oppose government censorship efforts. For example, in 2022, the Biden administration caved to public outcry and disbanded its Disinformation Governance Board (DGB) under its much-criticized director, Nina Jankowicz. What the public was never told when the DGB was disbanded was that there was a larger system in place, including other offices engaged in censorship efforts at Homeland Security. This included an estimated eighty FBI agents secretly targeting citizens and groups for disinformation. The administration also contributed to the funding of an "index" to warn advertisers to avoid what the index deemed to be dangerous disinformation sites. It turns out that all ten of the "riskiest" sites identified by the Global Disinformation Index (GDI) were popular with conservatives, libertarians, and independents. The index created a scoring and sanctioning system for sites based on their "reliability" to those in the political and media establishments. The GDI is a particularly insidious part of that effort. Partially funded by $330 million from the U.S. State Department through the National Endowment for Democracy (which contributes to GDI's budget), the GDI was designed to steer advertisers and subscribers away from "risky" sites that it says pose "reputational and brand risk" and to help companies avoid "financially supporting disinformation online."

The effort by the government and liberal groups to target Twitter over its anti-censorship efforts is familiar to many in the free speech community. It was reminiscent of how the Wilson administration established a Committee on Public Information (CPI) to identify those espousing dangerous thoughts. The CPI also demanded adherence with accepted positions on the war. Likewise, during the McCarthy period, blacklists were jointly assembled by government and corporate figures to stop the spread of harmful viewpoints. When McCarthy and others were blacklisting figures on the left, they also successfully orchestrated boycotts of corporate sponsors for free speech advocates like radio host Drew Pearson. In the most recent blacklisting efforts, companies were told that the flagged risky sites could damage their reputations and brands. The risky sites included the *New York Post*, Reason, RealClearPolitics, the Daily Wire, Blaze Media, One America News Network, the Federalist, Newsmax, the *American Spectator*, and the *American Conservative*. The index was breathtakingly biased. The inclusion of Reason was particularly glaring given the fact that it is a site that posts legal analysis from conservative and libertarian scholars. Conversely, some of the most biased sites on the political left are given higher rankings by the index. Indeed, GDI's definition of "disinformation" is heavily laden with subjective terms, including any site that GDI views as offering "adversarial narratives." Disinformation could include anything that is "financially or ideologically motivated" . . . "foster[s] long-term social, political or economic conflict" or simply creates "a risk of harm by undermining trust in science or targeting at-risk individuals or institutions."

Later, in the seventeenth release of the Twitter Files, journalist Matt Taibbi reported that the State Department's Global Engagement Center (GEC) may have supported a different disinformation blacklisting operation. The GEC controversy appears strikingly similar to the one involving the the National Endowment for Democracy (NED). Both have supported third-party organizations that carried out blacklisting. Taibbi contends that the GEC contracted with the Atlantic Council's Digital Forensic Research Lab (DFRLab), which sent suggested blacklists to Twitter.

At times, even Twitter censors reportedly balked at the size of the suggested blacklists and lack of supporting evidence. At one point, Yoel Roth, then Twitter's head of trust and safety, responded to the demands with "omg" and "what a total crock." Yet Twitter did take adverse actions against many of the citizens and groups targeted by the government.

The Twitter Files show that, as with intelligence operations, censorship programs are best carried out behind layers of third-party groups. For example, another such grant was identified in 2023 with various universities to combat "skepticism" over issues like vaccines and build "trust" in what the government and researchers maintain is the truth. It contained the same function as other grants in targeting citizens or groups spreading "doubts" about what the researchers viewed as true facts. The National Science Foundation reportedly awarded millions in grants in 2021 and 2022 for Course Correct to allow media and government officials to target misinformation on topics such as U.S. elections and COVID-19 vaccine hesitancy. The system used machine learning and other means to identify social media posts pertaining to electoral skepticism and vaccine hesitancy, including flagging at-risk online communities for intervention.

With the blacklisting grants, the government had come full circle from the McCarthy period. Once again, the government was seeking to blacklist groups and individuals to cut them off from support and visibility. While liberals and socialists were targeted in the 1950s, it is now conservatives who are being blacklisted.

Government officials quickly recognized the opportunity to use allies in social media to achieve indirectly what they were barred from achieving directly. Indeed, some universities pursued these contracts to play an active role in this censorship triad. For example, emails show University of Michigan's James Park pitching the school's WiseDex First Pitch program to government officials with a direct reference to the use of the school as a surrogate for censorship. Park promises that "our misinformation service helps policy makers at platforms who want to . . . push responsibility for difficult judgments to someone outside the company . . . by externalizing the difficult responsibility of censorship." The "difficult responsibility" of censorship made such academic cover irresistible for many in government and corporations.

The State Department, Homeland Security, and other agencies created initiatives, offices, and grants to regulate speech. For example, the Cybersecurity and Infrastructure Security Agency (CISA) was tasked with protecting our digital and internet "infrastructure." To join other agencies in regulating speech, its director, Jen Easterly, declared "the most critical infrastructure is our cognitive infrastructure" and pledged that "building that resilience to misinformation and disinformation, I think, is incredibly important." She expressly pledged to work with the private sector including social media companies changing our "cognitive infrastructure." Like content moderation, the use of this Orwellian euphemism does not disguise the government's effort to direct and control what citizens may read or say on public platforms. CISA and other agencies target misinformation, disinformation, and malinformation (MDM). The categories allowed virtually limitless censorship. The agency defined malinformation as "based on fact, but used out of context to mislead, harm, or manipulate." Thus, information can be true but can be censored if the government believes that it is being used for a misleading purpose. It is the ultimate example of how censorship worked like gas in a closed space. If you expand the space, government censorship, like gas, will expand to fill that space. In 2023, the United States Court of Appeals for the Fifth Circuit enjoined the CISA in *Missouri v. Biden* from continuing to "coerce or significantly encourage" tech companies to remove or reduce the spread of posts.

The use of social media companies to block those with dissenting views had an enormous impact on public discourse. Social media is the primary form of communication for Americans, far outstripping telephones. Given that dependency, social media bans have an even greater impact on citizens in silencing opposing views. Past bans for contesting government positions on the pandemic or climate change harken back to the censorship during the colonial period when laws, like the one in Plymouth Colony, declared that anyone who speaks "contemptuously of the laws . . . shall lose their freedom of this corporation." Indeed, the blacklisting on these companies for those accused of disinformation functioned much like the "exclusion" ordered for those accused of sedition—offenders were subject to "disfranchisement, banishment . . . under the rubric of 'exclusion penalties.'" Where the Crown controlled the licensing of publications, the government was now working with social media companies to effectively de-license speakers from using platforms for political or social dialogue.

The common purpose of the government and corporate executives raises serious constitutional concerns. The close relationship can create a legal agency that can trigger the First Amendment. Putting aside the direct action of the dozens of federal employees in these agencies, the government can be responsible for the actions of third parties who are partnering with the government on censorship. For example, in *Lombard v. Louisiana*, the Supreme Court in 1963 dealt with the denial of service to three Black students and one white student at a lunch counter in New Orleans reserved for white people. While there was no state statute or city ordinance requiring racial segregation in restaurants, the Court found that the local leaders made clear what they expected from businesses. The mayor and the superintendent of police publicly warned against any "sit-in demonstrations." The Court ruled that these officials "cannot achieve the same result by an official command which has at least as much coercive effect as an ordinance." While courts have rejected claims of agency by private parties over social media, these cases often turned on a lack of evidence of coordination and occurred before the release of the Twitter Files. For example, in *Rogalinski v. Meta Platforms, Inc.*, the court rejected a claim that Meta Platforms, Inc., violated the First Amendment when it censored posts about COVID-19. The court emphasized that there was no evidence that there was any input of the government to challenge the assertion that Meta's message was "entirely its own." There is now ample evidence that shows the government identifying individuals for censorship and then Twitter carrying out that task. It is direct coordination and funding from the government to carry out censorship by surrogate. Courts have found state action with far less. In one case, *Paige v. Coyner*, the Sixth Circuit found that a call from a government to an employer to complain about comments made by an employee at a public hearing was enough to trigger constitutional violations. Likewise, the Eighth Circuit found in *Dossett v. First State Bank* that there was state action when school board members pushed a bank to fire an employee. In the current censorship system, there is evidence of government officials targeting individuals or groups to be banned or censored or stripped of financial support.

The effort to undercut advertisers or revenue is a far more effective method of censorship. Barring social media postings can hinder the ability of a group to advocate, but blocking revenue can hinder the ability of that group to exist. In 2024, the Supreme Court heard arguments in *National Rifle Association of America v. Vullo*. In that case, the United States Court of Appeals for the Second Circuit ruled that the NRA had a viable free speech claim based on a state official's pressuring companies not to do business with the organization. The Second Circuit held that "although government officials are free to advocate for (or against) certain viewpoints, they may not encourage suppression of protected speech in a manner that 'can reasonably be interpreted as intimating that some form of punishment or adverse regulatory action will follow the failure to accede to the official's request.'" Under the Biden administration, a network of corporate and academic interests were supported in creating an extensive blacklisting system that pressured advertisers and funders to cut off support for those with opposing viewpoints.

Members of Congress reinforced this agency relationship by repeatedly threatening to punish social media companies if they did not expand their censorship efforts. Indeed, that pressure increased after Musk vowed to restore free speech protections and dismantle its censorship program. As Twitter's advertisers were targeted, the fear was that other companies might follow Musk's lead. To cut off that possibility, Representative Schiff—joined by Representatives André Carson (D-Ind.), Kathy Castor (D-Fla.), and Senator Sheldon Whitehouse (D-R.I.)—sent a letter to Facebook, warning it not to even consider reducing its censorship programs. Likewise, in prior hearings, social media executives were repeatedly warned of consequences for the failure to remove viewpoints were considered "disinformation."

The response of some of these same members to investigations into the government's censorship program quickly developed a familiar tone. Democrats have attacked journalists, experts, and other witnesses seeking to expose these programs. These attacks have included denouncing witnesses as "Putin lovers," "Russian assets," "communist lovers," and "insurrectionists." The ranking member of the Select Subcommittee on the Weaponization of the Federal Government, Delegate Stacey Plaskett (D-VI), even suggested that one journalist, Matt Taibbi, should be criminally charged. It is tragically ironic given the position of the party during the Red Scare, when Senator Joe McCarthy declared, "The Democratic Party [is] the bedfellow of international communism." During that period, blacklisting and public shaming were weapons used against the left. Federal agencies funded academic groups in blacklisting sites and seeking to drain the sites of revenue.

These hearings highlighted the abridged view of the First Amendment, including the functionalist rationale to justify censorship. That includes assertions that hate speech is not protected. That misunderstanding is consistent with the sliding scale of protections under functionalist rationales. At a major House hearing, Delegate Plaskett declared that "I hope that [all members] recognize that there is speech that is not constitutionally protected," and then referenced hate speech as an example. Likewise, Senator Ben Cardin (D-Md.), who is a lawyer, publicly insisted that "if you espouse hate . . . you're not protected under the First Amendment." Other politicians have voiced a similar view. Former Democratic presidential candidate Howard Dean has insisted that "hate speech is not protected by the First Amendment." This erroneous view is amplified in some dictionaries that define "hate speech" as "speech not protected by the First Amendment, because it is intended to foster hatred against individuals or groups based on race, religion, gender, sexual preference, place of national origin, or other improper classification."

If one treats free speech as a balancing of interests, it is understandable why hate speech would be viewed as unprotected. After all, in a balancing test, hate speech has a negative value as opposed to the concrete costs to society. Thus, even those who acknowledge that hate speech has been protected under the First Amendment fail to see the basis for such protection. Former journalist and Obama State Department official Richard Stengel insisted that while "the First Amendment protects the 'thought that we hate' . . . it should not protect hateful speech that can cause violence by one group against another. In an age when everyone has a megaphone, that seems like a design flaw." It is the same "bad tendency" rationale used for decades to deny the free speech to those deemed dangerous or disruptive.

Despite the Supreme Court protecting hate speech like that in *Brandenburg* by a KKK wizard, legislators continue to try to criminalize statements considered by the government to be hateful. For example, New York recently sought to ban "hateful conduct" on social media. It was a modern version of the New York law in 1902 that made it a felony to "advocate" anarchism or publishing anarchist literature was likewise a felony.

In *Volokh v. James*, U.S. district judge Andrew Carter Jr. correctly declared the law to be unconstitutional in 2023. The law defined "hateful conduct" as "the use of a social media network to vilify, humiliate, or incite violence against a group or a class of persons on the basis of race, color, religion, ethnicity, national origin, disability, sex, sexual orientation, gender identity or gender expression." Carter held that "speech that demeans on the basis of race, ethnicity, gender, religion, age, disability, or any other similar ground is hateful; but the proudest boast of our free speech jurisprudence is that we protect the freedom to express 'the thought that we hate.'"

Judge Carter was correct. However, again, the question is why. The answer inevitably comes back to the marketplace of ideas. The marketplace of ideas is needed to realize the full potential of the democratic process. However, this construct leads to the slippery slope of past crackdowns of speech. The Court in 1942 tied protection of speech directly to its perceived value: "There are certain well-defined and narrowly limited classes of speech, the prevention and punishment of which have never been thought to raise any Constitutional problem. These include the lewd and obscene, the profane, the libelous, and the insulting or 'fighting' words—those which by their very utterance inflict injury or tend to incite an immediate breach of the peace." For centuries, certain ideas have been deemed as dangerous in their "very utterance." Yet those seeking to exclude hate speech, disinformation, and other forms of low-value speech argue that the marketplace is enhanced, not undermined, by the elimination of such speech. Since the courts exclude some forms of speech as threatening imminent violence, it is relatively easy to argue that other speech incites insurrections or hate against vulnerable groups. That is why Holmes's theater analogy continues to be used as a mantra by those seeking to censor or sanction speech.

This is where that Rockwellian view comes into greater focus. Figures such as Justice Felix Frankfurter dismissed the notion of a single unified theory of free speech. As on so many constitutional issues, Frankfurter preferred more nuanced approaches that allowed the Court to make case-by-case judgments. He was the ultimate "constitutional connoisseur" in interpreting the First Amendment. As part of his approach, Frankfurter maintained in *Dennis* that not all speech is equal or protected. Instead, he insisted that "not every type of speech occupies the same position on the scale of values." Once you appoint yourself the arbiter on the inherent value of speech, you are free to profess a desire for less censorship while still allowing speech suppression when "the danger created by advocacy of overthrow justifies the . . . restriction of freedom of speech."

The alternative is to protect the speech due to its inherent worth to the speaker. That is understandably difficult to assert when the individual is a vile figure like Clarence Brandenburg spewing his twisted views of Blacks, Jews, and virtually every racial or religious group other than his own. Why should we care that some Klansman or neo-Nazi feels a need to express views that deny the existence or equality of others? The answer risks instant condemnation as a defender of extremism and hate. Citing the functionalist value of allowing speech to protect democratic norms avoids the need to address the speech itself. Yet it also allows for a dangerous ambiguity for many on when speech undermines democracy by marginalizing others or undermining the acceptance of elections. As we have seen, it is easy to define opposing views as hateful, particularly when uttered by the least popular among us. I expect Brandenburg would deny the right to speak to the wide array of people he viewed as subhuman, including my family.

Recognizing a human right in an inhuman person seems a contradiction in terms. It is not. It is not that his views have value to society, but that they have value to him. He has a right to expression even though others rightfully find those views disgusting and despicable. His ability to express views despised by most of us is the affirmation of the right of all humans to exercise a natural or autonomous right. Basing the right on that autonomous basis negates the balancing or devaluation inherent under functionalist rationales. Being offended, even intimidated, by the views of others is not a harm under this Millian approach. He is projecting his view of humanity and himself into society. While grotesque and hateful, it can be countered by our own countervailing speech. This classic liberal belief that the solution to bad faith is good faith is often rejected as naïve. It has not, many have argued, stopped the rise of Nazism or the spread of racism, anti-Semitism, and other hateful ideologies. Yet allowing free speech will not eradicate bad ideas any more than practicing democracy will eradicate the impulse for authoritarianism. Racism and prejudice will always be present in society. Moreover, extremist rhetoric is always likely to attract the most attention, even if it is the product of a small minority in society. Still, history has shown that censorship and speech suppression do little more than force such views underground. Germany has suppressed free speech for decades but still has a raging neo-Nazi movement. Indeed, censorship tends to fuel movements by creating self-professed victims. It also moves these movements into the shadows, where they can be harder to track and address. The fact that Brandenburg's speech has value to him does not mean that it has value to society beyond defending the right of free thought and expression for everyone as a human right.

If we oppose censorship and blacklisting, we should stop funding it. The government is always able to speak in its own voice to expressly combat false or misleading statements. That includes its own statements on social media to counter such speech. The creation of a ban on government funding or support of censorship systems would reestablish the United States as a bulwark against the growing anti–free speech movement sweeping over Europe. Most recently, the European Union passed the Digital Services Act (DSA) to systemize censorship. It is a nightmare for free speech. Under the DSA, users are "empowered to report illegal content online and online platforms will have to act quickly." This includes speech that is viewed not only as "disinformation" but also "incitement." European Commission executive vice president Margrethe Vestager has been one of the most prominent voices seeking international censorship. At the passage of the DSA, Vestager was ecstatic in declaring that it is "not a slogan anymore, that what is illegal offline should also be seen and dealt with as illegal online. Now it is a real thing. Democracy's back."

It is the same Orwellian logic that has been voiced by some in the United States. For example, when Musk took over Twitter, many figures, including Hillary Clinton, called upon European countries to use the DSA or similar laws to force him to censor citizens. Clinton warned that governments need to act now because "for too long, tech platforms have amplified disinformation and extremism with no accountability. The EU is poised to do something about it."

We can provide a rallying point for the world in offering an alternative to this race to the bottom in the position of free speech controls. Countries like Germany and France have spent decades criminalizing speech and proven the fallacy of changing minds through threatened prosecution. While one can sympathize with the Germans in seeking to end the scourge of fascism, their approach is not just a denial of free speech but a futile effort to stamp out extremism by barring certain symbols or rhetoric. Instead, extremists have rallied around an underground culture and embraced symbols that closely resemble those banned by the government.

Not only do neo-Nazis claim victim status, but these laws make it more difficult to identify and to track these hate groups and messaging. Censorship tends to direct these figures into the dark web, where they operate anonymously in a subterranean rage fest. Nevertheless, the Germans continue to double down on censorship rather than recognize that free speech itself is the best disinfectant. The German left has led this effort and the ruling Social Democratic Party of Germany (SPD) has called for more censorship before, to use Clinton's words, "it is too late." SPD members were alarmed that Twitter would now allow a greater range of free speech and curtail Twitter's massive censorship system. The SPD's Jens Zimmermann called for a crackdown on Twitter to prevent Musk from allowing greater speech with "stricter supervision" so that, "if Twitter does not meet the requirements, there are penalties not only against the company, but also against the managers responsible." Yet Germany has proven the fallacy of changing minds through threatened prosecution. I fail to see how arresting a man for a Hitler ringtone is achieving a meaningful level of deterrence, even if you ignore the free speech implications. None of this has put a dent in the ranks of actual fascists and haters. The true impact of these laws was evident in a poll of German citizens. Only 18 percent of Germans feel free to express their opinions in public. Fifty-nine percent of Germans did not even feel free expressing themselves in private among friends. And just 17 percent felt free to express themselves on the internet. The only true success of censorship has been the forced or compelled silence of those with opposing views. That pretense of social harmony is treated as success even though few minds are changed, as fewer voices are heard in society.

Barring the United States government from supporting censorship or blacklisting systems would reaffirm the rejection of the concept of speech as harm. While we will discuss criminal sanctions under sedition laws in chapter 29, the greatest threat today to free speech is coming from this triumvirate and its systemization of censorship by surrogate. It is possible to create higher legislative walls between the government and these groups. In that way, agencies can speak in their own voices but cannot seek to silence the voices of others.

Twenty-Eight

ACADEMIC ORTHODOXY AND THE RESTORATION OF FREE SPEECH IN HIGHER EDUCATION

A s professors, we often refer to ourselves as "academics" and our profession as the "academy." The terms derive from a small Athenian grove in an area dedicated to the goddess Athena in ancient Greece. Athena was the goddess of wisdom, and it was in this grove that Plato assembled his students to learn philosophy in c. 387 BCE. I have always been struck by the fact that this lush grove was once an arid and dry place that was transformed by Cimon, the general and statesman, into a place of sanctuary and beauty. The famed Plato's Academy mosaic shows the protected place for learning where students would gather to speak freely and openly.

The *academus* became the symbol of an intellectual sanctuary. It proved to be the very garden from which higher education would grow and spread for generations. It would become the model for unbridled intellectual pursuit: the search for knowledge and understanding essential to human development. The most important element was protection for free inquiry. It provided a safe space where forbidden thoughts or ideas could be explored without fear. Gathering in a circle, the students and the teacher literally formed a physical space for discourse, directing their

minds to the center of their discussions free from outside influence or pressures. The mosaic captures a space of pure reason and intellectual exchange—the ideal of higher education for centuries.

The grove, however, also holds a countervailing and darker symbolism of how the greatest danger to these protected places is often from within. The term *academus* is derived from the Greek hero Akademos. His story is a complex one. It appears that, years before she became the flashpoint for the Trojan War, Helen at age twelve was kidnapped by the Athenian king Theseus. Her brothers, Castor and Pollux, waged war to get her back, invaded Attica (the peninsula that included Athens), and threatened to burn Athens to the ground. Joining them was Tyndareus, the Spartan king who was both the father of Castor and stepfather of Helen. That is when Akademos "saved" Athens. He did so by betraying the confidence of his king and telling the enemy where she was hidden. The gratitude only extended so far. The Spartans laid waste to Attica and spared only the *Akademeia*.

The story of Akademos can take on a bitter element today for some of us who view the academy as yielding again to outside pressures and betraying our defining values. We have watched as professors are targeted for expressing dissenting views on subjects ranging from systemic racism to police abuse to gender identification to climate change. Many of their colleagues have remained silent. As faculty members are hounded out of the academy, some professors have even become modern-day "Akademics," pointing out colleagues to the mob and supporting efforts to fire or to suspend those with opposing views. In doing so, most of these faculty members believe that they and their institutions will be spared from the wrath of the mob. Indeed, some are leading the mob. Even law professors have supported shouting down speakers and barring others from campuses entirely because of their opposing views. Yet it is a sense of safety as illusory as that of Akademos. At most, it will spare this small space, but the mob can lay waste to the institution around it.

In the last decade, we have watched a new orthodoxy emerge on our campuses and, with it, an intolerance for opposing views or values. The justification for silencing others is a perverse harm principle where opposing views are treated as threatening or inherently violent. For example, law professor Mary Anne Franks countered free speech objections as failing to recognize that free speech itself is the problem:

> The true threat to free speech on college campuses is posed not by university norms on free speech, but by the attack on those norms by the Internet culture of free speech. The Internet model of free speech is little more than cacophony, where the loudest, most provocative, or most unlikeable voice dominates. . . . If we want to protect free speech, we should not only resist the attempt to remake college campuses in the image of the Internet, but consider the benefits of remaking the Internet in the image of the university.

What Franks considers a "cacophony" of loud and unlikeable voices is viewed by many as the manifestation of a free and open debate. It is the very "collision" that Mill referenced in the exercise of free speech. Instead, Franks suggests that there is a need on both the Internet and campuses to manage expressions and discussions. Once they are made extensions of the overseer—whether corporate or academic—unworthy ideas can then be suppressed for the protection or advancement of others: "While there are many competing ideas about the goal of higher education, and all universities fall short of the ideal, at the core of the educational project is the desire to learn more—about the world, about other people, about the nature of truth. That project requires discernment, not blind insistence on the value of hearing 'both sides.'"

In an article titled "Dear Administrators: Enough with the Free Speech Rhetoric! It Concedes Too Much to the Right-Wing Agenda," religious studies professor Richard Amesbury and history professor Catherine O'Donnell argue that free speech may be harming higher education by fostering "unworthy" ideas. While recognizing the value of free speech overall, they argue that "greater freedom of speech on campuses, however well-intentioned, risks undermining colleges' central purpose, namely, the production of expert knowledge and understanding, in the sense of disciplinarily warranted opinion." They further maintain that "[a] diversity of opinion—'intellectual diversity'—isn't itself the goal; rather, it is of value only insofar as it serves the goal of producing knowledge." Similar views are echoed throughout higher education today. Law professor Alexander Tsesis argues for censorship on a simple cost-benefit basis where "regulating intimidating and defamatory speech on campus outweighs the minimal burden it places on speakers." Once opposing views are declared harmful, scholars find themselves on a spectrum of censorship that runs from "discernment" in avoiding certain speakers to the more extreme "deplatforming" efforts by groups like Antifa. The extent of speech curtailment depends on the level of tolerance for opposing views at any given school. That level of tolerance appears to be dropping across the country.

For academics, what was once a protected space for viewpoint diversity has become a place for enforced orthodoxy. Those who are accused of "harmful" speech can be stripped of every cherished aspect of an intellectual life, including their academic positions. The loss for some is unbearable as shown by Dr. Mike Adams, a professor of sociology and criminology, who killed himself just days before he was to end his academic career. After years of litigation and cancel campaigns, he had finally agreed to surrender his position as a professor. He would leave the grove and the circle. He was forced out not by the students but by his own colleagues and the administration at the University of North Carolina, Wilmington. Removed from higher education, Adams literally would cease to exist. Sitting alone in a bedroom of his home, Adams, fifty-five, could no longer do the thing that he had spent his life to achieve in higher education. He took a gun and put a bullet in his head. Adams has not been the only suicide of faculty members facing discharges after controversies or investigations.

Few academics want to risk being targeted in a cancel campaign. For many years, this meant simply remaining silent as activists targeted colleagues for termination or condemnation. However, activists soon demanded more under the rationale that "silence is violence." Universities began to "break the cycle" or "change the culture" through mandatory or effectively compelled speech. Years ago, many were surprised to read the public testimonials from my own alma mater, Northwestern University Law School. In 2020, the acting dean of the law school began a diversity event by declaring, "I am James Speta, and I am a racist." He was followed by Emily Mullin, executive director of major gifts, who said, "I am a racist and a gatekeeper of white supremacy. I will work to be better." As individuals, these faculty members are free to offer such public allocutions. However, these recitations are increasingly expected as proof of being truly "antiracist."

There is a sense of urgency among some faculty not to be the last to condemn their prior selves. Indeed, some academics seem to stumble over each other to prove their bona fides to an increasingly demanding academic community. Others quickly censor their own words when subjected to cancel campaigns. For example, Ohio State University educational studies and student affairs professor Matthew Mayhew issued an abject apology after penning a column about "Why America Needs

College Football" for the magazine *Inside Higher Ed*. Mayhew argued that the return of college football could get the country through "uncharacteristically difficult times of great isolation, division and uncertainty." That did not sit well with some at the university, who called it racist for putting many Black players at risk. Mayhew published a cringing apology seeking forgiveness for the harm that he caused. He declared, "I was wrong. And even worse, I was uninformed, ignorant and harm inducing." He added, "I also don't want to write anything that suggests that antiracist learning is quick or easy. This is the beginning of a very long process."

If "silence is violence," remaining quiet no longer affords an academic protection. Many schools now require faculty to report annually on their efforts to combat racism or teach diversity principles in their classes and research. Those contesting such statements have found themselves under investigation or ordered to take sensitivity training. What began as voluntary statements have become either expressly or implicitly mandatory.

Take the "land acknowledgment statements" that now start many meetings and courses. George Brown College in Toronto requires faculty and students alike to agree to a land acknowledgment statement to even gain access to virtual classrooms. While such statements are portrayed as optional, they are often enforced as compulsory. The University of Washington encouraged faculty to add a prewritten "Indigenous land acknowledgment" statement to their syllabi. The recommended statement states that "The University of Washington acknowledges the Coast Salish peoples of this land, the land which touches the shared waters of all tribes and bands within the Suquamish, Tulalip and Muckleshoot nations." Computer science professor Stuart Reges decided to write his own statement. He declared, "Land acknowledgments are performative acts of conformity that should be resisted, even if it lands you in court." Reges questioned both the historical and philosophical basis for the statement. His own land acknowledgment stated, "I acknowledge that by the labor theory of property the Coast Salish people can claim historical ownership of almost none of the land currently occupied by the University of Washington." Reges was referring to an idea theory of John Locke's and his view of the state of nature where all was created in common by God. He was told that, while the university statement is optional, his statement was unacceptable because it questioned the indigenous land claim of the Coast Salish people. Reges's dissenting statement was removed, and the university emailed his students offering an apology for their professor's "offensive" opinion and advising them on "three ways students could file complaints against" him. Students in Reges's Computer Science and Engineering class were allowed to switch to a "shadow" class section, and 170 of his 500 students took that option.

The most important aspect about the original *academus* was the idea that it was a safe space for intellectual discourse—free from any threat of physical violence. It was an intellectual space where thoughts could flow freely without fear. Today, there is a constant threat of not just cancel campaigns but actual violence. Indeed, even faculty have participated in such violence against those with dissenting views—claiming that such views are "harmful" or "violent." For example, in 2023, Hunter College professor Shellyne Rodriguez trashed a pro-life display of students on campus as "violent" and "triggering." She berated the students and declared, "You're not educating s—t [. . .] This is f—king propaganda. What are you going to do, like, anti-trans next? This is bulls—t. This is violent. You're triggering my students." When one student tried to calm things down and actually apologized, it only seemed to make the professor angrier. She proceeded to trash the display while stating, "No, you're not—because you can't even have a f—king baby. So, you don't even know what that is. Get this s—t the f—k out of here."

What followed is all too familiar. Some faculty and students rallied around her, not the students whom she attacked. The PSC Graduate Center, the labor organization of graduate and professional schools at the City University of New York, declared that Rodriguez was "justified" in trashing the display, which the organization described as "dangerously false propaganda" and "disinformation." Hunter College itself refused to fire her but said that there would be consequences for further acts of violence. The next day, Rodriguez was caught on a second videotape holding a machete to the neck of a reporter who asked her for a comment at her apartment and threatened to chop him up. She then ran after the reporter and his photographer, chased them down the street, and kicked one in the shin. Finally, Hunter College fired the professor.

The problem is that many faculty have a reasonable expectation today that they will be lionized rather than penalized for attacking conservative, libertarian, or pro-life groups. Just before the Hunter College incident, a professor at the State University of New York at Albany, Renée Overdyke, shut down a pro-life display and then resisted arrest. One student is heard screaming, "She's a f—ing professor." That is, of course, the point. While the university maintains that faculty and students cannot stop others from speaking on campus, this faculty member was applauded for her actions by faculty and students.

Similarly, at the University of California, Santa Barbara, professors actually rallied around feminist studies associate professor Mireille Miller-Young, who physically assaulted pro-life advocates and tore down their display. She pleaded guilty to criminal assault but was not fired. Instead, she received overwhelming support from the students and faculty. Some called the pro-life display an act of terrorism and thus harmful to the students. She was later honored by the University of Oregon as a model for students.

Each of these incidents involved claims that the underlying speech was harmful and that the actions were justified as a matter of self-defense or righteous rage. Many insist that they are simply protecting the safe space for higher education; maintaining a marketplace of ideas where all feel welcomed. Conversely, it rejects the notion that these speakers have an autonomous or natural right to speak. While all speakers can be subject to uniform and reasonable conditions on time, place, and manner for expression, these speakers were denied their ability to engage others, including those who wanted to hear their views. This is why the narrow view of free speech is essential to those who seek to curtail free expression. By declaring speech as harmful, they give themselves license to stop views from being expressed. That includes the speech of fellow colleagues and the curtailment of academic freedom to "protect" students from harmful ideas.

The erosion of free speech in higher education is particularly alarming given the added protection for viewpoint diversity long guaranteed by academic freedom principles. Even academic freedom is being challenged or abridged in the name of combating harmful views and achieving greater diversity on campuses. There is an expanding effort to decouple academic freedom from the protections afforded by free speech. The concept of academic freedom can also be traced to the early Greek academy but, of course, the limits of such freedom were vividly demonstrated by a certain cup of hemlock and Plato's teacher, Socrates.

Modern academic freedom principles are usually traced to the Humboldtian reforms in the early nineteenth century in Prussia. Wilhelm von Humboldt instituted protections for the "freedom to teach" and the "freedom to learn." While it may surprise many, these were not the founding principles of most colleges, including those in the United States. The philosopher Charles Sanders Peirce in 1898 heralded the reforms as "the light of the whole world." Later, the American Association of University Professors (AAUP) issued its 1915 Declaration in the protection of both free speech and academic privilege. That Declaration was based on three defining principles in Germany: "teaching freedom" (*Lehrfreiheit*), "learning freedom" (*Lehrnfreiheit*), and "academic self-governance" (*Freiheit der Wissenschaft*). While all three were referenced in early drafts, the AAUP effectively dropped the learning freedom and academic self-governance parts in favor of teaching freedom (*Lehrfreiheit*). That freedom "protected the restiveness of academic intellect from the obedience norms of hierarchy." The Declaration was a critical moment for American higher education in reaffirming that academic freedom was meant to free our campuses from the demands of "an overwhelming and concentrated public opinion."

The Declaration reaffirmed that academic freedom was meant to protect professors from the "tyranny of public opinion." The ability to think and speak freely was the touchstone of the freedoms needed for higher education. It is the very antithesis of the current movement to silence or cancel professors for holding dissenting views. This nexus between free speech and academic freedom has been recognized by the courts.

However, again, the Court would abridge the right with limiting functionalist rationales. In 1957, in *Sweezy v. New Hampshire*, the Supreme
Court reviewed the conviction of Paul Sweezy, a Marxist and economist,
who refused to answer several questions of the state in an investigation
of "subversive persons." The plurality of the Supreme Court held that the
questioning violated due process because of the "broad and ill-defined"
delegation authority. The dicta defending academic freedom is strikingly
functionalist:

> The essentiality of freedom in the community of American universi-
> ties is almost self-evident. No one should underestimate the vital role
> in a democracy that is played by those who guide and train our youth.
> To impose any strait jacket upon the intellectual leaders in our colleges
> and universities would imperil the future of our Nation. . . . Schol-
> arship cannot flourish in an atmosphere of suspicion and distrust.
> Teachers and students must always remain free to inquire, to study
> and to evaluate, to gain new maturity and understanding; otherwise
> our civilization will stagnate and die.

The concurrence of Justice Felix Frankfurter, a former chaired Harvard law professor, was even more adamant that the questioning violated
core constitutional values, since "thought and action are presumptively
immune from inquisition by political authority." Joined by Justice Harlan,
Frankfurter ties "essential freedoms" to academic freedom:

> In a university knowledge is its own end, not merely a means to an
> end. A university ceases to be true to its own nature if it becomes
> the tool of Church or State or any sectional interest. A university is
> characterized by the spirit of free inquiry, its ideal being the ideal of
> Socrates—"to follow the argument where it leads." This implies the
> right to examine, question, modify or reject traditional ideas and be-
> liefs. Dogma and hypothesis are incompatible, and the concept of an
> immutable doctrine is repugnant to the spirit of a university. The con-
> cern of its scholars is not merely to add and revise facts in relation to

an accepted framework, but to be ever examining and modifying the framework itself.

. . . Freedom to reason and freedom for disputation on the basis of observation and experiment are the necessary conditions for the advancement of scientific knowledge. A sense of freedom is also necessary for creative work in the arts which, equally with scientific research, is the concern of the university.

. . . It is the business of a university to provide that atmosphere which is most conducive to speculation, experiment and creation. It is an atmosphere in which there prevail "the four essential freedoms" of a university—to determine for itself on academic grounds who may teach, what may be taught, how it shall be taught, and who may be admitted to study.

These freedoms support what Frankfurter insists is the essential "exclusion of governmental intervention in the intellectual life of a university." Notably, while this passage refers to knowledge being both a means and an end of higher education, what comes out of the Frankfurter concurrence is its underlying functionalist rationale for both free speech and academic freedom. Frankfurter refers to personal autonomy in free thought but explains that "For a citizen to be made to forego even a part of so basic a liberty as his political autonomy, the subordinating interest of the State must be compelling." He defends academic freedom in "the interest of wise government and the people's well-being."

The Court has repeatedly emphasized that academic freedom is protected under the First Amendment as a form of free speech, but it often ties this protection to the "marketplace of ideas" rationale. Thus, in 1967, in *Keyishian v. Board of Regents*, the Court found that the prohibition of Communist Party members being employed by the New York state government (including in teaching positions) was unconstitutionally vague and overbroad. Writing for the 5–4 majority, Justice William Brennan declared:

Our Nation is deeply committed to safeguarding academic freedom, which is of transcendent value to all of us, and not merely to the

teachers concerned. That freedom is therefore a special concern of the
First Amendment, which does not tolerate laws that cast a pall of orthodoxy over the classroom. "The vigilant protection of constitutional
freedoms is nowhere more vital than in the community of American
schools." . . . The classroom is peculiarly the "marketplace of ideas."
The Nation's future depends upon leaders trained through wide exposure to that robust exchange of ideas which discovers truth "out of a
multitude of tongues, [rather] than through any kind of authoritative
selection."

It is undeniable that academic freedom has a key function in fostering
free thought and advancing the progress of science and social sciences.
That in turn advances the interest of the nation. However, academic freedom is best considered a subset of free speech as a human right. Academics are no different from other citizens in their pursuit of reason and
creative expression. They are merely more focused and collaborative in
such efforts. Indeed, the Kantian pursuit of reason is more pronounced
and all-consuming for academics. They have an insatiable desire to follow their thoughts and ideas wherever they may lead. Yet that is the same
creative impulse that rests from other individuals in the process of self-
realization. The functionalist benefits from free thought do not negate an
underlying natural or liberty right. The Humboldtian reforms recognized
the necessity of academic privilege to maintain the essence of higher education, but that essence is the realization of human potential in science,
the humanities, and other fields. Moreover, the Court saw the threat as
coming from the government. A far greater threat today comes from the
narrow interpretation given to free speech within universities and colleges.

The erosion of free speech on campuses reflects the same conceptual
flaws discussed during speech crackdowns in the courts. It is a narrow
foundation supported by thoughtful academics who seem mired in their
own functionalist rationales. That in turn undermines the protections of
academic freedom. Consider the views of former Yale law dean Robert
Post in his 2012 book *Democracy, Expertise, and Academic Freedom: A*

First Amendment Jurisprudence for the Modern State. In fairness to Post, he explored why some speech has been protected under the Constitution and was making a case for academic freedom as one of those areas. The inquiry was narrower than exploring what free speech is or why it should be protected in a wide array of areas. Nevertheless, his analysis shows why even good-faith functionalist defenses of speech lay the seeds for their own destruction.

Post recognized three basic rationales for First Amendment protections: advancement of knowledge through the "marketplace of ideas," personal autonomy in the sense of "individual self-fulfillment [in reaching the] potentialities as a human being"; and, lastly, the political function of advancing democratic self-governance. He noted that the marketplace of ideas does not really support academic freedom, since academics must be able to declare some ideas as inherently wrong. While I do not base my own view of free speech on the marketplace rationale, I still value it and believe that Post dismissed it too readily in academia. While we do declare certain views or theories as flawed, we have different roles as educators than we do as intellectuals. Often our own work necessarily rejects the work of others. However, as educators, we are equally committed to teaching analytical thinking and allowing students to pursue their own truths. It is for that reason that I teach critical legal theory despite my own disagreement with these scholars. It is the reason I have supported "crits" for faculty positions, even though some have proven entirely hostile as faculty members to others with conservative or libertarian views. I want my students to be exposed to a variety of ideas and perspectives. That is also why I oppose state efforts to ban certain theories from being taught in schools. The marketplace rationale is linked inextricably to the educational values of the academy by guaranteeing a fully stocked marketplace of ideas.

Post also rejected the "ethical" or autonomy basis for free speech under the First Amendment because people are not treated equally in a variety of contexts. Here the focus on the First Amendment artificially limits the analysis, since there are many ways that individuals use free speech for self-fulfillment that are not protected under the amendment. That amendment is not the sole or exclusive definition of free speech.

While the First Amendment only protects against state action, there are also statutory means to protect free speech values that extend beyond the First Amendment. The first task should be to define the free speech values, not simply the protected zones under the First Amendment. If free speech is essential to fulfilling the most essential aspects of being human, it necessitates a wider array of protections that include both academic and nonacademic realms.

Post ultimately offered a powerful defense of the protection of academic freedom due to the final democratic rationale. He analogized academic freedom to producing the same value as areas like commercial speech. Both advance the interests of democratic governance by improving "democratic competence" through expert opinions and research. It is the same rationale embraced by the Court in previously discussed cases such as *Sweezy v. New Hampshire*. However, this "democratic competence" rationale lends itself to a rejection of broader free speech rights even on campuses. Indeed, if academic freedom is protected as a way of supplying expert knowledge to society, it can be used as an argument to curtail views deemed wrong or invalid.

The functionalist rationale is pushed to even greater extremes by others who seek to entirely decouple academic freedom from free speech protections. That is the thrust of the work of law professors Michael Bérubé and Jennifer Ruth, who argue for a narrower view of academic freedom in their 2022 book, *It's Not Free Speech: Race, Democracy, and the Future of Academic Freedom*. Citing Post, Ruth insisted that "the First Amendment has to do with democratic legitimation—that is, the belief that we can all participate in public debate without fear of repression or reprisal by the government—whereas academic freedom is about democratic competence, or the development of regimes of expertise that establish that some forms of speech are more knowledgeable and reliable and can function as resources for an informed citizenry." It is functionalism with an even narrower function: advancing the development of "true" knowledge to the benefit of citizens. That approach gives license to faculty rejecting calls for a diversity of ideologies and the barring of certain speakers on campuses. As they explain:

The First Amendment has no bearing on academic freedom, because the First Amendment has no relation to scholarly expertise. It forbids the prior restraint of speech by the state and certainly doesn't demand or expect that that speech be responsible or informed in any way. Moreover, free speech is an individual right. Whereas academic freedom, as a collective right of the faculty, insists that professorial research and teaching be autonomous from external influence—donors, trustees, legislators, journalists, passersby—because the professoriate has established rigorous systems of peer review that vet knowledge so that the search for truth (or justice, or goodness) is undertaken in intellectually legitimate ways.

If views are deemed wrong, the allowance of such speech does not further democratic competence. Indeed, this view demands that some views are actively suppressed as wrongheaded or ill-informed. The media has also picked up on this approach by columnists who insisted that hiring conservative law faculty is like hiring geocentrists to teach science.

As a threshold matter, this narrower view of academic freedom ignores the pedagogical purpose of higher education to teach critical thinking and expose students to a diversity of viewpoints. As Frankfurter stated in *Sweezy*, "It is the business of a university to provide that atmosphere which is most conducive to speculation, experiment and creation." The teacher-centric view of writers like Bérubé and Ruth treats the value of higher education as the "development of regimes of expertise," as opposed to a student-central purpose in nurturing of a generation of critically thinking and well-educated citizens. Not only does it dismiss autonomy-based rights in silencing some voices, but it also disavows aspects of the "learning freedom" (*Lehrnfreiheit*) element in the early understanding of academic freedom. The role of universities is vital to a democracy, but the role is advanced by allowing a diversity of opinion rather than an orthodoxy to control academic discourse. Courts have rejected the notion that the First Amendment is not implicated by limits on academic freedom as "fantastic." These theories on the basis of academic freedom highlight the vulnerability of functionalism in making trade-offs in free speech.

As with the reliance on the courts to curtail censorship by surrogate, there is little reason to expect academia to protect free speech given this history and the current composition of most faculties. Once again, Congress can reverse this trend and coerce universities to be more tolerant of a diversity of viewpoints. This is why "coercing free speech" can appear oxymoronic but is actually consistent with expanding individual freedoms. It returns to the concept of a protective circle that runs from the Athenian grove to Millian theory.

Mill wrote about the role of government supporting core rights. He generally divided governmental actions into authoritative and nonauthoritative acts. Naturally, for Mill, "the authoritative form of government intervention has a much more limited sphere of legitimate action than the other." Mill's vision of nonauthoritative action is particularly relevant as embracing the role of a government to protect the space of individual choice and action, "not meddling with them, but not trusting the object solely to their care, establishes, side by side with their arrangements, an agency of its own for a like purpose." There is even a role for authoritative action, but the burden is much higher, and it is excluded from areas that must be left to individual choice.

[Authoritative action] requires a much stronger necessity to justify it in any case; while there are large departments of human life from which it must be unreservedly and imperiously excluded. Whatever theory we adopt respecting the foundation of the social union, and under whatever political institutions we live, there is a circle around every individual human being, which no government, be it that of one, of a few, or of the many, ought to be permitted to overstep: there is a part of the life of every person who has come to years of discretion, within which the individuality of that person ought to reign uncontrolled either by any other individual or by the public collectively.

Free speech straddles the line of Millian authoritative and nonauthoritative action, particularly in higher education. Federal legislation can be used to protect, not reduce, the "circles" around individuals in their freedom of thought and expression.

From a classical liberal perspective, the notion of governmental action to protect free speech has a certain Hobbesian (or at least a Spinozan) appeal. After all, the reason to leave the state of nature was to no longer be ruled by the brutish and violent realities of stateless existence. The social contract to surrender powers to the state was based on the promise of protection from the violence and intimidation of others. The government can not only fulfill that purpose but also assure the public that it is not subsidizing the denial of free speech in higher education. It can do so by passing a law barring the receipt of government grants or funding at any university that denies core protections for free speech. Even without considering the billions in federal loan guarantees, the federal government spends billions on grants, projects, consultancies, and other support for academics and their institutions.

Congress has long conditioned the use of federal funds for a wide variety of purposes. The protection of this indispensable right would seem even more of a priority for Congress. Congress used such authority to condition the receipt of federal funds on schools allowing access for ROTC (Reserve Officer's Training Corps) programs and military recruitment under the "Solomon Amendments." In 2006, the Supreme Court upheld the law in *Rumsfeld v. Forum for Academic & Institutional Rights, Inc. (FAIR).* Many universities barred such access due to the discrimination of the military against homosexuals under the "Don't Ask, Don't Tell" policy. The schools argued that the pressure not to discriminate against military recruiters (and some students) was itself compelled speech. The Court rejected that claim. It found that the involvement of the law schools in dealing with recruiters through such channels as email was too inconsequential to constitute compelled association. The Court declared that such conditions "neither limits what law schools may say nor requires them to say anything. . . . As a general matter, the Solomon Amendment regulates conduct, not speech. It affects what law schools must do—afford equal access to military recruiters—not what they may or may not say."

Any federal effort to protect free speech and other rights must be narrowly tailored and enforced to avoid curtailing free speech in the name of protecting it. I have previously testified on ten simple conditions that could be required by law. This includes the expulsion or termination of students or faculty for physical assaults or attacks that would have seemed ridiculously obvious. It would also include the elimination of "free speech zones" that are used to deny the exercise of free speech. There should also be a requirement for speech neutrality rules, including a requirement that any speech sanctions be based on how speech is intended by a speaker rather than simply how speech is received by a listener. Many university rules define harmful speech in terms of how words or viewpoints impact others regardless of their intended meaning. It enables complaints based on "speech-as-harm" rationales by dismissing what a speaker meant rather than how speech was interpreted. These principles are designed to avoid intrusion into academic freedom or judgment, even when schools have abandoned ideological diversity on their faculties. There is no require-ment of ideological diversity on faculties, since enforcement would allow unwarranted government regulation based on ideology. However, Con-gress can require speech neutrality and due process in federally supported institutions. For those universities that value speech regulation more than federal funding, they are free to deny free speech so long as they can carry the costs. This law would also allow for an avenue for faculty and students to report denials of free speech, creating a public record of those schools with histories of speech intolerance.

The model for federal action should be the University of Chicago, which has been ranked as the number one free speech school in the coun-try. As an undergraduate at Chicago, I was thrilled by the range of divergent views and values at the university from Milton Friedman free marketers to Trotskyite Marxists. As most universities were issuing speech codes, creating free speech zones, and sanctioning microaggressions, Chicago took a stand. In 2020, its president, Robert Zimmer, sent all of the newly admitted students a letter warning them that at Chicago they would not be shielded from views that upset them and that, if they were seeking "safe spaces" in education, they had best go elsewhere. The letter declared that "our commitment to academic freedom means that we do not support so-called 'trigger warnings,' we do not cancel invited speakers because their topics might prove controversial, and we do not condone the creation of intellectual 'safe spaces' where individuals can retreat from ideas and perspectives at odds with their own." It became known as the Chicago Principles and should serve as the North Star for not just other universities but for Congress in finding a course back toward a more robust view of free speech and academic freedom.

If we are going to establish a new understanding of free speech, it will be a fight that will begin in our schools of secondary and higher education. We are raising a generation of speech phobics who have been taught that speech is harmful and that speech is protected according to its inherent value (or costs) in a democratic system. This narrow view of free speech has been embedded in the minds of these students from an early age. They have been insulated from opposing views while being taught that such speech is harmful. The result is a narrow range of viewpoints in what have become echo chambers of learning. It also produces a lasting change in how students perceive speech and tolerate opposing views. An analogy can be drawn to neurological changes discussed earlier. The hippocampus (used in creative thinking) can actually shrink from periods of monotony and isolation. The neuroscientist Nancy Andreasen noted the creative human brain requires "an environment full of intellectual richness and freedom." The plasticity of the brain requires a range of inputs, associations, and combination to fully develop. You can literally become less capable of creative thought over time. An analogous danger could be developing in our schools where free speech has been suppressed by a culture of orthodoxy and viewpoint intolerance. An analogy can be drawn to studies of prisoners in isolation reported a common sensory hypersensitivity to sounds and changes after relatively short periods of time. While obviously not as extreme or literal in its application to campuses, we have seen an increasing hypersensitivity among students who have been raised in a type of speech deprivation tank where opposing views are limited and treated as harmful. Simply knowing that opposing viewpoints are being expressed on campus becomes intolerable and threatening.

Speech hypersensitivity is evidenced in countless events where speakers are prevented from voicing opposing views. It is all "triggering" for students, including incidents where faculty have destroyed or disrupted pro-life displays. It was the same sensitivity that was evident at a recent controversy at Stanford Law School when Judge Stuart Kyle Duncan of the United States Court of Appeals for the Fifth Circuit was asked to speak on campus. However, liberal students found that a conservative judge speaking on campus was intolerable and set about to "deplatform" him by shouting him down.

Students prevented Duncan from speaking by screaming insults, and the judge asked for an administrator to allow the event to proceed. Stanford DEI (diversity, equity, and inclusion) dean Tirien Steinbach then took the stage and launched into a babbling attack on the judge for seeking to be heard despite such objections. Steinbach explained, "I had to write something down because I am so uncomfortable up here. And I don't say that for sympathy, I just say that I am deeply, deeply uncomfortable." It turned out that it was the free speech itself that was so stressful and painful for the law dean. Steinbach declared, "It's uncomfortable to say that for many people here, your work has caused harm." After a perfunctory nod to free speech, Steinbach proceeded to eviscerate it to the delight of the law students. She continued, "[A]gain I still ask, is the juice worth the squeeze? Is it worth the pain that this causes, the division that this causes? Do you have something so incredibly important to say about Twitter and guns and COVID that is worth this impact on the division of these people?"

Once again, no students were punished despite a statement from Stanford president Marc Tessier-Lavigne and law school dean Jenny Martinez denouncing the canceling of the judge. Other faculty and students supported the students. One such voice was the law professor Jennifer Ruth (coauthor with Michael Bérubé of the book *It's Not Free Speech*), who had previously argued against the centrality of free speech for academic freedom or higher education. She insisted that preventing Duncan from speaking prevented the harm from people "who have zero respect for the rules that govern democracies, and—if possible—even less respect for the rules that govern colleges and universities." Duncan, she said, should not be heard when he "participates in the now well-oiled judicial machinery of advancing political power through caricature, exaggeration, and doublespeak," and the Stanford Law protesters understood this—that "something existential is at stake." Thus, free speech is only viewed as essential for academia to the extent that it is used by faculty to advance correct ideas. It has no protection to the extent that it spreads harmful ideas. For example, Ruth defended her call for canceling Duncan by citing the Kalven Report, the influential study of academic freedom and free speech from the University of Chicago in 1967. The report was a powerful defense of the need to protect a diversity of thought and free inquiry in higher education: "The neutrality of the university as an institution arises then not from a lack of courage nor out of indifference and insensitivity. It arises out of respect for free inquiry and the obligation to cherish a diversity of viewpoints." Despite the fact that law professor Harry Kalven Jr. coined the term "heckler's veto" and opposed the cancellation of speakers, Ruth insists that the report supports preventing conservatives for speaking (and presumably teaching) on campus:

> From time to time instances will arise in which the society, or segments of it, threaten the very mission of the university and its values of free inquiry. In such a crisis, it becomes the obligation of the university as an institution to oppose such measures and actively to defend its interests and its values.

Thus, in the *Chronicle of Higher Education*, Ruth argued that a report heralding the "values of free inquiry" justifies censorship of conservative viewpoints. She simply declared Judge Duncan's views to be a threat to democracy and thus inimical to the educational mission.

Once decoupled from free speech moorings, the rest becomes easy. Academics will use their superior intellect and "professoriate" to judge the relative worth of ideas in establishing which can be voiced within a college or university. They are the "intellectual connoisseurs" for an unsophisticated audience in what Tom Wolfe might call the "Lawburg." As with citizens at large, students are not expected to have the discerning ability needed to judge such matters. They must be protected from their own ignorance or predilections. In addressing the need to combat disinformation generally, Michigan professor Barbara McQuade argues that today "there is something more at work than simply gullible people falling for lies. A significant number of Americans don't seem to care anymore whether the statement is true." As with earlier discussed groups, Ruth, Bérubé, and others reject the concept of "political neutrality" in allowing free speech to occur that is deemed harmful or inimical to democracy. Once declared as harmful, it is no longer free speech and is worthy of censorship or cancellation. It is that easy.

The conversion of college campuses from bastions of free speech to the current ideological echo chambers is arguably the greatest threat facing free speech. For some of us, the right to think and speak freely is something that belongs to each human. Locke described in his "labor theory" as allowing people to remove what was left in common and join it with something of their own. The creations of mankind are a projection of one's self into the world. Arguably, some of the greatest (if not the greatest) beneficiaries of this gift are intellectuals who try to understand and reshape the world around them. However, there is another part of Locke's theory. It ends with the words that these creations are yours as a natural right so long as there is "enough, and as good, left in common for others." "Locke's proviso," as it is called, reflects that you cannot deny others this divinely bestowed ability to create by denying to others what was left to you. It suggests that the accumulation of wealth can become so extreme as to prevent others from their own creations and pursuits. The proviso is a poignant reminder of what has occurred on campuses across the country. Faculty members who enjoyed tolerant institutions in pursuing their own writings and theories have sought to deny the same opportunities to others. In so doing, they have denied to others "enough and as good in common" when it comes to free speech.

The number of conservatives and libertarians on faculties has continued to fall in a virtual purging of academic ranks. Some schools have only a handful of such faculty members left. In a country roughly divided down the middle politically, less than 10 percent of faculty in all schools identify as conservative, and Democratic faculty outnumber Republican faculty by over ten times. In some schools this ratio goes up to roughly 30 to 1. At the same time, they have created environments of intolerance and orthodoxy where the majority of faculty and students now complain that they do not feel free to express themselves in classes or on campuses. A Wisconsin poll showed roughly 60 percent of students say that they fear speaking openly in class. That percentage is consistent with other polls taken across the country. The Buckley annual survey found that almost 60 percent of college students fear sharing an opinion in classrooms or on campuses. That tracks other polls by different groups. Yet colleges and universities continue to exclude Republican and conservative faculty members and maintain environments of speech intolerance. The poll shows a sharp increase from just last year with 63 percent reporting feeling intimidated in sharing opinions different than their peers. Likewise, a North Carolina poll found virtually the same percentage of those afraid to speak freely in our universities and colleges. The study confirmed how conservative students routinely "self-censor" and do not feel comfortable sharing their views in classes. An earlier poll at the University of North Carolina found that conservative students are three hundred times more likely to self-censor themselves due to the intolerance of opposing views on our campuses.

Given the ascendancy of such views in education, it is little surprise that, when students enter college, they believe that they should not have to tolerate views that upset or challenge them. If this pernicious view of free speech is to be challenged, it will have to be done at their source in our educational institutions. It has been roughly fifty years since the Kalven Report and roughly one hundred years since the AAUP Declaration. We now find ourselves fighting the same fight against those who seek to bar bad-tendency speech from our campuses. It is a view that has continued to rage due to the failure to recognize free speech as a transcendent right of individuals to pursue their own truth and identity. It is an intellectual pursuit that runs from Plato in the *academus* and continues to this day with professors in the modern academy. This is where the struggle for free thought took root, and we cannot yield this ground if we are to restore this indispensable right.

Academia will likely remain a battleground over the meaning of free speech, since faculties show little evidence that they will yield to calls for greater diversity of thought and expression. Despite stinging losses in the courts, colleges and universities remain a hardened silo of speech intolerance. That was made obvious in a decision handed down roughly a week later by the United States Court of Appeals for the Fourth Circuit in *Porter v. Board of Trustees of North Carolina State University*. The case involved a tenured professor, Dr. Stephen Porter, who was sanctioned for speaking out against diversity policies in hiring and scholarship. Judge Stephanie Dawn Thacker wrote an opinion declaring that the action was not a free speech matter because Porter was fired for being non-collegial. In other words, it was his conduct, not his speech, that was the cause for his discipline. It is an all too familiar rationalization. For many years, women and minorities were given low evaluations on grounds of collegiality as an excuse for denying them positions or advancement. The AAUP has warned that collegiality is often a coded or biased basis for discrimination, citing the lack of "'a constructive attitude' that 'will foster harmony.'" It was clear that Porter's view enraged his superiors and many of his colleagues, but the court converted the question into one of conduct rather than speech—the same thin rationalization used by the Supreme Court in denying protections to those opposing the draft or espousing dissenting political views in prior years. Ironically, back then, it was the left that was targeted as acting against the interests of the common good. The Fourth Circuit decision shows how fluid definitions of free speech can allow such opportunistic and artificial distinctions to justify anti–free speech measures. (Indeed, a law professor who was an outspoken critic of DEI policies at Ohio Northern University claims that he was also terminated on grounds of collegiality in 2023.) It also shows that universities continue to follow the same rationales used in abusive opinions like the dissenters in *Cohen v. California* in treating speech as conduct to circumvent constitutional protections. It is not a matter of free speech, just rejecting a more "cooperative relationship of colleagues" in voicing dissenting views. In the end, true collegiality is found in the tolerance and support of one's colleagues in holding opposing views. It is found in maintaining the Athenian circle that protects us all.

Twenty-Nine

SLAYING MADISON'S MONSTER: ENDING SEDITION AND SPEECH PROSECUTIONS

Friedrich Nietzsche once wrote that "whoever fights monsters should see to it that in the process he does not become a monster. And if you gaze long enough into an abyss, the abyss will gaze back into you." From the thirteenth century to today, one crime has lurked within our history as the menace of free speech and emerged during periods of "temporary panic." Madison described sedition prosecutions in his 1798 letter to Thomas Jefferson as the "monster that must forever disgrace its parents." Two years later, he would write his Report of 1800 to call his contemporaries to account for their re-embracing of the scourge of sedition. He warned how such laws would threaten the "free communication among the people thereon, which has ever been justly deemed, the only effectual guardian of every other right."

A return to a natural law or autonomy-based right would compel changes beyond the final rejection of sedition crimes, including a long-needed reexamination of prior cases on fighting words and obscenity. Indeed, other laws like the Comstock Act also warrant removal. Much like sedition, there are already redundant laws criminalizing the possession or mailing of child pornography. Beyond such well-defined crimes, criminalizing "obscene, lewd, lascivious, indecent, filthy or vile article, matter, thing, device, or substance" is an invitation for speech prosecutions. The law has been found unconstitutional in many respects, but Congress refuses to make a clean break from a law that was designed as a weapon to use against those with divergent or dissenting views on morality or social norms. Again, even if not widely used like the sedition offenses, the elimination of such laws would affirm that we have finally come to a reckoning with our past and reaffirmed the original purpose of the First Amendment—and the Revolution itself.

The long struggle over free speech in the United States fulfills Nietzsche's warning. Many of those who defied the British sedition laws would become the very thing that they despised. Madison's alarm over the Alien and Sedition Acts was in contrast to Jefferson, who (while opposing the abuses of the Adams administration) would use sedition against his own critics and countenance its use by the states. It was the first major crisis of faith for our constitutional system. With the ratification of the First Amendment, the United States adopted the single greatest protection of free speech in history. Yet within a few years, former Revolutionaries would reach for the same bludgeon to use against their own enemies. Even a Son of Liberty like Samuel Adams would label critics seditionists for engaging in protests closely analogous to the Boston Tea Party. It would begin two centuries of American sedition and speech criminalization. The most recent seditious conspiracy cases stemming from the January 6th riot continue that legacy. The January 6th prosecutions show how this crime is still relished by some for its stigmatizing effect on political opponents. As discussed later in this chapter, it is largely redundant with other charges offenses, but adds a charge that raises ideology as threat to the nation. Even though relatively few were charged with this crime among the hundreds arrested, it continues to serve the same purpose in punishing acts that do not qualify as treason—the very purpose of original sedition prosecutions brought before the Star Chamber. It is time to finally slay Madison's monster and put an end to American sedition.

As in the past, it is difficult to object to such charges without being accused of being a fellow traveler or seditious sympathizer. Indeed, it is difficult not to share the visceral anger against those who attacked our

Capitol building. Judges show the same natural impulse in the face of those who denigrate our institutions or shared values. Yet throughout our history, there were judicial figures who pushed back at the use of sedition charges as inimical to free speech—arguing that the government should focus on overt criminal acts. Even if the crime is not carried out, it is the attempt at the crime rather than the speech itself that can be criminalized. It is a distinction hard to see in periods of panic, let alone to draw as a judge. However, despite the litany of judges who failed to uphold the Constitution or even led the mob justice, there were exceptions like federal district judge George Bourquin of Montana. Bourquin was an example of how true justice is often an innate inclination. Bourquin never went to law school and instead studied law on his own. He would put up a shingle in Helena in 18̸ and then later take this legal practice to Butte. After Bourquin ser̸ short stint as a state judge, President William Taft would put him̸ federal bench in 1912. That made him a younger contemporary̸ Wendell Holmes.

The comparison between Bourquin and Holmes is stri̸ father, Oliver Wendell Holmes Sr., was the one who coi̸ "Boston Brahmins" to refer to the elite of that Eas̸ educated, Holmes had every advantage in the stud̸ losophy, and meaning of the Constitution. Yet ̸ narrow, lifeless view of free speech that expose̸ dissidents to arrest and incarceration.

Bourquin tried his hand at cowboyir̸ to study law. He was a large man who̸ irascible, yet merciful, fair, and just."̸ figure at social engagements with ̸

something of a recluse who ate alone (even having chairs removed or turned up to discourage anyone from trying to join him). He was known as a tough judge with a wry sense of humor and a frontier sense of justice. In one case, he found a man not guilty of a minor liquor violation, telling him, "The court finds you not guilty, but don't do it again." It was this self-educated Western lawyer who captured the meaning of free speech and saw a transcendent meaning that escaped Holmes.

During World War I, Bourquin was presented with a case involving a critic of a popular war. Montana had contributed more soldiers per capita to the war than any other state. Local politicians pushed to punish "slackers" who resisted the draft. Then, in 1918, the first case under the Espionage Act was brought in the state. The accused was a rancher named Ves Hall, who predicted that Germany "would whip the United States" and that "the United States was only fighting for Wall Street millionaires." He also denounced President Wilson as a "British tool, a servant of Wall Street millionaires, and the richest and crookedest-ever President." Despite the pressure to convict Hall, Bourquin acquitted him. And his ruling showed a sophisticated understanding of the Constitution and free speech.

Bourquin agreed with the federal government that Hall intended to deter recruitment efforts for the war. However, he insisted that criminalizing "loose talk" would return the nation to the dark days of sedition abuse of the Adams administration. He lamented that, despite "the genius of democracy and the spirit of our people," the country is still "unable to avoid greater evils than benefits from laws" in criminalizing speech. Bourquin construed the law narrowly and insisted that it was not meant to suppress criticism or denunciation, truth or slander, oratory or gossip, argument or loose talk, but only false facts, willfully put forward as true, broadly, with the specific intent to interfere with army or navy operations. Bourquin insisted that, if slanderous comments cause disruptions, should be prosecuted under state law for breach of the peace. That decision is concerning for free speech advocates, since governments always claim that it was the speaker, not the mob, who caused unrest. However, Bourquin hit on the key factor in "the law of attempts." He

insisted that the government needed to show a close nexus to a particular crime and the attempt to commit that crime:

> "It is settled law that attempts are efforts with specific intent to commit specific crimes and are of sufficient magnitude and proximity to the object of their operation that they are reasonably calculated to excite public fear and alarm that such efforts will accomplish the specific crimes if they do not fail."

Bourquin observed that these comments were made in "a Montana village of some 60 people, 60 miles from the railway, and none of the armies or navies within hundreds of miles." That is in sharp contrast to Holmes in cases like *Frohwerk*, where he dismissed the fact that the publisher actually collected most of the offending publications because "a little breath would be enough to kindle a flame, and that the fact was known and relied upon by those who sent the paper out." Holmes was describing a type of butterfly effect theory where "a butterfly can flutter its wings over a flower in China and cause a hurricane in the Caribbean" . . . or, in this case, a dissenting view spoken in "a small Montana village" can undermine a war effort thousands of miles away.

The response to Bourquin was fast and furious. In Washington, Montana senator Thomas J. Walsh, chair of the Senate Judiciary Committee, denounced Bourquin for his "notorious" decision and predicted it could "assist the cause of our enemies." Others warned that violence, even killing, would result from the anger. Newspapers called for Bourquin to be removed not from the bench (since "impeachment would take too long") but from the state.

Tying speech cases to the law of attempts can counter the constitutional butterfly effect theory. As law professor Geoffrey Stone noted, "The element of specific intent is essential because one 'cannot attempt . . . to do an act without the intent to do the act.' This seems self-evident, but it is critical. An individual who negligently or even recklessly creates a danger is not guilty of attempt." It would require a showing of a concrete effort to bring about a specific crime like a rebellion or riot. The alternative is evident in the World War I case where North Dakota banker John Wishek was charged with sedition for merely stating that "banks having large holdings in Liberty Bonds are unsafe to keep money in." In the Wishek case, another courageous jurist, Judge Charles Fremont Amidon, instructed the jury that such statements lack a necessary nexus to the crime of preventing or discouraging others from serving in the military. Yet the jury still deadlocked, 9–3, in favor of conviction, and Amidon was shunned by many for his handling of the case.

The problem with relying entirely on the law of attempt (rather than reframing the concept of free speech) is that it is still open to manipulation. Blackstone himself stated that the accused must be shown to have used speech that "could not fail of their mischievous effect." However, every publication is an effort to convince others. The greater the influence of the speaker, the more likely that minds will be changed and action could result. Likewise, the context can still be used to establish intent. The Court has struggled to preserve this type of case-by-case judgment.

The emphasis on attempt cases is useful, but these decisions still became muddled on the extremes of the application of the theory. Bourquin, Wishek, Hand, and others still recognized that speech could be criminalized if it were shown to cause a disruptive effect. In my view, that is the ultimate test of our commitment to free speech. Ideas alone cannot be criminalized, even if they are inimical to a war or other government actions. To put it bluntly, any nation that cannot withstand the competition of ideas lacks the foundation and legitimacy to be sustained. Even direct calls for rebellion are protected under this view. Consider, again, the case of anarchist Alexander Berkman, who declared around the same time as Hall that "when the time comes we will not stop short of bloodshed to gain our ends." Berkman was a violent agitator who later tried to assassinate a businessman. Writing about revolution is protected speech. That includes supporting such calls. However, when Berkman and his fellow anarchists set about to plan and build a bomb, they were squarely in the realm of attempts. The speech was part of a conspiracy to commit the murder of an individual. That was the crime, not the earlier ravings of these anarchists.

This view challenges not just crimes like seditious conspiracy (when based on speech alone) but also incitement. Governments have long defined certain speech as incitement (when it opposed the government) while tolerating other inflammatory speech in line with its policies. It is only speech that is intended to commit a specific crime that should be prosecuted when it evidenced that "sufficient magnitude and proximity" to qualify as an attempt. It cannot be the speech itself.

While the specific standards have evolved since Blackstone, speech prosecutions are based on the same butterfly effect theory of speech with the potential of building into an insurrection or rebellion. Courts have acknowledged that those prosecuted for speech opposing wars or drafts had little immediate impact on either effort. Many defendants stopped short of outright advocacy of violence or criminal conduct. As discussed earlier, Frank Shaffer is one such example. A member of the International Bible Students, Shaffer was prosecuted for publishing his book *The Finished Mystery*. Shaffer had held various jobs from farmer to rancher to storekeeper to postmaster. In 1917, he published his book with the Watch Tower Bible and Tract Society. It quoted a sermon by Reverend John Haynes Holmes that opposed the war, stating, "The war itself is wrong. Its prosecution will be a crime. There is not a question raised, an issue involved, a cause at stake, which is worth the life of one blue-jacket on the sea or one khaki-coat in the trenches." It was an innocuous passage from a speech given before the passage of the Espionage Act. However, the United States Court of Appeals for the Ninth Circuit dismissed the fact that this was little more than a butterfly flap in a little-read publication:

> It is true that disapproval of the war and the advocacy of peace are not crimes under the Espionage Act; but the question here . . . is whether the natural and probable tendency and effect of the words . . . are such as are calculated to produce the result condemned by the statute. . . .
>
> Printed matter may tend to obstruct the . . . service even if it contains no mention of recruiting or enlistment, and no reference to the military service of the United States. . . .
>
> To teach that patriotism is murder and the spirit of the devil, and that the war against Germany was wrong and its prosecution a crime,

is to weaken patriotism and the purpose to enlist or to render military service in the war. . . .

It is argued that the evidence fails to show that Shaffer committed the act willfully and intentionally. But . . . he must be presumed to have intended the natural and probable consequences of what he knowingly did.

It was the same "bad tendency" rationale. Like "clear and present danger," it proved the same wine in a different bottle. The "finish" for free speech was the same.

The argument for preemptive action against dangerous speech is a recurring theme on the Court. Many have long embraced the lazy logic of Justice Robert H. Jackson that "the Constitution is not a suicide pact." (Arguably the second most damaging line currently in vogue after Holmes's theater analogy.) Jackson made the observation in his dissent in *Terminiello v. Chicago*, though he actually said, "[I]f the Court does not temper its doctrinaire logic with a little practical wisdom, it will convert the constitutional Bill of Rights into a suicide pact." Notably, Jackson was objecting to the overturning of a conviction under a grossly unconstitutional ordinance that criminalized speech that "stirs the public to anger, invites dispute, brings about a condition of unrest, or creates a disturbance."

Jackson was not alone in calling for "practical" powers to silence some speakers before they influenced others in taking unlawful action. In *Dennis*, Chief Justice Vinson declared:

Obviously, the words cannot mean that before the Government may act, it must wait until the putsch is about to be executed, the plans have been laid and the signal is awaited. If Government is aware that a group aiming at its overthrow is attempting to indoctrinate its members and to commit them to a course whereby they will strike when the leaders feel the circumstances permit, action by the Government is required.

The problem, of course, is that leaders have always claimed that "circumstances . . . required" preemptive crackdowns to protect the nation.

It is not any attempted indoctrination but any attempted execution that should be the focus of prosecutions.

The United States must completely break from the concept of "bad tendency" rationales if it is going to fulfill the original promise of the First Amendment. Yet there remain lingering residues of this rationalization for contemporary prosecutions, including in some of the response to the January 6th riot. There are also striking historical comparisons, particularly with the Fries Rebellion. As discussed earlier, those participating in the Fries Rebellion did not believe that they were acting illegally in defying tax collection. It was no more of an actual rebellion than January 6th was an actual insurrection. The Pennsylvania farmers believed that they were allowed to constitute a militia and that there was law supporting their actions. As the historian Paul Douglas Newman observed, the Fries forces "wanted to be sure that they were recognizable as a company of militia, not a common mob, because the militia was a constitutionally sanctioned body." Some of the current sedition defendants also claim that they believed that they would be called to form a lawful militia by President Trump. Where the farmers had Reverend Jacob Eyermann assuring them that he was literally holding their legal authority in his hand, January 6th protesters had figures like John Eastman assuring the president and his followers that Congress (and Vice President Pence) could refuse certification.

Both groups were wrong on the law but believed that they had good-faith grievances and causes to act. In the Fries Rebellion, the farmers were following past practices in seizing tax collectors or assessors while demanding justice. The farmers actually cited not just constitutional claims but also the newly created First Amendment to support their actions. Many of these men fought in the Revolution and "believed that they had acted in accord with and in support of their Constitution, not against it." On the government side, there were even analogous claims of foreign interference before the Fries Rebellion. While Trump objected to critics declaring "Russia, Russia, Russia" in a foreign collusion, the Adams government was more inclined to cry "France, France, France." Even when it became clear that this was not a rebellion or treason in Pennsylvania, federalists still feared "Jacobin Phrenzy" like the chaos seen unfolding in the French Revolution. Where extremist groups like the Proud Boys have a history and reputation for violence, Pennsylvania had the Paxton Boys, who were notoriously violent and formed as a militia in prior years. Once again, the legal claims in both the Fries Rebellion and the January 6th riot were unsupported, and there were crimes committed by both groups. The issue is not the basis but their intent in the underlying protests for most of the participants. In both historical events, most protesters remained nonviolent as a minority lost control. In both events, criminal charges were warranted, but the question is the need for sedition charges to address such crimes.

On January 6th, there were clear crimes that were legitimately prosecuted, from trespass to assault. However, only roughly a dozen of the hundreds of cases prosecuted after January 6th included seditious conspiracy charges. The defendants associated with two extremist groups—the Oath Keepers and the Proud Boys—were charged with an array of crimes. In addition to the seditious conspiracy counts, the government commonly charged conspiracy to obstruct an official proceeding, obstruction of an official proceeding, and conspiracy to prevent members of Congress from discharging their official duties as well as lesser offenses.

Notably, seditious conspiracy, conspiracy to obstruct Congress, obstruction of Congress, and destruction of evidence have the same maximum potential sentence of twenty years in prison. Thus, with crimes generally running concurrently, the seditious conspiracy charge does not necessarily increase the ultimate sentences. More important, the sentencing provisions are not the only overlapping elements in these crimes. Seditious conspiracy under 18 U.S.C. § 2384 states:

> If two or more persons . . . conspire to overthrow, put down, or to destroy by force the Government of the United States, or to levy war against them, or to oppose by force the authority thereof, or by force to prevent, hinder, or delay the execution of any law of the United States, or by force to seize, take, or possess any property of the United States

contrary to the authority thereof, they shall each be fined under this title or imprisoned not more than twenty years, or both.

The law is different from the original sedition laws that made it a crime to "print, utter, or publish . . . any false, scandalous, and malicious writing or writings against the government of the United States, or either house of the Congress of the United States, or the President of the United States." The current law is broader to an absurd degree, allowing for the prosecution for conspiring "by force to prevent, hinder, or delay the execution of any law of the United States." The language allows for the use of sedition as part of count stacking, where the same offense is charged as separate offenses.

The redundancy of the seditious conspiracy claims with other crimes was evident in the Oath Keepers trial. On January 23, 2023, four members of the extremist group—Roberto Minuta, Joseph Hackett, David Moerschel, and Edward Vallejo—were convicted of conspiracy to obstruct an official proceeding, obstruction of an official proceeding, and conspiracy to prevent members of Congress from discharging their official duties. The Oath Keepers fashioned themselves as patriots who took an oath to defend the Constitution "against all enemies foreign and domestic." The indictment shows members storing weapons and organizing teams to march on the Capitol. Thus, they were convicted of a seditious conspiracy to obstruct proceedings *and* conspiracy to obstruct proceedings. If the dividing line is difficult to discern, it is because there is no real distinction. These men were rightfully charged with seeking to disrupt the presidential certification and should face incarceration. They claimed to believe the theory that Trump could and would invoke the Insurrection Act and call on militia members to stop the stealing of an election. It does not matter. They obstructed the proceedings and other related crimes. They could be sentenced to up to twenty years under some of the remaining counts.

The use of the sedition-based charge was meant to amplify the culpability of the defendants. It was based on their extremist views and conspiracy theories. However, thousands were at the protest, and hundreds entered the Capitol. Yet only a few individuals were charged with seditious conspiracy. The difficulty in separating these cases is evident in the prosecution of Guy Reffitt, who went to the Capitol with zip ties and carrying a gun. He was a member of the extremist group known as the Three Percenters. The group derived its name from a claim that only 3 percent of colonists actually fought the British in the American Revolution. He was convicted of five counts, including transport of a firearm in support of civil disorder and obstruction of an official proceeding. The government sought to increase the sentencing by claiming a terrorism enhancement because Reffitt was "planning to overtake our government." The Court balked and said that it was sufficient to treat him as a violent offender and imposed a heavy sentence of eighty-seven months in prison, three years of probation, $2,000 in restitution, and mandatory mental health treatment. The question is the distinction with the Proud Boys. While Reffitt would not enter the Capitol, that was not the key factor in the sedition-based cases. Moreover, Reffitt was captured on videotape stating that he wanted to drag lawmakers outside of the Capitol "kicking and screaming" and specifically wanted to see House Speaker Nancy Pelosi's head hit every stair on the way down. Prosecutors argued that he was a recruiter for the Three Percenters and wanted to turn volunteers "into an unstoppable force" against police officers. Before his own son turned him in, Reffitt told him and his sister that "if you turn me in, you're a traitor, and traitors get shot."

Reffitt's rage rhetoric was not enough to generate a sedition-based charge or a terrorism enhancement. He was legitimately prosecuted for his overt acts and the effort to disrupt the proceedings. For a small number of others, similar acts were charged under the same provisions, but with the addition of seditious conspiracy. These cases capture Holmes's ill-considered conversion of free speech issues into inchoate crimes to avoid addressing these issues. By using a sweeping criminalization of seeking "to prevent, hinder, or delay the execution of any law of the United States," the government could call the defendants seditionists. With many in the media and Congress still calling the riot an insurrection, the label helped mollify public demand for prosecution of individuals for their extremist views.

The January 6th protests produced three groups. The first group was protesters who were engaged in protected speech at the Ellipse and the Capitol. The second group was "rioters" like Reffitt who sought to obstruct proceedings. The third group was "seditionists" who sought to obstruct proceeding but did so with seditious intent. The last two groups both sought to disrupt, but one is labeled as doing so as a form of sedition. The distinction in these cases seems to be underlying speech and extremist advocacy of groups like the Oath Keepers. Rather than simply punish them for their overt acts, the government wanted to add charges that reflect seditious viewpoints. Notably, there are ample terrorism and treason charges that can be brought when warranted. However, as was the case under the Star Chamber proceedings, these are cases that do not meet the criteria for crimes like treason. Accordingly, the government uses the catch-all crime of conspiracy "to prevent, hinder, or delay the execution of any law."

Contemporary cases show that courts adopted the same rationales and rhetoric of early "panic periods." For example, in *United States v. Rahman*, the United States Court of Appeals for the Second Circuit considered a challenge to the seditious conspiracy offense in a 1999 terrorism case. Once again, there was ample evidence to convict the ten defendants on a variety of crimes such as conspiracy to commit terrorist acts like bombing and murder. However, the government found itself in the same position as the English government in its early treason cases. It could not establish the elements. So, it turned to sedition. Since there was no guideline for sedition sentencing, it asked the court to sentence as if the defendants were convicted of treason. The court agreed and, on appeal, the defendants insisted that the government should have to prove the elements of treason including betrayal of an allegiance. Among the defendants, Rahman also challenged on First Amendment grounds that he only engaged in political speech.

The Second Circuit upheld the use of the treason sentencing guideline (which allowed for the death penalty) to support a sentencing above the twenty-year maximum. It then upheld the conviction for Rahman's violent rhetoric. It ruled that "notwithstanding that political speech and religious exercise are among the activities most jealously guarded by the First Amendment, one is not immunized from prosecution for such speech-based offenses merely because one commits them through the medium of political speech or religious preaching." The court simply rationalized that the sedition crime "proscribes 'speech' only when it constitutes an agreement to use force against the United States." However, the government did not simply charge a conspiracy but chose sedition and then secured a sentencing akin to a treason conviction. The Justice Department achieved what the British Crown could not. Unable to prove treason, it was able to convict on the vague sedition crime and allowed to seek punishment for the very crime that it admitted it could not prove. While the trial court did give an instruction that political speech is still protected, the use of the treason guideline magnified the free speech concerns. What was equally troubling is that the court relied on the previously discussed 1951 decision in *Dennis v. United States*, where the Supreme Court upheld the constitutionality of the Smith Act's criminalization of the advocacy of (or conspiracy to advocate) the overthrow of the United States government by force or violence. The fractured Court upheld the conviction of ten defendants who wanted to form a Communist Party.

Dennis was a pure political speech case. In applying the *Schenck* standard, Judge Harold Medina instructed the jury members that they did not have to find that the speech of the defendants actually harmed the country. After the legendary Judge Learned Hand upheld the convictions, the Supreme Court magnified the damage in *Dennis*. Chief Justice Fred M. Vinson adopted an almost mocking distinction in noting that the Act "is directed at advocacy, not discussion." Vinson added a point that was impressively devoid of any sense of historical awareness or constitutional principle:

> Whatever theoretical merit there may be in the argument that there is a "right" to rebellion against dictatorial governments is without force where the existing structure of the government provides for peaceful and orderly change. We reject any principle of governmental helplessness in the face of preparation for revolution, which principle, carried to its logical conclusion, must lead to anarchy.

It was the same rationalization used by Samuel Adams to seek sedition charges against the defendants in Shays' Rebellion. Adams recognized that he and others committed similar acts in the Boston Tea Party, but he rejected the same challenges to the authority of the United States as manifestly illegitimate because "the man who dares rebel against the laws of a republic ought to suffer death." Vinson adopted the same convoluted logic that, because the United States was a democracy, it could prosecute citizens in a way condemned in other governments.

Dennis showed how little had changed in centuries of rationalization over sedition and speech controls. The greatest danger was not a small group of communists advocating a new political order. It was a larger group of courts enforcing censorship and criminalization of speech. The voice of clarity was heard in dissent and Justice Black's opinion is regrettably timeless in calling judges to account for their own roles in his ignoble history:

> These petitioners were not charged with an attempt to overthrow the Government. They were not charged with overt acts of any kind designed to overthrow the Government. They were not even charged with saying anything or writing anything designed to overthrow the Government. The charge was that they agreed to assemble and to talk and publish certain ideas at a later date. The indictment is that they conspired to organize the Communist Party and to use speech or newspapers and other publications in the future to teach and advocate the forcible overthrow of the Government. . . . So long as this Court exercises the power of judicial review of legislation, I cannot agree that the First Amendment permits us to sustain laws suppressing freedom of speech and press on the basis of Congress' or our own notions of mere "reasonableness." Such a doctrine waters down the First Amendment so that it amounts to little more than an admonition to Congress. The Amendment as so construed is not likely to protect any but those "safe" or orthodox views which rarely need its protection.
>
> Public opinion being what it now is, few will protest the conviction of these Communist petitioners.

Black's hope for a "later court" to correct such calls remains unfulfilled. After the Supreme Court upheld the convictions, the Justice Department rounded up communists and others. There were 131 persons indicted by May 2, 1956, and 98 were convicted. Only nine were acquitted.

The lack of clarity in the January 6th cases continued the dangerous selectivity and ambiguity of sedition prosecutions. Free speech demands bright lines to avoid the "chilling effect" that serves to achieve by self-censoring far more than can be achieved by direct censorship. Hundreds of years after Blackstone's defense of such prosecutions, vague seditious conspiracy standards can preserve for some the "perilous" potential for those challenging wars, pandemic measures, or other state-sanctioned viewpoints. For the government, sedition has always been an area of law that followed Oscar Wilde's rule on temptation: "The only way to get rid of a temptation is to yield to it. Resist it, and your soul grows sick with longing for the things it has forbidden to itself, with desire for what its monstrous laws have made monstrous and unlawful."

Madison's monster has been released time and time again because every generation believes that the rage rhetoric that it is facing represents an unprecedented or existential threat. Courts have been largely susceptible to the same temptation to yield—blinded by countervailing rage or irrationality. An age of rage is precisely when it is essential to have the brightest of bright lines protecting free speech. However, the one option—the one temptation—that must be denied to all sides is the ability to silence or sanction others for their viewpoints. Trump's Ellipse speech highlights the inherent danger of the functionalist view in criminalizing speech. Since advocates tie the protection of free speech to advancing the democratic process, a speech that challenges the results of elections or advances unfounded constitutional claims can be stripped of such protection as inimical to democracy. Likewise, courts can draw the same undiscernible distinction between "discussion" and "advocacy" of such views.

On January 6th, I was contributing to the coverage of the day and criticized Trump's speech while he was still giving it. Trump was wrong on his view of the election fraud claims and his view of the authority of Vice President Pence to block certification. However, Trump had every right to voice those views, and his supporters had every right to protest the certification vote. It is common for political groups to go to capitals to denounce votes or encourage allies to stand firm in opposition to legislative measures. Despite many law professors claiming that the speech could be the subject of criminal charges for incitement, prosecution on the basis of the speech would constitute a major erosion of free protections even under governing precedent. Trump's call for protesters to "peacefully" march on the Capitol to oppose certification did not come close to meeting the *Brandenburg* standard of a threat of "imminent lawless action and . . . likely to incite or produce such action." Prior such speeches supporting opposition by Democrats to the certification of Republican presidents were (correctly) not treated as incitement.

The danger of returning to the "bad tendency" rationales of prior years was evident in the first judicial treatment of Trump's Ellipse speech in *Eastman v. Thompson*. Judge David O. Carter in the U.S. District Court for the Central District of California considered the status of the speech in a civil rather than a criminal case involving Trump's private counsel. John Eastman withheld documents from the January 6th Committee. Many of us viewed this as an easy case. Eastman had to turn over the documents as part of the congressional investigation into the riot. While the exclusion of members appointed by the GOP led to a one-sided membership, the committee still had a legitimate interest in determining if there was any plan or conspiracy in the effort to stop the certification of the election. It should have been a simple and straightforward application of prior cases supporting such oversight authority. Instead, Carter wrote a sweeping opinion that was heavily imbued with rhetoric used to support claims of an insurrection. He dispenses with any suggestion of a riot and declares that this was "a coup in search of a legal theory."

Judge Carter declared that "[t]he illegality of the plan was obvious" on January 6th. The court concluded "it is more likely than not that President Trump corruptly attempted to obstruct the Joint Session of Congress on January 6, 2021." He rejected any claim that Trump could base his action on the legal advice of Eastman and others that Vice President Pence could refuse to certify the election and send the electoral votes back to the states.

Many of us had rejected that theory. However, there was no conclusive evidence to say that Eastman clearly knew that the theory was wrong as opposed to believing that it was novel, but unresolved. More important, this theory of criminality would demand not just a showing that Trump believed that the theory was meritless but also that he did not believe a court would find merit in it. Various presidents have made highly improbable arguments, even when they were not personally convinced of the merits. This includes excessive claims of executive or unilateral authority. In fact, Trump's successor, Joe Biden, was repeatedly found to have violated the Constitution in exceeding his authority, including ignoring the overwhelming opinion of legal advisers to embrace the lone view of one law professor. Nevertheless, Carter found that such legal advice failed under the "crime/fraud exception" because the president presumably knew there was no basis for such a challenge. Yet after acknowledging that Eastman still believed that the statute is unconstitutional as written, the Court simply brushes that aside and states the "ignorance of the law is no excuse" and "believing the Electoral Count Act was unconstitutional did not give President Trump license to violate it."

Despite my disagreement with the Eastman arguments, the implications of the ruling are chilling. Public interest lawyers often take novel arguments or seek to establish precedent despite prior judicial rejections. Some would lead to major new rulings by the Supreme Court. For example, *Brown v. Board of Education* was the culmination of a long line of cases attempting to establish that separate was not equal. This was clearly no *Brown* argument, but the question is the line of distinction for future cases in lawyers challenging prevailing legal views. Carter relies on legal memos laying out a legal strategy to send the certification back to the states as evidence of a "legal interpretation of the Electoral Count Act [being used as] a day-by-day plan of action." He simply interprets such legal memos as not a plan to challenge but a "plan to obstruct the joint session of Congress." Carter declares "the illegality of the plan was obvious." He further declares that, despite the protections of *Brandenburg*, Trump "more likely than not" committed federal crimes. Indeed, Carter does not cite *Brandenburg* once, let alone address the underlying free speech protections.

In declaring that Trump most likely committed crimes on January 6th, Carter simply brushes over the fact that Trump had every right to call his supporters to protest the election and to call for members to re-fuse to recognize the certification from particular states. Judge Carter recognized that the underlying theory had been discussed by others, but declared, "Their campaign was not confined to the ivory tower—it was a coup in search of a legal theory." So, Eastman could teach the theory in class, but it would become a "campaign to overturn a democratic nation" when repeated to a president or his followers. Carter's analysis reflects the same bad-tendency rationales that have characterized speech pros-ecutions since the trial of Henry Redhead Yorke and later trials. Carter treats the advocacy as the cause of the riot. Yet, if that were the case, one would expect more than a small number of sedition cases. All the protest-ers seemed to believe that the election was fraudulent and the certification was unlawful.

Eastman effectively declares presumptive guilt due to the effect of these legal arguments. It has elements of not just the "bad tendency" rationale but also seems to declare the legal theories as creating "clear and present danger" of a riot. Indeed, academics like Professor Dennis Baron directly relied on the now-discarded *Schenck* standard to insist that the speech alone constituted a crime. He explained that, under the First Amendment, "no . . . doesn't mean 'no.' Obscenity, fighting words, and threats have never been protected speech. Criminal conspiracy is not protected. Nei-ther is incitement to riot. Freedom of speech is never absolute." He added, "[F]reedom to speak doesn't protect speakers from the consequences of their speech," including how third parties respond to such speech. Like-wise, Berkeley Law dean Erwin Chemerinsky insisted during the second Trump impeachment that Trump's words were not protected under the First Amendment by citing *Schenck* and the defunct "clear and present danger" test. Chemerinsky also omitted any reference to Trump calling on supporters to "peacefully" protest. Chillingly, while also citing *Bran-denburg*, Chemerinsky noted that there was little real evidence against *Schenck*. Accordingly, Trump could be stripped of protection, since "a man could be punished for circulating a leaflet criticizing the draft during

World War I even though there was not a shred of evidence that it actually interfered with military enlistments." The thrust of the second Trump impeachment and calls for his criminal indictment were based on classic "bad-tendency" rationales. However, despite my disagreements with the use of what I called a "snap impeachment" against Trump, Congress is subject to a different standard in voting for impeachment. Yet Chemerinsky used the fact that "this is not a trial in a court of law" to dismiss the First Amendment concerns. As with academic institutions, Congress should act in conformity with free speech values regardless of whether it can be judicially compelled to do so.

The revival of *Schenck* in such writings—and invoked by members of Congress—magnifies the need for a bright line standard on free speech. *Schenck* was long opposed as a warmed-over "bad tendencies" decision, the theory that shaped the lower court rulings. The pamphlets clearly engaged in political speech but were deemed "calculated to cause . . . insubordination" and obstruction of the draft. Likewise, in *Frohwerk*, it was enough that a speech could be the "little breath . . . enough to kindle a flame." As noted by Chaffee, these cases allow for criminal prosecution of any speech where there is "some tendency, however remote, to bring about acts in violation of law." It is the constitutional butterfly effect theory long used to net those with extreme or unpopular views.

The fact that all three branches failed in periods of national unrest to protect free speech is well established. These failures are often rationalized as reflections of the times and the excess that occurs at times of war. Some, like Holmes and Jackson, suggested that there was room for greater leeway during such periods. This book suggests that those periods are the catalysts but not the cause of the regression of free speech rights. The cause is something more fundamental about the underlying view of free speech. The failure of the political branches is disappointing but hardly surprising. It is the failure of the judiciary in each of these periods that is more alarming. Functionalism lends itself to the division of beneficial and harmful speech. A review of the major free speech cases shows a familiar pattern. Rage rhetoric often triggered state rage in crackdowns on speech. Even the architects of these crackdowns would later look back with regret after the period of panic had passed. For example, Francis Biddle led crackdowns under Roosevelt but later wrote in *The Fear of Freedom* that "in times of panic" our greatest threat comes not from tyrannical leaders but "the people themselves . . . in fear of imagined peril." By "fanning fears," Biddle wrote, leaders followed the "harrowed practice" of confusing "panic with patriotism."

Figures such as Biddle failed to protect those values when such protection was unpopular. They failed to protect free speech when it counted the most. True defenders of free speech such as Justice Hugo Black knew that few have the courage in the critical moment to stand on principle. Instead, he hoped that, in the space between panic periods, citizens can act to remove powers that were previously abused: "There is hope, however, that in calmer times, when present pressures, passions and fears subside, this or some later Court will restore the First Amendment liberties to the high preferred place where they belong in a free society." We can only reach that "high preferred place" by abandoning the "harrowed practice" of speech criminalization when the rage subsides and reason returns.

The predictable defense of sedition is that it is rarely charged and, as shown in these cases, does not materially alter the actual sentencing in cases. However, neither objection is compelling. First, sedition cases have always gone through stretches of dormancy and then returned during periods of "panic politics." Even if used to "hoist a few wretches," the message is still clear that extreme views can be selectively punished under these laws. Panic makes speech prosecutions popular. Even the media celebrated the crackdowns. As thousands were rounded up on a single day in World War I, the *Washington Post* proclaimed, "[T]here is no time to waste on hairsplitting over infringement of liberty." The current seditious conspiracy prosecutions are equally popular despite their redundancy. Moreover, it is not necessarily true that such crimes have no practical impact. The addition of sedition charges is often used by prosecutors to seek higher sentences even if counts run concurrently. In such motions, the speech of the defendants often plays a critical role. Finally, just as sedition charges play an important symbolic role for the government, the removal of sedition from the criminal code would hold an even greater and more meaningful symbolic meaning. It would be the strongest declaration since the First Amendment that the United States was creating a bright line between overt acts and speech offenses. While the same conduct can be prosecuted under multiple provisions, the government would make a clean break from a long line of sedition cases used to crack down on political speech since the twelfth century.

The danger of the revival of American sedition was captured in the effort to use Section Three of the Fourteenth Amendment to remove Donald Trump from ballots in the 2024 presidential election as well as up to 120 Republican members of Congress. Some of us pointed out that the provision allows such a ban from federal office in cases of "insurrection or rebellion." January 6th was neither. It was a riot that was worthy of universal condemnation. However, it was not an insurrection or rebellion akin to the Civil War, which led to the ratification of this provision. When confronted with this argument, advocates turned to a chillingly familiar rationale. Various law professors argued that it really does not have to be an actual insurrection or rebellion so long as would qualify as sedition. They cite Noah Webster's first edition of his dictionary in 1828 as including "the open and active opposition of a number of persons to the execution of a law in a city or state," or sedition. In this way, insurrection can include any opposition to the execution of any law by a city or a state—and such opposition can allow candidates to be stripped from ballots. There are a host of objections that can be raised to this argument, including the adoption of the broadest possible interpretation of a given term in this constitutional context. Notably, the drafters were well aware of sedition but elected not to use that term. Moreover, even if Webster's is accepted as strong support for such a broad reading, the 1828 entry also equivocates to some degree in noting that insurrection "is equivalent to sedition, except that sedition expresses a less extensive rising of citizens." In this way, sedition would not only be revived but expanded to allow it to achieve the very purpose of royal governors in preventing citizens from being able to vote for those opposing laws. The logic becomes chillingly simple for many supporting this novel theory: "Specifically, I think an 'insurrection' is a 'riot' for the purpose of changing the outcome of 'an important political decision or event.'" Thus, any riot seeking to block an important political event is sedition, and any sedition can be used to limit the candidates in a given election. There remains a problem in the lack of a limiting principle. Presumably, other disruptive protests taken to stop official proceedings could also be viewed as a sedition-defined insurrection. For example, in April 2023, two legislators stopped the Georgia House of Representatives from voting in a protest over gun control. They were later expelled for obstruction of the official proceedings.

The Supreme Court was forced to weigh in to this question after the Colorado Supreme Court disqualified Trump from the ballot in 2024. Despite being entirely composed of democratically appointed justices, the Court split 4–3 in its ruling that January 6th was an insurrection and that Trump was barred under the Fourteenth Amendment. It was an outlier among the states, though disqualification was ordered by the Maine secretary of state and a lower court judge in Illinois. The Court ultimately did not have to address the sedition-based definition of insurrection or even whether an insurrection was attempted. Instead, in *Trump v. Anderson* the justices unanimously rejected the disqualification theory on the basis that the constitutional bar required action first by Congress. The right of states to unilaterally enforce the provision had been called "unassailable" by Harvard law professor Laurence Tribe and other legal experts, but was rejected by all nine justices as allowing a "patchwork" of state actions to dictate the outcome of elections. They added: "Nothing in the Constitution requires that we endure such chaos."

The use of sedition to expand the meaning of constitutional prohibitions reflects the same sedition addiction that plagued the country at its formation. For many academics on the left, they are even willing to adopt originalist arguments over the meaning of key terms to incorporate sedition into the Fourteenth Amendment. It remains the break-the-glass option for officials and advocates in periods of panic politics. The insistence of keeping sedition crimes on the books is analogous to the position of the Crown in the colonies. As the Revolution neared, sedition prosecutions over criticism of the government actually declined. The reason may have been that such criticism was increasingly common and the tensions with the colonials had become acute. Yet the Crown still valued the sedition laws to use selectively and "retained statutes proscribing seditious speech . . . as a clear reminder" of their authority to punish critics. The elimination of the crime of sedition would finish the work of James Madison and finally realize the potential of a revolution that sought to break from English tradition of speech criminalization. Writers like Zechariah Chafee long maintained that the First Amendment was "intended to wipe out the common law of sedition, and make further prosecutions for criticism of government, without any incitement to the law-breaking, forever impossible in the United States of America." Our history after the ratification of the First Amendment abandoned those principles and picked up the very cudgel wrestled from the hands of the king only years earlier. The rationalization for the criminalization of speech through the decades of crackdowns has remained the same. The elimination of the crime of sedition would represent one of the most powerful statements in favor of free speech since the ratification of the First Amendment. It would be a leap of faith that we can protect our Republic without the monster that has lurked in our criminal code for centuries.

Part V

CONCLUSION

I have called this our "age of rage," but it is hardly our first. We were born in rage as a nation. Democracy allows the venting of passions that are often expressed in rage rhetoric that can be alarming and threatening. The first victim in such periods is often free speech. Just as a desire for free expression is quintessentially human, so is rage. As shown throughout our history, rage is addictive. It bestows a certain license to shed the confining expectations of reason and civility. Perhaps the perfect epitaph for our age occurred in 2023 outside the House floor as Representative Jamaal Bowman (D-N.Y.) was filmed screaming at the top of his lungs about gun control as his colleagues filed out after a vote. Various Democratic members tried to calm Bowman. However, after Representative Thomas Massie (R-Ky.) asked him to stop yelling, Bowman shouted, "I was screaming before you interrupted me." At times, our politics seem like a collective primal scream session where only the loudest prevail. Yet, for some, the license to rage goes beyond the amplification of their own views and becomes a demand for the silencing of others.

The rage at the start of our Republic was not new and certainly was not what distinguished that moment from what came before. Rather, it was also the birth of a quintessential new concept of free speech, a uniquely American concept at the time. The Framers extended the horizonal view of free speech to embody something more than simply the functional. They articulated a truly American right that adhered to all citizens as human beings.

While we have faced anti–free speech movements throughout our history, the current movement has unique elements that arguably make it far more dangerous for the country. The alliance of academic, media, and corporate interests with the government has created an existential threat to this indispensable right. Yet the most dangerous aspect to this movement is a crisis of faith in free speech. A terrible by-product of freedom is that it can sometimes be taken for granted; a people that has long enjoyed liberty can assume it a fixed part of their lives or, worse yet, a nonessential element.

Indeed, the loss of support for free speech has migrated to a broader lack of faith in the constitutional system as a whole. Violence is again viewed as warranted to suppress those with opposing or dangerous views. A 2023 poll by the University of Virginia Center for Politics captured this crisis of faith with more citizens doubting our constitutional system and each other. The poll showed that 52 percent of Democrats believed that Republicans are now a threat to American life, while 47 percent of Republicans felt the same about Democrats. Moreover, among Biden supporters, 41 percent now believe violence is justified "to stop [Republicans] from achieving their goals." An almost identical percentage, 38 percent, of Trump supporters now embrace violence to stop Democrats. Thirty-one percent of Trump supporters and 24 percent of Biden supporters also believe that the nation should explore alternative forms of government. Roughly a quarter (24 percent) of Biden supporters also question the viability of democracy.

Free speech can be an abstraction to those who have never known its absence. This is a global struggle over the erosion of free speech among countries that helped define this human right. Today, around the world, free speech is sinking in a sea of relativism as other countervailing interests are balanced against the narrower function of free speech. For those of us in the free speech community, this is the moment that we have long feared would come. We have been watching a movement building around the world that has left free speech in a virtual free fall, even among our closest allies. In Canada, human rights commissions routinely arrest individuals for speaking against homosexuality and other issues. Canadian prime minister Justin Trudeau has pursued a scorched-earth campaign against protesters. He has pushed for expanded prosecutions under changes to the Criminal Code and the Canadian Human Rights Act that criminalize any "communication that expresses detestation or vilification of an individual or group of individuals on the basis of a prohibited ground of discrimination." That regulation of speech was criticized for the vague terms with which it seeks to prevent "social media platforms, [from being] used to threaten, intimidate, bully and harass people, or used to promote racist, anti-Semitic, Islamophobic, misogynistic and homophobic views that target communities, put people's safety at risk and undermine Canada's social cohesion or democracy." Even under the prior standard, free speech had become conditional in Canada. A comedian was even arrested for trash-talking with heckling women in the audience in a comedy club. In 2024, the government was pushing legislation to make certain speech crimes punishable with life sentences while increasing any speech promoting hatred to five years in prison. In the United Kingdom, you can be arrested for language deemed "threatening, abusive, insulting" or "likely to cause . . . harassment, alarm, or distress." A court upheld the conviction of a man for holding "toxic ideologies," a literal thought crime. The country has also seen the arrest of a woman for simply praying outside of an abortion clinic as well as the arrest of individuals who criticize homosexuality, "misgender" others, wear anti-police T-shirts, or espouse a host of other views deemed offensive.

In France, laws criminalize speech under vague standards referring to "inciting" or "intimidating" others based on race or religion. For example, in 2011, fashion designer John Galliano was found guilty in a French court on charges of making anti-Semitic and sexist comments in a Paris bar. The father of French conservative presidential candidate Marine Le Pen was fined because he called people from the Roma minority "smelly." Religious writers have been arrested for denouncing homosexuality. In Ireland, the proposed 2023 Criminal Justice (Incitement to Violence or Hatred and Hate Offences) Act criminalized "incitement to violence or hatred against" people with "protected characteristics," as well as "condoning, denying or grossly trivialising genocide, war crimes, crimes against humanity and crimes against peace." It was defended by Green Party chairwoman Pauline O'Reilly as justified in seeking the arrest of anyone who causes "deep discomfort" in others. After all, she insisted, "when one thinks about it, all law and all legislation is about the restriction of freedom. This is exactly what we are doing here. We are restricting freedom, but we are doing it for the common good."

Germany has long criminalized speech, but prosecutions are expanding

from earlier cases involving Nazi symbols or speech. A German conservative politician was placed under criminal investigation for a tweet in
which she accused police of appeasing a "barbaric gang raping Mus-
lim hordes of men." German justice minister Heiko Maas was censored
under his own laws for calling an author an "idiot" on Twitter. The long
crackdown on Nazi symbols and speech has morphed and expanded,
leading to absurd cases like the arrest of a man for having the voice of
Adolf Hitler as his ringtone. Germany has proven the fallacy of changing
minds through threatened prosecution. These laws have proven ineffec-
tive in stopping neo-Nazis and extreme speech, but have been effective in
curtailing free speech. With only 17 percent of its population reporting
a sense of freedom of speech in public, Germany has achieved what authoritarian systems have long sought—the suppression of speech. What
is truly alarming is that it has eviscerated free speech in the name of protecting democracy.

The tide of this global anti–free speech movement has reached our
shores and found eager advocates for the criminalization and censorship
of speech among fellow citizens. The same functionalist trade-offs are
again being used to rationalize speech limits. While the government has
sought to silence critics and political dissidents in the past, it is now being
joined by groups that have historically been protective of free speech. In a
departure from earlier crackdowns on free speech in our nation, the current movement is supported by an unprecedented alliance of academic,
corporate, and government forces. The success of the current anti–free
speech movement cannot be denied. Once the targets of the McCarthy
period, the political left has rotated 180 degrees and are now proving
themselves adept at using corporate, media, and academic allies to isolate
and silence opposing viewpoints. The United States represents the final
line of defense for free speech. It is here that free speech can take a stand
and serve, again, as a beacon to the world.

The legislative and regulatory reforms suggested in this book could
give us critical breathing space during this difficult period, but free
speech will continue to decline without a reawakening of a lost faith. Even
the core figures who seemed to embody the liberty-based right had their

own crises of faith. For example, Thomas Paine, who most embodied the rights of the free press and free speech, seemed to equivocate on those protections during the French Terrors. Paine spent much of his life being pursued for sedition and other offenses in Great Britain, the colonies, the United States, and France. In France, where he was welcomed as a hero and made a member of the National Convention, Paine took no time in lashing out at those who abused their offices or corrupted the goals of the Revolution. He fled a sedition charge in Great Britain, but a manuscript of his was found in the archives, one that included a letter from Paine to Georges Danton, a leading Jacobin and head of the Committee of Public Safety. While Danton would ultimately become a victim of "the Terrors" himself, the Committee was the vehicle for the arrest and execution of thousands of dissenters. It was, therefore, crushing to read Paine's May 1793 letter in which he encouraged Danton to crack down on "calumnia-tors," or those who spread lies and treachery. Paine explained that "cal-umny is a species of Treachery that ought to be punished as well as any other kind of treachery." He accused such speakers of spreading vice "be-cause it is possible to irritate men into disaffection by continual calumny who never intended to be disaffected." It is not a position that Paine took publicly, but it is still disheartening to read such a view in private corre-spondence. Paine would experience the full terror of the Revolution when he was pulled from his bed late at night on December 28, 1793, to be sent to the infamous Luxembourg Prison. There he would share a cold, wet, ten-by-eight-foot cell with other prisoners with virtually no light. Each day, he would await the chalk mark on his door to signal that he would join the long line of prisoners to be guillotined that day. (On one such oc-casion, he was designated for death, but the guards missed the mark when the door was left open to help cool his raging fever.) He was spared only when the Terrors ended with the death of Maximilien Robespierre on the guillotine and the intervention of then United States minister to France, James Monroe.

Thomas Paine is an example of how we can lose our faith, if only for a critical moment, in periods of rage. A moment is all that it takes for orthodoxy or authoritarianism to take hold. In such periods, dissent becomes disloyalty, and disloyalty becomes dangerous. Even the greatest among us can yield to a desire to be rid of meddlesome voices. Oliver Wendell Holmes is one of the most troubling examples of the resistible impulse to punish speech. It is notable that free speech, as discussed by Holmes and others, is often analogized to fire. It was not just the fire in a theater. Holmes wrote of the danger of that speech to "kindle a flame" of dissent. Under this view, free speech, like fire, is a necessity, but dangerous to democracy when not controlled.

The fear of free speech reflects the view that this right may be indispensable, but only to the extent that it supports the democratic process. It is, therefore, indispensable but divisible. While we often offer a rote attestation of faith to this right, we continue to reject its very essence, the very thing that makes it so indispensable for humankind. We speak as devout believers in free speech but remain agnostics on its foundation or quintessence.

The rise in speech regulation is often defended on the basis that free speech itself is a danger. It is the "harm principle" of John Stuart Mill, with a lethal twist. Despite the Millian references, it is a construct that is neither faithful to Mill's writing nor logical in its application. Yet that same rationale has been used by social media companies as the foundation for the robust censorship programs now enforced across the media in what is often called the "post-truth" environment. Mill anticipated that his principle could be misused since "[h]ow (it may be asked) can any part of the conduct of a member of a society be a matter of indifference to the other members? No person is an entirely isolated being." Yet Mill recognized the essentiality of free speech "being almost of as much importance as the liberty of thought itself, and resting in great part on the same reasons, is practically inseparable from it." For those who view free speech as a natural or autonomous right, this harm is narrowly defined when connected to overt acts or offenses like fraud or conspiracy. For others, Mill's harm principle can be read as part of a general utilitarian philosophy where utility favors functionalist limits on free speech and other values. At its most extreme, this view can reduce protections to the exclusion for entirely harmless acts or views. However, Mill was also clear that free speech is an essential right. Notably, he believed that the threat to free speech in democracies was not the state, but the "social tyranny" of other citizens.

The growing anti–free speech movement is undeniably successful. It has fueled a variety of forms of speech controls and assembled arguably the greatest alliance of institutional forces in history against free expression. Terms like *disinformation* and *content moderation* have allowed the repackaging of age-old rationales for speech codes and controls, particularly on our college campuses. It is especially alarming for those of us who remember educational institutions with few limits on viewpoints or values. It was an awakening for each of us who found a world of endless intellectual possibilities and pursuits. When I went to the University of Chicago in the 1980s, free speech was still an all-you-can-eat feast of viewpoints, from the grand to the grotesque. I lived in a vegetarian cooperative where the Spartacus League (a group of Trotskyites and communists) would vent in the basement while militant vegans would debate upstairs and libertarians gathered next door. It was thrilling. Today that intellectual smorgasbord often seems like little more than a McDonald's Happy Meal—prepackaged, uniform, and self-contained . . . except that no one seems particularly happy. As universities remove views deemed "harmful," what is left is an artificially contented campus with greatly reduced intellectually nutritional content. While it is enough to achieve immediate political and social goals, it is not enough to sustain us. If some of us are right about the inherent need for free thought and free expression to be fully human, it cannot succeed. Indeed, while speech is being limited to protect students from the "harm" of opposing views, it has not made our students or our campuses any happier. Like junk food, it tends only to make us feel worse about ourselves and others. Schools have yielded to the rage. The result is more than the decline of reason. It is a steady diet that leads to an addiction to rage.

The concept of shaping speech came easily to some, particularly in academia. For years, professors have discussed how to "nudge" citizens into making "optimal" decisions. It is an effort to "frame" or structure decision-making. Psychologist Herbert Simon explained: "If we wish to know what form gelatin will take when it solidifies, we do not study the gelatin; we study the shape of the mold in which we are going to pour it. . . . The same strategy can be used to construct a psychology of thinking." This "bounded rationality" can be used to shape human conduct and choices in each environment. It is the very purpose of much of the censorship and blacklisting carried out by government agencies and their allies in the private sector. The government has often sought to pour the gelatin of free speech into a structured mold to produce better decisions among citizens, including the use of enlightened algorithms to direct users to better choices of reading. This "choice architecture" and "choice intervention" has been the rage for many in academia, but it is now being used to shape our very social and political discourse. Through "bounded rationality," citizens can be coaxed to make the right choices by "organizing the context in which people make decisions." Thus, according to Harvard law professor Cass Sunstein, it "nudges interventions that steer people in particular directions but that also allow them to go their own way."

When used in the area of free speech, this framing of the public debate places society on the slippery slope of state and private censorship. Over time, nudges can become shoves. In fairness to Sunstein, he was focused on interventions that "[do] not impose significant material incentives (including disincentives). A subsidy is not a nudge; a tax is not a nudge; a fine or a jail sentence is not a nudge. To count as such, a nudge must fully preserve freedom of choice." However, once the government is in the business of framing free speech, censorship can be rationalized as a nudge even when it is more of a nullification of speech. Those engaging in censorship often speak of the need to bound or to frame the choices or views being considered by users. Stanford's Virality Project is illustrative. The project insisted even true stories needed to be censored because "true stories . . . could fuel hesitancy" over taking the vaccine or other measures. This includes censoring postings on "celebrity deaths after vaccine" or the closure of a central New York school. The fact that the stories were true does not matter when you are framing the context for decision-making.

To use Rockwell's *Freedom of Speech* painting, Jim Edgerton could speak about a new school on social media but not about COVID protocols in those schools.

Those seeking to limit speech today, particularly in academia, show the same dangerous assumptions in creating a type of "bounded rationality" in the public debate. These theories assume that the correct answer is clear, as determined by the government. However, it is also possible to nudge citizens toward bad choices. It has been a rationale throughout the historical periods discussed in this book. For example, the Federalists believed that the public were easily swayed and misled if left to their own devices. As Newman wrote, "[T]o most conservative Federalists of the 1790s, American society hinged on a paternalistic social elite that extended patronage and demanded deference from common people." The same paternalistic voice is heard now in those demanding that harmful views be censored on the internet. Senator Elizabeth Warren made this plain when she called for using enlightened algorithms to steer average people away from bad choices in their reading material.

When used in the context of free speech, the government can reinforce bad public policy by treating dissenting views as bad speech. The most obvious example is the debate over COVID-19 and the pandemic measures. Various experts, including those who signed the Great Barrington Declaration, were banned from social media and shunned from academic conferences and publications. They raised questions that would later be recognized as legitimate over aspects for the pandemic, including the necessity of shutting down schools for young children or the efficacy of masks. Numerous experts were suspended or banned for challenging these very claims while the media labeled them dangerous or fringe figures. The Twitter Files showed how many of these actions were taken at the behest of the government, including the Centers for Disease Control and Prevention (CDC). The debate was framed by what experts decided was the bounded rationality of the pandemic. They were wrong, and the result was that the public debate (and development of public policies) was significantly curtailed.

The manipulation of public debate can be rationalized under a functionalist approach as simply enhancing the value of public debate to the democratic process by eliminating harmful or false claims. Indeed, it proved an ironic twist on Oliver Wendell Holmes once dismissing free speech objections by telling Judge Learned Hand that free speech "stands no differently than freedom from vaccination." In the pandemic, free speech did become the same as vaccination—subject to the whim of the majority. The only difference is that vaccinations became mandatory and debate about vaccinations became discretionary. Yet the pandemic shows how, even under a functionalist theory, these censorship and blacklisting efforts proved inimical to the democratic process. In the name of combating disinformation, the government and its corporate allies suppressed divergent views later found credible. The narrow view of free speech facilitated these abuses.

Basing free speech on a broader autonomous foundation is not a rejection but a restoration of the original American view of this indispensable right. It was often expressed as a matter of natural rights or personal liberty. For example, the Pennsylvania Declaration of Rights affirmed "certain natural, inherent and inalienable rights" and expressly stated that "the people have a right to freedom of speech, and of writing, and publishing their sentiments." This natural rights premise for government found expression in early American documents like the Virginia Declaration of Rights and Declaration of Independence. Back then, as today, it was a radical concept. Embracing a broader understanding of free speech requires a leap of faith. After years of "content moderation" and deplatforming, many believe that free speech is simply too dangerous to be allowed to spread unregulated or unmonitored. It is a paternalistic view that the public needs to be protected from false or harmful ideas. It is the same rationale that existed in colonial times when sedition prosecution targeted "false news." The suppression of speech has often been cloaked in terms of protecting citizens and society from our own worst impulses. That was evident in the Court's long adherence of the view that "bad tendency" speech should be curtailed in the public interest.

An autonomous view of free speech minimizes such intrusions into free speech. It could not be based solely on the claim that the speech is harmful because it is misleading, false, or triggering. From political to artistic speech, these are many creations or statements that are deemed flawed or harmful by third parties. However, these views are projections of individuals of values or views in the world around them. They can be challenged or dismissed in the exercise of the same right held by third parties. However, they are based on a right tied to the individual rather than the democratic process.

For Supreme Court Justice Benjamin N. Cardozo, "freedom of expression is the matrix, the indispensable condition, of nearly every other form of freedom." His statement was strikingly close to the statement of Justice Louis Brandeis that free speech is the indispensable right. In Brandeis's exposition, free speech was both "an end and a means." His view of free speech as "indispensable" was echoed by the Court in 2023 in the *303 Creative* decision. Yet it was a beautiful sentiment that escaped Brandeis and Holmes in their concurrence in *Whitney*. It was Whitney, not Brandeis, who got free speech right. She sounded almost Millian in declaring that expression alone cannot be considered a public harm: "If believing in equality is a crime against my country, then I am guilty. If belief in self-expression that does not interfere with the lives of others is criminal, then I am criminal."

We began this book with the observation of George Bernard Shaw that history is always made by unreasonable people. In many ways, our history of free speech is the history of unreasonable people. We are a nation of unreasonable people who refused to accept that status quo, refused to conform their beliefs and their speech to the demands of others. Figures like John Lilburne, Anita Whitney, John Callender, Harry Croswell, Ida B. Wells-Barnett, Eugene Debs, and others were wonderfully unreasonable people who refused to yield to the coercion of public officials and public opinion. From the Boston Tea Party that rallied the nation, our history has proven true the observation of Brandeis in *Whitney* that "those who won our independence believed . . . courage to be the secret of liberty." Whether they were Whigs, "Wobblies," or "Workies," these characters tested us time and time again. They were nonconformists like Victoria Claflin Woodhull and "Tennie" Claflin, who insisted on living and writing without fear. Many, in my view, were fundamentally wrong in their views, but we shared a common article of faith in the right to express those views. They are often, even today, treated as villains, as opposed to the heroes of our Republic. The true villains are John Adams, Anthony Comstock, Mitchell Palmer, and others who betrayed those values in the name of the public good.

Just as Montesquieu believed that "one must consider man before the establishment of societies," that same is true for free speech. One must consider humanity before one considers the place of free speech in the establishment of societies. The drive to think and speak freely existed in the state of nature before society because it is an essential impulse of human beings. Any "social contract" was based on the desire to secure the benefits of society in realizing the potential of our own humanity. The drive to create—in speech and form—has been shown to be irresistible even at the risk of one's own liberty or life. It is all-consuming precisely because it is elemental. Brandeis understood that the right was indispensable, but not why it was indispensable. It was the same lack of faith that led leaders immediately after the Revolution to embrace the very powers that they opposed under English rule. Our current crisis of faith over free speech is due to that original sin after the American Revolution. Our centuries of struggle with free speech proved Montesquieu and Madison right. The failure to consider the essence of free speech to being fully human led to centuries of conflicted and often abusive laws and opinions. It allowed the government to respond to rage rhetoric with its own form of rage.

There is one great advantage to believing in a natural or autonomous basis for free speech: a certain optimism. This anti–free speech movement cannot entirely change us. We are hardwired for free speech with a psychological and even a physiological impulse to create. If you believe that free thought and expression are the essence of being human, that impulse cannot be entirely extinguished. While we can lose our appetite for free speech, we never truly lose our taste for it. In the end, our faith in free speech is really a faith in each other. A faith that we do not have to fear opposing viewpoints, but rather the inclination to silence others. There may be bad-tendency speech, but the worst tendency is found in the effort to protect society from harmful thoughts. This is indeed an age of rage. However, rage is not what defines us. It is free speech that defines us.

Acknowledgments

This is not the first book on free speech. It is not even the hundredth such book. Indeed, it took me thirty years of thinking and writing in this area to get up the gumption to add another book to this ample supply. In doing so, I recognize that none of us write on a blank slate. As discussed in the book, there are masterful prior works that I recommend for those who want to pursue different aspects of the legal and historical background on free speech. That includes the work of Professor Geoffrey R. Stone, including his exhaustive study in *Perilous Times: Free Speech in Wartime from the Sedition Act of 1798 to the War on Terrorism* (New York: W. W. Norton, 2004). I also want to acknowledge the work of scholars such as Professor Larry D. Eldridge in *A Distant Heritage: The Growth of Free Speech in Early America* (New York: New York University Press, 1994), as well as Professor Stephen D. Solomon in *Revolutionary Dissent: How the Founding Generation Created the Freedom of Speech* (New York: St. Martin's Press, 2016). While I refer to the work of these and other leading scholars in the book, any errors or conclusions that I draw from this work are entirely my own.

I also want to acknowledge the work of the many law students at schools ranging from Harvard to Georgetown to George Washington who have assisted me in decades of research and writing on the theories and cases discussed in this book. That includes my assistant, Seth Tate, who has supplied essential support for years.

This book is decades in the making but required particularly intense periods of near total absorption in the last two years. That commitment of time was only possible due to the support of my wife, Leslie, and my four children, Benjamin, Jack, Aidan, and Madie. It may be vanity or a fear of mortality, but every author hopes to leave something more lasting than himself in this world. I hope that this book will explain my own long, and at times unpopular, fight for free speech rights. However, my most cherished legacy is found not in these pages but in my family members, who have stood by me throughout this long journey. The only true limits to free speech are found in the inability to express the profound gratitude for those who love us unconditionally.

Notes

EPIGRAPH

vii   *"I like a little rebellion"*: Letter from Jefferson to Abigail Adams (Feb. 22, 1787), in
The Papers of Thomas Jefferson, vol. 11, edited by Julian P. Boyd (Princeton, NJ:
Princeton University Press, 2018), 174.

INTRODUCTION

1   *"for raising this sea-storm"*: William Shakespeare, *The Tempest*, act I, sc. 3 (1611).

1   *"a little rebellion now and then"*: Letter from Thomas Jefferson to James Madison
(Jan. 30, 1787), in *The Papers of Thomas Jefferson*, vol. 11, 93 ("I hold it that a little
rebellion now and then is a good thing, and as necessary in the political world as
storms in the physical").

1   *"the spirit of resistance"*: Letter from Thomas Jefferson to Abigail Adams (Feb. 22,
1787).

2   *"reign of the witches"*: Letter from Thomas Jefferson to John Taylor (June 4, 1798),
Founders Online, https://founders.archives.gov/documents/Jefferson/01-30-02
-0280 ("[A] little patience, and we shall see the reign of witches pass over, their
spells dissolve, and the people recovering their true sight, restor[ing] their government to it's [*sic*] true principles").

2   *"[a] little patience"*: Letter from Thomas Jefferson to John Taylor (June 4, 1798).

3   *"reclaim America from Constitutionalism"*: Ryan D. Doerfler & Samuel Moyn, "The
Constitution Is Broken and Should Not Be Reclaimed," *New York Times*, Aug. 19, 2022.

3   *just dump it*: Imami Gandy, "I Agree with Elie Mystal. The Constitution Is Trash,"
Rewire News Group, Mar. 11, 2022.

3   *indispensabity*: 303 Creative LLC v. Elenis, 600 U.S. 570, (2023).

4   *one of the longest-serving justices*: Al Richmond, *Native Daughter: The Story of
Anita Whitney* (Anita Whitney 75th Anniversary Committee, 1942), 17–21.

4   *fitting motto for the young girl*: See generally Haig A. Bosmajian, *Anita Whitney,
Louis Brandeis, and the First Amendment* (Vancouver, BC: Fairleigh Dickinson
University Press, 2010).

5 *at the settlement*: Bosmajian, *Anita Whitney*, 36.

5 *"ignorance, sickness, and vice"*: Bosmajian, *Anita Whitney*, 36.

5 *"dread of being thought different"*: Lisa Rubens, "The Patrician Radical: Charlotte Anita Whitney," *California History* 65, no. 3 (Sept. 1986): 160.

5 *"ameliorate poverty"*: Rubens, "Patrician Radical," 161.

6 *"anarchists and Wobblies"*: Bosmajian, *Anita Whitney*, 46.

6 *"all progress is made by unreasonable people"*: George Bernard Shaw, *Man and Superman: A Comedy and a Philosophy* (London: Archibald & Co., 1907), 238.

6 *"a challenge, a puzzle"*: Rubens, "Patrician Radical," 159.

6 *"I wanted to help change it"*: Rubens, "Patrician Radical," 161.

6 *"It's in the blood"*: Rubens, "Patrician Radical," 161.

7 *"children will it so"*: Rubens, "Patrician Radical," 164.

7 *"effecting any political change"*: Whitney v. California, 274 U.S. 357, 360 (1927) (quoting Cal. Stats. 1919).

7 *"lawless and disorderly"*: Rubens, "Patrician Radical," 164.

8 *"done nothing wrong?"*: Rubens, "Patrician Radical," 164.

8 *others have questioned*: See generally David Skover & Ronald Collins, "A Curious Concurrence: Justice Brandeis' Vote in *Whitney v. California*," *Supreme Court Review* 333 (2005).

9 *"The Right to Privacy"*: Samuel D. Warren & Louis D. Brandeis, "The Right to Privacy," *Harvard Law Review* 4 (1890): 193, 194.

9 *"We may have democracy"*: Raymond Lonergan, *Mr. Justice Brandeis, Great American*, edited by Irving Dillard (St. Louis, MO: Modern View Press, 1941), 42.

9 *Supreme Court victories*: Muller v. Oregon, 208 U.S. 412 (1908).

9 *"making others uncomfortable"*: Albert Lawrence, "Biased Justice: James C. McReynolds of the Supreme Court of the United States," *Journal of Supreme Court History* 30, no. 3 (2005): 244, 248.

10 *"the Court with another Jew"*: David G. Dalin, *Jewish Justices of the Supreme Court: From Brandeis to Kagan* (Waltham, MA: Brandeis University Press, 2017); Drew Pearson & Robert S. Allen, *The Nine Old Men* (Garden City, NY: Doubleday, Doran & Co., 1937), 98.

10 *"a Jew, or both"*: Pearson & Allen, *Nine Old Men*, 225.

11 *"assembly should be guaranteed"*: Whitney v. California, 274 U.S. 357, 375–76 (1927) (Brandeis, J., concurring).

12 Chaplinsky v. New Hampshire: Chaplinsky v. New Hampshire, 315 U.S. 568 (1942).

12 *"order and morality"*: Chaplinsky, 315 U.S. at 572.

12 Brandenburg v. Ohio: Brandenburg v. Ohio, 395 U.S. 444 (1969).

13 *our political discourse*: See generally Jonathan Turley, "The Right to Rage: Free Speech and Rage Rhetoric in American Political Discourse," *Georgetown Journal of Law & Public Policy* 21, no. 2 (2023).

13 *public discord*: See, e.g., Gitlow v. New York, 268 U.S. 652, 667 (1925).

13 *politics to the arts*: See, e.g., Magnificent Montague & Bob Baker, *Burn, Baby!*

Burn!: The Autobiography of Magnificent Montague (Champaign: University of Illinois Press, 2009).

13 *prelude to reform*: Sylvester Monroe, "'Burn Baby Burn': What I Saw as a Black Journalist Covering the L.A. Riots 25 Years Ago," *Washington Post*, Apr. 28, 2017.

14 *"trial by combat"*: Ed Pilkington, "Incitement: A Timeline of Trump's Inflammatory Rhetoric Before the Capitol Riot," *Guardian*, Jan. 7, 2021.

14 *"get confrontational"*: Steven Nelson, "Biden Praises Polarizing Rep. Waters," *New York Post*, Oct. 13, 2022.

14 *"released the whirlwind"*: Jonathan Turley, "From Court Packing to Leaking to Doxing: White House Yields to National Rage Addiction," *Res Ipsa* blog (www.jonathanturley.org), May 9, 2022.

14 *animated video*: Lisa Hagen, "Paul Gosar Censured, Removed from Committees Over Violent Post About Democrats," *US News & World Report*, Nov. 17, 2021.

14 *assaulting a CNN figure*: "Donald Trump Posts Video of Him Beating CNN in Wrestling," BBC, July 2, 2017.

14 *can mean vastly different things*: "Rage," *Merriam-Webster*, https://www.merriam-webster.com/dictionary/rage (last visited June 11, 2023).

14 *"rage against the machine" in music*: Rage Against the Machine, "New Millennium Homes" on *The Battle of Los Angeles* (Epic Records, 1999), track 10.

14 *"rage against racism"*: "Dublin March Against Racism," *Irish Times*, Sept. 11, 1997.

14 *"the dying of the light"*: Dylan Thomas, "Do Not Go Gentle into That Good Night," in *The Poems of Dylan Thomas*, edited by Daniel Jones (New York: New Directions, 2003), 239.

15 *"rage supplies [us] with weapons"*: Virgil, *The Aeneid*, bk. I, 150.

15 *"Letting off steam"*: Roger Fisher & Willian Ury, *Getting to Yes: Negotiating Agreement Without Giving In*, 2nd ed. (New York: Houghton Mifflin, 1991), 31.

15 *a level of catharsis*: Others have questioned or rejected this catharsis theory. See Stephen Diamond, "Anger and Catharsis: Myth, Metaphor, or Reality," *Psychology Today*, Sept. 28, 2009. See generally Turley, "Right to Rage."

15 *more lasting damage*: Josh Cohen, "The Meaning of Anger," *Aeon*, Jan. 6, 2022, https://aeon.co/essays/anger-is-a-state-of-agitated-enervation-that-moves-the-world.

15 *"and the somatic"*: Cohen, "Meaning."

15 *"oppose their government"*: "Seditious," *Cambridge Dictionary*, https://dictionary.cambridge.org/us/dictionary/english/seditious (last visited June 11, 2023).

17 *violent protests*: Jennifer A. Kingson, "$1 Billion-Plus Riot Damage Is Most Expensive in Insurance History," *Axios*, Sept. 16, 2020.

17 *"The One Un-American Act"*: William O. Douglas, "The One Un-American Act," *Nieman Reports* 7, no. 1 (Jan. 1953): 20, https://niemanreports.org/wp-content/uploads/2014/03/Spring-1953_150.pdf.

18 Schenck v. United States: Schenck v. United States, 249 U.S. 47 (1919).

PART I. THE INDISPENSABLE RIGHT

1. FREE EXPRESSION AND THE HUMAN CONDITION

24   *"liberty of expression"*: Larry D. Eldridge, *A Distant Heritage: The Growth of Free Speech in Early America* (New York: New York University Press, 1994), 1, citing Leonard W. Levy, *Emergence of a Free Press* (New York: Oxford University Press, 1985), 28.

24   *"mixed with his labor"*: John Locke, *Second Treatise on Civil Governments*, edited by Lester DeKoster (Grand Rapids, MI: W. B. Eerdmans: 1978), 26.

24   *"good" for others*: Locke, *Second Treatise*.

25   *"the divine Michelangelo"*: Nancy C. Andreasen, *The Creative Brain* (New York: Plume Books, 2005), 6.

26   *uniquely human*: Marc Bekoff, "Scientists Conclude Nonhuman Animals Are Conscious Beings," *Psychology Today*, Aug. 10, 2012; see also Marc Bekoff, *The Emotional Lives of Animals: A Leading Scientist Explores Animal Joy, Sorrow, and Empathy—And Why They Matter* (Novato, CA: New World Library, 2007), 10–12.

26   *great apes*: Chris Deziel, "Animals That Share Human DNA Sequences," *Sciencing*, July 20, 2018.

26   *"human and complex parts"*: Andreasen, *Creative Brain*, 73.

26   *"survival through deception"*: Dahlia W. Zaidel, "Creativity, Brain, and Art: Biological and Neurological Considerations," *Frontiers in Human Neuroscience*, June 2, 2014.

26   *"creativity in humans"*: Zaidle, "Creativity."

27   *curiosity and creativity*: Jaak Panksepp, "Emotional Foundations for Creativity: The Brain's SEEKING System" in *Secrets of Creativity: What Neuroscience, the Arts, and Our Minds Reveal*, edited by Suzanne Nalbantian and Paul M. Matthews (New York: Oxford University Press, 2019), https://doi.org/10.1093/oso/9780190462321.003.0011.

28   *changed man*: See John Darrell Van Horn et al., "Mapping Connectivity Damage in the Case of Phineas Gage," *PLoS One* 7, no. 5 (May 16, 2012): e37454, https://journals.plos.org/plosone/article?id=10.1371/journal.pone.0037454.

29   *"'no longer Gage'"*: John M. Harlow, "Recovery from the Passage of an Iron Bar Through the Head," *Boston Medical and Surgical Journal* 39, no. 20 (Dec. 13, 1848), https://www.proquest.com/docview/127950580?pq-origsite=gscholar&fromopenview=true&sourcetype=Scholarly%20Journals.

29   *emotional processing*: Jon Hamilton, "Why Brain Scientists Are Still Obsessed with the Curious Case of Phineas Gage," NPR, May 21, 2017.

29   *cerebral cortex*: Van Horn et al., "Mapping Connectivity Damage."

29   *through his head*: Van Horn et al., "Mapping Connectivity Damage."

29   *changes in personality*: See Kieran O'Driscoll & John Paul Leach, "'No Longer Gage': An Iron Bar Through the Head," *BMJ* 317, no. 7174 (Dec. 19, 1998): 1673.

29   *"neurological organization"*: Zaidel, "Creativity."

29   *"abstract thinking"*: Leonardo C. de Souza et al., "Frontal Lobe Neurology and the Creative Mind," *Frontiers in Psychology* 5 (2014): 761.

30   *dissecting corpses*: R. Douglas Fields, "Michelangelo's Secret Message in the Sistine Chapel: A Juxtaposition of God and the Human Brain," *Scientific American*, May 27, 2010.

30   *the human brain*: See F. L. Meshberger, "An Interpretation of Michelangelo's Creation of Adam Based on Neuroanatomy," *Journal of the American Medical Association* 264 (1990): 1837.

30   *forms of mental illness*: Karamet Reiter et al., "Psychological Distress in Solitary Confinement: Symptoms, Severity, and Prevalence in the United States, 2017–2018," *American Journal of Public Health* 110 (2020): 556–62, https://pubmed.ncbi.nlm.nih.gov/31967876/.

30   *"a perceived loss of identity"*: Reiter et al., "Psychological Distress."

30   *psychological, but physiological*: Julian Strong, "The Body in Isolation: The Physical Health Impacts of Incarceration in Solitary Confinement," *PLoS One* 15 (2020): e0238510.

31   *isolation of Antarctic expeditioners*: A. C. Stahn, "Brain Changes in Response to Long Antarctic Expeditions," *New England Journal of Medicine* 381 (Dec. 2019): 2273–75.

31   *shrinking hippocampus*: Stahn, "Brain Changes."

31   *"bilateral hippocampus"*: Roger E. Beaty, "The Creative Brain," *Cerebrum* (Jan.–Feb. 2020), https://www.ncbi.nlm.nih.gov/pmc/articles/PMC7075500/.

31   *"whence and how they come"*: Andreasen, *Creative Brain*, 76.

31   *"neural level associations"*: Andreasen, *Creative Brain*, 128.

2. ANCIENT SPEECH AND NATURAL LAW

32   *throne of Thebes*: See Sophocles, *Antigone*, reprinted in *Nine Greek Dramas by Æschylus, Sophocles, Euripides and Aristophanes*, edited by Charles W. Eliot, translated by E. H. Plumptre (New York: P. F. Collier and Son, 1909).

32   *"not of today nor yesterday"*: Sophocles, *Antigone*, 269.

33   *"practice philosophy"*: Plato, *Apology 29d*, reprinted in *Plato: Complete Works*, edited by John M. Cooper (London: Hackett, 1997), 17, 27.

33   *Plato's Apology*: Plato, *Apology*.

34   isegoria *and* parrhesia: Teresa M. Bejan, "The Two Clashing Meanings of 'Free Speech,'" *Atlantic*, Dec. 2, 2017, https://www.theatlantic.com/politics/archive/2017/12/two-concepts-of-freedom-of-speech/546791/.

34   *"equality, not freedom"*: Bejan, "Two Clashing Meanings."

34   *"use of one's reason"*: Immanuel Kant, "An Answer to the Question: 'What is Enlightenment?,'" in *Kant: Political Writings*, edited by Hans Reiss, translated by H. B. Nisbet (Cambridge, UK: Cambridge University Press, 1970), 54–55.

35   *"cornerstone of democracy"*: Kurt A. Raaflaub, *The Discovery of Freedom in Ancient Greece* (Chicago: University of Chicago Press, 2004), 230.

36   *"really freedom"*: Jonathan I. Israel, *Spinoza: Life and Legacy* (London: Oxford University Press, 2023), 591.

36   *exercise of natural rights*: Edward I. Pitts, "Spinoza on Freedom of Expression,"
     Journal of the History of Ideas 47 (1986): 26–27.

36   *"saying what they think"*: Elwes, *Chief Works*, 264.

36   *"act as he pleased"*: Elwes, *Chief Works*, 264.

36   *right of the government*: Mayton, "Seditious Libel," 28.

36   *"say what he thinks"*: R. H. M. Elwes, *The Chief Works of Benedict de Spinoza*,
     vol. 1 (Mineola, NY: Dover, 1951); see also William T. Mayton, "Seditious Libel
     and the Lost Guarantee of a Freedom of Expression," *Columbia Law Review* 84
     (1984): 91.

36   *"day of judgment"*: Matthew 12:36 (KJV).

37   *"evil from Israel"*: Deuteronomy 17:12-13 (NKJV).

37   *"of thy people"*: Exodus 22:28 (KJV).

37   *"ruler of thy people"*: Exodus 22:28.

37   *"nonsense upon stilts"*: Jeremy Bentham, *The Works of Jeremy Bentham*, vol. 2,
     edited by J. Bowring (Edinburgh: William Tait, 1843), 501.

37   *"short of actual revolt"*: Jeremy Bentham, *A Fragment on Government*, edited by J.
     H. Burns and H. L. A. Hart (Cambridge, UK: Cambridge University Press, 1988),
     97–98.

3. THE BRITISH EXPERIENCE: THE STAR CHAMBER, BLACKSTONE, AND "THE NONCONFORMISTS"

38   *"great men of the realm"*: The Statute of Westminster, The First (1275), 3 Edward I,
     ch. 34, Statutes at Large, I, 53.

38   *"false bruits and rumors"*: John C. Lassiter, *Scandalum Magnatum: The "Scandal
     of Magistrates" in English Law, Society, and Politics*, thesis, 1974, 5.

38   *Hugh of Crepping*: George Osbourne Sayles, ed., *Select Cases in the Court of King's
     Bench, Volume 55* (London: B. Quaritch, 1936).

38   *"in a short time"*: Lassiter, *Scandalum Magnatum*, 9.

39   *"great officers of the realm"*: Thomas Starkie and Thomas Huntington, *Treatise on
     the Law of Slander: Libel Scandalum Magnatum and False Rumors* (Bloomington,
     IN: Indiana University Press, 1832), 104.

39   *"punished in all ages"*: William Hudson, "A Treatise of the Court of Star Chamber"
     (written c. 1620), in *Collectanea Juridica*, edited by F. Hargrave (London, 1792),
     vol. 2, 102.

39   *"King and his people"*: Stephen D. Solomon, *Revolutionary Dissent: How the
     Founding Generation Created the Freedom of Speech* (New York: St. Martin's Press,
     2016), 37.

40   *absence of any cited authority*: William T. Mayton, "Seditious Libel and
     the Lost Guarantee of a Freedom of Expression," *Columbia Law Review* 84
     (1984): 104.

40   *Archbishop John Whitgift*: Larry D. Eldridge, *A Distant Heritage: The Growth of
     Free Speech in Early America* (New York: New York University Press, 1994), 23.

40   *"dieth not"*: *Case de Libellis Famosis* (1605), 5 Co. Rep. 125b, 77 ER 251.

40 *"Subjects under him?"*: *Case de Libellis Famosis* (1605), 5 Co. Rep. 125b, 77 ER 251; see also Eldridge, *Distant Heritage*, 133.

41 *charges were read aloud*: Eldridge, *Distant Heritage*, 94.

41 *"the best government"*: M. Searle Bates, *Religious Liberty: An Inquiry* (New York: Harper & Bros., 1945), 327.

41 *"level their estates"*: "The Statement of the Levellers (1649)," Paul Brians, Washington State University, https://brians.wsu.edu/2016/11/04/statement-of-the-levellers -1649/ ("We profess that we never had it in our thoughts to level men's estates").

41 *before the Star Chamber*: Nathan Dorn, "John Lilburne, Oaths and the Cruel Trilemma," *In Custodia Legis* blog, Library of Congress, Apr. 25, 2013.

41 *"get to Liberty"*: Mark A. Graber & Howard Gillman, *The Complete American Constitutionalism*, vol. 1 (New York: Oxford University Press, 2015), 499.

42 *"above all liberties"*: J. Milton, *Areopagitica: A Speech for the Liberty of Unlicensed Printing to the Parliament of England* (1644) (London: Noel Douglas, 1927), 35.

42 *"from our knowledge"*: Milton, *Areopagitica*.

42 *"scandalous libels"*: William Blackstone, *Commentaries on the Laws of England*, vol. 2, (New York: Cavendish, 2001), 151–52.

43 *"religious pamphleteers"*: Frederick Seaton Siebert, *Freedom of the Press in England, 1476–1776: The Rise and Decline of Government Control* (Urbana, IL: University of Chicago Press, 1965), 117.

43 *whipping and body mutilation*: Judith Schenck Koffler & Bennett L. Gershman, "National Security and Civil Liberties: The New Seditious Libel," *Cornell Law Review* 69 (1984): 816, 820. See generally Mayton, "Seditious Libel."

43 *Pine's Case*: Pine's Case, 79 Eng. Rep. 703, 703 (K.B. 1628).

43 *"king than Hickwright"*: Pine's Case.

43 *"not treason"*: Pine's Case, 711; see also Mayton, "Seditious Libel," 104.

43 *treason offenses*: Mayton, "Seditious Libel," 104.

43 *intriguing character*: See generally Amanda Goodrich, *Henry Redhead Yorke, Colonial Radical: Politics and Identity in the Atlantic World, 1772–1813* (London: Routledge, 2019).

43 *other than Thomas Paine*: Goodrich, *Henry Redhead*.

44 *"in his company"*: "Henry Redhead Yorke and Thomas Paine," *paineandfriends* blog, Jan. 29, 2018, https://paineandfriends.com/2018/01/29/henry-redhead-yorke-and -thomas-paine/.

44 *"perhaps more so"*: "Henry Redhead," *paineandfriends*.

44 *"a settled melancholy"*: "Henry Redhead," *paineandfriends*.

44 *threat of sedition prosecution*: See generally W. H. G. Armytage, "The Editorial Experiences of Joseph Gales, 1786–1794," *North Carolina Historical Review* 28 (1951): 28.

44 *"all human polity"*: See "Trial of Henry Redhead, Otherwise Henry Yorke, Gentleman, for Conspiracy (1795)," in *A Complete Collection of State Trials and Proceedings for High Treason and Other Crimes and Misdemeanors, 1794–1796*, vol. 25, edited by Thomas Jones Howell (London: T. C. Hansard, 1818), 1017.

44 *"happiness of mankind"*: Howell, "Trial."

45 *"tumults therein"*: Howell, "Trial."

45 *"cause of peace"*: Howell, "Trial."

45 *"Commons House of Parliament"*: Howell, "Trial," 1012.

45 *intent to cause disorder*: Howell, "Trial," 1015.

45 *imprisonment and fines*: Howell, "Trial," 1016.

46 *"perhaps to bloodshed"*: Blackstone, *Commentaries*, 150.

46 *publishers and dissenters*: See generally I. Brant, *The Bill of Rights: Its Origin and Meaning* (Indianapolis, IN: Bobbs-Merrill, 1965), 217.

46 *"corrupt or wicked Magistrates"*: Solomon, *Revolutionary Dissent*, 39.

47 *"good opinion of it"*: Thomas Jones Howell, ed., *A Complete Collection of State Trials and Proceedings for High Treason and Other Crimes and Misdemeanors, 1794–1796*, vol. 25, (London: T. C. Hansard, 1818), 1128; see also Edward Walford, *Speeches of Thomas Lord Erskine*, vol. 1 (1870), 200.

47 *condemnation of Blackstone's view*: Joseph Priestley, *Remarks on Some Paragraphs in the Fourth Volume of Dr. Blackstone's Commentaries on the Laws of England Relating to the Dissenters* (London: J. Johnson and J. Payne, 1769).

47 *"persecuting Spirit"*: Priestley, *Remarks.*

47 *"English Liturgy"*: Priestley, *Remarks.*

47 *"Danger of the Laws"*: Priestley, *Remarks.*

48 *"not the tendency"*: Philip Furneaux, *Letters to the Honourable Mr. Justice Blackstone, Concerning his Exposition of the Act of Toleration and Some Positions relative to Religious Liberty* (London: T. Cadell, 1770).

48 *the Rights of Man and the Citizen*: Declaration of the Rights of Man and Citizen, art. 11 (1789), reprinted in Frank Maloy Anderson, *Constitutions and Other Select Documents Illustrative of the History of France, 1789–1901* (Minneapolis, MN: H. W. Wilson, 1904), 58, 60.

48 *"defined by law"*: Anderson, *Constitutions.*

4. THE AMERICAN REVOLUTION AND MADISON'S MONSTER

49 *Free speech . . . was alienable*: Steven J. Heyman, "Righting the Balance: An Inquiry into the Foundations and Limits of Freedom of Expression," *Boston University Law Review* 78 (1998): 1275, 1292.

49 *"secured under this Constitution"*: 1 Annals of Cong. 449 (Joseph Gales & William Seaton eds., 1834) (remarks of Rep. Madison).

49 *"establishment of societies"*: See Montesquieu, *The Spirit of the Laws*, edited and translated by Anne M. Cohler et al. (Cambridge, UK: Cambridge University Press, 1989).

50 *"abridging the freedom of speech"*: U.S. Constitution, amend. I.

50 *"no law abridging"*: Mishkin v. State of N.Y., 383 U.S. 502, 518 (1945) (Black, J., dissenting).

50 *"ecclesiastical and civil" tyrannies*: John Adams, "A Dissertation on the Canon and the Feudal Law" (1765), in *Papers of John Adams*, vol. 1, edited by Robert J. Taylor (Cambridge, MA: Harvard University Press, 1977), 111–15.

50   *"settlement of America"*: Taylor, *Papers of John Adams*, vol. 1, 111–15.

50   *"the great Legislator of the universe"*: Taylor, *Papers of John Adams*, vol. 1, 111–15.

50   *"two calves, and a turkey"*: Larry D. Eldridge, *A Distant Heritage: The Growth of Free Speech in Early America* (New York: New York University Press, 1994), 5.

51   *"of ill fame"*: Eldridge, *Distant Heritage*, 6.

51   *"on the Lord's Day"*: Eldridge, *Distant Heritage*, 5.

51   *colonial courts*: Eldridge, *Distant Heritage*, 3.

51   *new American ethos*: See generally Jerome McGann, "'Christian Charity,' A Sacred American Text," *Textual Cultures* 12 (2019): 27–52.

51   *"others mean and in subjection"*: John Winthrop, "A Model of Christian Charity" (1630; Hanover, IN: Hanover Historical Texts Project, 1996).

51   *"authority from God"*: Winthrop, "Model."

51   *"divine vengeance"*: Eldridge, *Distant Heritage*, 11.

52   *"his Lieutenant Governor"*: Stephen D. Solomon, *Revolutionary Dissent: How the Founding Generation Created the Freedom of Speech* (New York: St. Martin's Press, 2016), 18.

52   *"such high contempt shall deserve"*: Solomon, *Revolutionary Dissent*, 25.

52   *"times of danger"*: See generally Eldridge, *Distant Heritage*, 36.

52   *"tumult and rebellion"*: Eldridge, *Distant Heritage*, 36.

52   *royal colony*: Eldridge, *Distant Heritage*, 50.

52   *"damn them all"*: Eldridge, *Distant Heritage*, 69.

52   *public floggings*: Eldridge, *Distant Heritage*, 91.

53   *rifle butts*: Eldridge, *Distant Heritage*, 95.

53   *"well laid on"*: Eldridge, *Distant Heritage*, 10.

53   *"sharply inflicted"*: Eldridge, *Distant Heritage*, 92.

53   *tied to his legs*: Eldridge, *Distant Heritage*, 96.

53   *the prison porch in Newport*: Eldridge, *Distant Heritage*, 101.

54   *"beyond all bounds"*: Chaim M. Rosenberg, *The Loyalist Conscience: Principled Opposition to the American Revolution* (Jefferson, NC: McFarland, 2018), 193.

54   *criminal defamation*: Josiah Quincy Jr., ed., *Reports of Cases Argued and Adjudged in the Superior Court of Judicature of the Province of Massachusetts Bay, Between 1761 and 1772* (Boston: Little, Brown, 1865), 244–45; Solomon, *Revolutionary Dissent*, 1–2.

55   *harsh penal laws*: Vincent Buranelli, "Governor Cosby and His Enemies," *New York History* 37 (1956): 365, 366.

55   *"meeting obstacles"*: Buranelli, "Governor Cosby," 365, 366.

55   *paid for his service*: Solomon, *Revolutionary Dissent*, 31.

55   *while in England*: Buranelli, "Governor Cosby," 389.

56   *"Justice in his room"*: Buranelli, "Governor Cosby," 370–71.

57   *"a Thousand thanks"*: Solomon, *Revolutionary Dissent*, 43.

57   *"wretches can invent"*: Buranelli, "Governor Cosby," 375.

57   *to speak freely*: Solomon, *Revolutionary Dissent*, 51.

57   *"writing the truth"*: Marvin R. Summers, *Free Speech and Political Protest* (Lexington, MA: D. C. Heath, 1967), 19.

58   *"the right of another"*: John Trenchard & Thomas Gordon, *Cato's Letters or Essays on Liberty, Civil and Religious, and Other Important Subjects*, edited by Ronald Hamowy (Indianapolis, IN: Liberty Fund, 1995) (1755), 110. See also Wendell Bird, *Press and Speech Under Assault: The Early Supreme Court Justices, the Sedition Act of 1798, and Campaign Against Dissent* (New York: Oxford University Press, 1986), 10–11.

58   *freedom of thought*: See, e.g., Thomas Gordon, *Of Freedom of Speech: That the Same Is Inseparable from Publick Liberty*, no. 15 (1721), reprinted in *Cato's Letters: Essays on Liberty, Civil and Religious, & Other Important Subjects* (New York: Da Capo Press, 1971) (1755), 96.

58   *protection of free speech*: Steven D. Smith, "Skepticism, Tolerance, and Truth in the Theory of Free Expression," *Southern California Law Review* 60 (1987): 649, 703.

58   *freedom of speech*: John Locke, *An Essay Concerning Human Understanding*, edited by Peter H. Nidditch (Oxford, UK: Clarendon Press, 1975) (1690), 353 ("[T]hough Men uniting into politick Societies, have resigned up to the publick the disposing of all their Force . . . yet they retain still the power of Thinking. . . .").

58   *"what you thought"*: Trenchard & Gordon, *Cato's Letters*, vol. 15, 113.

59   *"Prejudice of another"*: Trenchard & Gordon, *Cato's Letters*, vol. 2, 248.

59   *"purposes of ministers"*: *Works of James Wilson*, edited by McCloskey (Cambridge, MA: Belknap Press, 1967), vol. 2, 663–64, 650.

59   *"democratic revolution"*: R. R. Palmer, *The Age of the Democratic Revolution* (Princeton, NJ: Princeton University Press, 1959, 1964); see also David M. Rabban, "The Ahistorical Historian: Leonard Levy on Freedom of Expression in Early American History," *Stanford Law Review* 37 (1985): 795.

59   *inquiry and reason*: Richard Ashcraft, *Revolutionary Politics & Locke's Two Treatises of Government* (Princeton, NJ: Princeton University Press, 1986), 66–67.

59   *"free, rational, and willing" inquiry*: John Trenchard & Thomas Gordon, *The Independent Whig*, vol. 2, 7th ed. (London: J. Peele, 1743), 27.

59   *"Natural or Revealed"*: Trenchard & Gordon, *Cato's Letters*, vol. 2, 462, 468. For further discussion of these sources, see Steven J. Heyman, "Reason and Conviction: Natural Rights, Natural Religion, and the Origins of the Free Exercise Clause," *University of Pennsylvania Journal of Constitutional Law* 23 (2021): 48–56.

60   *"range of political interest"*: Dennis v. United States, 341 U.S. 494, 521 (1951) (Frankfurter, J., concurring).

60   *"oil upon the flames"*: Wendell Bird, "The Sedition Act and the Assault on Freedoms of Press and Speech: The Missing Half of the Sedition Cases," in *Press and Speech Under Assault: The Early Supreme Court Justices, the Sedition Act of 1798, and the Campaign Against Dissent* (New York: Oxford University Press, 2016); Solomon, *Revolutionary Dissent*, 291.

61   *"respecting the American cause"*: Solomon, *Revolutionary Dissent*, 231.

61   *hold in the colonies*: See generally Jonathan Turley, "The Right to Rage: Free Speech and Rage Rhetoric in American Political Discourse," *Georgetown Journal of Law & Public Policy* 21, no. 2 (2023): 498.

61   *"tolerated by the magistrate"*: John Locke, "A Third Letter for Toleration," ch. 1 (1692), reprinted in *The Works of John Locke*, vol. 5, 12th ed. (London: Rivington, 1824) 139, 156–57.

61   *"judges of the matter"*: Thomas Paine, *The Writings of Thomas Paine, 4 Vols.* (New York: E. G. Putnam & Sons, 1894), 476.

61   *libertarian view of free speech*: See Leonard Levy, *Legacy of Suppression: Freedom of Speech and Press in Early American History* (Cambridge, MA: Belknap Press, 1960); see also Leonard W. Levy, *Emergence of a Free Press* (New York: Oxford, 1985); see also Rabban, "Ahistorical Historian," 795–804. But see Vincent Blasi, "The Checking Value in First Amendment Theory," *Law and Social Inquiry* 2 (1977): 521, https://www.jstor.org/stable/827945.

61   *the common law*: Levy, *Legacy of Suppression*, 233–34.

61   *"actual meaning of the instrument"*: The Debates in the Several State Conventions on the Adoption of the Federal Constitution as Recommended by the General Convention at Philadelphia in 1787, vol. 4, edited by Jonathan Elliot (1836), 569–73.

62   *"to be apprehended"*: J. Stuart Mill, *On Liberty*, edited by D. Spitz (New York: W. W. Norton, 1975), 17; see generally William W. Van Alstyne, "Congressional Power and Free Speech: Levy's Legacy Revisited," *Harvard Law Review* 99 (1986): 1091.

62   *"temporary panic"*: Jonathan Turley, "Harm and Hegemony: The Decline of Free Speech in the United States," *Harvard Journal of Law and Public Policy* 45 (2022): 600–610.

62   *"the symptoms of apparent panic"*: Letter from Learned Hand, Judge, U.S. District Court, Southern District of New York, to Oliver Wendell Holmes, Assoc. Justice, U.S. Supreme Court (Nov. 25, 1919), reprinted in Gerald Gunther, "Learned Hand and the Origins of Modern First Amendment Doctrine: Some Fragments of History," *Stanford Law Review* 27 (1975): 719, 760.

63   *"auxiliary precautions"*: The Federalist No. 51, at 322 (James Madison) (Clinton Rossiter ed., 1961).

63   *"power in terrorem"*: Geoffrey R. Stone, *Perilous Times: Free Speech in Wartime: From the Sedition Act of 1798 to the War on Terrorism* (New York: W. W. Norton, 2004), 64.

64   *the 1800 election*: Stanley Elkins & Eric McKitrick, *The Age of Federalism* (New York: Oxford University Press, 1993), 722.

64   *"raised against them"*: The Works of John Adams, vol. 9, edited by Charles Francis Adams (Boston: Little, Brown & Co., 1854), 161.

64   *"Government over the people"*: Solomon, *Revolutionary Dissent*, 267.

65   *cause of free speech*: Papers of James Madison, vol. 17, edited by Robert A. Rutland et al. (Charlottesville: University of Virginia Press, 1977), 205, 336.

65 *"the absolute sovereignty"*: New York Times Co. v. Sullivan, 376 U.S. 254 (1964) (quoting 4 *Elliot's Debates* 569 [1876]) (citation omitted in original).

65 *"both responsible"*: Elliot, *The Debates*, vol. 4, 569–70.

65 *"faithful discharge of its duty"*: Elliot, *The Debates*, vol. 4, 575.

65 *"yielding the proper fruits"*: James Madison, "The Virginia Report," in *The Mind of the Founder: Sources of the Political Thought of James Madison*, rev. ed., edited by Marvin Meyers (Waltham, MA: Brandeis University Press, 1981), 231, 243.

66 *"the lowest class of slaves"*: Solomon, *Revolutionary Dissent*, 266.

66 *"liberty of speech and of the press"*: Henry Schofield, *Essays on Constitutional Law and Equity and Other Subjects* (Boston: Chipman Law, 1921), 521.

66 *"criticism of the government"*: Solomon, *Revolutionary Dissent*, 4.

PART II: THE AGES OF RAGE AND CRUCIBLE OF FREE SPEECH

69 *"cannot be honest"*: Thomas Paine, "A Response to Cato's Fourth Through Seventh Letters," Thomas Paine, "The Forester's Letters, Letter III—'To Cato,'" 24 *Pennsylvania Journal* (April 1776).

69 *"shall be inviolable"*: 1 Annals of Cong. 434 (1789).

70 *participatory government*: Stephen D. Solomon, *Revolutionary Dissent: How the Founding Generation Created the Freedom of Speech* (New York: St. Martin's Press, 2016), 23.

70 *"freeborn English men"*: Solomon, *Revolutionary Dissent*, 21.

70 *"a face from the ancient gallery"*: The Doors, "The End," *The Doors* (Elektra Records, 1967).

71 *"been born and bred"*: Geoffrey R. Stone, *Perilous Times: Free Speech in Wartime from the Sedition Act of 1798 to the War on Terrorism* (New York: W. W. Norton, 2004), 41.

71 *this "darling privilege"*: Stone, *Perilous Times*, 41.

71 *the world around them*: George Bernard Shaw, *Man and Superman: A Comedy and a Philosophy* (London: Archibald & Co., 1907), 238.

5. THE BOSTON TEA PARTY AND AMERICA'S BIRTH IN RAGE

73 *seeking outright rebellion*: Benjamin L. Carp, *Defiance of the Patriots: The Boston Tea Party & the Making of America* (New Haven, CT: Yale University Press, 2011), 2–5.

73 *"against the British Crown"*: Carp, *Defiance of the Patriots*, 2.

73 *one million pounds of tea a year*: Benjamin Woods Labaree, *The Boston Tea Party* (New York: Oxford University Press, 1964), 7.

73 *illegally from Holland*: Labaree, *Boston Tea Party*, 7.

73 *Boston, New York, and Philadelphia*: Labaree, *Boston Tea Party*, 8.

74 *"America prostate at his feet"*: Labaree, *Boston Tea Party*, 39.

74 *"enliven your Appearance"*: Theodore Draper, *A Struggle for Power: The American Revolution* (New York: Knopf Doubleday, 1997), 394.

75 *paid within twenty days*: Labaree, *Boston Tea Party*, 126–27.

75 *"our just Resentment"*: Labaree, *Boston Tea Party*, 133.

76   *trapped in the harbor*: Labaree, *Boston Tea Party*, 138–39.

76   *Coercive Acts against Boston*: Cedric W. Porter, "Lord Dartmouth and the Boston Tea Party," *Dartmouth Alumni Magazine*, March 1, 1965; Labaree, *Boston Tea Party*, 139.

76   *punish him for his treachery*: Labaree, *Boston Tea Party*, 140.

76   *Old South Meeting House*: Labaree, *Boston Tea Party*, 141.

76   *"a childish fantasy"*: Carp, *Defiance of the Patriots*, 121.

76   *taking direct action*: Carp, *Defiance of the Patriots*, 5.

76   *just ten to twelve chests*: Labaree, *Boston Tea Party*, 8.

77   *dump more tea*: Labaree, *Boston Tea Party*, 8.

77   *"tea for the fishes"*: Harlow Giles Unger, *American Tempest: How the Boston Tea Party Sparked a Revolution* (Cambridge, MA: Da Capo Press, 2011), 6.

77   *by the Parliament*: Jonathan Turley, "The Right to Rage: Free Speech and Rage Rhetoric in American Political Discourse," *Georgetown Journal of Law & Public Policy* 21, no. 2 (2023): 487.

77   *"British rule in America"*: Unger, *American Tempest*, 169.

78   *"Epocha [sic] in History"*: Archive of the Diary of John Adams, "1773. Dec. 17th," in National Archives, Founders Online, https://founders.archives.gov/documents/Adams/01-02-02-0003-0008-0001, accessed June 11, 2023.

78   *"destroy private Property"*: Benjamin Franklin to the Massachusetts House Committee of Correspondence, Feb. 21, 1774, National Archives, Founders Online, https://founders.archives.gov/documents/Franklin/01-21-02-0023, accessed June 10, 2023.

78   *"Crown of Great Britain"*: Thomas Fleming, *The First Stroke* (Washington, DC: U.S. Department of Interior, 1978), 13.

78   *"we have any authority"*: Fleming, *First Stroke*, 13.

78   *"other places to tumults"*: Fleming, *First Stroke*, 13.

79   *"her best days"*: William Stanhope Taylor & Captain John Henry Pringle, *Correspondence of William Pitt*, vol. 4 (1839) 337.

6. SHAYS' REBELLION AND THE RISE OF AMERICAN SEDITION

80   *difficult for farmers*: Charles River Editors, *Shays' Rebellion and the Whiskey Rebellion* (Scotts Valley, CA: CreateSpace, 2017), 6.

81   *"state senate and governor's office"*: Leonard Richards, *Shays's Rebellion: The American Revolution's Final Battle* (Philadelphia: University of Pennsylvania Press, 2002), 74.

81   *their homes confiscated*: Richards, *Shays's Rebellion*, 10.

81   *"redress for their grievances"*: Howard Zinn, *A People's History of the United States* (New York: HarperCollins, 2005), 6.

81   *"necessary to prevent it"*: James Warren to John Adams, April 30, 1786, in *Papers of John Adams*, vol. 18 (Cambridge, MA: Massachusetts Historical Society, 2023).

82   *soldier in the Revolution*: James M. Greene, "Ethan Allen and Daniel Shays: Contrasting Models of Political Representation in the Early Republic," *Early American Literature* 46, no. 1 (2013): 126; Richards, *Shays's Rebellion*, 5.

82   *"so extraordinary a Mandate"*: Benjamin Woods Labaree, *The Boston Tea Party* (New York: Oxford University Press, 1964), 113.

82   *demand relief*: Richards, *Shays's Rebellion*, 10.

83   *riot in Northampton*: Richards, *Shays's Rebellion*, 9.

83   *"violent and riotous proceedings"*: Tom Cutterham, *Gentlemen Revolutionaries: Power and Justice in the New American Republic* (Princeton, NJ: Princeton University Press, 2017), 130.

83   *"ringleaders and abettors"*: Cutterham, *Gentlemen Revolutionaries*, 130.

83   *"disorderly, riotous, and seditious persons"*: Zinn, *A People's History*, 93.

84   *"dangerous insurrection"*: Joseph Parker Warren, "The Confederation and the Shays Rebellion," *American Historical Review* 11, no. 1 (Oct. 1905): 50–51.

84   *coin for the tax*: Gary Shattuck, "The Groton Riots of 1781," *Journal of the American Revolution*, uploaded May 29, 2014, https://allthingsliberty.com/2014/05/the-groton-riots-of-1781/. See also Gary Shattuck, *Artful and Designing Men: The Trial of Job Shattuck and the Regulation of 1786–1787* (Mustang, OK: Tate, 2013).

84   *"Capt. Sheple for rates"*: Shattuck, "Groton Riots," 2014.

84   *he should not come again*: Shattuck, "Groton Riots," 2014.

84   *personified the crisis*: Sean Condon, *Shays's Rebellion: Authority and Distress in Post-Revolutionary America* (Baltimore: Johns Hopkins University Press, 2015), 54.

84   *"government of the Commonwealth"*: Shattuck, "Groton Riots," 2014.

84   *"Staves and Clubbs"*: Shattuck, "Groton Riots," 2014.

84   *"supporting and protecting it"*: "Springfield, Sept. 27," *New-Haven Gazette*, Sept. 27, 1786.

85   *much of the debt*: Richards, *Shays's Rebellion*, 23, 78, 85–86.

85   *"could not now look back"*: David P. Szatmary, *Shays's Rebellion* (Amherst: University of Massachusetts Press, 1980), 97.

86   *the Stamp Act riots*: Labaree, *Boston Tea Party*, 104.

86   *unload their goods*: Labaree, *Boston Tea Party*, 127.

86   *"Obstinacy rendered necessary"*: Labaree, *Boston Tea Party*, 148.

86   *"ought to suffer death"*: William Pencak, "Play as Prelude to Revolution," in *Riot and Revelry in Early America*, edited by William Pencak et al. (University Park: Pennsylvania State University Press, 2002), 4.

7. THE WHISKEY REBELLION AND "HAMILTON'S INSURRECTION"

88   *listen to their grievances*: Thomas P. Slaughter, *The Whiskey Rebellion: Frontier Epilogue to the American Revolution* (New York: Oxford University Press, 1986), 18–19.

88   *war debt*: Slaughter, *Whiskey Rebellion: Frontier*, 95–96.

88   *"their intemperate use"*: Ernest Hurst Cherrington, *The Evolution of Prohibition in the United States of America* (Cambridge, MA: Harvard University Press, 1920) 53.

89   *"the minds of the members"*: 1 Annals of Cong. 1921 (Joseph Gales, ed., 1790).

89   *annually in revenue*: Slaughter, *Whiskey Rebellion: Frontier*, 97.

89   *worthless currency*: Slaughter, *Whiskey Rebellion: Frontier*, 71.

89   *viable form of currency*: Slaughter, *Whiskey Rebellion: Frontier*, 73.

89   *roughly $16 in profit*: William Hogeland, *The Whiskey Rebellion: George Washington, Alexander Hamilton and the Frontier Rebels Who Challenged America's Newfound Sovereignty* (New York: Scribner, 2006), 67.

89   *six cents per gallon*: Slaughter, *Whiskey Rebellion: Frontier*, 148–54

89   *paid in cash*: Slaughter, *Whiskey Rebellion: Frontier*, 73.

90   *violent agitation*: Bruce E. Stewart, *Redemption from Tyranny: Herman Husband's American Revolution* (Charlottesville: University of Virginia Press, 2020), 2.

90   *Benjamin Franklin*: Hogeland, *Whiskey Rebellion: George Washington*, 91.

90   *unloading tea in Boston*: Labaree, *Boston Tea Party*, 101.

91   *hardened tar from his body*: Hogeland, *Whiskey Rebellion: George Washington*, 20–24.

91   *redress for the taxes*: Hogeland, *Whiskey Rebellion: George Washington*, 123, 163.

92   *"a display of strength"*: Thomas Ladenburg, "Chapter 5: The Whiskey Rebellion," Digital History, University of Houston, 2007, 22, https://www.digitalhistory.uh .edu/teachers/lesson_plans/pdfs/unit3_5.pdf.

92   *"undoubtedly prove very meek"*: Labaree, *Boston Tea Party*, 178.

92   *"their worst fears"*: Hogeland, *Whiskey Rebellion: George Washington*, 126.

92   *out of business*: Hogeland, *Whiskey Rebellion: George Washington*, 98–104.

93   *held out for negotiations*: Hogeland, *Whiskey Rebellion: George Washington*, 125.

93   *"high offices and salaries"*: Hogeland, *Whiskey Rebellion: George Washington*, 172.

93   *taken locally*: Hogeland, *Whiskey Rebellion: George Washington*, 219.

94   *barefoot*: Hogeland, *Whiskey Rebellion: George Washington*, 221.

94   *unheated tavern cellar*: Hogeland, *Whiskey Rebellion: George Washington*, 221–22.

94   *information on their charges*: Hogeland, *Whiskey Rebellion: George Washington*, 237.

94   *played roles in the violence*: Hogeland, *Whiskey Rebellion: George Washington*, 238.

94   *pardoned both men*: Hogeland, *Whiskey Rebellion: George Washington*, 238.

94   *bears his name*: Jeff Cioletti, "Whiskey's New Rebellion," SevenFiftyDaily, Aug. 9, 2017, https://daily.sevenfifty.com/whiskeys-new-rebellion/.

95   *"we will adhere to"*: Jefferson to Madison, Monticello, Dec. 28, 1794, in *The Papers of Thomas Jefferson*, edited by John Catanzariti (Princeton, NJ: Princeton University Press, 2000), 28, 228–30.

95   *"Hamilton's Insurrection"*: Jefferson to Madison, Jan. 1, 1797, in National Archives, Founders Online, https://founders.archives.gov/documents/Jefferson/01 -29-02-0196-0002.

95   *"storms in the physical"*: Jefferson to Madison, Paris, Jan. 30, 1787, in National Archives, Founders Online, https://founders.archives.gov/documents/Jefferson/01 -11-02-0095.

8. FRIES AND THE FAUX REBELLION

96   *around a liberty pole*: Shira Lurie, *The American Liberty Pole: Popular Politics and the Struggle for Democracy* (Charlottesville, VA: University of Virginia, 2023), 100.

96 *"Laws, Liberty or Death"*: Paul Douglas Newman, "Fries's Rebellion and American Political Culture, 1798–1800," *Pennsylvania Magazine of History and Biography* 119, nos. 1/2 (Jan.–Apr. 1995): 53.

96 *"Tories"*: Newman, "Fries's Rebellion," 47.

97 *preserve American liberties*: Benjamin Woods Labaree, *The Boston Tea Party* (New York: Oxford University Press, 1964), 148.

97 *windows in a dwelling*: Newman, "Fries's Rebellion," 31.

97 *unconstitutional and unenforceable*: Newman, "Fries's Rebellion," 41, 55.

97 *nullify unconstitutional acts*: Newman, "Fries's Rebellion," 41.

97 *Federalists to the Republicans*: Newman, "Fries's Rebellion," 46–48.

97 *heard in Congress*: Newman, "Fries's Rebellion," 11.

97 *Revolutionary War veterans*: Newman, "Fries's Rebellion," 19.

98 *release the livestock*: Paul Douglas Newman, *Fries's Rebellion: The Enduring Struggle for the American Revolution* (Philadelphia: University of Pennsylvania Press, 2004), 116.

98 *unconstitutional and unfair*: Newman, *Fries's Rebellion: The Enduring Struggle*, 50.

98 *the district from the Federalists*: Newman, *Fries's Rebellion: The Enduring Struggle*, 49.

99 *business partners*: Charles M. Sandwick Sr., "Historical Research: The Henry Family, IV," *Jacobsburg Record*, Oct.–Nov. 1976, 1.

99 *seeking federal intervention*: William Watts Hart Davis, *The Fries Rebellion 1798–99* (Doylestown, PA: Doylestown Pub. Co. Printers, 1899), 44–47.

99 *Bethlehem, Pennsylvania*: Dwight F. Henderson, "Treason, Sedition, and Fries' Rebellion," *American Journal of Legal History* 14, no. 4 (Oct. 1970): 310–11.

99 *invoked the First Amendment*: Newman, *Fries's Rebellion: The Enduring Struggle*, 101.

99 *half were armed*: Henderson, "Treason, Sedition," 311.

99 *peacefully to the tavern*: Newman, "Fries's Rebellion," 57.

99 *"fired on first"*: Newman, "Fries's Rebellion," 58.

99 *ball before the powder*: Newman, "Fries's Rebellion," 128.

100 *dispersed a week earlier*: Henderson, "Treason, Sedition," 308, 309–11.

100 *"laws of their country"*: Henderson, "Treason, Sedition," 311.

100 *assessor Stephen Balliott*: Henderson, "Treason, Sedition," 311.

100 *"levying war against the United States"*: Henderson, "Treason, Sedition," 312.

100 *local Federalist candidate*: Wendell Bird, *Press and Speech Under Assault: The Early Supreme Court Justices, the Sedition Act of 1798, and the Campaign Against Dissent* (New York: Oxford University Press, 2016), 380–81.

100 *mounted company from Philadelphia*: Newman, *Fries's Rebellion: The Enduring Struggle*, 162.

100 *"splayed another in two"*: Newman, *Fries's Rebellion: The Enduring Struggle*, 163.

101 *"war against the United States"*: Carlton F. W. Larson, "The Forgotten Constitutional Law of Treason and the Enemy Combatant Problem," *University of Pennsylvania Law Review* 154, no. 4 (Apr. 2006): 863, 906.

101   *contradiction to his other actions*: Henderson, "Treason, Sedition," 312–13.

101   *"pronouncing sentence on him"*: Henderson, "Treason, Sedition," 313.

102   *"want of military weapons"*: Larson, "Forgotten Constitutional Law," 907.

102   *"suppress future insurrections"*: Henderson, "Treason, Sedition," 313.

102   *"they were of our laws"*: Newman, *Fries's Rebellion: The Enduring Struggle*, 183.

102   *"rebels" on May 21, 1800*: Henderson, "Treason, Sedition," 316.

103   *these men from death*: Newman, "Fries's Rebellion," 68.

9. ADAMS AND THE RETURN OF "THE MONSTER"

104   *swing from the gallows*: Stephen D. Solomon, *Revolutionary Dissent: How the Founding Generation Created the Freedom of Speech* (New York: St. Martin's Press, 2016), 281.

105   *"rascally seditious crew"*: Richard N. Rosenfeld, *American Aurora: A Democratic-Republican Returns: The Suppressed History of Our Nation's Beginnings and the Heroic Newspaper That Tried to Report It* (New York: St. Martin's Press, 2014), 179.

105   *"King, Pitt, and Liberty"*: Bob Ruppert, "The Battle of Golden Hill—Six Weeks Before the Boston Massacre," *Journal of the American Revolution* (Oct. 2014).

105   *he was arrested*: Solomon, *Revolutionary Dissent*, 282.

105   *"insurrection and civil war"*: Solomon, *Revolutionary Dissent*, 282; see also Wendell Bird, "The Sedition Act and the Assault on Freedoms of Press and Speech: The Sitting Supreme Court Justices and the Trials," in *Press and Speech Under Assault: The Early Supreme Court Justices, the Sedition Act of 1798, and the Campaign Against Dissent* (New York: Oxford University Press, 2016).

105   *"power in terrorem"*: Geoffrey R. Stone, *Perilous Times: Free Speech in Wartime from the Sedition Act of 1798 to the War on Terrorism* (New York: W. W. Norton, 2004), 64.

106   *"Strength to Government"*: Adams to Jefferson, Grosvenor Square, Nov. 30, 1786, in National Archives, Founders Online, https://founders.archives.gov/docu ments/Jefferson/01-10-02-0419.

106   *"no severities from their governments"*: Jefferson to Madison, Paris, Jan. 30, 1787, in National Archives, Founders Online, https://founders.archives.gov/docu ments/Jefferson/01-11-02-0095.

106   *"two Juries pronounced it"*: Adams to Jefferson, June 30, 1813, in National Archives, Founders Online, https://founders.archives.gov/documents/Jefferson/03 -06-02-0216#TJ522675_14.

107   *"urged the insurrection"*: 4 Annals of Cong. 899 (1794).

107   *"the objects of legislation"*: 4 Annals of Cong. 899 at 934.

107   *"government over the people"*: 4 Annals of Cong. 899 at 122.

107   *"speaking and publishing, are sacred"*: William T. Mayton, "Seditious Libel and the Lost Guarantee of a Freedom of Expression," *Columbia Law Review* 84 (1984) (quoting Rep. Giles's speech in the *Philadelphia Aurora* of December 8, 1794).

108   *"stirrer up of sedition"*: Solomon, *Revolutionary Dissent*, 273.

108   *the pompous and the corrupt*: Arthur Scherr, "Inventing the Patriot President:

Bache's *Aurora* and John Adams," *Pennsylvania Magazine of History and Biography* 119, no. 4 (Oct. 1995): 369–99.

108   *"all denominations"*: Michael Kent Curtis, *Free Speech: The People's Darling Privilege* (Durham, NC: Duke University Press, 2000), 63.

108   *"peace and safety of this country"*: Curtis, *Free Speech*, 64.

108   *"power or persecution"*: Rafi Andonian, "The Adamant Patriot: Benjamin Franklin Bache as Leader of the Opposition Press," Penn State University Libraries, https://libraries.psu.edu/about/collections/unearthing-past-student-research -pennsylvania-history/adamant-patriot-benjamin.

108   *prosecutions of his opponents*: William Dudley, *The Bill of Rights: Opposing Viewpoints* (San Diego: Greenhaven Press, 1994), 54.

109   *"our construction of it"*: Jefferson to Mrs. Adams, Sept. 11, 1804, in *Memoirs, Correspondence, and Private Papers of Thomas Jefferson*, vol. 4, edited by Thomas Jefferson Randolph (London: Henry Colburn and Richard Bentley, 1829), 27, 28.

109   *"integrity of the presses"*: Jefferson to Thomas McKean, Feb. 19, 1803, in *Freedom of the Press from Zenger to Jefferson*, edited by Leonard W. Levy (Durham, NC: Carolina Academic Press, 1966), 327, 364.

109   *early comments on sedition*: See, e.g., "Address of the General Assembly to the People of the Commonwealth of Virginia," in *The Writings of James Madison*, edited by Gaillard Hunt (New York: G. P. Putnam's Sons, 1908), 333–34. (Madison during the Virginia Resolutions debate to his opponents: "Every libelous writing or expression might receive its punishment in the state courts.")

109   *"querulous ADAMS"*: Solomon, *Revolutionary Dissent*, 271.

109   *"rogues to assist them"*: Alan M. Dershowitz, *America on Trial: Inside the Legal Battles That Transformed Our Nation* (New York: Grand Central, 2004), ii.

109   *not once but twice in Britain*: J. Potter, "William Cobbett in North America," *Bulletin of the British Association for American Studies*, no. 2 (Mar. 1961): 17.

109   *hypocrisies in the new nation*: Potter, "William Cobbett," 12.

110   *persisted in his own country*: Potter, "William Cobbett," 20.

110   *critics like Thomas Cooper*: James Morton Smith, *Freedom's Fetters: The Alien and Sedition Laws and American Civil Liberties* (Ithaca, NY: Cornell University Press, 1956), 231; see also James Morton Smith, "President John Adams, Thomas Cooper, and Sedition: A Case Study in Suppression," *Mississippi Valley Historical Review* 42, no. 3 (Dec. 1955): 438.

110   *"principles we have rejected"*: Smith, *Freedom's Fetters*, 231.

110   *"ought to be prosecuted"*: Smith, *Freedom's Fetters*, 231.

111   *"President of the United States"*: Sedition Act of 1798, ch. 74, 1 Stat. 596 (1798) (expired 1801).

111   *under the First Amendment*: David Jenkins, "The Sedition Act of 1798 & the Incorporation of Seditious Libel into First Amendment Jurisprudence," *American Journal of Legal History* 45, no. 2 (Apr. 2001): 154, 165.

111   *regulations of the press*: Solomon, *Revolutionary Dissent*, 275.

111   *"proven by evidence?"*: Stone, *Perilous Times*, 10.

111 *"temporary panic"*: The Alien Act was not used to the same extent as the Sedition Act, but it gave the president the power to expel any alien deemed "dangerous to the peace and safety of the United States." Alien Act of 1798, ch. 58, 1 Stat. 570, 570–71 (1798).

111 *wholesale crackdown on dissent*: Andrew Burnstein & Nancy Isenberg, *Madison and Jefferson* (New York: Random House, 2010), 335.

111 *the allies of the French*: Peter Onuf, "Thomas Jefferson: Campaigns and Elections," Miller Center, University of Virginia, https://millercenter.org/president /jefferson/campaigns-and-elections. (The Jeffersonians were demonized by the Federalists, including declarations that "[m]urder, robbery, rape, adultery, and incest will be openly taught and practiced, the air will be rent with the cries of the distressed, the soil will be soaked with blood, and the nation black with crimes.") The Federalists were equally vicious in their account of their political opponents. Francis Wharton, *State Trials of the United States During the Administrations of Washington and Adams* (Philadelphia: Carey and Hart, 1849), 689, 322–32. (Federalist journalist William Cobbett called Jeffersonians "frog-eating, man-eating, blood-drinking cannibals" and the "refuse of nations.")

111 *monarchist or mob tyranny*: Stone, *Perilous Times*, 26.

111 *protect public safety*: 8 Annals of Cong. 2147–48 (Gales & Seaton, eds. 1851).

112 *to sort out the truth*: Stone, *Perilous Times*, 33.

112 *"a contagious disease"*: Stone, *Perilous Times*, 34.

112 *"selfish avarice"*: Wharton, *State Trials*, 333; see also Charles Slack, *Liberty's First Crisis: Adams, Jefferson and the Misfits Who Saved Free Speech* (New York: Atlantic Monthly Press, 2015), 114, 127–28; see also Smith, *Freedom's Fetters*, 23.

112 *prison and a fine*: When then-president Thomas Jefferson would later learn of the sentence, he remarked, "I know not which mortifies me most, that I should fear to write what I think or my country bear such a state of things." Jefferson to John Taylor, Nov. 26, 1798, in National Archives, Founders Online, https://founders .archives.gov/documents/Jefferson/01-30-02-0398.

112 *uttered similar thoughts*: Wendell Bird, "New Light on the Sedition Act of 1798: The Missing Half of the Prosecutions," *Law and History Review* 34, no. 3 (Aug. 2016): 514.

112 *"head of his master"*: Stone, *Perilous Times*, 17.

112 *"poor people's pockets"*: Stone, *Perilous Times*, 18.

112 *at the courthouse*: Stone, *Perilous Times*, 48.

112 *"principle of Presidential infallibility"*: Stone, *Perilous Times*, 49.

113 *"hosts of invading foes"*: Stone, *Perilous Times*, 50.

113 *lead and convicted*: Stone, *Perilous Times*, 51.

113 *"unlicensed abuse of government"*: John C. Morgan, *Resisting Tyranny: The Story of Matthew Lyon, Early American Patriot* (Eugene, OR: Wipf & Stock, 2018), 8.

114 *"the prisoner's misery"*: Stone, *Perilous Times*, 51.

114 *treatment of Lyon*: John Spargo, *Anthony Haswell: Printer, Patriot, Ballader* (Rutland, VT: Tuttle Co., 1925), 60.

114   *"unprincipled sedition"*: Stone, *Perilous Times*, 63.

114   *tavern critics*: Bird, "New Light," 518.

114   *the Biden election*: Merrill D. Peterson, *Thomas Jefferson and the New Nation: A Biography* (New York: Oxford University Press, 1970), 630.

115   *"even that of England"*: Peterson, *Thomas Jefferson*, 163–64 (citing letter from Thomas Jefferson to John Taylor, Nov. 26, 1798, in Bernard Schwartz et al., *The Bill of Rights: A Documentary History*, vol. 2 (New York: Chelsea House, 1971).

115   *the laws in 1800*: Eugene H. Roseboom, *A Short History of Presidential Elections* (Springfield, OH: Collier Books, 1967), 11–19.

115   *"free to combat it"*: Noble E. Cunningham, *In Pursuit of Reason: The Life of Thomas Jefferson* (New York: Random House, 1993), 239–40.

115   *"any in the Union"*: St. George Tucker to John Marshall, Nov. 6, 1800, in *The Papers of John Marshall 1800–1807*, edited by Charles Hobson (Durham: University of North Carolina Press, 1990), 4–5; see generally Kurt T. Lash & Alicia Harrison, "Report: John Marshall and the Defense of the Alien and Sedition Acts," *Ohio State Law Journal* 68, no. 2 (2007): 435.

115   *crackdown on political dissent*: Bird, "New Light," 544.

115   The Prospect Before Us: Bird, "New Light," 541, 544.

115   *"Chase's Bloody Circuit"*: Stone, *Perilous Times*, 69.

115   *British imperialism*: James Thomson Callender, *The Political Progress of Britain* (Charlottesville: University of Virginia Special Collections, 1795), https://encyclopediavirginia.org/11436hpr-0e2c8ea779f56fd/.

116   *questionable finances and associations*: Stone, *Perilous Times*, 61.

116   *"hoary headed incendiary"*: Stephen Presser & Jamil S. Zainaldin, *Law and Jurisprudence in American History* (Eagan, MN: West Group, 2000), 238; Stone, *Perilous Times*, 49.

116   *Callender fled to Virginia*: James Morton Smith, "Sedition in the Old Dominion: James T. Callender and the Prospect Among Us," *Journal of Southern History* (May 1954): 157, 159.

116   *"circulation of truth"*: Smith, "Sedition in the Old Dominion," 164.

116   *"use of it he pleased"*: Smith, "Sedition in the Old Dominion," 165.

117   *as a vagrant*: Smith, "Sedition in the Old Dominion," 165; see also Albert J. Beveridge, *The Life of John Marshall: Conflict and Construction* (Washington, DC: Beard Books, 2000), 37.

117   *"differs from his opinions"*: Bruce A. Ragsdale, *The Sedition Act Trials* (Washington, DC: Federal Judicial Center, 2005), 62.

117   *"obscure and friendless foreigner"*: Smith, "Sedition in the Old Dominion," 170.

117   *"people against him?"*: Smith, "Sedition in the Old Dominion," 171; see also Stephen Presser, "Samuel Chase: In Defense of the Rule of Law and Against the Jeffersonians," *Vanderbilt Law Review* 62, no. 2 (2009): 349, 356–63.

118   *novel* Scandalmonger: William Safire, *Scandalmonger* (New York: Mariner Books, 2001).

118   *utter abandon*: Solomon, *Revolutionary Dissent*, 283.

118   *Adams refused*: Solomon, *Revolutionary Dissent*, 284.

119   *criticizing Adams*: *United States v. Cooper* (Chase, Circuit Justice, C.C.D. Pa. 1800), reprinted in Thomas Cooper, *An Account of the Trial of Thomas Cooper of Northumberland* (Philadelphia: John Bioren, 1800), 19.

119   *"licentiousness of the press"*: Lucas Powe, *The Fourth Estate and the Constitution: Freedom of the Press in America* (Berkeley: University of California Press, 1991), 59, http://ark.cdlib.org/ark:/13030/ft6t1nb4fx/.

119   *"disgrace its parents"*: Andrew Burnstein & Nancy Isenberg, *Madison and Jefferson* (New York: Random House, 2013), 333.

10. JEFFERSON AND *THE WASP*

120   *found unconstitutional*: Geoffrey R. Stone, *Perilous Times: Free Speech in Wartime from the Sedition Act of 1798 to the War on Terrorism* (New York: W. W. Norton, 2004), 71.

120   *"safeguard of the public liberty"*: Letter to Edward Carrington, Jan. 16, 1787, in *Jefferson: Writings*, edited by M. Peterson (New York: Library of America, 1984), 880.

120   *"foreign nations"*: Stephen D. Solomon, *Revolutionary Dissent: How the Founding Generation Created the Freedom of Speech* (New York: St. Martin's Press, 2016), 264.

121   *the Jefferson administration*: Leonard Levy, *Jefferson and Civil Liberties: A Darker Side* (Cambridge, MA: Belknap Press, 1963), 70–71.

121   *George Washington and John Adams*: Michael Durey, *With the Hammer of Truth: James Thomson Callender and America's Early National Heroes* (Charlottesville: University of Virginia Press, 1990), 117, 119–21; Stephen Presser & Becky Baur Hurley, "Saving God's Republic: The Jurisprudence of Samuel Chase," *University of Illinois Law Review* (1984): 771, 809.

121   *"profligacy and . . . usury"*: Francis Wharton, *State Trials of the United States During the Administrations of Washington and Adams* (Philadelphia: Carey and Hart, 1849), 689, 322–32.

122   *"he had attempted it"*: Thomas Fleming, "Verdicts of History IV: 'A Scandalous, Malicious, Seditious Libel,'" *American Heritage* 19, no. 1 (Dec. 1967).

122   *"as of the United States"*: People v. Croswell, 3 Johns. Cas. 337 (N.Y. Sup. Ct. 1804).

122   *as a defense witness*: Fleming, "Verdicts of History IV," 19.

123   *conviction to stand*: Terri Diane Halperin, *The Alien and Sedition Acts of 1798: Testing the Constitution* (Baltimore: Johns Hopkins University Press, 2016), 126.

123   *"their fundamental rights"*: Croswell, 3 Johns. Cas. at 391.

123   *"with bad motives"*: Croswell, 3 Johns. Cas. at 394.

123   *"by worthy motives"*: Croswell, 3 Johns. Cas. at 392.

123   *voted for Croswell*: Kate Elizabeth Brown, *Alexander Hamilton and the Development of American Law* (Lawrence: University of Kansas Press, 2017), 193–95.

123   *by Jefferson*: Doug Clouatre, *Presidents and Their Justices* (Lanham, MD: University Press, 2012), 167.

123   *truth as a defense*: An Act Concerning Libels, ch. 90, 1805 N.Y. Sess. Laws 450.

124   *Jeffersonian judges*: People v. Freer, 1 Cai. R. 518, 518–19 (N.Y. Sup. Ct. 1804).

124 *contempt of the court*: See Paul Finkelman, "Thomas Jefferson, Original Intent, and the Shaping of American Law," *New York University Annual Survey of American Law* 62, no. 1 (May 2006): 45, 78.

124 American Sphinx: Joseph Ellis, *American Sphinx: The Character of Thomas Jefferson* (New York: Vintage Books, 1998).

125 *"a selected one"*: Jefferson to McKean, Washington, Feb. 19, 1803, in National Archives, Founders Online, https://founders.archives.gov/documents/Jefferson/01-39-02-0461.

11. JACKSON AND THE "LURKING TRAITORS" AMONG US

126 *the War of 1812*: Jonathan Turley, "Tribunals and Tribulations: The Antithetical Elements of Military Governance in a Madisonian Democracy," *George Washington Law Review* 70, no. 4 (Aug. 2002): 649.

127 *the young nation*: See generally Matthew Warshauer, *Andrew Jackson and the Politics of Martial Law* (Knoxville: University of Tennessee Press, 2006).

127 *"authority but his own"*: Robert Remini, *Andrew Jackson and the Course of American Empire, 1767–1821* (New York: Harper & Row, 1977).

127 *"dealt with accordingly"*: Daniel Feller, ed., "General Orders to New Orleans Citizens and Soldiers" (Dec. 15, 1814), in *The Papers of Andrew Jackson*, vol. 3 (Charlottesville: University of Virginia Press, 2015), 205.

128 *"those of Great Britain"*: Letter from James Monroe to Andrew Jackson, Library of Congress, https://www.loc.gov/item/maj005092/.

128 *"a free city"*: Matthew Warshauer, *Andrew Jackson and the Politics of Martial Law* (Knoxville: University of Tennessee Press, 2006), 33.

129 *"making the Constitution respected"*: A. S. Colyar, *Life and Times of Andrew Jackson: Soldier-Statesman-President*, vol. 1 (Nashville: Marshall & Bruce, 1904), 355.

129 *"armies of the United States"*: Stanley Clisby Arthur, *The Story of the Battle of New Orleans* (New Orleans: Louisiana Historical Society, 1915), 255.

129 *"too long secretly fomenting"*: Warshauer, *Andrew Jackson*, 282.

130 *"victory and triumph"*: Warshauer, *Andrew Jackson*, 284.

130 *ancestral homelands*: Brian Hicks, "The Cherokees and Andrew Jackson," *Smithsonian*, March 2011.

131 *"yield to its mandate"*: Letter from Andrew Jackson to John Coffee (Apr. 7, 1832), in *Correspondence of Andrew Jackson, 1829–1832*, vol. 4, edited by John Spencer Bassett (Washington, DC: Carnegie Institute of Washington, 1929), 429, 430.

131 *chief of the Cherokee Nation*: Walter H. Conser Jr., "John Ross and the Cherokee Resistance Campaign, 1833–1838," *Journal of Southern History* 44 (1978): 191, 193.

131 *supported the action*: Steve Inskeep, *Jacksonland: President Andrew Jackson, Cherokee Chief John Ross, and a Great American Land Grab* (New York: Penguin, 2016), 292.

131 *regulations and criminalization*: Andrew Jackson, "Seventh Annual Message to

Congress, Dec. 8, 1835," American Presidency Project, https://www.presidency
.ucsb.edu/documents/seventh-annual-message-2.

12. LINCOLN AND THE COPPERHEADS

133   *the nineteenth century*: Jonathan Turley, "History Repeating Itself? Biden and
       Trump Not the First to Use 'Rage Rhetoric' for Political Gain," *The Hill*, Sept. 10,
       2022.

133   *"endure forever"*: Nicholas Gachon, *Abraham Lincoln and the US Constitution,
       1861–1865: The Presidential War* (Newcastle upon Tyne, UK: Cambridge Schol-
       ars, 2022), 101.

134   *"Copperheads"*: Phillip Shaw Paludan, *The Presidency of Abraham Lincoln* (Law-
       rence: University of Kansas Press, 1994), 155.

134   *"in this Department"*: Geoffrey R. Stone, "Abraham Lincoln's First Amendment,"
       New York University Law Review 78, no. 1 (April 2003): 5, quoting General Order
       No. 38 (Apr. 13, 1863), in *The Trial of Hon. Clement L. Vallandigham by a Military
       Commission* (Cincinnati: Rickey & Carroll, 1863), 7.

134   *"power of the government"*: Stone, "Abraham Lincoln's First Amendment," 5.

135   *"evils of disruption"*: James L. Vallandigham, *A Life of Clement L. Vallandigham*
       (Baltimore: Turnbull Bros., 1872), 144.

135   *"power, and prosperity"*: Marion Mills Miller, *Great Debates in American History:
       The Civil War* (New York: Current Literature, 1913), 264.

135   *"Fredericksburg and Vicksburg answer"*: See generally Stone, "Abraham Lincoln's
       First Amendment," Chicago Unbound, 2003, 7–8, https://chicagounbound.uchi
       cago.edu/cgi/viewcontent.cgi?referer=&httpsredir=1&article=2953&context=jour
       nal_articles.

135   *"paramount law"*: Geoffrey R. Stone, *Perilous Times: Free Speech in Wartime from
       the Sedition Act of 1798 to the War on Terrorism* (New York: W. W. Norton, 2004),
       103.

136   *"masses of the people"*: *Ex parte Vallandigham*, 28 F. Cas. 874, 923 (C.C.D. Ohio 1863).

136   *"prisoner of war"*: "Vallandigham. Another Account of His Transfer to Rebel Ter-
       ritory," *New York Times*, May 28, 1863.

136   *"shot myself"*: Jeremy Clay, "Victorian Strangeness: The Man Who Shot Himself
       Proving His Case," BBC, Aug. 16, 2014, 2–14.

136   *"men be allowed?"*: Augustus Woodbury, *Major General Ambrose E. Burnside and
       the Ninth Army Corps: A Narrative* (Providence, RI: Sidney S. Rider and Brother,
       1867), 511.

137   *deeply offensive*: Stone, *Perilous Times*, 107.

137   *"to suppress it"*: Stone, *Perilous Times*, 113.

13. THE GILDED AGE AND THE MOBBING OF "FREE SPEECH"

138   *thirty-four Black citizens*: Donald E. Reynolds, "The New Orleans Riot of 1866,
       Reconsidered," *Louisiana History* 5, no. 1 (Winter 1964): 13.

139   *valued education*: See generally Gary Dorrien, *The New Abolition: W. E. B. DuBois and the Black Social Gospel* (New Haven, CT: Yale University Press, 2015).

139   *against her*: Chesapeake, Ohio & Southwestern Railroad Co. v. Wells, https://www.lib.uchicago.edu/ead/pdf/ibwells-0008-011-02.pdf.

140   *Booker T. Washington*: David M. Tucker, "Miss Ida B. Wells and Memphis Lynching," *Phylon* 32, no. 2 (1971): 112–22.

140   *Memphis in 1892*: Damon Mitchell, "The People's Grocery Lynching, Memphis, Tennessee," JSTOR Daily, Jan. 24, 2018.

141   *her friends*: See generally Linda O. McMurry, *To Keep the Waters Troubled: The Life of Ida B. Wells* (New York: Oxford University Press, 2000).

141   *"their women"*: Ida B. Wells, *Memphis Free Speech*, May 21, 1892.

141   *did nothing*: See Neely Tucker, "The Truth and Mighty Will Prevail," Library of Congress blog, Feb. 20, 2020, https://blogs.loc.gov/loc/2020/02/truth-is-mighty-and-will-prevail-ida-b-wells/.

141   *"the elite"*: "A Colored Corday," *Columbia Herald*, Dec. 23, 1892.

141   *"obscene filth"*: "Colored Corday," Dec. 23, 1892.

141   *"The Free Speech"*: Editorial, *The Appeal*, Aug. 20, 1982. See also https://tennesseehistory.org/ida-b-wells-international-appeal-the-1893-worlds-columbian-exposition/.

14. COMSTOCK AND THE OBSCENITY OF DISSENT

143   *speech deemed immoral*: David M. Rabban, "The Free Speech League, the ACLU, and Changing Conceptions of Free Speech in American History," *Stanford Law Review* 45, no. 1 (Nov. 1992): 100.

143   *use of profanity*: Helen Lefkowitz Horowitz, "Victoria Woodhull, Anthony Comstock, and Conflict Over Sex in the United States in the 1870s," *Journal of American History* 87, no. 2 (Sep. 2000): 403, 405.

144   *"Probably"*: Amy Sohn, *The Man Who Hated Women: Sex, Censorship, and Civil Liberties in the Gilded Age* (New York: Macmillan, 1973).

144   *"God's garden"*: Moira Donegan, "An Anti-Obscenity Law from 1873 Was Discarded for Decades. Now the Anti-Abortion Movement Wants It Back," *Guardian*, Apr. 19, 2023.

144   *masturbation to obscenity*: David M. Rabban, "The Ahistorical Historian: Leonard Levy on Freedom of Expression in Early American History," *Stanford Law Review* 37 (1985): 28–29.

144   *"sin and wickedness"*: See generally Amy Beth Werbel, *Lust on Trial: Censorship and the Rise of American Obscenity in the Age of Anthony Comstock* (New York: Columbia Press, 2018).

145   *"free lusters"*: Rabban, "Ahistorical Historian," 31.

145   *"Devil traps"*: Horowitz, "Victoria Woodhull," 403, 420.

145   *"Tennie" Claflin*: Marcia E. Stockmeyer, "Anthony Comstock: A Man on a Mission," SSRN, Nov. 12, 2010, 5–6, https://ssrn.com/abstract=1500669.

146   *masquerade ball*: Horowitz, "Victoria Woodhull," 429.

146 *used for printing*: Horowitz, "Victoria Woodhull," 431.

147 *Suppression of Vice*: Horowitz, "Victoria Woodhull," 433.

147 *"second-rate country-town civilization"*: Ellen Wexler, "The 150-Year-Old Comstock Act Could Transform the Abortion Debate," *Smithsonian*, June 15, 2023.

147 *fifteen people to suicide*: Wexler, "The 150-Year-Old Comstock."

15. "WOBBLIES" AND WORLD WAR I

148 *the Workingmen's Party*: See generally Paul Avrich, *When Justice Fails: The Haymarket Tragedy* (Princeton, NJ: Princeton University Press, 1984).

148 *line of police officers*: Avrich, *When Justice Fails*, 204–10. (Before the throwing of the bomb, the Chicago mayor described the event as peaceful, but a commander decided toward the end of the day to clear the square.)

148 *public statements*: Seven were sentenced to death, though two later had their sentences commuted. One died just before his execution and four were hanged. Avrich, *When Justice Fails*, 204.

149 *"wanton murders done"*: Joseph E. Gary, "The Chicago Anarchists of 1886: The Crime, the Trial, and the Punishment," *Century* 45, no. 6 (Apr. 1893): 803, 837.

149 *workers showed up*: Parker, "Report on Wheatland Hop-Field Riot," U.S. Senate Committee on Education and Labor, 1914, 20070.

150 *organize a strike*: See generally Greg Hall, *Harvest Wobblies: The Industrial Workers of the World and Agricultural Workers of the American West 1905–1930* (Corvallis: Oregon State University Press, 2001).

150 *"pistol were gone"*: Ryan McCarthy, "Hop Riots' Aftermath Echoes in Wheatland, 97 Years Later," *Appeal-Democrat*, Sept. 7, 2010.

151 *McKinley in 1901*: See generally Sidney Fine, "Anarchism and the Assassination of McKinley," *American Historical Review* 60, no. 4 (July 1955): 777.

151 *"ideals of anarchism"*: Paul Avrich, "The Anarchists in the Russian Revolution," *Russian Review* 26, no. 4 (Oct. 1967): 341, 343; see also D. Novak, "Anarchism and Individual Terrorism," *Canadian Journal of Economics & Political Science* 20, no. 2 (May 1954): 176–84.

151 *"on fire"*: "The Assassin Makes a Full Confession," *New York Times*, Sept. 8, 1901, A1; see generally Julia Rose Krause, "Global Anti-Anarchism: The Origins of Ideological Deportation and the Suppression of Expression," *Indiana Journal of Global Legal Studies* 19, no. 1 (Winter 2012): 169.

151 *violent anarchists*: Edwin P. Hoyt, *The Palmer Raids, 1919–1920: An Attempt to Suppress Dissent* (New York: Seabury Press, 1969), 6.

151 *"our ends"*: Geoffrey R. Stone, *Perilous Times: Free Speech in Wartime from the Sedition Act of 1798 to the War on Terrorism* (New York: W. W. Norton, 2004), 142.

151 *three times*: Alexander Berkman, "On the Shooting of Henry Clay Frick," Anarchy Archives, n.d., http://dwardmac.pitzer.edu/Anarchist_Archives/goldman/frick.html; see also Paul Avrich & Karen Avrich, *Sasha and Emma: The Anarchist Odyssey of Alexander Berkman and Emma Goldman* (Cambridge, MA: Harvard University Press, 2012), 65–67, 77.

152 *"unnecessary"*: Emma Goldman, "Anarchism: What It Really Stands For," in *Anarchism and Other Essays* (Port Washington, NY: Kennikat Press, 1910), 53, 56.

152 Freiheit *(Freedom)*: Krause, "Global Anti-Anarchism," 176.

152 *"poison and dynamite"*: Krause, "Global Anti-Anarchism," 176.

152 *"against the anarchist"*: Theodore Roosevelt, "State of the Union Address," Infoplease, Dec. 3, 1901, https://www.infoplease.com/primary-sources/government/presidential-speeches/state-union-address-theodore-roosevelt-december-3-1901.

152 *"in certain cases"*: People v. Most, 73 N.Y.S. 220, 222 (Ct. Spec. Sess. 1901).

153 *"stern repression"*: Stone, *Perilous Times*, 137.

153 *"are unreasonable"*: John Milton Cooper, *Reconsidering Woodrow Wilson* (Baltimore: Johns Hopkins University Press, 2008), 191; see also Woodrow Wilson, *Constitutional Government in the United States* (London: Routledge, 2017).

153 *"itself into action"*: Wilson, *Constitutional Government*, 39.

153 *undermined national unity*: Stone, *Perilous Times*, 149.

153 *"right to civil liberties"*: Stone, *Perilous Times*, 137.

154 *espousing dangerous thoughts*: Stone, *Perilous Times*, 153.

154 *"fact by speaking"*: Woodrow Wilson, "Address at the Institute of France" (May 10, 1919), in *Selected Literary and Political Papers and Addresses of Woodrow Wilson*, vol. 2 (New York: Grosset & Dunlap, 1925), 330, 333.

154 The Finished Mystery *by mail*: Geoffrey R. Stone, *War & Liberty: An American Dilemma: 1790 to the Present* (New York: W. W. Norton, 2007), 54.

154 *"in the trenches"*: Shaffer v. United States, 255 F. 886, 887 (9th Cir. 1919); see also Stone, *Perilous Times*, 943.

154 *political speech*: *Schaffer*, 255 F. at 888–89.

154 *"in the war"*: *Schaffer*, 255 F. at 888.

154 *free love*: David M. Rabban, "The Free Speech League, the ACLU, and Changing Conceptions of Free Speech in American History," *Stanford Law Review* 45 (Nov. 1992): 47, 53.

155 *"violent or 'incendiary'"*: Hal D. Sears, *The Sex Radicals: Free Love in High Victorian America* (Lawrence: University Press of Kansas, 1977), 79.

155 *views a crime*: Robert K. Murray, *Red Scare: A Study in National Hysteria, 1910–1920* (Minneapolis: University of Minnesota Press, 1955), 233–34.

155 *likewise a felony*: N.Y. Penal Law §§ 160–61 (1909). See generally Stewart Jay, "The Creation of the First Amendment Right to Free Speech from the Eighteenth to the Mid-Twentieth Century," *William Mitchell Law Review* 34, no. 3 (Apr. 2008): 863.

155 *infamous Palmer raids*: Jonathan Turley, "Harm and Hegemony: The Decline of Free Speech in the United States," *Harvard Journal of Law and Public Policy* 45 (2022): 602–03.

155 *Thousands were arrested*: Turley, "Harm and Hegemony," 602–03; see also Hoyt, *Palmer Raids*.

155 *thirty-three cities*: Stone, *Perilous Times*, 223.

155 *"newspaper photographers"*: Stone, *Perilous Times*, 225–26.

155 *engaging in free speech*: Stone, *Perilous Times*, 233.

155 *Adams administration*: Jack A. Gottschalk, "'Consistent with Security': A History of American Military Press Censorship," *Communications & the Law* 5 (1983): 38.

156 *"avenging government"*: "All Disloyal Men Warned by Gregory," *New York Times*, Nov. 21, 1917. For a discussion of this period see Geoffrey R. Stone, "Free Speech and National Security," *Indiana Law Journal* 84, no. 3 (Oct.–Dec. 2009).

156 *"their political views"*: American Civil Liberties Union (ACLU) Bulletin 63, "Civil Liberty and the Courts: Obscenity and Political Opinions," November 1928, in *American Civil Liberties Union Records and Publications, 1917–1975* (Glen Rock, NJ: Microfilming Corporation of America, 1977); see also Laura M. Weinrib, "The Sex Side of Civil Liberties: *United States v. Dennett* and the Changing Face of Free Speech," *Law and History Review* 30, no. 2 (May 2012): 325.

156 *"sort may fall"*: Regina v. Hicklin, L.R. 3 Q.B. 360, 371 (1868).

156 *other social reforms*: United States v. Bennett, 16 Blatchf. 338 (C.C.S.D.N.Y. 1879); see also Weinrib, "The Sex Side," 358.

156 *other causes*: David M. Rabban, *Free Speech in Its Forgotten Years* (New York: Cambridge University Press, 1997), 24.

156 *New York's obscenity law*: Rabban, *Free Speech in Its Forgotten Years*, 8.

156 Young People: United States v. Dennett, 39 F.2d 564 (2nd Cir. 1930); see also Rabban, *Free Speech in Its Forgotten Years*, 8.

157 *other social ills*: Jonathan Turley, "Can FIRE Be the New ACLU? Hopefully Not, But It Can Be the Old ACLU," *Res Ipsa* blog (www.jonathanturley.org), June 16, 2022.

157 *Margaret Sanger's*: Rabban, *Free Speech in Its Forgotten Years*, 25.

157 *social harmony*: Rabban, "Free Speech League," 52–53.

16. THE BUND AND THE BIDDLE: SEDITION IN WORLD WAR II

158 *deemed disloyal*: Geoffrey R. Stone, "Free Speech in World War II: 'When Are You Going to Indict the Seditionists?'," *International Journal of Constitutional Law* 2 (Apr. 2004): 334.

158 *"colored racial traces"*: Geoffrey R. Stone, *Perilous Times: Free Speech in Wartime from the Sedition Act of 1798 to the War on Terrorism* (New York: W. W. Norton, 2004), 245.

159 *it was defeated*: Richard W. Steele, *Free Speech in the Good War* (New York: St. Martin's Press, 1999), 29.

159 *"soft, pudgy democracy"*: Stone, *Perilous Times*, 336; Steele, *Free Speech in the Good War*, 38.

159 *"embarrassment"*: Stone, *Perilous Times*, 336.

159 *"expression of opinion"*: Stone, *Perilous Times*, 336 (citing 9 76th Cong., 3d Sess. (Mar. 4, 1940), 86 Cong. Rec. SA1840 (Apr. 3, 1940).

159 *"Zionist Jews"*: Terminiello v. Chicago, 337 U.S. 1, 37 (1949) (Jackson, J., dissenting).

160 *"at the stars'"*: Terminiello, 337 U.S. at 14.

160 *"a suicide pact"*: Terminiello, 337 U.S. at 37.

160 *English sedition trials*: "The Press: Coughlin Quits," *Time*, May 18, 1942, https://content.time.com/time/subscriber/article/0,33009,849845,00.html.

160 *"at war"*: Stone, *Perilous Times*, 338; see also address of Francis Biddle, "The Power of Democracy: It Can Meet All Conditions," Yosemite National Park, California, Sept. 18, 1941, https://www.justice.gov/sites/default/files/ag/legacy/2011/09/16/09 -18-1941.pdf.

160 *in Minneapolis*: Claudius O. Johnson, "The Status of Freedom of Expression Under the Smith Act," *Western Political Quarterly* 11, no. 3 (Sept. 1958): 469, https://www.jstor.org/stable/444561.

161 *"chief executive in Washington"*: Stone, *Perilous Times*, 338.

161 *"Marxist lingo"*: Stone, *Perilous Times*, 338, quoting Francis Biddle, *In Brief Authority* (Garden City, NY: Doubleday, 1962), 152.

161 *"cool, blue space"*: Stone, *Perilous Times*, 258.

161 *"cut your throat"*: Leo P. Ribuffo, *The Old Christian Right: The Protestant Far Right from the Great Depression to the Cold War* (Philadelphia: Temple University Press, 1983), 180, 182; Stone, *Perilous* Times, 336.

162 *Jews deported*: Jason Daley, "The Screenwriting Mystic Who Wanted to Be the American Führer," *Smithsonian*, Oct. 3, 2018.

162 *"being seditious"*: Stone, *Perilous Times*, 341.

162 *"vile publications"*: Steele, *Free Speech in the Good War*, 151.

162 *"anti-war talk stopped"*: Stone, *Perilous Times*, 257.

162 *"do the fighting"*: Margaret A. Blanchard, *Revolutionary Sparks: Freedom of Expression in Modern America* (New York: Oxford University Press, 1992), 203.

162 *"talk of the author"*: United States v. Pelley, 132 F.2d 170, 179 (7th Cir. 1942).

17. MCCARTHY AND THE RED SCARE

164 *detention of dissidents*: David Cole, "The New McCarthyism: Repeating History in the War on Terrorism," *Harvard Civil Rights-Civil Liberties Law Review* 38 (2003): 1.

164 *coerce their associates*: David J. Fine, Comment, "Federal Grand Jury Investigation of Political Dissidents," *Harvard Civil Rights-Civil Liberties Law Review* 7, no. 2 (Mar. 1972): 432, 442.

164 *threat to the Constitution*: Carl Auerbach, "The Communist Control Act of 1954: A Proposed Legal-Political Theory of Free Speech," *University of Chicago Law Review* 23, no. 2 (Winter 1956): 173, 184, 189.

164 *"impose totalitarianism"*: Auerbach, "Communist Control Act of 1954," 189.

165 *out of the voters*: Geoffrey R. Stone, "Free Speech in the Age of McCarthy: A Cautionary Tale," *California Law Review* 94, no. 5 (Oct. 2005): 1387, 1389.

165 *federal positions*: Exec. Order No. 9835, 12 Fed. Reg. 1935 (Mar. 25, 1947).

165 *political reforms*: Stone, "Free Speech in the Age of McCarthy," 1391.

166 *"parlor punks"*: Geoffrey R. Stone, *Perilous Times: Free Speech in Wartime from the Sedition Act of 1798 to the War on Terrorism* (New York: W. W. Norton, 2004), 336.

166 *"the United States Senate"*: Stone, *Perilous Times*, 389.

166 *"vitals of America"*: "Text of Address by Truman Explaining to Nation His Actions in the White Case," *New York Times*, Nov. 17, 1953, 26.

166 *"'almost unchallenged'"*: Stone, "Free Speech in the Age of McCarthy," 1400.

166   *"bulwark of the Communist Party"*: Edwin R. Bayley, *Joe McCarthy and the Press* (Madison: University of Wisconsin, 1981), 206.

166   *"no sense of decency?"*: Bayley, *Joe McCarthy*, 206.

167   *mores and laws*: Clare Carlisle, "Bertrand Russel on Individualism and Self-control," *Guardian*, Dec. 16, 2013.

167   *contrarian and libertine parents*: Ray Monk, *Bertrand Russell: The Spirit of Solitude, 1872–1921* (New York: Simon & Schuster, 1996), 189.

167   *"values are concerned"*: Bertrand Russell, "John Stuart Mill," British Academy Lecture, 1955 (Oxford, UK: Oxford University Press, 2009).

168   *"courageously and honestly"*: Bertrand Russell & Bradley Trevor Grieve, *In Praise of Idleness* (New York: Thomas Dunne Books, 1996), 11.

18. DAYS OF RAGE: RACE, RHETORIC, AND REBELLION IN THE 1960S

169   *"busy swinging"*: Malcolm X, "At the Audubon," in *Malcolm X Speaks*, edited by George Breitman (New York: Grove, 1990), 9.

169   *Democratic Society (SDS)*: Bryan Burrough, *Days of Rage: America's Radical Underground, the FBI and the Forgotten Age of Revolutionary Violence* (New York: Penguin Books, 2015).

170   *"COINTELPRO"*: See generally Nelson Blackstock, *Cointelpro: The FBI's Secret War on Political Freedom* (New York: Pathfinder, 1988).

170   *enraged many groups*: David J. Garrow, "The FBI and Martin Luther King," *Atlantic*, July/Aug. 2002, https://www.theatlantic.com/magazine/archive/2002/07/the-fbi-and-martin-luther-king/302537/.

170   *crackdowns in various states*: Robert J. Cottrol & Raymond T. Diamond, "'Never Intended to Be Applied to the White Population': Firearms Regulation and Racial Disparity—The Redeemed South's Legacy to a National Jurisprudence?," *Chicago-Kent State Law Review* 70 (1995): 1307; Robert J. Cottrol & Raymond T. Diamond, *The Second Amendment: Toward an Afro-Americanist Reconsideration*, *Georgetown Law Journal* 80 (1991): 309.

170   *"fight back!"*: Kwame Ture & Charles V. Hamilton, *Black Power: The Politics of Liberation in America* (New York: Vantage, 1992), 52–53.

171   *"you need a revolution"*: Breitman, *Malcolm X Speaks*, 9.

171   *"embrace as their own"*: James H. Cone, "Martin and Malcolm on Nonviolence and Violence," *Phylon* 49 (2001): 173, 181.

171   *"white homes and businesses"*: Burrough, *Days of Rage*, 29.

172   *for their own protection*: David Stout, "Robert F. Williams, 71, Civil Rights Leader and Revolutionary," *New York Times*, Oct. 19, 1996.

172   Negroes with Guns: Robert F. Williams, *Negroes with Guns* (Detroit: Wayne State University Press, 1962).

172   *(SNCC) secretary*: "Camichael Is Sentenced for Black Panther Rally," UPI, Nov. 30, 1966.

173   *"as cherry pie"*: Burrough, *Days of Rage*, 41.

173 *violent speech to violent action*: Burrough, *Days of Rage*, 41.

173 *"comparably rare"*: Burrough, *Days of Rage*, 26.

174 *"logical next step"*: Burrough, *Days of Rage*, 81.

174 Cohen v. California: Cohen v. California, 403 U.S. 15 (1971).

174 *into a frenzy*: Thomas G. Krattenmaker, "Looking Back at *Cohen v. California*: A 40-Year Retrospective from Inside the Court," *William & Mary Bill of Rights Journal* 20 (2012): 651, 654.

174 *the Supreme Court*: Krattenmaker, "Looking Back," 655.

174 *"fact of communication"*: *Cohen*, 403 U.S. at 18.

19. ANTIFA, MAGA, AND THE AGE OF RAGE

175 *ethical and legal issues*: See, e.g., Jonathan Turley, "Government Ethics and the Russian Investigation," *Res Ipsa* blog (www.jonathanturley.org), July 24, 2017.

175 *promise of greater censorship*: Jonathan Turley, "Running on Censorship: California Candidate Seeks to Ride Anti–Free Speech Wave," *Res Ipsa* blog (www.jonathanturley.org), Nov. 7, 2023.

176 *"my type!"*: Axios (@axios), Twitter, Oct. 18, 2018.

176 *"the shooting starts"*: Grace Panetta, "Trump Claims His 'When the Looting Starts, the Shooting Starts' Remarks Weren't a Call to Violence but Instead a 'Fact,'" *Business Insider*, May 29, 2020.

177 *before World War II*: Jonathan Turley, "The Right to Rage: Free Speech and Rage Rhetoric in American Political Discourse," *Georgetown Journal of Law & Public Policy* 21, no. 2 (2023): 492.

177 *undefined structures*: *The Right of the People Peacefully to Assemble: Protecting Speech by Stopping Anarchist Violence, Before the S. Comm. on the Judiciary*, 116th Cong., 2020 (testimony of Professor Jonathan Turley).

177 *act of self-defense*: Mark Bray, "Antifa Isn't the Problem. Trump's Bluster Is a Distraction from Police Violence," *Washington Post*, June 1, 2020, 6:00 a.m.

177 The Anti-Fascist Handbook: Mark Bray, *Antifa: The Anti-Fascist Handbook* (Brooklyn, NY: Melville House, 2017).

177 *"communists, socialists, anarchists"*: Benjy Sarlin, "Antifa Violence Is Ethical? The Author Explains Why," NBC News, Aug. 26, 2017.

178 *"set ablaze"*: Bray, *Antifa*, 116.

178 *"three were admitted"*: "Statement from United States Park Police Acting Chief Gregory T. Monahan," June 4, 2020, available at https://www.nps.gov/subjects/uspp/6_2_20_statement_from_acting_chief_monahan.htm.

179 *his legal defense*: Jonathan Turley, "Antifa Member Who Took Axe to Senate Office Given Probation and His Axe Back," *Res Ipsa* blog (www.jonathanturley.org), Nov. 26, 2021.

179 *"this dramatic rebellion"*: Bray, "Antifa Isn't the Problem."

179 *"Movement is winning"*: *Right of the People*, 116th Cong.; see also Jonathan Turley, "The Movement Is Winning: Alleged Ringleader in Statute Attacks Claims Victory in Public Comments," *Res Ipsa* blog (www.jonathanturley.org), July 4, 1990.

179 *"stand by"*: Jonathan Turley, "Proud Boys and Antifa Emerge as the Winners from the Presidential Debate," *Res Ipsa* blog (www.jonathanturley.org), Sept. 30, 2020.

179 *"focused on"*: Jonathan Turley, "'You Might Be the Fascist': MSNBC Host Joy Reid Defends Antifa Despite Its Violent Anti–Free Speech History," *Res Ipsa* blog (www.jonathanturley.org), Sept. 9, 2002.

20. JANUARY 6TH AND THE REVIVAL OF AMERICAN SEDITION

181 *constitutional process*: Jonathan Turley, "The Desecration of Democracy," *The Hill*, Jan. 7, 2021.

181 *"one-off cases"*: Jonathan Turley, "The FBI Comes Up Empty-Handed in Its Search for an Insurrection," *Res Ipsa* blog (www.jonathanturley.org), Aug. 23, 2021.

181 *Kevin McCarthy*: Jonathan Turley, "No Friend of Congress: Pascrell Seeks to Block 120 House Republicans from Being Seated in Retaliation for Signing Supreme Court Amicus Brief," *Res Ipsa* blog (www.jonathanturley.org). Dec. 12, 2020.

181 *died in combat*: "New Estimate Raises Civil War Toll," *New York Times*, Apr. 3, 2012.

182 *the* Dobbs *decision*: Jonathan Turley, "Insurrection or Advocacy? Chicago Mayor Lightfoot Issues Call to Arms After Leaking Abortion Ruling," *Res Ipsa* blog (www.jonathanturley.org), May 10, 2022.

182 *"enemy within"*: Seth McLaughlin & Dave Boyer, "Nancy Pelosi Says House GOP Is 'the Enemy Within' Congress, Slams Rep. Taylor Greene," *Washington Times*, Jan. 28, 2021.

182 *state of Ohio*: Jonathan Turley, "The Death Star Strategy: Is Trump Contemplating the Ultimate Constitutional Trick Shot?" *Res Ipsa* blog (www.jonathanturley.org), Nov. 23, 2020.

182 *"witnessing Democracy at work"*: House Republicans (@HouseGOP), Twitter, June 23, 2022.

182 *"in many States"*: 151 Cong. Rec. S41–S56 (Thursday, Jan. 6, 2005) (statement of Senator Durbin).

183 *"your voices heard"*: Jonathan Turley, "'What-aboutism'—Ruling Against Trump Leaves More Questions Than Answers on Free Speech," *The Hill*, Feb. 19, 2022.

184 *"produce such action"*: Brandenburg v. Ohio, 395 U.S. 444, 448–449 (1969).

184 *"indefinite future time"*: Hess v. Indiana, 414 U.S. 105, 108 (1973).

184 *necks of opponents*: NAACP v. Claiborne Hardware Co., 458 U.S. 886, 934 (1982).

184 *assaulted an officer*: Brie Stimson, "Nebraska Police Arrest Six at State Capitol," Fox News, May 19, 2023.

184 *"peaceful protest"*: Jonathan Turley, "Lafayette Park and the Revision of History," *Res Ipsa* blog (www.jonathanturley.org), Jan. 9, 2021.

185 *any insurrection*: Jonathan Turley, "Harvard Study: J6 Rioters Were Motivated by Loyalty to Trump, Not Insurrection Against the Constitution," *Res Ipsa* blog (www.jonathanturley.org), July 31, 2022.

185 *not an insurrection*: Jonathan Turley, "Preserve the Narrative: The Public Rejects the Insurrection Claim in New Polling," *Res Ipsa* blog (www.jonathanturley.org), Jan. 1, 2022.

185   *attempted murder of Pence*: Bob Brigham, "Will Merrick Garland Be the One to
       Criminally Charge Trump?," Salon, June 17, 2022.

185   *the* Schenck *decision*: Schenck v. United States, 249 U.S. 47 (1919).

185   *nothing happened*: Jonathan Turley, "What Ever Happened to the Prosecution of
       Donald Trump for Incitement?," *Res Ipsa* blog (www.jonathanturley.org), Jan. 6,
       2022.

185   *American sedition*: See generally Jonathan Turley, "The Right to Rage: Free Speech
       and Rage Rhetoric in American Political Discourse," *Georgetown Journal of Law
       & Public Policy* 21, no. 2 (2023): 481; Jonathan Turley, "Rage Rhetoric and the Re-
       vival of American Sedition," *William & Mary Law Review* 65 (forthcoming 2024).

186   *"an avenging government"*: "All Disloyal Men Warned," *New York Times*, Nov. 21,
       1917, 3, available at https://www.nytimes.com/1917/11/21/archives/all-disloyal
       -men-warned-by-gregory-criminal-courts-will-handle.html. For a discussion of
       this period, see Geoffrey R. Stone, "Free Speech and National Security," *Indiana
       Law Journal* 84 (2009): 939.

186   *"we're gonna get charged"*: Scott Pelley, "Inside the Prosecution of the Capitol
       Rioters," CBS, Mar. 22, 2021, https://www.cbsnews.com/news/capitol-riot-inves
       tigation-sedition-charges-60-minutes-2021-03-21/.

186   *"power* in terrorem*"*: Stone, *Perilous Times*, 64.

186   *"restraint of public opinion"*: Geoffrey R. Stone, *Perilous Times: Free Speech in
       Wartime from the Sedition Act of 1798 to the War on Terrorism* (New York: W. W.
       Norton, 2004), 170.

186   *"the former President"*: Jordan Williams, "Judges Says Trump's False Elections
       Claims Still Pose Threat Months Later," *The Hill*, May 27, 2021.

187   United States v. Alvarez: United States v. Alvarez, 567 U.S. 709 (2012).

187   *debate and math clubs*: Ariel Zilber, "The Rise and Fall of the QAnon Shaman,"
       Daily Mail, Nov. 17, 2021.

188   *"captivated and entranced"*: Zilber, "Rise and Fall."

188   State of Illusion: Jacob Angeli, *One Mind at a Time: A Deep State of Illusion* (self-
       pub., 2020).

188   *"sphere of influence"*: Angeli, *One Mind*.

189   *"conspiracy culture"*: Jules Evans, "A Closer Look at the 'QAnon Shaman' Lead-
       ing the Mob," Medium, Jan. 7, 2021, https://gen.medium.com/the-q-shaman
       -conspirituality-goes-rioting-on-capitol-hill-24bac5fc50e6.

189   *"liberated minds"*: Evans, "A Closer Look."

189   *"Divine Creator God"*: Evans, "A Closer Look."

189   *"Justice Is Coming!"*: Tio Armus & Rachel Weiner, "'QAnon Shaman's' Note to
       Pence Cited as Evidence of 'Assassination' Plot Before Prosecutors Walk Back
       Claim," *Washington Post*, Jan. 15, 2021.

189   *"United States government"*: Jenni Fink, "QAnon Shaman Jacob Chansley Loses
       Bid for Freedom Ahead of Capitol Riot Trial," *Newsweek*, July 6, 2021.

190   *"this whole event"*: Jonathan Turley, "Did the 'QAnon Shaman' Get the Shaft on
       Sentencing?," *Res Ipsa* blog (www.jonathanturley.org), Mar. 8, 2008.

190   *"meant to create"*: Josh Gerstein & Kyle Cheney, "'QAnon Shaman' Jacob Chansley Is Sentenced to 41 Months in Prison," Politico, Nov. 17, 2021.

190   *National Public Radio explored*: Domenico Montanaro, "What Is the Insurrection Act That Trump Is Threatening to Invoke?," National Public Radio, June 6, 2020.

191   *rule of law*: Newman, "Fries's Rebellion," 41.

192   *"against the same"*: Jonathan Turley, "The Disqualification of Donald Trump and Other Legal Legends," *The Hill*, Aug. 19, 2023.

192   *action from Congress*: Griffin's Case, 11 F. Cas. 7 (C.C.D. Va. 1869) (No. 5,815).

192   *"taking it again"*: Worthy v. Barrett, 63 N.C. 199, 204–05 (1869).

193   *judge Francis Mathew in 2022*: New Mexico ex rel. White, 2022 N.M. Dist. LEXIS 1.

193   *on insurrectionists*: In re Charge to Grand Jury, 62 F. 828 (N.D. Ill. 1894).

193   *the abuses of the period*: Richard Cahan, *A Court That Shaped America: Chicago's Federal District Court from Abe Lincoln to Abbie Hoffman* (Evanston, IL: Northwestern University Press, 2002), 42.

PART III. HOLMES AND DOUSING THE FIRE OF FREE SPEECH

21. HOLMES AND THE "ROUTE TO HELL"

198   *"it has been experience"*: Oliver Wendell Holmes, *The Common Law* 1 (S. J. Parkhill, 1909) (1881).

199   *dissenting free speech*: Frohwerk v. United States, 249 U.S. 204 at 209 (2019).

199   *"mark of a civilized man"*: Oliver W. Holmes, "Ideals and Doubts," *Illinois Law Review* 10 (1915): 1, 3.

199   *"chastity [of] intellectual style"*: Stephen Budiansky, *Oliver Wendell Holmes: A Life in War, Law, and Ideas* (New York: Norton, 1923), 59–60.

199   *"process of thought itself"*: Budiansky, *Oliver Wendell Holmes*, 60.

199   Buck v. Bell: Buck v. Bell, 274 U.S. 200 (1927).

199   *"imbeciles are enough"*: *Buck* at 207.

200   *"ordinary ugly people"*: Budiansky, *Oliver Wendell Holmes*, 431.

200   Fox v. Washington: Fox v. Washington, 236 U.S. 273 (1915).

200   *nude swimming*: Fox at 277.

200   *"conventional society"*: See generally Justin Wadland, *Trying Home: The Rise and Fall of an Anarchist Utopia on Puget Sound* (Corvallis: Oregon State University Press, 2014).

200   *"courts of justice"*: Fox at 275 (quoting Wash. Rem. & Bal. Code § 2564 [1910]).

201   *"drawn by the law"*: Fox at 277.

201   *"nonsense on stilts"*: Jeremy Bentham, "Anarchical Fallacies," in *Works of Jeremy Bentham*, vol. 2 (Edinburgh: William Tait, 1843), 501.

201   *social interests*: David M. Rabban, *Free Speech in Its Forgotten Years* (New York: Cambridge University Press, 1997), 184.

201   *"gets very little"*: Roscoe Pound, "Do We Need a Philosophy of Law?," *Columbia Law Review* 5 (1905): 339, 348.

201 *that criticism*: Oliver Wendell Holmes, "Natural Law," *Harvard Law Review* 32 (1918): 40.

201 *"universal validity"*: Holmes, "Natural Law," 42.

201 *"ultimate symbol"*: Letter from Oliver Wendell Holmes to Harold J. Laski (May 12, 1927), in "The Correspondence of Mr. Justice Holmes and Harold J. Laski, 1916–1935, vol. 2" *Texas Law Review* 31 (1953): 925, 942.

201 *"for his bone"*: Holmes, "Natural Law," 42.

202 *"an ought not"*: David Hume, *A Treatise of Human Nature*, edited by L. A. Selby-Bigge (1739; Oxford: Clarendon Press, 1896), 469–70.

202 *"I don't"*: Letter from Oliver Wendell Holmes Jr. to Harold Laski (Sept. 15, 1929) in *The Essential Holmes*, edited by Richard A. Posner (Chicago: University of Chicago Press, 1992), 116.

202 *"inexorable moral laws"*: Peter C. Myers, "Seed-Time and Harvest-Time: Natural Law and Rational Hopefulness in Frederick Douglass's Life and Times," *Journal of African American History* 99 (2014): 56, 59.

202 *"unchangeable and eternal"*: Meyers, "Seed-Time," 59.

202 *"not postponed"*: Meyers, "Seed-Time," 58.

203 *"distress you"*: Budiansky, *Oliver Wendell Holmes*, 57, citing "Books," *Harvard Magazine* 4 (December 1858).

203 *intellectual evolution*: Jonathan Turley, "The Military Pocket Republic," *Northwestern University Law Review* 97 (2002): 1–134.

203 *"like the other"*: Budiansky, *Oliver Wendell Holmes*, 35.

203 *"have asked"*: Budiansky, *Oliver Wendell Holmes*, 33.

203 *"spirit of enquiry"*: Ronald Collins, "Oliver Wendell Holmes: A Heart Touched by Fire," *American Heritage*, Spring 2019, 64.

204 *"nonconformist"*: Collins, "Heart Touched by Fire."

204 *dangerous and immoral*: Collins, "Heart Touched by Fire."

204 *"pretty convinced abolitionist"*: Collins, "Heart Touched by Fire."

204 *"leading families"*: Collins, "Heart Touched by Fire."

205 *"youth and delicacy"*: Budiansky, *Oliver Wendell Holmes*, 74.

205 *"happen is best"*: Budiansky, *Oliver Wendell Holmes*, 87.

207 *"which was it?"*: Oliver Wendell Holmes Sr., "My Hunt After 'the Captain,'" *Atlantic*, Dec. 1862.

207 *for his son*: Holmes Sr., "My Hunt."

207 *"store of strength"*: Holmes Sr., "My Hunt."

207 *"muddy heeltaps"*: Holmes Sr., "My Hunt."

207 *resented his article*: Holmes Sr., "My Hunt."

207 *return to Massachusetts*: Budiansky, *Oliver Wendell Holmes*, 97.

207 *"M.D. Boston"*: Budiansky, *Oliver Wendell Holmes*, 99.

208 *"superincumbent dead"*: Collins, "Heart Touched by Fire"; see also Ronald K. L. Collins, ed., *The Fundamental Holmes* (Cambridge, UK: Cambridge University Press, 2010).

208 *"apart by our experience"*: James Marten, *Sing Not War: The Lives of Union and*

Confederate Veterans in Gilded Age of America (Chapel Hill: University of North Carolina, 2011), 257.

208 *"elastic as I was"*: Marten, *Sing Not War.*

208 *"brooding omnipresence in the sky"*: S. Pac. Co. v. Jensen, 244 U.S. 205, 222 (1917) (Holmes, J., dissenting).

208 *"can be identified"*: S. Pac. Co., 244 U.S.

208 *"the established lines"*: Collins, "Heart Touched by Fire."

208 *"power-focused philosophy"*: Albert W. Alschuler, *Law Without Values: The Life, Work, and Legacy of Justice Holmes* (Chicago: Chicago University Press, 2000), 10.

208 *"absolute truth"*: Letter from O. W. Holmes to Albert Einstein (June 1, 1905), reprinted in *The Holmes-Einstein Letters*, edited by J. P. Peabody (New York: St. Martin's Press, 1964),16.

209 *stands out*: Budiansky, *Oliver Wendell Holmes*, 76.

209 *"brutish, and short"*: Thomas Hobbes, *Leviathan*, edited by Richard Tuck (1651; Cambridge, UK: Cambridge University Press, 1991), 89.

209 *"peace and defence"*: Hobbes, *Leviathan*, 176–85.

209 *"named Blood Lane"*: Collins, "Heart Touched by Fire."

209 *"smacked of Darwinism"*: Collins, "Heart Touched by Fire."

210 *"dead or wounded"*: Collins, "Heart Touched by Fire."

210 *"demand it"*: Oliver Wendell Holmes, "Natural Law," *Harvard Law Review* 32 (1918): 41–42.

210 *"a kind of rage"*: Budiansky, *Oliver Wendell Holmes*, 376.

210 *"rights of man"*: Letter from Oliver Wendell Holmes to Harold Laski (Sept. 15, 1916), in *Holmes-Laski Letters*, vol. 1, edited by Mark DeWolfe Howe (Cambridge, MA: Harvard University Press, 1953), 21.

210 *"Natural Law"*: Holmes, "Natural Law," 40.

210 *"all men everywhere"*: Holmes, "Natural Law," 41.

210 *"to death"*: Holmes, *The Common Law*, 43.

211 *"'They are gone'"*: See Oliver Wendell Holmes Sr., *The Last Leaf: Poem* (Legare Street Press, 2022).

22. HOLMES AND SCHENCK: THE SOCIALIST IN A CROWDED THEATER

212 *"It's my job"*: Letter from Oliver Wendell Holmes to Harold J. Laski (Mar. 4, 1920), in *Holmes-Laski Letters*, edited by Mark DeWolfe Howe (Cambridge, MA: Harvard University Press, 1953), vol. 1, 249.

213 *resist conscription*: Bill Lynskey, "Reinventing the First Amendment in Wartime Philadelphia," *Pennsylvania Magazine of History and Biography* 131 (2007): 33, 50–53.

213 *"Constitution of the United States"*: Richard A. Parker, *Free Speech on Trial* (Tuscaloosa: University of Alabama Press, 2003), 21.

213 *"sinking of the Lusitania"*: Lynskey, "Reinventing the First Amendment," 53.

213 *"the National Army"*: Lynskey, "Reinventing the First Amendment," 53, quoting "Treason Is Charged to Raid Prisoners," *Evening Bulletin*, Aug. 29, 1917.

213 *the organization*: Lynskey, "Reinventing the First Amendment," 53.

213 *"work in the morning"*: Lynskey, "Reinventing the First Amendment," 58.

214 *"the main purpose"*: Schenck, 249 U.S. at 51.

214 *channeling Blackstone*: Schenck, 249 U.S. at 47–49.

214 *"entirely of reflections"*: Fred D. Ragan, "Justice Oliver Wendell Holmes Jr., Zechariah Chafee Jr., and the Clear and Present Danger Test for Free Speech: The First Year, 1919," *Journal of American History* 58 (1971): 24, 26.

214 Commonwealth v. Blanding: Commonwealth v. Blanding, 3 Pick [Mass] 304 (1825).

215 *"the main purpose"*: Commonwealth, 3 Pick. [Mass] at 50.

215 *obstructing the draft*: Commonwealth, 3 Pick. [Mass] at 51–52.

215 *"tumults therein"*: See "The Trial of Henry Yorke, for a Conspiracy" (1795), in *A Complete Collection of State Trials and Proceedings for High Treason*, vol. 25, edited by Thomas Bayly Howell & Thomas Jones Howell (London: T. C. Hansard, 1816–28).

216 *"right to prevent"*: Schenck v. United States, 249 U.S. 47, 52 (1919).

216 *"people, not places"*: Katz v. United States, 389 U.S. 347, 351 (1967).

216 Katz v. United States: *Katz*, 389 U.S. 347 (1967).

216 *"unsafe doctrine"*: Ernst Freund, "The *Debs* Case and Freedom of Speech," *New Republic*, May 3, 1919, 14.

216 *curtail free speech*: Jonathan Turley, "How the Western World Is Limiting Free Speech," *Washington Post*, Oct. 12, 2012; see also Carlton F. W. Larson, "Shouting Fire in a Crowded Theater: The Life and Times of Constitutional Law's Most Enduring Analogy," *William & Mary Bill of Rights Journal* 24 (2015): 181.

217 *"brigaded with action"*: Brandenburg v. Ohio, 393 U.S. 444, 456 (Douglas, J., concurring).

217 *noise regulations*: N.A.A.C.P. v. Claiborne Hardware Co., 458 U.S 886, 927 (1982) (threats); F.C.C. v. Pacifica Found., 438 U.S. 726, 744 (1978) (indecency); Cox v. La., 379 U.S. 559, 563 (1965) (picketing); Kunz v. N. Y., 340 U.S. 290, 298 (1951) (Jackson, J., dissenting) (prior restraints); Kovacs v. Cooper, 336 U.S. 77, 86 (1949) (noise regulations).

217 *"theater or something"*: David L. Hudson Jr., "Fixed Stars: Famous First Amendment Phrases and Their Indelible Impact," *Charleston Law Review* 15 (Fall 2020): 189, 195.

217 *"few or locked"*: Zechariah Chafee Jr., "Freedom of Speech in War Time," *Harvard Law Review* 32 (1919): 932, 944.

23. HOLMES AND THE "DEBS REBELLION"

218 Frohwerk v. United States: Frohwerk v. United States, 249 U.S. 204, 206 (1919).

218 Missouri Staats Zeitung: Lee C. Bollinger & Geoffrey R. Stone, *The Free Speech Century* (New York: Oxford University Press, 2018), 34.

219 *"at war"*: Frohwerk, 249 U.S. at 208.

219 *"the paper out"*: Frohwerk, 249 U.S. at 209.

219 Debs v. United States: Debs v. United States, 249 U.S. 211 (1919).

219 *"charged with murder"*: Larson, "'Shouting "Fire" in a Theater.'"

220 *"the human race"*: Editorial, *New York Times*, July 9, 1894, 4.

220 *arrest of socialists*: Fred D. Ragan, "Justice Oliver Wendell Holmes Jr., Zechariah Chafee Jr., and the Clear and Present Danger Test for Free Speech: The First Year, 1919," *Journal of American History* 58 (1971): 32.

220 *"especially their lives"*: Ragan, "Justice Oliver Wendell Holmes," 33, citing Ray Ginger, *The Bending Cross: A Biography of Eugene Victor Debs* (New Brunswick, NJ: Rutgers University Press, 1949), 358.

220 *"by the people"*: E. V. Debs, "The Canton, Ohio, Speech, Anti-War Speech," *Call*, June 16, 1918, https://www.marxists.org/archive/debs/works/1918/canton.htm.

221 *"into their own"*: Michael E. Deutsch, "The Improper Use of the Federal Grand Jury: An Instrument for the Internment of Political Activists," *Journal of Criminal Law and Criminology* 75 (1984): 1159, 1173.

221 *"Time will tell"*: Eugene Victor Debs, *Writings and Speech of Eugene V. Debs* (New York: Hermitage Press, 1948), 436.

221 *in the war*: Debs, 249 U.S. at 216.

222 *"obstruct recruiting"*: Debs, 249 U.S. at 214.

222 *"the books"*: Debs, 249 U.S. at 216.

223 *"criminal intent"*: "Harding Frees Debs and 23 Others Held for War Violations," *New York Times*, Dec. 24, 1921, 1.

223 *Masses Publishing Co. v. Patten*: Masses Publishing Co. v. Patten, 244 F. 535, 539 (S.D.N.Y.), rev'd 246 F. 24 (2d Cir. 1917).

223 *free speech jurisprudence*: Gerald Gunther, "Learned Hand and the Origins of Modern First Amendment Doctrine: Some Fragments of History," *Stanford Law Review* 27 (1975): 719; *Teacher's Manual to Accompany Ideas of the First Amendment*, edited by Vincent Blasi (Eagan, MN: Thomson West, 2006), 171.

223 *"our own"*: Letter from Hand to Holmes (June 22, 1918), reprinted in Gunther, "Learned Hand," 755.

224 *"its improbability"*: United States v. Dennis, 183 F.2d 201, 212 (2d Cir. 1950).

224 *Abrams v. United States*: Abrams v. United States, 250 U.S. 616, 625 (1919) (Holmes, J., dissenting).

24. THE GOOD HOLMES AND THE ABANDONMENT OF *SCHENCK*

225 *United States v. Schwimmer*: United States v. Schwimmer, 279 U.S. 644 (1929).

225 *"we hate"*: Schwimmer, 279 U.S. at 654–55 (Holmes, J., dissenting).

225 *"burning themes"*: Thomas Healy, *The Great Dissent: How Oliver Wendell Holmes Changed His Mind—and Changed the History of Free Speech in America* (New York: Metropolitan Books 2013), 70.

226 *"side of freedom"*: Sheldon Novick, "The Unrevised Holmes and Freedom of Expression," 1991 *Supreme Court Review* (1992), 303, 389.

226 *the challenge*: Novick, "The Unrevised Holmes," 1231.

226 *"we don't like"*: Budiansky, *Oliver Wendell Holmes*, 375.

227   *"CAPITALISM"*: Abrams v. United States, 250 U.S. 616 (1919), at 620.

227   *"for freedom"*: Laura Weinrib, "Power and Premises: The Contested Meanings of the Abrams Dissent," *Seton Hall Law Review* 5 (2000): 61, 64–66.

228   *"up to fight"*: *Abrams*, 250 U.S. at 622.

228   *"of the war"*: Sedition Act of 1918, 40 Stat. 553 (1918).

228   *"his own"*: Weinrib, "Power and Premises," 74, citing "Bolshevist Witness Curbed by Court," *New York Times*, Oct. 22, 1918.

229   *"the Government"*: *Abrams*, 250 U.S. at 622.

229   *"in this country"*: *Abrams*, 250 U.S. at 623.

229   *"ammunition factories"*: Abrams v. United States, 250 U.S. 616 (1919), at 624.

229   *"it imposed"*: *Abrams*, 250 U.S. at 630 (Holmes, J., dissenting).

230   *"save the country"*: *Abrams*, 250 U.S. at 630 (Holmes, J., dissenting).

230   *"United States of America"*: Zechariah Chafee Jr., *Free Speech in the United States*, ch. XIII (Cambridge, MA: Harvard University Press, 1941); T. Emerson, *The System of Freedom of Expression* (New York: Random House, 1970), 21.

230   *"at other times"*: *Abrams*, 250 U.S. at 627.

231   Dennis v. United States: Dennis v. United States, 341 U.S. 494 (1951).

231   *"living instrument"*: *Dennis*, 341 U.S. at 523.

231   *"'good order'"*: *Dennis*, 341 U.S. at 590.

231   Brandenburg v. Ohio: Brandenburg v. Ohio, 395 U.S. 444 (1969) (per curiam).

232   *"revengance [sic] taken"*: *Brandenburg*, 395 U.S. at 446.

232   *that purpose*: *Brandenburg*, 395 U.S. at 444–45.

232   *"produce such action"*: *Brandenburg*, 395 U.S. at 447; Jonathan Turley, "The Right to Rage: Free Speech and Rage Rhetoric in American Political Discourse," *Georgetown Journal of Law & Public Policy* 21, no. 2 (2023): 507.

232   *"Free Speech?"*: Christopher Finan, "Was Oliver Wendell Holmes Right About Free Speech?," *Publishers Weekly*, Nov. 8, 2019.

232   *blacklisting and censorship*: Jonathan Turley, "Turley Testifies at Censorship Before House Select Subcommittee," *Res Ipsa* blog (www.jonathanturley.org), Feb. 9, 2023.

232   *most jarring*: Jonathan Turley, "'Putin Apologists': Former Sen. Claire McCaskill Denounces Senators Calling for Investigations of FBI Abuses," *Res Ipsa* blog (www.jonathanturley .org), Feb. 10, 2023.

233   *"a law class here"*: See "Hearing on Oversight of Justice Department," C-SPAN, Feb. 9, 2023.

PART IV. RESTORING THE INDISPENSABLE RIGHT

25. ROCKWELLIAN FREE SPEECH

237   *"everywhere in the world"*: President Franklin D. Roosevelt, "Annual Message to Congress" (Jan. 6, 1941), in 87 Cong. Rec. 44, 46 (1941), available at http://www .fdrlibrary.marist.edu/4free.html.

237   *Jim Edgerton*: See generally Susan E. Meyer, *Norman Rockwell's People* (New York: Abrams, 1981).

237 *school construction plan*: Greg Sukiennik, "Arlington and Rockwell: An Enduring Relationship," *Manchester Journal*, July 11, 2018.

238 *"our times"*: Clement Greenberg, "Avant-Garde and Kitsch" (1939), 10, https:// cpb-us-e2.wpmucdn.com/sites.uci.edu/dist/d/1838/files/2015/01/Greenberg -Clement-Avant-Garde-and-Kitsch-copy.pdf; see also Richard Lewis, "When Clement Greenberg Met Norman Rockwell," Lewis Art Cafe (Jan. 26, 2022).

238 *piece of art*: *Rockwell and Realism in an Abstract World*, Norman Rockwell Museum, https://www.nrm.org/2012/09/rockwell-and-realism-in-an-abstract -world/ (last visited June 28, 2023).

238 *"Abstract expressionism!"*: Lewis, "When Clement Greenberg."

239 Art Gallery Guide: See Wanda M. Corn, "Ways of Seeing," http://www.columbia .edu/itc/barnard/arthist/wolff/pdfs/week13_corn.pdf.

239 *unapologetically Rockwellian*: I am also a great fan of Andrew Wyeth's, who has also been criticized for his "narrative" art and previously compared his style to constitutional interpretation. Jonathan Turley, "Art and the Constitution: The Supreme Court and the Rise of the Impressionist School of Constitutional Interpretation," *Cato Supreme Court Review*, (2004): 57–83.

240 *"not have noticed"*: Lori Stranger, "Norman Rockwell 1894–1978," *HASTA*, Feb. 3, 2020.

240 *"social orders"*: Greenberg, "Avant-Garde and Kitsch."

240 *"I understood"*: Corn, "Ways of Seeing."

241 *"no law abridging"*: Smith v. California, 361 U.S. 147, 157 (1959) (Black, J., concurring).

241 *valuation of artists*: Tom Wolfe, *The Painted Word* (New York: Farrar, Strauss and Giroux, 1975).

242 *"solidarity and individuality"*: Mark Tushnet, "An Essay on Rights," *Texas Law Review* 62 (1984): 1386, 1382–83 .

242 *"common ground"*: Mary Ann Glendon, *Rights Talk: The Impoverishment of Political Discourse* (New York: Free Press, 1991), 14.

242 *"speech of women"*: Catharine McKinnon, *Feminism Unmodified: Discourses on Life and Law* (Cambridge, MA: Harvard University Press, 1987), 155–56.

242 *American journalism*: David Mindich, *Just the Tacts: How "Objectivity" Came to Define American Journalism* (New York: New York University Press, 2000), 1.

242 *"social justice"*: Zadie Winthrop, "Should Journalists Rethink Objectivity? Stanford Professors Weigh In," *Stanford Daily*, Aug. 20, 2020, https://stanforddaily .com/2020/08/20/should-journalists-rethink-objectivity-stanford-professors -weigh-in/.

242 *reactionary and harmful*: Leonard Downie Jr., "Newsrooms that Move Beyond 'Objectivity' Can Build Trust," *Washington Post*, Jan. 30, 2023.

242 *"got to go"*: See Jonathan Turley, "'Objectivity Has Got to Go': News Leaders Call for the End of Objective Journalism," *Res Ipsa* blog (www.jonathanturley.org), Feb. 1, 2023.

243 *"meritocracy"*: Mari J. Matsuda et al., *Words That Wound: Critical Race Theory,*

Assaultive Speech, and the First Amendment (Boulder, CO: Westview Press, 1993), 6.

243 *"revisionist histories"*: Matsuda et al., *Words That Wound*.

243 *"being interpreted"*: Hans-Georg Gadamer, *Truth and Method*, translated by Joel Weinsheimer & Donald G. Marshall, 2nd rev. ed. (London: Continuum, 1989), 309.

243 *political context*: Jacques Derrida, *Writing and Difference*, translated by A. Bass (Chicago: University of Chicago Press: 1978) (1967).

243 *"freedom, and play"*: Joan C. William, "Critical Legal Studies: The Death of Transcendence and the Rise of the New Langdells," *New York University Law Review* 62 (1987): 429, 461.

243 *"a moral sense"*: Oliver Wendell Holmes, "The Path of the Law," *Harvard Law Review* 10 (1897): 457, 460.

243 *"public interests"*: Roscoe Pound, "Interests of Personality," *Harvard Law Review* 28 (1915): 343, 344.

243 *marketplace of ideas*: Abrams v. United States, 250 U.S. 616, 630 (1919) (Holmes, J., dissenting) (valorizing the "free trade in ideas").

244 *"the individual interest"*: Pound, "Interests of Personality," 445, 453.

244 *"free belief and free speech"*: Pound, "Interests of Personality," 456.

244 *"open expression"*: Levy, *Emergence of a Free Press*, 281.

244 *view of free speech*: See Levy, *Legacy of Suppression* (1960); see also Leonard W. Levy, *Emergence of a Free Press* (New York: Oxford, 1985); see also David M. Rabban, "The Ahistorical Historian: Leonard Levy on Freedom of Expression in Early American History," *Stanford Law Review* 37 (1985): 795–804. But see Vincent Blasi, "The Checking Value in the First Amendment Theory," *Law and Social Inquiry* (1977), 521.

244 *"long time"*: Adam Liptak, "Leonard Levy, 83, Expert on Constitutional History Dead," *New York Times*, Sept. 1, 2006.

244 Self-Government *(1948)*: Alexander Meiklejohn, *Free Speech and Its Relation to Self-Government* (New York: Harper & Brothers, 1948).

245 *"may not be abridged"*: Meiklejohn, *Free Speech*, 22–25.

245 *"costs and benefits"*: United States v. Stevens, 130 S. Ct. 1577, 1585 (2010).

246 *"statements of fact"*: Gertz v. Robert Welch, Inc., 418 U.S. 323, 339–40 (1974).

246 *that should be discarded*: Imami Gandy, "I Agree with Elie Mystal. The Constitution Is Trash," Rewire News Group, Mar. 11, 2022.

246 *marginalizing ideas*: See, e.g., Mary Ellen Gale, "Reimagining the First Amendment: Racist Speech and Equal Liberty," *St. John's Law Review* 65 (1991): 119.

246 *"for none"*: Harold Kalven, "Upon Rereading Mr. Justice Black on the First Amendment," *UCLA Law Review* 14 (1967): 428, 432.

247 *"against silence"*: Harry Kalven Jr., "The Metaphysics of the Law of Obscenity," 1960 *Supreme Court Review*, 1, 19.

247 *"democratic experiment"*: Gale, "Reimagining."

247 *"false idea"*: *Gertz*, 418 U.S. at 339–40.

247 *"can be prohibited"*: Kalven Jr., "Metaphysics," 11.

248 *"Achilles Heel"*: Alexander Hall, "Law Professor: First Amendment Can Be 'Achilles Heel,' Makes U.S. 'Particularly Vulnerable to Disinformation,'" Fox News, Feb. 28, 2024.

248 *"political agenda"*: Barbara McQuade, *Attack from Within: How Disinformation Is Sabotaging America* (New York: Seven Stories Books, 2024) 5.

248 *"statements of fact"*: *Gertz*, 418 U.S. at 339–40.

249 United States v. Alvarez: United States v. Alvarez, 567 U.S. 709 (2012).

249 *"speech and expression"*: *Alvarez*, 567 U.S. at 730.

249 *"overcome the lie"*: *Alvarez*, 567 U.S. at 709.

249 *"their own right"*: Geoffrey R. Stone, *Perilous Times: Free Speech in Wartime from the Sedition Act of 1798 to the War on Terrorism* (New York: W. W. Norton, 2004), 271.

249 *Mexican television star*: Jonathan Turley, "The Better Part of Valor: Should Lying About Medals Be a Crime?," *Res Ipsa* blog (www.jonathanturley.org), Feb. 19, 2012.

250 Snyder v. Phelps: Snyder v. Phelps, 562 U.S. 443 (2011).

250 *"circumstances of the case"*: *Snyder* 562 U.S. at 451.

26. FINDING THE FORTY-TWO OF FREE SPEECH

252 *complex questions*: Jonathan Turley, "The Hitchhiker's Guide to CLS, Unger, and Deep Thought," *Northwestern University Law Review* 81 (1988): 593.

253 *"one's reason"*: Immanuel Kant, "An Answer to the Question: 'What is Enlightenment?'" in *Kant: Political Writings*, edited by Hans Reiss, translated by H. B. Nisbet (Cambridge, UK: Cambridge University Press, 1970), 54–55.

254 *safety but freedom*: John Locke, *A Letter Concerning Toleration*, edited by Oskar Piest (1950), 45–46.

254 *"in the making"*: John Milton, *Areopagitica and of Education with Autobiographical Passages and Other Prose Works*, edited by George H. Sabine (New York: Wiley-Blackwell, 1951), 50.

254 *"only an idea"*: C. Montesquieu, *The Spirit of the Laws*, translated by T. Nugent (New York: Hafner, 1949), 193–94.

254 *"special protection"*: Connick v. Myers, 461 U.S. 138, 145 (1983).

254 *"the community"*: *Connick*, 461 U.S. at 147.

254 *same-sex wedding*: 303 Creative LLC v. Elenis, 600 U.S. 570 (2023).

254 *"spread of political truth"*: *303 Creative LLC*, 600 U.S. 570, 143 S. Ct. 2298, 2311 (2023) (quoting *Whitney v. California*, 274 U.S. 357, 375, 47 S. Ct. 641, 71 L. Ed. 1095 (Brandeis, J., concurring)); see also Jonathan Turley, "The Unfinished Masterpiece: Speech Compulsion and the Evolving Jurisprudence of Religious Speech," *Maryland Law Review* 83 *Maryland Law Review* 145 (2023).

255 *"inalienable human rights"*: Turley, "Unfinished Masterpiece."

256 *"compulsion and control"*: James Fitzjames Stephen, *Liberty, Equality, Fraternity*, edited by R. J. White (1873; Chicago: University of Chicago Press, 1991), 85.

256 *"harm to others"*: John Stuart Mill, *On Liberty*, edited by John Gray (1859; Oxford, UK: Oxford University Press, 1991), 14.

256	*in journalism*: Jonathan Turley, "'A Harm Reduction Model': CNN's Brian Stelter Offers a Perfectly Orwellian Attack on Free Speech and Freedom of the Press," *Res Ipsa* blog (www.jonathanturley.org), Feb. 2, 2021.

256	*"far beyond them"*: John Stuart Mill, *On Liberty* (1859; New York: Penguin, 1974), 146–47.

256	*"inseparable from it"*: Mill, *On Liberty*, 146–47.

257	*"a remarkable American"*: Charles Larabee Street, *Individualism and Individuality in the Philosophy of John Stuart Mill* (Milwaukee: Morehouse, 1926), 98.

257	*"individual selfish system"*: Richard Gunderman, "The Failure of a Socialist Dreamer," *Law & Liberty* magazine, May 14, 2021.

257	*the communal life*: David M. Rabban, "The Ahistorical Historian: Leonard Levy on Freedom of Expression in Early American History," *Stanford Law Review* 37 (1985): 26.

258	*"self-preservation"*: Ann Caldwell Butler, "Josiah Warren and the Sovereignty of the Individual," *The Journal of Libertarian Studies* 4 (1980): 433, 441.

258	*"INTERESTS OF OTHERS"*: Butler, "Josiah Warren," 434.

258	*"individual is sovereign"*: Butler, "Josiah Warren," 436.

258	*"for all concerned"*: John Stuart Mill, *Utilitarianism*, in *10 Collected Works of John Stuart Mill*, edited by J. M. Robson (1861; Toronto: University of Toronto Press, 1963), 218.

258	On Liberty: John Stuart Mill, *On Liberty*, edited by David Spitz (1859; New York: W. W. Norton, 1975).

259	*"the instigation"*: Mill, *On Liberty*.

259	*"some mischievous act"*: Mill, *On Liberty*.

259	*"form of a placard"*: Mill, *On Liberty*.

259	*harm but expediency*: See generally Steven D. Smith, "Is the Harm Principle Illiberal?," *American Journal of Jurisprudence* 51 (2006): 1.

259	*"exercise its power"*: Gerald Dworkin, "Devlin Was Right: Law and the Enforcement of Morality," *William & Mary Law Review* 40 (1999): 927, 934.

259	*between these extremes*: See David A. J. Richards, "Symposium on Taking Legal Rights Seriously: Constitutional Legitimacy, the Principle of Free Speech, and the Politics of Identity," *Chicago-Kent Law Review* 74 (1999): 779, 789.

259	*to choose from*: John Stuart Mill, "On Liberty" (1859), reprinted in John Stuart Mill, *On Liberty, Utilitarianism, and Other Essays*, new ed., edited by Mark Philp & Frederick Rosen (New York: Oxford University Press, 2015), 52, 19.

259	*"restraint, is evil"*: Mill, "On Liberty," 623.

260	*"expression of opinion"*: Mill, "On Liberty," 19.

260	*"influence of example"*: John Stuart Mill, "Principles of Political Economy," in *The Collected Words of John Stuart Mill*, vol. 3, edited by J. M. Robson (1848; Toronto: University of Toronto Press, 1965), 938.

260	*orthodox values*: Mill, "On Liberty," 23 (the "peculiar evil of silencing the expression of an opinion is, that it is robbing the human race").

260	*coercive government measures*: Jonathan Turley, "The Loadstone Rock: The Role of Harm in the Criminalization of Plural Unions," *Emory Law Journal* 64 (2015): 1905.

260   *unhealthy or harmful*: The famous Hart-Devlin was triggered by the release of the Report of the Committee on Homosexual Offenses and Prostitution ("Wolfenden Report"), which declared that criminal law must be used to deter immoral ideas and advocacy. Patrick Devlin, *The Enforcement of Morals* 2 (1965), quoting *Report of the Committee on Homosexual Offences and Prostitution* ¶ 13 (1957).

261   *"means of the law"*: Mill, "Principles of Political Economy," 938.

261   *to speaking areas*: Jonathan Turley, "Schapiro's Unsafe Zone: Northwestern University Students Attack Police in Defending Police," *Res Ipsa* blog (www.jonathanturley.org), Nov. 2, 2020.

261   *"character and conduct"*: Mill, "On Liberty," 52.

261   *"little of that"*: Mill, "On Liberty," 37.

262   *"collision with error"*: Mill, "On Liberty," 19.

262   *under Mill's approach*: Jeremy Waldron, *Mill and the Value of Moral Distress, in Liberal Rights: Collected Papers, 1981–1991* (1993), 115; see also J. Cobbe, "Algorithmic Censorship by Social Platforms: Power and Resistance," *Philosophy & Technology* 34 (2020): 739, 740. ("From their earliest days, many social platforms adopted a hands-off approach and promoted the apparent benefits of connecting people, sharing information, and the free exchange of ideas.")

262   *"actually taking place"*: Waldron, *Mill and the Value*, 125. But see Jeremy Waldron, "Dignity, Rights, and Responsibilities," *Arizona State Law Journal* 43 (2012): 1107.

263   New York Times v. Sullivan: New York Times Co. v. Sullivan, 376 U.S. 254 (1964).

263   *defamation cases*: *Sullivan*, 376 U.S. at 277.

263   *the democratic process*: Despite such functionalist rationales, Brennan publicly eschewed positivism. William J. Brennan Jr., "Address at the Annual Survey of American Law at New York University Law School," Apr. 15, 1982 ("The vogue for positivism in jurisprudence—the obsession with what the law is . . . had to be replaced by a jurisprudence that recognizes human beings as the most distinctive and important feature of the universe which confronts our senses, and the function of law as the historic means of guaranteeing that pre-eminence"), in Honorable Daniel J. O'Hern, "Some Reflections on the Roots of the Differing Judicial Philosophies of William J. Brennan, Jr. and Joseph Weintraub," *Rutgers Law Review* 46 (1994): 1049, 1058.

263   *"'collision with error'"*: *Sullivan*, 376 U.S. 254, 279 (quoting John Stuart Mill, "On Liberty").

263   Citizens United v. Federal Election Commission: Citizens United v. Federal Election Commission, 558 U.S. 310 (2010).

264   *"group of individuals"*: Virginia v. Black, 538 U.S. 343, 359 (2003).

264   *the political context*: See, e.g., *Black*, 538 U.S. at 359; see also R.A.V. v. City of St. Paul, Minn, 505 U.S. 377, 388 (1992); see also Watts v. U.S., 394 U.S. 705, 707 (1969).

27. "FALSE NEWS" AND CENSORSHIP BY SURROGATE

265 *"great men of the realm"*: Larry D. Eldridge, *A Distant Heritage: The Growth of Free Speech in Early America* (New York: New York University Press, 1994), 20.

266 *treason of the colony*: Matthew Kruer, *Time of Anarch: Indigenous Power and the Crisis of Colonialism in Early America* (Cambridge, MA: Harvard University Press, 2022), 136.

266 *five months in prison*: Noeleen McIlvenna, *A Very Mutinous People: The Struggle of North Carolina, 1660–1713* (Chapel Hill: University of North Carolina Press, 2009), 65–66.

266 *"false and dangerous reports"*: Eldridge, *Distant Heritage*, 19.

266 *"intensify social conflict"*: "The Danger of Fake News in Inflaming or Suppressing Social Conflict," Center for Information Tech. & Society, https://www.cits.ucsb.edu/fake-news/danger-social, accessed on June 28, 2023.

267 *associated with France*: Newman, "Fries's Rebellion," 66–67.

267 *"the Grand Orient of FRANCE"*: Newman, "Fries's Rebellion," 67.

267 *call disinformation*: Geoffrey R. Stone, *Perilous Times: Free Speech in Wartime from the Sedition Act of 1798 to the War on Terrorism* (New York: W. W. Norton, 2004), 67.

268 *"wires of jugglers"*: Newman, "Fries's Rebellion," 199.

268 *among the young*: Donna St. George, "American Students' Test Scores Plunge to Levels Unseen for Decades," *Washington Post*, Sept. 1, 2022.

269 *she called "racist"*: Jonathan Turley, "'Please Don't Write About It': *New York Times* Science Reporter Declares Lab Leak Theory 'Racist,'" *Res Ipsa* blog (www.jonathanturley.org), May 28, 2021.

269 *may be true*: Jonathan Turley, "Fear Free Speech: Biden Denounces Big Tech as 'Killing People' by Not Censoring Speech," *Res Ipsa* blog (www.jonathanturley.org), July 17, 2021.

269 *"who can be heard"*: Jonathan Turley, "From Shadow Bans to Black Lists, Musk Forces a Free-Speech Reckoning for Politicians and Pundits," *Res Ipsa* blog (www.jonathanturley.org), Dec. 12, 2022.

270 *discuss censorship programs*: Mike Issac & Kellen Browning, "Zuckerberg and Dorsey Face Harsh Questioning from Lawmakers," *New York Times*, Nov. 17, 2020.

270 *"threats to our world"*: Jonathan Turley, "Harm and Hegemony: The Decline of Free Speech in the United States," *Harvard Journal of Law and Public Policy* 45 (2022): 616.

270 *possible congressional backlash*: See generally Turley, "Harm and Hegemony," 616.

271 *other businessmen*: Jonathan Turley, "Companies Join Call to Suspend Advertising with Twitter," *Res Ipsa* blog (www.jonathanturley.org), Nov. 26, 2022.

271 *individuals and groups*: *Censorship Laundering: How the U.S. Department of Homeland Security Enables the Silencing of Dissent: Hearing Before the H. Subcomm. on Oversight, Investigation, and Accountability*, 118th Cong. (2023) (testimony of Professor Jonathan Turley); *Hearing on the Weaponization of the Federal Government:*

Hearing Before the H. Select Subcomm. on the Weaponization of the Federal Government, 118th Cong. (2023) (testimony of Professor Jonathan Turley).

272　*platforms like Facebook*: David Molloy, "Zuckerberg Tells Rogan That FBI Warning Prompted Biden Laptop Story Censorship," BBC, Aug. 26, 2022, https://www.bbc.com/news/world-us-canada-62688532.

272　*March 18, 2021*: Jonathan Turley, "Twitter's 'Tricky' Timing Problem; Lawsuit Reveals Back Channel in CDC to Coordinate Censorship," *Res Ipsa* blog (www.jonathanturley.org), Aug. 24, 2022.

273　*censorship by surrogate*: *Fanning the Flames: Disinformation and Extremism in the Media: Hearing Before the Subcomm. on Commc'n & Tech. of the H. Comm. on Energy & Com.*, 117th Cong. (2021) (statement of Jonathan Turley).

273　*"do for itself"*: *Misinformation and Disinformation on Online Platforms: Hearing Before the Subcomm. on Commc'n & Tech. and Subcomm. on Consumer Protection of the H. Comm. on Energy & Com.*, 117th Cong. (2021) (question from Rep. Robert Latta).

273　*the Twitter Files*: Turley, "From Shadow Bans to Black Lists."

273　*hundreds of millions of*: "Twitter Revenue and User Statistics," Business of Apps, Jan. 31, 2023, https://www.businessofapps.com/data/twitter-statistics/.

273　*Snapchat, and Pinterest*: "Most Popular Social Networks," Statista, https://www.statista.com/statistics/272014/global-social-networks-ranked-by-number-of-users/, accessed on June 28, 2023.

273　*"who can be heard"*: Turley, "From Shadow Bans to Black Lists."

273　*"can speak freely?"*: Turley, "From Shadow Bans to Black Lists."

274　*Nina Jankowicz*: Jonathan Turley, "Biden's Disinformation Nanny: Why Nina Jankowicz Is 'Practically Perfect in Every Way,'" *Res Ipsa* blog (www.jonathanturley.org), May 2, 2022.

274　*espousing dangerous thoughts*: Stone, *Perilous Times*, 153.

274　*host Drew Pearson*: Stone, *Perilous Times*, 379.

275　*maintain is the truth*: Jonathan Turley, "Combating 'Skepticism': Federal Grant Funds New Effort to Combat 'Misinformation,'" *Res Ipsa* blog (www.jonathanturley), Mar. 22, 2023.

276　*"responsibility of censorship"*: Jonathan Turley, "Externalizing the Difficult Responsibility of Censorship," *Res Ipsa* blog (www.jonathanturley.org), Feb. 7, 2024.

276　*"incredibly important"*: Maggie Miller, "Cyber Agency Beefing Up Disinformation, Misinformation Team," *The Hill*, Nov. 10, 2022, https://thehill.com/policy/cybersecurity/580990-cyber-agency-beefing-up-disinformation-misinformation-team/.

276　*"harm, or manipulate"*: "Foreign Influence Operations and Disinformation," CISA, https://www.cisa.gov/topics/election-security/foreign-influence-operations-and-disinformation (last visited June 29, 2023).

277　*spread of posts*: Jonathan Turley, "Fifth Circuit Enjoins Biden Censorship Program," *Res Ipsa* blog (www.jonathanturley.org), Oct. 4, 2023.

277　*"freedom of this corporation"*: Eldridge, *Distant Heritage*, 28.

277   *"exclusion penalties"*: Eldridge, *Distant Heritage*, 104.

277   Lombard v. Louisiana: Lombard v. Louisiana, 373 U.S. 267 (1963).

277   *"an ordinance"*: *Lombard*, 373 U.S. at 273.

278   *over social media*: O'Handley v. Padilla, 579 F. Supp.3d 1163, 1192-93 (N.D. Cal. 2022).

278   Rogalinski v. Meta Platforms, Inc.: Rogalinski v. Meta Platforms, Inc., 2022 U.S. Dist. LEXIS 142721 (August 9, 2022).

278   *"entirely its own"*: *Rogalinski*, 2022 U.S.

278   Paige v. Coyner: Paige v. Coyner, 614 F.3d 273 (6th Cir. 2010).

278   *at a public hearing*: *Paige*, 614 F.3d at 276.

278   Dossett v. First State Bank: Dossett v. First State Bank, 399 F.3d 940 (8th Cir. 2005).

278   National Rifle Association of America v. Vullo: National Rifle Association of America v. Vullo, 49 F.4th 700, 715 (2d Cir. 2022).

278   *with the organization*: *National Rifle Association*, 49 F.4th at 715.

278   *"the official's request"*: *National Rifle Association*, 49 F.4th, quoting Hammerhead Enters., Inc. v. Brezenoff, 707 F.2d 33, 39 (2d Cir. 1983).

279   *its censorship programs*: Jonathan Turley, "Censor or Else: Democratic Lawmakers Warn Facebook Not to 'Backslide' on Censorship," Fox News, Dec. 18, 2022.

279   *criminally charged*: Jonathan Turley, "Lock Him Up! Ranking Democrat Suggests Possible Criminal Charges Against Journalist Matt Taibbi," *Res Ipsa* blog (www.jonathanturley.org), Apr. 22, 2023.

280   *"other improper classification"*: "Hate Speech," YourDictionary, https://www.yourdictionary.com/hate-speech, accessed on June 28, 2023.

280   *"like a design flaw"*: Richard Stengel, "Why America Needs a Hate Speech Law," *Washington Post*, Oct. 29, 2019, https://www.washingtonpost.com/opinions/2019/10/29/why-america-needs-hate-speech-law/.

280   *likewise a felony*: N.Y. Penal Law §§ 160–61 (1909). See generally Stewart Jay, "The Creation of the First Amendment Right to Free Speech from the Eighteenth to the Mid-Twentieth Century," *William Mitchell Law Review* 34, no. 3 (Apr. 2008): 863.

280   Volokh v. James: Volokh v. James, No. 22-CV-10195 (ALC), 2023 WL 1991435 (S.D.N.Y. 2023).

280   *"gender expression"*: N.Y. Gen. Bus. Law § 394-ccc(1)(a).

281   *"breach of the peace"*: Chaplinsky v. State of New Hampshire, 315 U.S. 568, 571–72 (1942).

281   *"scale of values"*: Dennis v. United States, 341 U.S. 494, 544 (1951) (Frankfurter, J., concurring).

281   *"freedom of speech"*: *Dennis*, 341 U.S. at 550–51.

283   *"Democracy's back"*: Jonathan Turley, "Elon Musk Buying Twitter Is Good for Free Speech," *USA Today*, Apr. 25, 2022.

283   *"something about it"*: Jillian Deutsch, "Tech Giants Face Landmark Fines Under EU's New Content Rules," Bloomberg, Apr. 22, 2022.

284 *free speech implications*: Jonathan Turley, "Mein Ringtone: Man Arrested for Having Hitler Speech as Ringtone," *Res Ipsa* blog (www.jonathanturley), July 2, 2010.

28. ACADEMIC ORTHODOXY AND THE RESTORATION OF FREE SPEECH IN HIGHER EDUCATION

286 *"saved" Athens*: John Carr, *Sparta's Kings* (Barnsley, UK: Pen & Sword, 2012).

287 *their opposing views*: Jonathan Turley, "Washington & Lee Professors Join Students in Seeking to Ban Conservative Speaker," *Res Ipsa* blog (www.jonathanturley.org), Mar. 28, 2023.

287 *"image of the university"*: Mary Anne Franks, "The Miseducation of Free Speech," *Virginia Law Review Online* 15 (2019): 218; see also Mary Anne Franks, "Free Speech Elitism: Harassment Is Not the Price 'We' Pay for Free Speech," *HuffPost: The Blog*, Jan. 23, 2014.

287 *free and open debate*: Jonathan Turley, "Harm and Hegemony: The Decline of Free Speech in the United States," *Harvard Journal of Law and Public Policy* 45 (2022): 586.

288 *fostering "unworthy" ideas*: Richard Amesbury & Catherine O'Donnell, "Dear Administrators: Enough with the Free Speech Rhetoric! It Concedes Too Much to the Right-Wing Agenda," *Chronicle of Higher Education*, Nov. 13, 2023.

288 *"producing knowledge"*: Amesbury & O'Donnell, "Dear Administrators."

288 *"places on speakers"*: Alexander Tsesis, "Burning Crosses on Campus: University Hate Speech Codes," *Connecticut Law Review* 43 (2010): 617, 671–72.

289 *in his head*: Greg Lukianoff & Rikki Schlott, *The Canceling of the American Mind* (New York: Simon & Schuster, 2023), 348.

289 *controversies or investigations*: Jonathan Turley, "Princeton Professor Commits Suicide After Termination of Contract," *Res Ipsa* blog (www.jonathanturley.org), Apr. 22, 2011.

289 *"I am a racist"*: Jonathan Turley, "The Real Conversation on Racism Is Much More Difficult But Necessary," *The Hill*, Sept. 12, 2020.

290 *magazine* Inside Higher Ed: Matthew J. Mayhew & Musbah Shaheen, "Why America Needs College Football," *Inside Higher Ed*, Sept. 23, 2020.

290 *that he caused*: Matthew J. Mayhew, "Why America Needs College Football—Part 2," *Inside Higher Ed*, Sept. 28, 2020.

290 *an academic protection*: Jonathan Turley, "How 'Silence Is Violence' Can Become Compelled Speech," *Res Ipsa* blog (www.jonathanturley.org), Aug. 31, 2020.

290 *virtual classrooms*: Jonathan Turley, "George Brown College Under Fire for Requiring a 'Land Acknowledgment Statement' for Access to Zoom Event," *Res Ipsa* blog (www.jonathanturley.org), June 5, 2022.

291 *students took that option*: Jonathan Turley, "'Performative Acts of Conformity': Professor Sues University of Washington Over Land Acknowledgment Statement," *Res Ipsa* blog (www.jonathanturley.org), July 14, 2022.

291 *"violent" and "triggering"*: Jonathan Turley, "The Machete Standard: The Firing of

an Activist Professor Leaves More Questions Than Answers," *Res Ipsa* blog (www .jonathanturley.org), May 25, 2023.

291 *"out of here"*: Turley, "Machete Standard."

292 *"f—ing professor"*: Jonathan Turley, "'She's a . . . Professor!': Albany Professor Arrested After Obstructing Pro-Life Display and Resisting Arrest," *Res Ipsa* blog (www.jonathanturley.org), May 4, 2023.

292 *down their display*: Jonathan Turley, "California Professor Charged with Battery and Theft in Confrontation with Pro-Life Protestors," *Res Ipsa* blog (www.jona thanturley.org), Mar. 21, 2014.

292 *model for students*: Jonathan Turley, "California Professor Who Assaulted Pro-Life Advocates Is Featured by Oregon to Help Students 'Embrace . . . the Radical Potential of Black Feminism in Our Everyday Lives,'" *Res Ipsa* blog (www.jona thanturley.org), Oct. 17, 2018.

293 *free speech and academic privilege*: American Association of University Professors, Appendix A: "General Report of the Comm. on Academic Freedom and Academic Tenure" (1915), reprinted in *Freedom and Tenure in the Academy*, edited by William W. Van Alstyne (Durham: Duke University Press, 1993), 393, 397.

293 Freiheit der Wissenschaft: American Association of University Professors, Appendix A: "General Report"; see also Walter P. Metzger, "Profession and Constitution: Two Definitions of Academic Freedom in America," *Texas Law Review* 66 (1988): 1265, 1266; see also Rebecca S. Eisenberg, "Academic Freedom and Academic Values in Sponsored Research," *Texas Law Review* 66 (1988): 1363, 1365.

293 Lehrfreiheit: Metzger, "Profession," 1266.

293 *"norms of hierarchy"*: Metzger, "Profession," 1266.

293 *"concentrated public opinion"*: American Association of University Professors, "The A.A.U.P.'s 'General Declaration of Principles,' 1915," in *American Higher Education: A Documentary History*, vol. 2, edited by Richard Hofstadter & Wilson Smith (Chicago: University of Chicago Press, 1961), 860.

293 *"tyranny of public opinion"*: American Association of University Professors, "The A.A.U.P.'s 'General Declaration of Principles'"; see also Judith Areen, "Understanding the First Amendment Protection of Academic Freedom and Governance," *Georgetown Law Journal* 97 (2009): 945.

294 Sweezy v. New Hampshire: Sweezy v. New Hampshire, 354 U.S. 234 (1957).

294 *"stagnate and die"*: *Sweezy*, 354 U.S. at 250.

295 *"admitted to study*: *Sweezy*, 354 U.S. at 276.

295 *"life of a university"*: *Sweezy*, 354 U.S. at 262.

295 Keyishian v. Board of Regents: Keyishian v. Board of Regents, 385 U.S. 589, 603 (1967).

296 *"authoritative selection"*: *Keyishian*, 385 U.S. 589, 603 (1967).

297 the Modern State: Robert C. Post, *Democracy, Expertise, and Academic Freedom: A First Amendment Jurisprudence for the Modern State* (New Haven, CT: Yale University Press, 2012).

298 Academic Freedom: Michael Bérubé & Jennifer Ruth, *It's Not Free Speech: Race,*

Democracy, and the Future of Academic Freedom (Baltimore: Johns Hopkins University Press, 2022).

298   *"an informed citizenry"*: Scott Jaschik, "A Narrower Definition of Academic Freedom," *Inside Higher Ed*, May 5, 2022, https://www.insidehighered.com /news/2022/05/06/new-book-argues-narrower-definition-academic-freedom.

299   *"legitimate ways"*: Jaschik, "A Narrower Definition."

299   *to teach science*: See, e.g., Joe Patrice, "Again, People Pointing Out That You're Stupid Is Not an Attack on Freedom of Speech," *Above the Law*, Sept. 27, 2022.

299   *"experiment and creation"*: Sweezy, 354 U.S. at 234, 262–63 (Frankfurter, J., concurring in the result).

299   *freedom as "fantastic"*: Scallet v. Rosenblum, 911 F.Supp. 999, 1013–14 (W.D.Va.1996); see also Minarcini v. Strongsville City Sch. Dist., 541 F.2d 577, 582 (6th Cir.1976).

300   *"than the other"*: John Stuart Mill, "Principles of Political Economy," in *The Collected Words of John Stuart Mill*, vol. 3, edited by J. M. Robson (1848; Toronto: University of Toronto Press, 1965), 19.

300   *"a like purpose"*: Mill, "Principles of Political Economy," 19.

300   *"public collectively"*: Mill, "Principles of Political Economy," 19.

301   *academics and their institutions*: "The Federal Investment in Higher Education," Datalab, accessed June 28, 2023, https://datalab.usaspending.gov/colleges-and -universities/. ("In 2018, higher education institutions received a total of $1.068 trillion in revenue from federal and non-federal funding sources. Investments from the federal government were $149 billion of the total, representing 3.6% of federal spending.")

301   *"Solomon Amendments"*: 10 U.S.C. 983 (2022).

301   Institutional Rights, Inc. (FAIR): Rumsfeld v. Forum for Academic and Institutional Rights, Inc., 547 U.S. 47 (2006).

301   *"Don't Ask, Don't Tell" policy*: Claudio Sanchez, "U.S. Government Punishes Schools That Ban Military Recruiting," NPR, June 1, 2005.

301   *itself compelled speech*: Rumsfeld, 547 U.S. at 62–63.

301   *compelled association*: Rumsfeld, 547 U.S. at 62.

301   *"may or may not say"*: Rumsfeld, 547 U.S. at 60.

302   *required by law*: See *The Right of the People Peacefully to Assemble: Protecting Speech by Stopping Anarchist Violence Before the S. Comm. on the Judiciary*, 116th Cong. (July 27, 2020) (testimony of Professor Jonathan Turley). The list includes (1) guaranteeing that speakers appear on campus under the same costs and conditions, regardless of their views (or opposition to their views); (2) committing to disciplinary action of students or faculty who block classes, lectures, or speeches by violent acts or threats of violence; (3) committing to the expulsion or termination of students or faculty who physically assault speakers or others seeking to exercise free speech or the right to peaceful assembly; (4) committing to disciplinary action of students or faculty who block classes, lectures, or speeches through disruptive conduct inside classrooms, halls, or other spaces reserved for

such presentations; (5) enforcing a presumption that the exercise of free speech outside of the school (including statements on social media) for faculty or students is generally not a matter for school sanctions or termination; (6) committing to a process for due process of students and faculty who are disciplined for exercising free speech rights, including the right to discovery of patterns of bias or inconsistent treatment in other controversies; (7) barring restrictive "free speech zones" and other exclusionary zones for free expression (other than rules barring demonstrations, disruptions, or exhibits in classrooms, halls, or other spaces used for lectures, presentations, and events); (8) barring student governments or organizations from sanctioning or censuring fellow students for their exercise of free speech without a clear and narrowly tailored standard as well as the approval of a university body; (9) barring faculty from sanctioning, censoring, or retaliating against students for their political, social, or religious statements or values (subject to protected exceptions for religious-based institutions); and (10) barring faculty from requiring that students adhere to, adopt, or endorse political, social, or religious positions as a condition for any class, program, or benefit (subject to protected exceptions for religious-based institutions).

302   *diversity on faculties*: Turley, "Harm and Hegemony," 689–90.

302   *in the country*: Jonathan Turley, "UChicago Ranked as Top Free Speech School While Columbia, Georgetown, Penn Rank at the Very Bottom," *Res Ipsa* blog (www.jonathanturley. org), Sept. 15, 2022.

303   *"with their own"*: Pete Grieve, "University to Freshmen: Don't Expect Safe Spaces or Trigger Warnings," *Chicago Maroon*, Aug. 23, 2016.

303   *"intellectual richness and freedom"*: Nancy C. Andreasen, *The Creative Brain* (New York: Plume Books, 2005), 128.

303   *fully develop*: Andreasen, *Creative Brain*, 159.

303   *short periods of time*: Karamet Reiter et al., "Psychological Distress in Solitary Confinement: Symptoms, Severity, and Prevalence in the United States, 2017–2018," *American Journal of Public Health* 110 (2020): S56, S58.

304   *canceling of the judge*: Jonathan Turley, "Stanford Orders Mandatory Free Speech Sessions for the Law School but Will Not Hold Students Accountable for Disrupting Judge's Remarks," *Res Ipsa* blog (www.jonathanturley. org), Mar. 23, 2023.

305   *"is at stake"*: Jennifer Ruth, "Why Stanford Law Students Were Right to Protest," *Chronicle*, Mar. 23, 2023.

305   *"and its values"*: Kalven Committee, *Report on the University's Role in Political and Social Action*, University of Chicago, Nov. 1967, https://provost.uchicago.edu/reports/report-universitys-role-political-and-social-action.

305   *conservative viewpoints*: Ruth, "Why Stanford."

306   *"statement is true"*: Barbara McQuade, *Attack from Within: How Disinformation Is Sabotaging America* (New York: Seven Stories Books, 2024) 6.

306   *"common for others"*: John Locke, *The Second Treatise of Government: An Essay Concerning the True Original Extent and End of Civil Government*, 15.

306   *identify as conservative*: Scott Jaschik, "Professors and Politics: What the

Research Says," *Inside Higher Ed*, Feb. 27, 2017, https://www.insidehighered.com/news/2017/02/27/research-confirms-professors-lean-left-questions-assumptions-about-what-means.

306   *over ten times*: Mitchell Langbert et al., "Faculty Voter Registration in Economics, History, Journalism, Law and Psychology," *Econ Journal Watch* 13 (2016): 422, 425, fig. 2.

306   *roughly 30 to 1*: Mitchell Langbert, "Homogenous: The Political Affiliations of Elite Liberal Arts College Faculty," *Academic Questions* 31 (2018): 186, 192–93, tbl. 2.

307   *across the country*: Jonathan Turley, "Wisconsin Survey Finds Almost 60 Percent of Students Fear to Speak Openly in Class," *Res Ipsa* blog (www.jonathanturley.org), Feb. 2, 2002.

307   *universities and colleges*: Jonathan Turley, "University of North Carolina Study Finds Conservative Students Engage in Self-Censorship on Campus," *Res Ipsa* blog (www.jonathanturley.org), Aug. 30, 2022.

307   *on our campuses*: Jonathan Turley, "Study: UNC Stifles Free Speech and Conservative Students Are 300 Times More Likely to Self-Censor Views," *Res Ipsa* blog (www.jonathanturley.org), Feb. 19, 2020.

308   Porter v. Board of Trustees of North Carolina State University: Porter v. Board of Trustees of North Carolina State University, 72 F.4th 573 (2023).

308   *"will foster harmony"*: American Association of University Professors, "On Collegiality as a Criterion for Faculty Evaluation," at http://www.aaup.org/statements/Redbook/collegia.htm.

308   *collegiality in 2023*: Scott Gerber, "DEI Brings Kafka to My Law School," *Wall Street Journal*, May 9, 2023.

308   *dissenting views*: "Collegiality," *Merriam-Webster*, https://www.merriam-webster.com/dictionary/collegiality.

29. SLAYING MADISON'S MONSTER: ENDING SEDITION AND SPEECH PROSECUTIONS

309   *"gaze back into you"*: Friedrich W. Nietzsche, *Beyond Good and Evil*, translated by Walter Kaufmann (New York: Vintage, 1989), 89.

309   *"disgrace its parents"*: Andrew Burnstein & Nancy Isenberg, *Madison and Jefferson* (New York: Random House, 2013), 333.

309   *"every other right"*: James Madison, "The Virginia Report," in *The Mind of the Founder: Sources of the Political Thought of James Madison*, rev. ed., edited by Marvin Meyers (Waltham, MA: Brandeis University Press, 1981), 231, 243.

311   *Bourquin of Montana*: Arnon Gutfeld, *Treasure State Justice: Judge George M. Bourquin, Defender of the Rule of Law* (Lubbock: Texas Tech University Press, 2013).

311   *"fair, and just"*: Arnon Gutfeld, "The Ves Hall Case, Judge Bourquin, and the Sedition Act of 1918," *Pacific Historical Review* 37 (1968): 163.

312   *"don't do it again"*: Gutfeld, "Ves Hall Case," 165.

312   *"Wall Street millionaires"*: Geoffrey R. Stone, *Perilous Times: Free Speech in*

Wartime from the Sedition Act of 1798 to the War on Terrorism (New York: W. W. Norton, 2004), 161.

312   *"crookedest-ever President"*: Gutfeld, "Ves Hall Case," 167.

312   *Adams administration*: United States v. Hall, 248 F. 150, 154 (D., Mont. 1918).

312   *"army or navy operations"*: *Hall*, 248 F. at 153.

313   *do not fail*: *Hall*, 248 F. at 152.

313   *"hundreds of miles"*: *Hall*, 248 F. at 152.

313   *"the paper out"*: Frohwerk v. United States, 249 U.S. 204, 209 (1919).

313   *"in the Caribbean"*: Jamie L. Vernon, "Understanding the Butterfly Effect," *American Scientist* 105, no. 3 (Jan. 2017): 130.

313   *"of our enemies"*: Stone, *Perilous Times*, 169.

313   *from the state*: Stone, *Perilous Times*, 169.

313   *"guilty of attempt"*: Stone, *Perilous Times*, 175.

314   *serving in the military*: Stone, *Perilous Times*, 163.

314   *handling of the case*: Jeffrey Brandon Morris, *Establishing Justice in Middle America* (Minneapolis: University of Minnesota Press, 2007), 93.

314   *"their mischievous effect"*: William Blackstone, *Commentaries on the Laws of England*, vol. 4 (New York: Cavendish, 2001), vol. 4, 35–37.

314   *"gain our ends"*: Geoffrey R. Stone, *Perilous Times: Free Speech in Wartime from the Sedition Act of 1798 to the War on Terrorism* (New York: W. W. Norton, 2004), 142.

315   *"khaki-coat in the trenches"*: Denise Ohio, "Shaffer, Frank (1877–1950?)," Historylink, Oct. 20, 2021, https://www.historylink.org/File/21334.

316   *"he knowingly did"*: Shaffer v. United States, 255 F. 886 (9th Cir. 1919).

316   *"a suicide pact"*: Terminiello v. Chicago, 337 U.S. 1, 37 (Jackson, J., dissenting).

316   *"Government is required"*: Dennis v. United States, 341 U.S. 494, 509 (1951).

317   *"constitutionally sanctioned body"*: Paul Douglas Newman, *Fries's Rebellion: The Enduring Struggle for the American Revolution* (Philadelphia: University of Pennsylvania Press, 2004), 135.

317   *could refuse certification*: Newman, *Fries's Rebellion: The Enduring Struggle*, 41.

317   *support their actions*: Newman, *Fries's Rebellion: The Enduring Struggle*, 101.

317   *"not against it"*: Newman, *Fries's Rebellion: The Enduring Struggle*, 141.

317   *"France, France, France"*: Newman, *Fries's Rebellion: The Enduring Struggle*, 153.

318   *the French Revolution*: Newman, *Fries's Rebellion: The Enduring Struggle*, 47.

318   *in prior years*: Newman, *Fries's Rebellion: The Enduring Struggle*, 42–43.

319   *"President of the United States"*: Sedition Act of 1798, Ch. 74, 1 Stat. 596 (1798) (expired 1801).

319   *their official duties*: "Four Oath Keepers Found Guilty of Seditious Conspiracy Related to U.S. Capitol Breach," U.S. Department of Justice, Jan. 23, 2023.

319   *"enemies foreign and domestic"*: *Oath Keepers Indictment*, 3. United States Department of Justice, Indictment, Jan. 12, 2022, ¶ 3, at 3.

319   *march on the Capitol*: Rebecca Beitsch, "Oath Keepers Stockpiled 30 Days of Supplies, Rifles Ahead of Jan. 6," *The Hill*, Jan. 19, 2022.

320   *"overtake our government"*: Beitsch, "Oath Keepers Stockpiled."

320   *mental health treatment*: Eric Neugeboren, "Texan Who Prosecutors Say 'Lit the Match' of Jan. 6 Riot Sentenced to More Than 7 Years in Prison," *Texas Tribune*, Aug. 1, 2022.

320   *the way down*: Neugeboren, "Texan Who Prosecutors Say."

321   *a 1999 terrorism case*: United States v. Rahman, 189 F.3d 88, 115 (2d Cir. 1999).

322   *"religious preaching"*: *Rahman*, 189 F.3d at 117.

322   Dennis v. United States: *Dennis*, 341 U.S. at 494.

322   *force or violence*: *Rahman*, 189 F.3d at 114.

322   *"advocacy, not discussion"*: *Dennis*, 341 U.S. at 502.

322   *"lead to anarchy"*: *Dennis*, 341 U.S. at 501.

323   *"to suffer death"*: William Pencak, "Play as Prelude to Revolution," in *Riot and Revelry in Early America*, edited by William Pencak et al. (University Park: Pennsylvania State University Press, 2002).

323   *"these Communist petitioners"*: *Dennis*, 341 U.S. at 581; see also Michael P. Downey, Note, "The Jeffersonian Myth in Supreme Court Sedition Jurisprudence," *Washington University Law Quarterly* 76 (1998): 683, 700–704.

324   *nine were acquitted*: Claudius O. Johnson, "The Status of Freedom of Expression Under the Smith Act," *Western Political Quarterly* 11 (1958): 469, 470.

324   *state-sanctioned viewpoints*: Zechariah Chafee Jr., *Free Speech in the United States* (Cambridge, MA: Harvard University Press, 1941), 51.

324   *"monstrous and unlawful"*: Oscar Wilde, *The Picture of Dorian Gray*, edited by Isobel Murray (New York: Oxford University Press, 1974), 18.

325   Eastman v. Thompson: Eastman v. Thompson, 2022 U.S. Dist. LEXIS 59283 (March 29, 2022).

325   *on January 6th*: *Eastman*, 2022 U.S. at 52.

325   *"January 6, 2021"*: *Eastman*, 2022 U.S. at 52.

326   *one law professor*: Jonathan Turley, "Ragefully Wrong: A Response to Professor Laurence Tribe," *Res Ipsa* blog (www.jonathanturley.org), Sept. 8, 2023.

326   *"to violate it"*: Turley, "Ragefully Wrong."

327   *"never absolute"*: Dennis Baron, "Trump's Words on Jan. 6th Were a Clear and Present Danger," *Web of Language* blog, Feb. 16, 2021, https://blogs.illinois.edu/view/25/502281961.

327   *"clear and present danger" test*: Erwin Chemerinsky, "Trump's Incitement Is Not Protected Speech," *San Francisco Chronicle*, Feb. 8, 2021.

328   *"bad-tendency" rationales*: Jonathan Turley, "The Right to Rage: Free Speech and Rage Rhetoric in American Political Discourse," *Georgetown Journal of Law & Public Policy* 21, no. 2 (2023): 523.

328   *against Trump*: Jonathan Turley, "How a Snap Impeachment Could Shatter Our Constitutional Balance," *Res Ipsa* blog (www.jonathanturley), Jan. 11, 2011.

328   *obstruction of the draft*: Schenck v. United States, 249 U.S. 47, 51 (1919).

328   *"kindle a flame"*: Frohwerk v. United States, 249 U.S. 204, 208–09 (1919).

328 *"violation of law"*: Zechariah Chafee Jr., *Freedom of Speech in Wartime*, 32 HARV. L. REV. 932, 948 (1919).

329 *"imagined peril"*: Francis Biddle, *The Fear of Freedom* (Garden City, NY: Double-day, 1951), 18.

329 *"panic with patriotism"*: Biddle, *Fear of Freedom*; see also Stone, *Perilous Times*, 293.

329 *"a free society"*: Dennis v. United States, 341 U.S. 494, 581 (1951).

329 *"infringement of liberty"*: Stone, *Perilous Times*, 224.

330 *qualify as sedition*: Steven Calabresi, "Section 3 of the Fourteenth Amendment," *Reason*, Oct. 12, 2023, https://reason.com/volokh/2023/10/12/section-3-of-the-fourteenth-amendment/.

331 *over gun control*: Josh Christenson, "What Happens Next to Tennessee House Democrats Who Were Expelled?," *New York Post*, Apr. 7, 2023, https://nypost.com/2023/04/07/what-happens-next-to-the-expelled-tennessee-house-democrats/.

332 *to punish critics*: Larry D. Eldridge, *A Distant Heritage: The Growth of Free Speech in Early America* (New York: New York University Press, 1994), 137.

332 *"United States of America"*: Zechariah Chafee Jr., *Freedom of Speech* (New York: Harcourt, 1920), 23–24.

331 *first by Congress*: Trump v. Anderson, 610 U.S. ___ (2024).

331 *called "unassailable"*: Jonathan Turley, "Supreme Court Ensures Democracy Is Winner," *USA Today*, March 5, 2024.

331 *"endure such chaos"*: Trump, 610 U.S. ___, *6.

PART V. CONCLUSION

335 *filed out after a vote*: Jonathan Turley, "'I Was Screaming Before You Interrupted Me,'" *Res Ipsa* blog (www.jonathanturley), March 30, 2023.

336 *and each other*: Jonathan Turley, "America's Crisis of Faith," *Res Ipsa* blog (www.jonathanturley), Oct. 23, 2023.

336 *"ground of discrimination"*: See "Canada Proposes Another 'Hate Speech' Law and This One Is Just as Threatening to Free Speech," June 28, 2021.

337 *"cohesion or democracy"*: Jonathan Turley, "Oh Canada: Trudeau's Government Condemns Cuba Over Free Speech," *Res Ipsa* blog (www.jonathanturley.org), Feb. 19, 2022.

337 *five years in prison*: Jonathan Turley, "Oh Canada: The Parliament Moves to Impose Life Sentences for Speech Crimes," *Res Ipsa* blog (www.jonathanturley.org), March 14, 2024.

337 *"harassment, alarm, or distress"*: Criminal Justice and Public Order Act § 154 (1994).

337 *"crimes against peace"*: Jonathan Turley, "'We Are Restricting Freedom . . . for the Common Good': Irish Green Party Calls for Limiting Free Speech," *Res Ipsa* blog (www.jonathanturley.org), June 18, 2023.

338 *"hordes of men"*: Joanna Plucinska, "German MP's Anti-Muslim Tweets Spark Account Suspension, Outcry," Politico, Jan. 2, 2018.

339 *"other kind of treachery"*: Charles Walton, "Thomas Paine: Enemy of Free Speech?," University of Warwick, June 2022, https://warwick.ac.uk/fac/arts/history/ecc/blog/thomaspaine/.

340 *"kindle a flame" of dissent*: Frohwerk v. United States, 249 U.S. 209 (1919).

340 *a lethal twist*: Jonathan Turley, "The Loadstone Rock: The Role of Harm in the Criminalization of Plural Unions," *Emory Law Journal* 64 (2015): 1905.

340 *logical in its application*: See, e.g., Jason Pontin, "The Case for Less Speech," *Wired*, Nov. 11, 2018, https://www.wired.com/story/ideas-jason-pontin-less-speech/.

340 *social media companies*: Julia Angwin & Hannes Grassegger, "Facebook's Secret Censorship Rules Protect White Men from Hate Speech but Not Black Children," ProPublica, June 28, 2017. (Former "content moderation director" Dave Willner said Facebook used Millian harm principles as the foundation for its censorship program, but admitted that the use of the principle was "more utilitarian than we are used to in our justice system. It's fundamentally not rights oriented.")

340 *"post-truth" environment*: Cynthia Kroet, "'Post-Truth' Enters Oxford English Dictionary," Politico, June 27, 2017. (*Post-truth* has been defined as "circumstances in which objective facts are less influential in shaping public opinion than appeals to emotion and personal belief.")

340 *"entirely isolated being"*: John Stuart Mill, *On Liberty* 23 (Boston: Ticknor & Fields 1863) (1959), 154.

340 *"inseparable from it"*: Mill, *On Liberty*, 13.

340 *acts or views*: See generally Steven D. Smith, "Is The Harm Principle Illiberal?," *American Journal of Jurisprudence* 51 (2006): 1.

342 *"psychology of thinking"*: Herbert A. Simon, "Invariants of Human Behavior," *Annual Review of Psychology* 41 (Feb. 1990): 6.

342 *in each environment*: Herbert A. Simon, *Models of Thought* vol. 1 (New Haven, CT: Yale University Press, 1979), 1.

342 *social and political discourse*: See Jonathan Turley, "Madisonian Tectonics: How Function Follows Form in Constitutional and Architectural Interpretation," *George Washington University Law Review* 83 (2015): 305.

342 *"people make decisions"*: Richard H. Thaler & Cass R. Sunstein, *Nudge: Improving Decisions About Health, Wealth and Happiness* (New York: Penguin Books, 2009), 3.

342 *"their own way"*: Cass Sunstein, "The Ethics of Nudging," *Yale Journal on Regulation* 32 (2015): 413, 417.

343 *"from common people"*: Newman, "Fries's Rebellion," 50.

343 *their reading material*: Turley, "Enlightened Algorithms."

344 *this indispensable right*: See generally Philip A. Hamburger, "Natural Rights, Natural Law, and American Constitutions," *Yale Law Journal* 102 (1993): 907, 922.

344 *"inherent and inalienable rights"*: Pennsylvania Constitution of 1776, art. I (1776).

344 *"publishing their sentiments"*: Pennsylvania Constitution of 1776, art. XII.

344 *Declaration of Independence*: David Bogan, "The Origins of Freedom of Speech and Press," *Maryland Law Review* 42 (1983): 429, 451.

345   *"form of freedom"*: Palko v. Connecticut, 302 U.S. 319 (1937).

345   *the indispensable right*: Whitney v. California, 274 U.S. 357, 379 (1927).

345   303 Creative *decision*: 303 Creative LLC v. Elenis, 600 U.S. 570 (2023).

345   *"I am criminal"*: Melvin I. Urofsky, *100 Americans Making Constitutional History* (Washington, DC: CQ Press, 2004), 207.

345   *by unreasonable people*: George Bernard Shaw, *Man and Superman: A Comedy and a Philosophy* (London: Archibald & Co., 1907), 238.

Image Credits

PHOTOS THROUGHOUT

Page 27 Photograph by Jack and Beverly Wilgus of daguerreotype originally from their collection, and now in the Warren Anatomical Museum, Center for the History of Medicine, Francis A. Countway Library of Medicine, Harvard Medical School

Page 63 White House Collection/White House Historical Association

Page 198 National Photo Company

PHOTO INSERT

Image 2 Samuel Johnson Woolf

Image 4 White House Collection/White House Historical Association

Image 8 Special Collections Research Center, University of Chicago Library

Image 10 Courtesy of Special Collections, Fine Arts Library, Harvard University

Index

About the Author

JONATHAN TURLEY is a law professor, columnist, television analyst, and litigator. Since 1998, he has held the Shapiro Chair for Public Interest Law at George Washington University Law School. He has served as counsel in some of the most notable cases in the last two decades, including representing members of Congress, judges, whistleblowers, five former attorneys general, celebrities, accused spies and terrorists, whistleblowers, journalists, protesters, and the workers at the secret facility Area 51. Turley has testified before Congress more than one hundred times, including during the impeachments of Presidents Bill Clinton and Donald Trump. He was also lead counsel in the last judicial impeachment in U.S. history. He has written for the *New York Times*, *Wall Street Journal*, *Washington Post*, *Los Angeles Times*, and *USA Today*. Called the "dean of legal analysts" by the *Washington Post*, Turley has worked as a legal analyst for CBS, NBC, BBC, and Fox. In a study by Judge Richard Posner, Turley was found to be thirty-eighth in the top one hundred most cited "public intellectuals" (and the second most-cited law professor).